BEN HOGAN

The Myths Everyone Knows,
The Man No One Knew

TIM SCOTT

ISBN: 978-1-62937-096-5

This book is available in quantity at special discounts for your group or organization. For further information, contact:

Triumph Books LLC
814 North Franklin Street
Chicago, Illinois 60610
(312) 337–0747
www.triumphbooks.com

Printed in U.S.A.

"If you never met Hogan, you never really got to know who Hogan was."

– Ken Venturi

"I would say the people who knew Ben, closely, liked him very much. The people that just saw what was said about him, in the papers, about him being tough and being hard to know and so forth, why, they probably didn't think he had a very good personality."

– Byron Nelson

"If you've been reading about Ben Hogan over the years, you've probably seen a lot of negative reports about his relations with people. Some have described him as cold… But take it from someone who knows him well— he is also a fine, courageous, and warmhearted human being."

– Jimmy Demaret

"He kept the world at bay. But he could be fun-loving, a wonderful dinner companion to share a pre-meal martini with."

– Jim Murray

DEDICATION

To all the young boys and girls who have lost their fathers: While it's a much more difficult path without a father, Ben Hogan's example shows that you too can become successful in life.

CONTENTS

FOREWORD

The best athletes demonstrate passion, commitment, and hunger for the game which undeniably describes the great Ben Hogan which author, Tim Scott, passionately depicts in this myth busting book, *Ben Hogan: The Myths Everyone Knows, The Man No One Knew.*

Scott paints the true picture of Ben Hogan the man, while also offering first hand glimpses into the championship golfer's drive to be the best. Scott's firsthand experience of working closely with Hogan for over a decade is what offers him the ability to write such a dynamic book.

Within the pages of this book, Scott takes readers on a fantastic journey as they learn about the real Ben Hogan as seen by his family, friends, fellow golfers, and employees. The reader will find themselves letting go of the media myths and experience a paradigm shift in their view of Hogan.

I personally found this book to be one of the most real, and honestly expressed stories of Ben Hogan ever written. It is not only an enjoyable read for golf fans, but even the casual reader will find this story of Hogan to be an inspirational one. The true test of a good book is to be universal. This book is that and then some.

Brad VanFossan,
Editor, *The Vindicator Newspaper*
Freelance Writer, FanVsFan

Acknowledgements

This twenty year effort to bring to light the non-public side of Ben Hogan could not have been done without the valuable assistance of my Ben Hogan Company colleagues who were instrumental in recalling their personal episodes with Mr. Hogan. I would especially like to thank Archie Allison, Morgan Barofsky, Chip Bridges, Ray Coleman, Bernie Coyle, Shirley Givant, Rosemary Godwin, Charles Harris, Dennis Iden, Frank Mackey, Pat Martin, Doug McGrath, Jeff Price, Sharon Rea, Phil Romaine, Bill Shake, Gene Sheeley, Mike Sieverson, Barry Simpter and Tom Stites.

Many others who contributed and to whom I am thankful are Phil Bartholomew, Jim Bartlett, Jimmy Burch, Steve Cain, Joe Cates, Dr. David Cook, Ben Dickson, Bob Dickson, Jim Eagle, John Ferries, Stuart Fitts, Bill Flynn, Dick Ford, John P. Grace, Willie Mae Green, Craig Harmon, Ernie Horn, Jimmie Hudson, Randy Jacobs, Tommy John, Rodney Johnston, Buck Jordan, Ted Katula, Marty Leonard, Joe Matthews, John McMackin, Eldridge Miles, Jim Moore, Linda McCoy-Murray, Kevin McMullen, Alex McNab, Gary Player, Gary Randall, George Reich, Ron Reimer, Fred Reynolds, Dr. Todd Samuelson, Chuck Scherer, Coleen Sowden, Judy Stemple, Mike Towle, Dr. Wym Van Wyk, Tom Weiskopf, William White, Jay Whitney, Marge Williams, Congressman Roger Williams, Randy Wolff, Mike Wright and Cynthia Zordich.

Many thanks helping me with the facts on Ben Hogan's record to Tim Benton and Dave Lancer from the PGA Tour; Angela Howe, Senior Heritage & Museum Curator, The Royal & Ancient; Patty Moran of the USGA library and Claribel Kelly, Ben Hogan's secretary.

Much gratitude is extended to those organizations and individuals who assisted in gathering photos and in providing the photos used in this book. They are the Merion Golf Club, Ms. Christine Pooler, and Mr. John Capers III, for use of the cover photo of Mr. Hogan, and for Mr. Capers' assistance with the manuscript. To Colonial Country Club and the Historical Preservation Committee at Colonial Country Club, for photos from their collections, and to Dennis Roberson and Ben Matheson for their time and help in the collection process. To Shady Oaks Country Club for use of the painting of

Mr. Hogan and Max, to Lisa Scott and Robert Stennett of the Ben Hogan Foundation for access to Mr. Hogan's photo collection, the extraordinary help with the pictures, and for reviewing and assisting with the manuscript. To the Fitz-Symms Photography Company who provided a photo from the Fitz-Symms Photography collection as did the *Tribune Chronicle* of Warren, Ohio. To Marty Leonard for photos from her collection, Mark Angle for photos from the Lee Angle Photography collection, Jeff Price for use of photos from his collection, Martha Theis for the photo from the Theis collection and to Doug McGrath for his contribution of photos from his collection and helping locate other photos.

Many thanks for assistance on the A.S. Barnes & Company lawsuit information to author Al Barkow who was especially helpful with insightful contributions, to Steve Hayes, Todd Sailor, and Dan McMullen for tracking down the case law information on the Hogan lawsuit, its outcome and on the related cases that show the significance of the Hogan case decision.

For reviewing my manuscript and offering their comments and suggestions on the material my special thanks to Don Callahan, Instructor, Butch Harmon School of Golf; Robert Stennett, Executive Director, Ben Hogan Foundation; Lindy Miller, PGA Teaching Professional, Shady Oaks Country Club and Ben Matheson, Chairman, Historical Preservation Committee at Colonial Country Club.

I am especially grateful to Ken Venturi, Henry Picard, Jim McKay, Shelley Mayfield, Dick Harmon, Nick Seitz, Gene Smyers and Gordon Boswell, Jr. who helped a new, inexperienced author wannabe with not only helpful material for the book, but also with enthusiastic assistance, encouragement and support that helped me feel that I could do this; to Ted Katula for his coaching and special influence on me to play golf, to Professor Kenneth R. Davis for his summer internship to research and write case studies, and to all those who have been praying for me for guidance and direction, that my first manuscript and photos would help to provide insight and understanding of Ben Hogan, the man we were privileged to know.

A very special thank you to —

My very special wife, Rosey, and to my son, Jordan, and daughter, Heather, and the rest of the family who put up with all the inconveniences and missed times together over the many years I was working on the manuscript, for their understanding and faith in me. To my mother, Ruth, who instilled values in my brother Doug and me that helped us throughout life.

BEN HOGAN

The Myths Everyone Knows,
The Man No One Knew

Ben Hogan speaks to the crowd welcoming him back to Fort Worth after winning the British Open, July 1953. (PHOTO COURTESY OF *FORT WORTH STAR-TELEGRAM*, SPECIAL COLLECTIONS, THE UNIVERSITY OF TEXAS AT ARLINGTON LIBRARY, ARLINGTON, TEXAS)

INTRODUCTION

When Ben Hogan returned to Fort Worth following his 1953 British Open victory at Carnoustie, Scotland, the minister at his church, Reverend Granville Walker, had this to say about the man, Ben Hogan:

"If there is anything more important about Ben Hogan than the remarkable record he has made, it is simply that Hogan the Man has been the sort of person who could do what he has done...

You cannot be true to the facts and attribute what this man has done to luck, unless you define luck as the place where preparation and opportunity meet. Ben Hogan has had every reason for quitting more than once. He has known what it means to fight the dread spectre of poverty, to be hungry and still not cease to dream. He has known what it means to enter the lists and lose, and then make of the loss an occasion to re-examine his game, discipline himself once more and try again. He has known what it means to see things he gave his life to broken and stoop and build 'em up with worn out tools...

There is no question that Ben Hogan's rise to fame had its humble beginnings in a dream. It was a dream of genuine achievement, and instead of being mastered by it, he mastered it, by keeping his feet firmly on the ground. He set his heart on a goal knowing what it would cost to reach it, and then dedicated himself to paying the price of reaching it...

Anyone who knows Ben Hogan knows that the British Open was not won on the Carnoustie course. That was merely the place where the great exhibition of skill took place. The tournament was won on the practice greens and fairways where relentless hard work paid off in competence. When Paul wrote that the pressures of life produce staying power, and staying power produces competence, he was talking about how to be a champion in the business of living. That is the path Ben Hogan has followed to the fulfillment of a great ambition...

It is impossible to separate Ben the Sportsman from Ben the Man, for the qualities that have made Ben Hogan what he is, were lived in the context of a great career in golf. The record of that career is unique. It is a record in which his friends take pride, for somehow each of us feels he belongs to us. But Ben the man is something more than the record. He is indomitable ambition, dogged willingness to work, impeccable honesty of soul and spirit, high intelligence, dauntless courage, relentless fortitude and genuine religious faith, and the world's best golfer wrapped in a single package. If there is anything more remarkable than Ben Hogan's record, it is Ben Hogan."

Hogan's record was indeed remarkable. He won 64 tournaments on the PGA Tour, which puts him fourth on the all-time list. He won nine major championships, including an unprecedented sweep of all three he played in 1953 and a record-tying four (some say a record-setting five) U.S. Opens. He is one of only five players to have won the Masters, the U.S. and British Opens, and the PGA Championship- the modern-day four majors-in his career. All that despite losing two years of competition in his prime to serve during World War II, and another year following a near-fatal car-bus collision in 1949. After the accident, Hogan never played more than seven events a year, and usually no more than three or four in any single season because of the lifetime-long effects of his injuries from the accident.

Golf aficionados regard Hogan as golf's greatest striker of the ball, both before and after the accident. His solid swing was unique. He seemed concreted to the ground, with every muscle unleashed at the ball at the point of impact. Despite the compensations for injuries he had to make, Hogan hit the golf ball with an authority like no other.

Hogan was a man ahead of his time. He invented practice on the pro tour as we know it today, and his craftsmanship and ingenuity regarding golf equipment would have multiplied manifold with today's electronic engineering methods. His meticulous attention to the smallest of details, his almost scientific investigation to find what was really taking place in the golf swing or with a golf club, set him apart from others. Hogan was perhaps the most focused person ever to play the game of golf, and certainly the most focused person I've ever known. He wanted to pursue, evaluate and resolve things that had him preoccupied, and he wanted to do it right then while it was fresh in his mind. That helped him set his priorities, and he rarely deviated from them. He looked for answers many times when others did not see the question.

Few people, however, have heard witness of Ben Hogan the man like those remarks by the Reverend Granville T. Walker of University Christian Church. If you believed everything you read or watched or heard about Hogan, you would picture him as a solitary, unapproachable, brusque individual, one devoid of feelings; a selfish man who took from the game of golf, but gave little or nothing in return. Even today, accounts in the media have portrayed the man, Ben Hogan, as cold, demanding, unfriendly, rude, even surly or mean.

Typical are the ESPN Classic and ESPN's Top Athletes of the Century series. ESPN's Fifty Greatest Athletes video begins by recalling Hogan as "a great golfer and a difficult man," stating that Hogan had "spooky eyes that were hard to look at," and quoting golfer Paul Runyan as describing Hogan as "the most self-centered great champion I've ever known." Later, announcer Jimmy Roberts recounts another familiar story: "One day Jimmy Demaret came into the clubhouse, and he saw Hogan sitting alone at a table, and he said to the rest of the golfers he was with, 'Hey, there's Ben Hogan sitting with all his friends.'"

Among other oft-repeated, negatively-framed Hogan stories about his dealings with fellow golfers are ones about Gary Player, Ben Crenshaw and Claude Harmon. Player called Hogan on the phone seeking swing advice. Hogan asked Player if he was affiliated with a club manufacturer, and when Player answered, Dunlop, Hogan said, "Call Mr. Dunlop." When Crenshaw was a standout at the University of Texas and a friend tried to arrange a game with Hogan, Hogan replied that he "didn't want to play golf with a long-haired hippie." And when Hogan and Harmon, who were good friends, played together in the 1947 Masters Tournament and they walked toward the green of the par-3, 12th hole together, Hogan, as usual, did not say a word. Only when they moved off the green did Hogan speak, remarking that it was the first birdie 2 he had ever made on the 12th during the tournament, before preparing to play his tee shot first on 13. Harmon, stunned, had to tell Hogan it wasn't his honor. Harmon had just made a hole in one on the same hole (12), but Hogan hadn't acknowledged his ace.

Even Hogan's nickname, "The Hawk," gives the impression of an individual looking for innocents to devour in his quest for survival. Indeed, Hogan was a tough competitor, perhaps one of the fiercest competitors in the game, a man who stalked golf courses, and devised ways to reduce his score to win tournaments. In his mind, that's what competitive golf was all about, shooting lower scores and winning tournaments. Hogan's expressive eyes and face reflected his moods, from warm and friendly in lighter moments, to serious and determined in moments of intense reflection or concentration, to dour and piercing stares when provoked or upset. His determined, unyielding focus during competition on the course was undoubtedly more of the look of a predator than that of a friendly competitor.

In their book *The Sacred Romance*, Brent Curtis and John Eldredge argue that life is not a combination of sentences, a list of propositions, rather a series of dramatic scenes and episodes that speak through the emotions and images of stories.

In short, life is a continuum, an ongoing story. Too frequently stories told about individuals are taken out of the context of the continuum of that person's life. As a result, those stories take on a tone different from one remembered or told given the context of the continuum of a life. The out-of-context story, as it gets repeated, becomes a myth. Ben Hogan's life was an ongoing story, with a beginning and an end. One must remember the context of the story to appreciate the man, Ben Hogan.

Take those oft-told Hogan stories. The truth lies beyond the abbreviated versions, and shedding a different light on the man. For example, Jimmy Demaret, in his book, *My Partner Ben Hogan*, reflects on Hogan as a person… "He is a man of strong character and fine qualities. He is difficult to know for a couple of reasons. One, he is an introvert, plain and simple. The other is that he spends most of his time on the golf course…. But take it from someone who knows him well, he is also a fine, courageous, and warm human being".

Gary Player had once been set to sign with the Hogan Company before taking a different offer without telling Hogan, which violated Hogan's code of respect. Player shared with me, "I can't say as I blame him. Hogan was a proud person and he had never offered that [a contract] to anyone else, so he probably thought I would sign with him." Shaggy hair (and not just college-aged Crenshaw's), Hogan felt, could hurt golf's popularity and code of decorum, but when Crenshaw was struggling as a pro years later, he received custom clubs from Hogan, and he considered one of his prize possessions a photograph of Hogan kissing his infant daughter Katherine.

Harmon was simply a victim of Hogan's singular focus on Hogan's own golf game, which precluded his registering his friend's perfect shot while he still had a putt to make for a 2.

Claude Harmon's son Dick, who at the time was teaching at his own golf school near Houston, shared this about Hogan... "Of all the men I've met, Ben Hogan's words meant the most to me. He wasn't into small talk very much, so when he did say something it usually meant he had something worthwhile to say. And he was an incredible speaker. I was at the staff pro dinner one year and he gave a wonderful speech. He just spoke from the heart as if he were speaking to us one on one." Yes, Ben Hogan, like all other living human beings, could be cold, demanding, unfriendly, rude, and even surly or mean. But that was by no means the totality of his personality.

One of Ben Hogan's biggest tour rivals, who knew Hogan from their caddying days at Glen Garden Country Club in Fort Worth was Byron Nelson. He probably best summed up opposing views of Ben Hogan, "I would say the people that knew Ben, closely, liked him very much. The people that just saw what was said about him, in the papers, about him being tough and being hard to know and so forth, why, they probably didn't think he had a very good personality."

The truth lies beyond the abbreviated versions. It reflects a vastly different side of Ben Hogan and sheds a different light on the man. Descriptions and examples of his human side, his lighthearted, intense, compassionate, principled side, have been left wanting, and sometimes completely ignored. Ben Hogan was a complex and private person, one of the hardest-working athletes ever to compete in professional sport, driven to succeed when almost all others, perhaps all others, would have given up in failure.

In short, Ben Hogan had another side that needs to be known. The purpose of *Ben Hogan: The Myths Everyone Knows, The Man No One Knew* is to provide firsthand accounts, episodes that help depict the man, Ben Hogan-as opposed to the myth, the mystique, and the mystery surrounding him.

As an eleven-year-old boy in the mid-1950s, I was encouraged to take up golf by Leonard Theis, one of my school friends, whose father, Virgil, was the golf professional at the Warren Avalon Golf Course, a public course near Warren, Ohio. I asked my mom about it, who was a single mother after Dad's death, when I was six and my brother three. She dug out his old clubs, some with wooden shafts, some with steel shafts, and I started to play golf. Dad had died in May of 1950 when he suffered a heart attack while fighting a fire as a volunteer fireman. Dad's clubs, having gone unused for at least five years, were a bit rusty, but a little polish took away most of the corrosion. I used Dad's metal-shafted 2 and 3 woods to qualify for the state Jaycees tournament as a teenager, and they stayed in my bag until my senior year in high school.

Virgil's summer junior program included a golf league, and each week the 9-hole match results, including every kid's scores, were published in the local newspaper, the *Tribune-Chronicle* in Warren, Ohio. To encourage the kids to keep up with the sport, each team had to be named after a professional golfer. New to the game, I knew little about the players or its history, but my teammates David Lozner and Mike Blake and I decided to call our team "Ben Hogan," after a guy who was nearly killed in an auto accident, and then came back to play again, becoming the best there was in the game. I also started caddying at nearby Squaw Creek Country Club and hunted golf balls in the woods surrounding the shortholes par-3 course, in my hometown of Vienna, Ohio. However, golf was the third sport on my list, following basketball and baseball. I spent countless hours shooting hoops.

When I was a freshman in high school, I caddied for Ed Theis, Virgil's oldest son, in the Youngstown Open, and met Ted Katula, who was paired with Ed in the 36-hole tournament. Katula finished as the low amateur, second only to the professional winner, Eddie Griffith. While we were on the course, Katula mentioned he was leaving the next day to go to some small college in Indiana as an assistant football coach. Six years later, when a knee injury ended my varsity basketball career at DePauw University in Greencastle, Indiana, the golf coach asked me to try out for the team. The coach was the

Ben Hogan's foursome finishing on 18 at the Avalon Golf Course, Vienna Ohio in 1951-- the course where the author started playing golf in 1955. (PHOTO COURTESY OF *THE TRIBUNE CHRONICLE*, WARREN, OHIO)

Virgil Theis (right), who introduced the author to golf, with Ben Hogan and Tom Banish (left) after their round at Avalon Golf Course, 1951, Vienna, Ohio. (PHOTO COURTESY OF *THE TRIBUNE CHRONICLE*, WARREN, OHIO)

same Ted Katula I had met at the Youngstown Open. "Katman" as he was called, helped me develop my game, and golf became my number one sport. Six years later, after finishing graduate school, I went to work for the Ben Hogan Company in Fort Worth, Texas. I worked there for thirteen years, the last eight as the Vice President of Sales & Marketing.

Mr. Hogan was fifty-six years old and active in the high-end golf equipment company that bore his name, when I first met him. I only saw him play three rounds of competitive golf: when I was a teenager during the 1960 PGA Championship at Firestone Country Club in Akron, Ohio, and later, when I was with the Ben Hogan Company, during the 1970 Colonial National Invitation Tournament in Fort Worth. Hogan may have mellowed from his competitive tour days, and especially following his accident, but the same forces from within that drove him toward perfection on the golf course drove his efforts at the Ben Hogan Company.

Hogan was a man of black and white, with very little gray. He walked a narrow path. As a young man fresh out of graduate school, I found him friendly yet intimidating, open yet forceful, humorous yet dour, engaging yet distant, inviting yet solitary, a perfectionist yet forgiving, a technician yet a motivating, inspirational person. He was also a man of strong principles, and from those he rarely, if ever, deviated. Whether on the golf course, his company, or in his personal life, Hogan consistently lived by those principles, as well as unwavering standards and values.

Hogan was a very private individual. He did not do things for personal publicity, nor for personal adulation. His private life was his private life, and he and those immediately surrounding him-his wife Valerie, and his secretaries through the years, Claribel Kelly, Rosemary Godwin, Doxie Williams, Sharon Rae and Pat Martin-went to great lengths to keep it that way. Make no mistake; Hogan could be a distant, cold individual. But he could also be warm and friendly, with a smile that made his blue eyes twinkle and his whole countenance beam. He had an expressive face. When he smiled, his whole face seemed to light up, and his laugh was deep and infectious, reflecting sheer delight. (In fact, "delighted" was one of Hogan's favorite words. In speeches he would pause in the middle of the word to emphasize the "light" syllable... "I am de-LIGHTED", to express his personal joy at whatever had given him pleasure or enjoyment).

But that same expressive face with those same blue eyes could become the infamous Hogan glare. Those "steely blues," accentuating his sullen, angrily piercing outrage, could bore a hole through the self-assured, and leave those with lesser self-security gasping for air. However, in the thirteen years that I was around him at the Ben Hogan Company, and the numerous times I saw him after that, I witnessed it infrequently. Perhaps I was just lucky that I never had the wrath of Ben Hogan directed at me. He and I had several significant differences of opinion, but while Hogan was unyielding in his position, he listened to my line of reasoning, articulated his position and stated his conclusions, and we moved on from there.

While I worked frequently with Mr. Hogan at the company, we were not personal or social friends, though I was a member and active golfer at Shady Oaks Country Club, his home course. He did invite me to play golf with him half a dozen times, and was enjoyable to play with on each occasion. Perhaps losing my father at a young age, however, helped me relate to him and better understand some of the things he did, or didn't do. Hogan lost his father to suicide at age nine.

Hogan, whose youth was almost totally void of acceptance, lived life as a struggle for survival. He was the kid who was picked on because he was small, the struggling boy who never seemed to get a break. Those experiences toughened him and ingrained in him the determination not only to survive but ultimately to succeed to such a level to be respected as a person. People's perception of him was not his concern--respect was. His search for acceptance with no fatherly praise or advice, with no assistance from anyone in his young life, left an emptiness a lifetime of success couldn't fill, only mollify. Hogan wanted to succeed, had to succeed, to such a level that people would give him the respect he never had as a youngster.

During a course for our men's group at church, Tom Wilson in leading us through a series entitled "Manhood," had this to say about boys without relationships with their father:

"When a boy fails to connect with his dad in one way or another, demons of one kind or another will often fill the void. If you don't get what you need from your dad growing up, you will fill it with other things." Hogan filled it with a drive to be the best at golf. I worked hard at basketball. He used anger to drive away fear. I used anger when relating to unfairness, sometimes even driving away made up villains. (I slowly learned in life that "fair" is where you go to ride the rides and play games of chance). As I've written this book, I've thought about an unspoken, even unrealized connection there. I never knew about his father until a number of years after my tenure at the Hogan Company, but there was something there that I related to with the man that made it different.

Some say that Hogan was a different man after his accident, that the outpouring of sympathy and support for him tore down the walls built up by his hard childhood and his having to scratch everything out for himself the hard way, alone on the practice range. That may be. His accident occurred twenty years before I arrived at the Hogan Company, and his playing career was essentially finished. Other than a slight limp when he walked, and his shoulder surgery in the late 1960s, no other signs of that near-fatal experience were noticeable. In the years I worked for the company and the numerous times I saw him after my tenure there, he never mentioned that accident. Hogan had to work extremely hard to regain his golf ability after the crash. Once, among a very small group, he related that he had to dramatically revise his swing to accommodate his damaged left knee because he could no longer put the same stress on his left side as he did prior to the accident. On a couple of occasions, while playing golf with him at Shady Oaks, I saw him muff shots when the lie demanded significantly more than the normal amount of stress on his left knee. He didn't comment on it, and uttered no excuse. He sternly moved to his next shot and played on. By then Hogan was in his 60's, but the grimace of pain at those moments was noticeable.

Much of what the media have presented to the public regarding Hogan's personality has been negative. His privacy did not mesh with many sportswriters' and sportscasters' desires to make public his private side. The media thought their hold on access to the public demanded favorable treatment from Hogan. Consequently, they either ignored him or stayed with their trite, negative characterizations of him. His seclusion after his playing days only further aggravated his image as a non-caring person. He wasn't interested in whether you liked him or not, just whether you respected him. Whether the negative media didn't bother him enough to cause concern, or his Irish nature caused him to bridle at any thought of yielding to their wishes to improve his image, is an unanswered question. But Hogan chose to do it his way, regardless of the consequences to his image.

On several occasions before I left the company in 1982, I anxiously asked Hogan to work with someone on his autobiography. I even bought legendary test pilot Chuck Yeager's autobiography and gave it to him, hoping it would interest him enough to tell his life story. Henry Picard, the golf professional to whom Hogan dedicated his 1948 book *Power Golf*, in a handwritten note to me wished me luck. He too, had the "good idea" of encouraging Hogan to write his autobiography, but Picard said in his note, "I did not win."

Hogan had, on occasion, discussed doing an autobiography with various people, including veteran golf writer and author Al Barkow, who contacted three publishers about the project. Gordon Boswell Jr., a Shady Oaks acquaintance of Hogan's, made notes with the thought of possibly writing a Hogan biography himself. Boswell's notes recalled that Hogan knew that his story was inspirational for many who had experienced one of life's tragedies, and that he and Valerie had discussed writing a book "just to help others." In every case, Hogan declined, saying it would be too time consuming and too much work. His modesty may have been another problem, Boswell noted, because Hogan worried, "I'm afraid people would think I was bragging."

During the 1980s and '90s, I heard numerous references about Hogan as a solitary, brusque, surly, selfish man, totally unapproachable and devoid of feelings. These terms were incongruent with the man I had worked with for nearly a decade and a half. I was able to observe Hogan first hand on many occasions. I also got to know people who knew him in various capacities: friends, golf professionals, Hogan Company co-workers and people in the golf industry. I started putting together notes of personal experiences, expanded those to the recollections of others he knew and, in so doing, was encouraged to talk to additional people for new material. In 1999 I contributed a story about a dog named Max to *I Remember Ben Hogan*, a book published in 2000. That tale was selected by Paul Harvey as the basis for one of his "The Rest of the Story" radio episodes, which encouraged me to continue.

Ben Hogan: The Myths Everyone Knows, The Man No One Knew is not meant to be another biography of Ben Hogan, although it begins with a summary of his life story. It focuses on little-known public things that give the reader better answers to the questions, what was the man like? And, how different was he from the predominant public image of him as a cold, calculating championship golfer?

Making the bricks for his house on site; selecting the china and flatware for a country club; demanding an ad agency be fired for the "f" word in a commercial outtake; concerned about a little boy's "l'il toofies"; taking a collection for a waitress; giving a speech while wearing a woman's wig; having a stray dog watch his every practice stroke; telling a shag boy not to catch the golf balls because he might break a small bone in his finger; complimenting a sportscaster as the very best at what he does; winning a lawsuit that contributes to the game and professional sports: these are not typical topics connected with the mythic golfer Ben Hogan. But they are very much the man Ben Hogan.

Some of the stories I was a part of, some I was just a spectator. Still others were related to me by individuals who had no reason to embellish them. I've also included some episodes published in previous works, with the same objective of providing insight into the man, Ben Hogan. Some of the stories, had I not been there myself, I would not have believed.

It was the man, Ben Hogan, who lived his values and principles regardless of the cost. It was the man, Ben Hogan, whose grit and determination kept him returning to the pro tour despite his numerous failings. It was the man's courage and resolution that pushed him to play on bandaged legs when someone less driven, less compelled would have faltered, quit or demanded the rules be made more accommodating. It was the man, Ben Hogan, whose desire to provide superior golf equipment and whose ingenuity moved the industry up a level with the lightweight steel shaft, the forerunner to graphite. It was also the man, Ben Hogan, who had a friendly personal side, an engaging sense of humor, and a sense of compassion for those who had suffered the physical misfortunes of accidents or disease. My hope is that this collection of life episodes fills in the gaps in an understanding of the man, Ben Hogan.

Nick Seitz wrote a feature story on Hogan in the September 1970 issue of *Golf Digest*. Hogan told him, "I got credit for a lot of things I didn't do, but I did dedicate myself to the game. And I loved every minute of it. And I'm the same person today as I was then." Seitz, after spending a week with Hogan, confessed in the article, "In that time I think I came to know somewhat a Ben Hogan only remotely related to the single-dimensional, distant figure I had been led to expect."

Ken Venturi, one of Hogan's closest friends, felt that if you never met Ben Hogan, you really never got to know who he was. He succinctly summed up his feelings about Ben Hogan when he noted, "Why did Ben Hogan take me under his wing? He wasn't someone in search of companionship. He was in search of perfection, and he came as close as anyone to achieving it. Yet Hogan gave me his time, and his wisdom, also without any conditions. I saw Hogan's strengths and his weaknesses, and both made me a better golfer and a better man. I was proud to call him my friend."

As one who met Ben Hogan, worked with him, played a few rounds of golf with him and observed him for many years, I got to know him as the man, not the myth.

Ben Hogan talks to Sam Snead during the 1950 Colonial NIT. (PHOTO COURTESY, *FORT WORTH STAR-TELEGRAM*, SPECIAL COLLECTIONS, THE UNIVERSITY OF TEXAS AT ARLINGTON LIBRARY, ARLINGTON, TEXAS)

ONE:
HOGAN – CHARACTER TOUGH

MYTH: *Ben Hogan was just a mean person, an aloof recluse who cared only for himself.*

MAN: "Ben was a tough little guy who learned to fend for himself and maybe by the sheer force of his will made himself a success. Heaven knows, there was very little in his young life that would make you want to think he would later become one of the greatest golfers in the history of the game." - Sam Snead

Ben Hogan was nine years old when his father, Chester Hogan, who had been in bad health for more than a year, shot himself in the family home with a .38 caliber pistol. Conflicting accounts of the tragedy place Ben's brother, Royal, three days shy of thirteen, or Ben, age nine, in the room at the time of the suicide. The real story never got outside the family, which later included his wife, Valerie. Regardless, the whole family was in the small house and the very loud explosion of the gunshot and the horror of their father as he lie dying would have been traumatic for the whole family. "In all the years we were married, he only talked about his father's death a few times, about how he remembered his father.... I didn't know about it until after we had been married for some time," Valerie Hogan said. "Somebody in his family mentioned his father's suicide and I said, 'What are you talking about?' Ben's father was his idol, and his father's death just hurt Ben so much. I was told that at his father's funeral they were not able to get Ben to go into the church, he couldn't bear to see the casket."

Ben idolized his father, and his death was traumatic. In the late 1980s Hogan revealed a guarded secret in a conversation with Kris Tschetter, Hogan's friend and TCU golfer and later LPGA professional. "'Tough time?' he said quietly. 'I'll tell you about a tough time. Imagine a little boy walking into a room as...' His voice trailed off, but he stuck out his index finger like a gun and made the unmistakable gesture of a man shooting himself. He looked at me as if surprised by what he just

The Hogan kids - sister, Princess 5; young Ben 2; and the oldest, brother Royal 7. (PHOTO COURTESY HOGAN ESTATE)

said. Tears welled up in his eyes. He had this hollow, shattered look on his face, one that I had never seen from him before and one that I will never forget. His eyes fell to the floor and then into the distance. It was as if he thought focusing on something far off would push the words and memories away. His father's suicide affected him and he knew it. It still brought tears to his eyes sixty-five years later."

Hogan's father's death left his wife Clara, her two boys and their sister Princess, age 15, in difficult financial circumstances, requiring the two boys to help with the household income and basically ending their childhood. Royal, in the sixth grade when his dad died, quit school before long and got a job selling the *Fort Worth Star-Telegram*. He enlisted younger brother Ben to help. Selling newspapers on the street corner or at the train station back then was a tough business. Both Hogan boys learned quickly, learned to think quickly and learned to defend themselves and their favorite newspaper spots, on the street corner and the train station. They often used their fists to fend off other newsboys who often tried to run them off. The boys also would try to make a little extra money by carrying passengers' bags on and off the trains. However, only "Redcaps," the porters employed by the train station, were supposed to carry luggage. On one occasion the two were caught by a Redcap and they took off. Seeing the Redcap gaining ground the two dropped their bags and bolted.

Ben Hogan rarely discussed those early difficult years. A Shady Oaks colleague, Gordon Boswell, Jr., was present on a few rare occasions when he did talk about those days. Boswell recalled, "Ben's early life was tough. His mother worked as a seamstress to support the family. One of his favorite stories was recalling how he and Royal met for a hamburger and a coke after selling newspapers in town at night. His face would always light up recalling the old Greek restaurant owner who would always ask, 'Do you want any picklies?'"

Boswell added, "After selling newspapers for a short time, Hogan found out he could make more money caddying at the Glen Garden Country Club in Fort Worth, than he could selling newspapers so he headed for Glen Garden to caddie. During his caddying days Ben learned about people, and because of his smallness in stature, he had to fight the kids there who picked on him."

The Glen Garden caddie yard was a rough place to break in. Picking on new kids was standard fare to drive off competition for toting bags. After numerous hazing episodes, which ranged from kangaroo court, to being rolled down a hill in a barrel, or made to run through a line where he was whacked on the backside, sometimes with belts. Hogan had to take on one of the larger caddies in a fistfight. The undersized newsboy, who had learned to use his "dukes" to protect his newspaper spot, gave the bigger boy a going over. Little Bennie Hogan had learned to be tough and unyielding when it came to survival. He even stuffed his pockets full of mushy, almost tasteless red hawberries on the way to caddy at Glen Garden so he could have some lunch.

Gardner Dickinson related a story that Hogan later confirmed that as a little boy, each night he would sell all but two of his newspapers. He would take them out to Glen Garden Country Club where he was a caddie. He would spread one of them in the bottom of a bunker near the eighteenth green and cover himself with the other, and then he would sleep there so he could be the first in line to caddie. He thought that he might make more money by getting two loops in one day. When a couple of the bigger caddies arrived and saw little Ben first in line, the bigger boys would grab him and toss him to the end of the line. Dickinson, and the caddie who told him the story, surmised that such treatment could have contributed to Hogan's developing a mean streak.

Clara Hogan was an excellent seamstress. For her, failure was not an option, only a sign of giving up too soon or not working hard enough. She was a tough woman, one who demanded that her boys do quality work. If they were going to do anything, it had to be done right. They did not want to let her down. Following her example both ended up successful businessmen (Royal in office supplies) with strong work ethics, high quality standards, and tempers that rose to anyone who challenged those standards.

While Clara Hogan stood only 5' 2", she was not one to be trifled with. Chester Hogan's death was not a topic for open conversation, even in private family settings. Valerie Hogan noted that she and Ben had been married many years before she found out about it and that it was only when she overheard a discussion between her sister-in-law Princess Hogan and Mama Hogan. It wasn't until books were written about Ben Hogan, that some of his friends learned that his father had committed suicide.

Trying to help with the household expenses, young Ben Hogan was committed to doing whatever he needed to do to be a caddie, including fighting other caddies if it came to that. In their spare time, the caddies had a game of whacking golf balls with a club, and whoever hit his ball the shortest distance had to retrieve the balls for the entire group. Hogan, though undersized, joined in the game and quickly grew tired of fetching the balls. He learned to hit the ball far enough so he wouldn't have to run out and pick up the balls each time.

While he did not possess a natural golf swing, Bennie Hogan worked at it and became one of the best players in the caddie pen. He later revealed that his brother, Royal, switched him from playing golf left-handed to right-handed, telling him that no athlete was ever successful playing left-handed. Being a natural left-hander and playing golf from the right side gave Hogan the ability to generate a great deal of power due to his strong left side.

At Glen Garden Hogan started caddying for Marvin Leonard, a local businessman nearly 20 years his senior. While Leonard originally thought his time too valuable to chase a little white ball, he was told by doctors in 1927 at the age of 32 that for health reasons he needed to strike a balance between work and leisure activities, so Leonard pulled out some old golf clubs he had and started playing golf in earnest. He scheduled nine-holes of golf into his daily routine by trying to play nine-holes at sunup every morning, and there to carry his bag at that early hour was 15 year old Bennie Hogan. Golf restored Leonard's health but it also established a relationship between the young man and the teenager. Leonard had four daughters, but he had no son, and Bennie Hogan had no father figure in his life. The relationship would become very important to both men throughout their lives. Young Bennie's main competition among the Glen Garden caddies, amazingly enough, was Byron Nelson. Two of golf's greatest stars of their era started in the same caddie ranks at Glen Garden Country Club in Fort Worth, Texas.

At the age of 15 Hogan and Nelson squared off in the annual 9-hole caddie tournament. Nelson sank a long putt on the ninth and final green to tie Hogan. Someone said they should play sudden death to break the tie. Hogan won the first hole, and presumably the match, with a par. But then someone else suggested the playoff should be a full nine holes. Hogan thought he had been had, that someone changed the rules so Nelson could win, but he said nothing and went on with the full 9-hole playoff. Nelson again sank another long putt on the last green, this time to beat Hogan by a shot. There was a party at the country club after the tournament. Bennie Hogan, for whatever reason, did not attend.

Within the next several months Glen Garden offered a prized Junior Membership to one caddie; it was given to Nelson. About the same time, Hogan, who was then 16 and too old by the club rules to caddie, asked if he could practice at the club. He was refused. Hogan was given a part-time position of shop assistant at Glen Garden by Ted Longworth working late into the night on the weekends, but even then, wasn't allowed to play or practice at the club. Longworth took Byron Nelson to the PGA Championship in Dallas that year to watch it, but not Bennie Hogan.

Hogan had to go to several daily-fee golf courses to practice and play. His determination and hard work resulted in Hogan becoming one of the top two amateur players in North Texas. The other was Byron Nelson. There were not many amateur tournaments at that time to offer sufficient challenge to Hogan's game, and to really develop his skills and to earn some money, so Hogan decided to try the professional circuit. However, dogged by a recurring hook Hogan came home broke after each attempt of several tries at the circuit.

In 1932, for example, Hogan headed for California with $75 in his pocket to play on the winter tour. He had to sell his clubs to get back to Fort Worth.

At one point during the next few years, to make money for his next tour attempt, Hogan rented the golf shop at Fort Worth's 9-hole Oakhurst Country Club, anticipating his golfing friends would frequent his shop. "No friend ever showed up," Hogan told golf writer Herbert Warren Wind 23 years later. Said Wind, "I've never heard a man so bitter." Hogan had to take other jobs to supplement his Oakhurst income to save enough money for another try at the tournament circuit.

The lessons of his childhood that implanted the seeds of a self-reliant attitude were only reinforced by the lack of support from people he considered friends once he tried to make the professional golf tour. It hardened Hogan's wariness of people, fomented a lack of acceptance of people, and left him suspicious of the motives of others. Only his brother, Royal, and his friend, Marvin Leonard, financially helped or encouraged Hogan. Both loaned him money so he could continue his quest to win on golf's professional circuit. Beyond that, Hogan was strictly on his own.

Consequently, he did not to expect help from his competitors. He was a quiet, hard worker who devoted a great deal of time to practice rather than socializing with the other professionals, so none of them offered advice, assistance or support, and Hogan was too shy or too turned inward to ask them for help.

In 1935 Ben Hogan married Valerie Fox, whom he'd known since she was 14 years old. Clara Hogan for some reason did not care for Valerie Fox, and did not attend the wedding. The two never would get along. Together, Ben and Valerie chased after Hogan's dream to be a professional golfer. On the tournament trail he was lonely, and he wanted Valerie with him for both companionship and moral support.

After having failed in 1932, 1933, 1934, yet again in 1936, in 1937, Hogan still wasn't cutting it financially. He and Valerie couldn't afford for both of them to continue on the tour. His total winnings in 1937 were just over $1,100, so Valerie insisted he go on without her. But he would have none of that. If she didn't go, he wasn't going without her. Hogan was so completely discouraged he was ready to give it all up.

At a Fort Worth hotel the Hogans were animatedly discussing their financial problem and neither was giving in. Henry Picard, who happened to be at the hotel, noticed the discussion and sensed the seriousness of it. Picard, one of the most respected and successful players then on the tour, walked over and gave some timely encouragement. He also offered his financial support should Hogan need it for both of the Hogans to continue traveling the tour. Picard's magnanimous offer of financial support at least at this point gave the Hogans the opportunity to continue on in search of a dream.

Heading to the 1938 Oakland Open, the Hogans were about broke. He had won just $142 in the first four tournaments, and Oakland was his last hope. Ben and Valerie Hogan had made a "deal" that they would take the $1,400 they had saved and play the tour until the money ran out, and if they ran out of money Hogan agreed to sell his clubs and not talk about professional golf again.

In Oakland the Hogans once again stayed at the least expensive hotel they could find. The morning of the first day of the tournament as Hogan left the hotel to drive to the tournament, he found his car jacked up on rocks, the wheels had been stolen off of his car. Hogan bummed a ride to the tournament with Byron Nelson, arriving just in time to tee off, but not having time to practice before his round. Hogan finished sixth, winning $285. In 1983 Hogan told CBS' Ken Venturi that he felt it was the biggest check he ever saw in his life, since it enabled him to continue his golf career.

Still struggling financially, Hogan was given another boost with the quiet assistance of Henry Picard. Picard recommended Hogan for the assistant professional position at Century Golf Club in Purchase, New York, and Hogan was hired at $500 a month, plus what he earned giving lessons. This also gave Hogan an opportunity to work on his golf swing.

By 1939, he had still failed to win a tournament. Picard, knowing Hogan's struggle with his demon hook, offered him some swing advice. "Go out there and learn to slice," Picard said. "That's right, lift the ball and slice it…. begin slamming it hard, with the same slicing motion. It'll straighten out and you'll be unbeatable." Hogan took Picard's advice, and worked on changing his swing. In 1940 Hogan won his first tournament, the North and South Open at Pinehurst, North Carolina, and immediately followed it with successive wins at Greensboro and Asheville.

However, despite a remarkable stretch of golf another demon haunted Hogan's progress to win tournaments the way he felt he was capable of winning; distraction by the crowds. Hogan was unnerved by the distractions' negative effect on his game, and he could not practice away the crowds and their negative impact on his ability to play his best.

Again, Hogan's approach was to mentally define his problem and seek a solution. He set his mind to conquer the obstacle that obstructed his path to success. Since the crowd distraction unnerved him and negatively affected his game, he had to find a way to block it out. This he did by focusing totally on the immediate challenge before him—the hole, the shot, the conditions, and where he wanted the ball for his next shot. By focusing totally on the task before him, Hogan was able to block out any distractions that might break his concentration. Hogan once told a friend that he used anger to drive away fear, to more intently focus and to help put up a wall around him. In so doing, he so deeply fixed his attention on his shots and game plan that he might not even recognize Valerie, his wife, in the gallery, even if he looked directly at her.

In all, from 1940 through 1942 Hogan won 15 tournaments, and was the leading money winner on the tour all three years. In 1941, Henry Picard again recommended Hogan for a club job, this time at the Hershey Country Club, as the playing representative for the Hershey Candy Company. The Hershey job provided a substantial increase in income, and only required that Hogan socialize with the members when in town, leaving plenty of time for practice on his schedule.

While totally dominating the pro tour, Hogan had also developed the persona of a mechanical man, one of all strokes and no feelings. He couldn't engage with the crowds and concentrate on his game. It seemed that it had to be one or the other, and he believed, rightly or wrongly, that the right choice was to win golf tournaments. Hogan had chosen the perfect formula to win golf tournaments, but the wrong formula to win friends and fans, and he didn't win the affection of the media, either.

After several tournament wins Hogan left town without allowing the press to interview him. Hogan offered the explanation that he hadn't meant to offend anyone, and that he was just eager to get to the next tournament stop, but that didn't satisfy the press. One influential columnist complained to his readers, "Hogan may have the game to win a number of golf tournaments, but not yet the grace to be a champion." The media felt Hogan uncooperative, and Hogan's blunt short answers weren't the type of responses they wanted. An adversarial grudge was building between Hogan and the media, and that's usually a losing proposition for an athlete. Some golf writers thought Hogan took perverse pleasure in making their life difficult and vowed to punish him for his short responses and apparent slights of the media. Hogan wasn't wired to fraternize with the media, and he wasn't about to let them get close enough to intrude into his personal life and the family secret he shared with no one.

Hogan became particularly upset when he felt he was misquoted. Consistent with his personality and his family upbringing Hogan had also been his perfectionistic self with the media, and they disliked it. His early fights with the press because he felt he was misquoted and misunderstood put him on the outs with reporters, and being without recourse, Hogan withdrew. He was a private person to begin with, the whole Hogan family was. His life experiences had made him wary of others, and his run-ins with the media only drove him further from the spotlight, made him less available to the media, and elevated his distrust for the fourth-estate.

In 1943, with World War II raging, Hogan joined the Army Air Forces. He was discharged in 1945. Returning to the pro tour late in the 1945 season, he won five tournaments.

Despite winning the wartime Hale America Open in 1942, and losing the Masters that same year to Byron Nelson in a playoff, Hogan had yet to win a recognized major championship as he hit his stride in 1946. At both the Masters and the U.S. Open that year, he three-putted the 72nd green to lose. Losing in such heart-breaking fashion in not just one, but to have the first two opportunities in your grasp to win a major championship only to be three-putted away, would be such a bitter defeat that it would devastate most golfers, but not Hogan. He had suffered major setbacks in his life many times before, and he again responded. Again, Hogan called upon that inner strength to figure out his problem, work on a solution, and work, work, and work some more on perfecting the newly acquired solution.

Discouraged, he left the tour and returned to Fort Worth to regroup. Hogan's nemesis, the terrible hook, was slipping back into his game and wreaking havoc with his ability to win. Hogan noted, in an article he wrote in the August 8th, 1955 issue of *Life* magazine, "I was finishing in the money and occasionally winning a tournament, even with a terrible game. But the handwriting was on the wall. If I was going to stay and make a living, something had to be done." Mulling over in his scientific mind what technique or techniques could he try to eliminate the devastating hook without giving

Valerie Hogan pins the bars of a 2nd Lieutenant on the collar of her husband as he gets his commission after graduating from the Officer Candidate School of the Army Air Forces. Nov. 13, 1943. (A/P WORLDWIDE)

Ben Hogan practices his putting in the hotel room. (GETTY IMAGES)

up any yardage on his shots Hogan didn't pick up a golf club for three or four days. All those solutions cut down on his distance by five to ten yards, and to Hogan's thinking, "Five yards is a long way. You can't give anybody five yards. You can't correct a fault with a fault."

One night Hogan, while lying awake in bed, began thinking about an old technique, that along with two adjustments he devised, he would later call his "secret." It was a combination of an old Scottish technique called pronation, a rolling of the hands during his swing to manipulate the clubface, the face of the club opens with this roll of the hands on the backswing. Hogan experimented with the second of two added adjustment techniques, the bending the left wrist back and inward at the top of the backswing which further opened the clubface and made it impossible to close the clubface fast enough for Hogan to hook the ball. The other adjustment was a modification of his grip, "moving my left hand one-eighth to one-fourth inch to the left so the thumb was almost directly on top of the shaft."

Hogan tested the new combination of techniques for a week or so with spectacular results, the ball "had a slight fade to the right. It came down light as a feather. The harder I hit the better it worked. There was no loss of distance." Hogan felt he had to put the new technique to a real test. That test would be playing in a tension-packed tournament. Would it withstand the pressure of tournament golf?

It did. Hogan won the 1946 PGA Championship at the Portland Country Club. In the semifinals of the match-play tournament, he faced his friend Jimmy Demaret. Hogan shot 33-32-31 to beat Demaret 10 up; they didn't even have to play the final nine holes of the match. Hogan was sharply criticized for beating his best friend on the tour so badly. One writer called him "ruthless, cold-blooded, and the least compassionate" golfer on the tour, further stating, "He doesn't merely want to beat you, he wants to trample you underfoot." After winning the finals against Porky Oliver, Hogan said during the awards ceremonies, "It is impossible to explain how much this means to me," his sentence tapering off with emotion, "So I'll just say thank you to the PGA and my wife, Valerie."

As far as the "secret" was concerned, Hogan won 8 of the final 12 tournaments in 1946, something had improved. During one stretch Hogan won 7 of 8 tournaments, including 6 in a row. Immediately prior to the first victory in that run, the PGA Championship, he finished 2nd in the Philadelphia Inquirer Open. Following his PGA Championship victory, he finished 2nd at Colonial, where a victory would have enabled Hogan to piece together a victory string of 8 tournaments in a row as he won the next 6 tournaments after the Colonial.

Prior to the PGA Championship, in late 1946, a growing rift between the tournament players and the PGA Association threatened to split the two organizations apart. The tournament players wanted to control their own affairs, with less interference from the PGA. The tournament players were struggling to make enough money to meet their expenses, and PGA members felt they had the right to play in any tournament they qualified for. While Hogan was a scourge as far as the press was concerned, and was not one of the most-liked players on the tour, he was one of the tournament players selected to represent them. Hogan and Gene Sarazen had been the two strongest proponents of the tournament players' demands. Herb Graffis, golf writer and the PGA official historian noted, "Sarazen and Hogan are, on the record, the coldest, toughest, most defiant proponents of the policy that tournament golf is a problem whose answers are worked out by clubs, balls and the scorecard, instead of being a playground of the welfare state." So while Hogan wasn't one of the most liked by his tournament player peers, when it came to their professional interests and helping to establish the basic foundations of the beginning of the modern professional golf tour, Ben Hogan was one they selected and counted on to represent them.

The following year (1947), Hogan won 6 tournaments, including his second Los Angeles Open, and was selected to be the Ryder Cup team's playing captain. The U.S. Ryder Cup Team, under Hogan's leadership, proved a formidable group—Sam Snead, Jimmy Demaret, Herman Barron, Lew Worsham, Lloyd Mangrum, Byron Nelson, Dutch Harrison, Herman Kaiser, Ed Oliver, and playing captain, Hogan. The Americans won the most lopsided Ryder Cup victory ever, 11-1.

Hogan started the 1948 season by winning the Los Angeles Open on one of his favorite courses, Riviera Country Club. He also won his second PGA Championship, beating club professional Mike Turnesa 7 and 6 in the finals. Most likely remembering the criticism he had received just two years earlier when he drubbed Jimmy Demaret in the 1946 semifinal match, Hogan, as he accepted the PGA Trophy, uncharacteristically offered some of his feelings to those in attendance. "I know you all think I'm the great stone face…but this is a competitive game. I know the other fellow doesn't expect any quarter from me, and I don't give it. You probably think I'm happy over winning this tournament, but I'm not. I hate to beat these men. They go back to their clubs and tell how they were beaten."

Biographer James Dodson reported what followed Hogan's words in *Ben Hogan An American Life*: "For one of the few times ever, Hogan let down his guard and peeled back the curtain on his complex psyche, aiming to show compassion for the challenge facing young club pro Mike Turnesa. In the aftermath of these remarks, he was dismayed to read that some reporters actually found his comments to be ungracious and condescending, an example of classic Hogan gamesmanship, possibly even a carefully worded effort to humiliate an up-and-coming competitor. It was exactly these kinds of distortions, or simple misinterpretations that contributed to increasingly chilly relations between Hogan and some members of the press corps."

For a person who wanted it exactly right, Hogan deeply resented those who twisted his words or made them out to mean something he had not intended. Making his heartfelt remarks out to be a humiliation of a young pro only deepened Hogan's distrust of the media, and his disdain for some of the people in it. Oddly in 1948, the PGA was played prior to the U.S. Open. The Open was at the Riviera Country Club where Hogan had won the Los Angeles Open at the start of the season. He returned to Riviera and won the Open shooting 276, breaking the tournament scoring record by five strokes. His U.S. Open victory was the first of five consecutive wins—the Inverness Four-Ball, Motor City Open, Reading Open, and the last being the Western Open. Hogan was the first player ever to win the PGA, U.S. Open and the Western Open, the three then considered majors, all in the same year. Nevertheless he continued to earn criticism in the press, such as after finishing early in the Denver tournament Hogan felt his score wouldn't win so he raced to the train station to catch the train for Salt Lake City,

Ben Hogan talks to reporters. (PHOTO COURTESY, *FORT WORTH STAR-TELEGRAM*, SPECIAL COLLECTIONS, THE UNIVERSITY OF TEXAS AT ARLINGTON LIBRARY, ARLINGTON, TEXAS)

site of the next tournament. But he had won, so he missed the award presentation ceremony. He called the tournament headquarters to extend his apologies. Still, the *Rocky Mountain News* blasted Hogan and the Associated Press sent out a report of Hogan's no show. Hogan was again branded as a prima donna, an enigmatic star, one who had no care or concern for the fans. In October of 1948 Hogan capped a marvelous year on the golf course by winning the Glendale Open, his 10th tournament victory of the year. He was sought by TV hosts, and he raised his exhibition fees, pushing the previous ceiling up substantially.

In February 1949, after two early wins on the California tour which gave Hogan eleven wins and four second place finishes in his last 17 tournaments, he and Valerie decided to return to Fort Worth. They had recently purchased a new home, and Hogan needed the rest. He was now 36 years old and did most of his traveling by train, but he and Valerie had driven to California. In an interview with *Time* magazine Hogan said he was tired and going home, "It's not the golf, it's the traveling," he said. "I want to die an old man, not a young man."

In less than three and a half years, from 1945 through 1948 he had won a total of 34 tournaments. And from 1940 – 1948, with 2 full years in the military (1943 & 1944), he was the leading money winner 5 times: 1940, 1941, 1942, 1946 and 1948. In 1945, after returning from the military in August, he was 3rd on the money list. He had the low stroke average on tour the same years he was the leading money winner. He won the Vardon Trophy in 1940, 1941, and 1948, but no Vardon Trophy was awarded in 1942 or 1946. And during that 9-year period (actually six and a half golf years for Hogan) he won 49 official PGA tournaments.

On their way home to Fort Worth, the Hogans stopped at the same motel in Van Horn, Texas that they usually stayed at on this trip. The next morning, dense patches of fog enveloped the highway severely reducing visibility. Having difficulty seeing the road, Hogan slowed to a crawl as they proceeded east toward Fort Worth.

Traveling west on the same Highway 80 was a Greyhound bus. Running behind schedule, the driver was trying to make up time but had come up behind a slower moving freight hauler. When the bus driver thought he had a clear opportunity to pass, he sped up and swung out into the oncoming lane. Less than an eighth of a mile ahead, the Hogans were coming up a slight rise onto a bridge. Suddenly there were four headlights side by side in the roadway in front of them. Hogan instantly looked for an escape route, a place to swerve off the road, but the bridge abutments left no room.

As the bus was about to crash into their car, Hogan flung himself in front of his wife to protect her. The left front of the bus slammed head-on into the left front of the Hogans' car and drove it backward on the bridge then off the side of the road into the culvert. Hogan's reaction to dive to his right to protect his wife most certainly saved his life and probably hers also. As the 25,000 pounds of bus, passengers and luggage rammed Hogan's Cadillac, the impact with the bus drove the car's steering wheel through the front seat. Had Hogan not dove to the right the steering wheel would have crushed his chest. As it was, the steering wheel caught Hogan's left shoulder, fracturing it, and the impact of the bus pushed the car's engine and dashboard back into the front seat, leaving Hogan with a broken left ankle, two crushed legs, crushed pelvis, a broken rib, broken shoulder and bladder injuries. The dashboard also smashed into Hogan's head causing injuries, particularly on the left side of his head.

After being pulled from the car, Hogan lay motionless on the ground. Several people thought he was dead and tried to cover him with a blanket. But a few moments later Hogan groaned and moved a little. Before fading again into unconsciousness Hogan complained that his left leg felt cold. Then he passed out and went into shock, with a dropping blood pressure and pulse rate, and loss of consciousness.

In the confusion and chaos it was more than an hour and a half after the accident before an ambulance arrived. In the meantime, Hogan was in and out of consciousness and his condition growing worse. It took four hours to get Hogan to a hospital in El Paso, more than 100 miles away. Initially doctors gave Hogan only a slim chance to live. If he survived, they gave him little chance of ever walking again. Jimmy Demaret went to see him within days of the accident and indicated the doctors made no secret of their opinion that Hogan was never going to be able to play golf again. Virtually nobody believed his legs would withstand the physical stress of professional tournament golf.

Hogan started to recover. His condition was gradually upgraded from critical to fair to good. While he had nothing to say to reporters, Valerie Hogan talked with them to describe the accident and how Ben had flung himself in front of her to protect her during the collision. The story, plus pictures of Hogan's mangled car, went out to the newspapers and suddenly the image of Ben Hogan began to change. Hogan had risked his own life to save his wife. It was a different picture from the insensitive, uncaring man with ice in his veins that the press had presented.

Severe pain in Hogan's chest, and X-rays led to a diagnosis that blood clots had formed in his left leg and had moved toward his chest. Despite doctors' efforts to thin his blood, clots still developed. Hogan's condition was downgraded to critical. If a large clot reached his lungs it could cause death. Doctors decided to perform a dangerous operation. Tying off the vena cava vein, which returns blood to the heart, to save the legs and eliminate the blood clots from reaching the lungs was not a common surgery in 1949, and the long-term effects were unknown. The surgery, if successful, would leave Hogan with severely impaired circulation in his legs and his badly damaged left knee. If he ever did walk again there would likely be swelling and persistent pain in his legs for the rest of his life. Hogan's odds for survival were assessed at one in three. Doing nothing, however, most probably would mean he would die.

Dr. Alton Ochsner from New Orleans, one of the leading vascular surgeons in the country, was selected to do the surgery. But poor weather conditions in Louisiana meant that no airplane connections were available. Valerie and Royal Hogan convinced Brig. General David Hutchison of the Army Air Forces in El Paso, who had seen Hogan just a few days before, to fly a B-29 to New Orleans to bring the surgeon to perform the surgery on the former Army Air Forces captain. After two hours of surgery Dr. Ochsner described the surgery as successful. It was thought that Hogan's life had been saved, but at the expense of his golf career. Almost all the doctors felt he would never walk again without assistance, and swinging a golf club, playing professional golf was totally out of the question.

With no large vein to carry the blood in his legs back to his heart, Hogan's blood had to be forced through smaller veins in his legs. Tight bandages and elastic hose

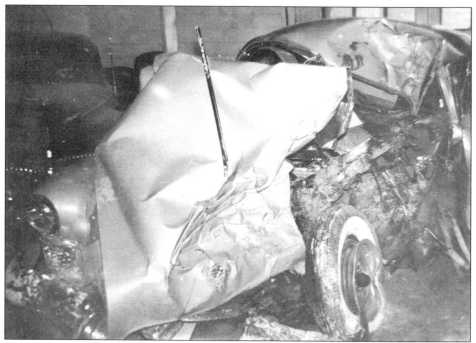

Ben & Valerie Hogan's car after being hit head on by a bus, February 1949. (A/P WORLDWIDE)

Ben & Valerie Hogan's car in front of Leonard's Department Store, shortly after their February 1949 head on collision with a bus. (PHOTO COURTESY HISTORICAL PRESERVATION COMMITTEE, COLONIAL COUNTRY CLUB)

were used to force the blood through the smaller vessels, in an effort to enlarge them sufficiently to handle the larger flow. This resulted in, not surprisingly, very poor circulation to Hogan's legs, which plagued him the rest of his life.

In addition to his leg problem, Hogan's collarbone had been broken by the steering wheel and his head's left side hurt by the dashboard. Hogan himself said his nervous system had been shot by the accident, and he didn't know if he could readjust it for competition.

Meanwhile, the switchboard at the Hotel Dieu Hospital was flooded with phone calls, and cards, letters and telegrams arrived in batches. The outpouring of sympathy and encouragement impacted Hogan greatly. Until then he believed, possibly correctly, that no one gave a damn about him. Now, he realized there were people out there who cared. Valerie Hogan told the *Fort Worth Star-Telegram*, "If there's one good thing out of this accident, it's been that Ben realizes how many good friends he has everywhere. People have been wonderful." Later when Hogan traveled the tour, then with a severely reduced schedule, he visited some of the people who had written to him and told him of their own struggles. Hogan did his best to keep such visits private. Indeed, throughout his life Hogan was a charitable man, giving donations to numerous charities, organizations, and individuals, but always keeping it very private.

Despite prevailing opinion, Hogan took a different view of his future, "Golf was my business, and I just didn't think I had to get out of it. You can do a lot if you have determination, the will, and faith. Very seldom do I take another person's word that I can't do something. I had to be convinced that I couldn't play again. I had to see for myself."

While still hospitalized in El Paso he called on his inner strength and faith to methodically day-by-day, step-by-step, rebuild his mangled body. First he squeezed little rubber balls to strengthen his wrists and forearms and had a small gymnasium bar suspended from the ceiling above his hospital bed to build his upper body. He had to start with his right arm because of his broken left collarbone. Twelve days after his surgery, his legs started to heal, and he got himself out of bed unaided. It was the first time in six weeks that he had put both feet on the floor. Several weeks later he rode by train to Fort Worth, and an ambulance took him to his new home, the one he had left the tour in California for, to get some much needed rest.

At home, Hogan again set his feet on the floor, gritted his teeth and stood up. Initially, he could take only a step or two. "It hurt, but I had to do it to get well," he said. He gradually increased the distance he walked, once, then twice around the bed, then around the room, then down the walk, and later around the block. During that tortuous ordeal he started putting a golf ball, then pitching golf balls inside the house.

That Fall Hogan made the trip to England to be the non-playing captain of the U.S. Ryder Cup team. He still had difficulty walking. Leonard Crawley, of the *Daily Telegraph*, thought Hogan looked like a cripple. He and Henry Longhurst of the *Times* talked with Hogan for hours, listening to him tell his plans to play again and win more championships. When Hogan left, both writers said together, "How pathetic."

Hogan's physical impairment did not diminish him mentally or emotionally. With his Ryder Cup team down, going into the last day's play, it looked like the British and Irish team might take the Cup away. Hogan gave a strong motivational speech that lit a patriotic fire under the American team lifting it to a 7-5 victory via a strong 6-2 final day thus retaining the Cup and bringing it back with them on the *Queen Mary*. When he returned home a determined Hogan restarted his daily workout regimen, painfully regaining his ability to walk. "I was fortunate that my profession was golf," Hogan said, "I just had to walk." He got to where he could walk five miles. It was at that point that he first started to take practice swings with his clubs. It was December, just ten months after his accident.

Even the warmth of public affection following his accident did not eliminate his suspicion of the motives of others. That, plus his desire for privacy, was indelibly etched into Hogan's psyche. However, the little kindness and support that was offered to him was remembered and greatly appreciated by him.

Little chance had been given that Hogan would ever walk again, let alone play golf, and competitive golf at the professional level was beyond hope. Yet, the fire inside the man demanded he overcome, challenging his capabilities and his physical limitations, while putting back the pieces to his golf swing that had brought him this far. Hogan's grim determination and will to succeed drove him, not only to play again, but also to play at a level some say no one could match. Hogan's legs could no longer take the active schedule he had played before, so he would never return to the double-digit victory years that preceded his accident. And despite a very limited tournament schedule due to the lasting effects of the accident, Hogan pushed his legacy to still further heights.

Once more, Hogan had dedicated himself to overcoming the obstacle set before him. He subtly changed his golf swing, a swing that had just won thirty-four tournaments in thirty-seven months, and that commanded the top money spot on the tour for nearly a decade. He could no longer put the same stress on his left side, could no longer transfer his weight as strongly as before onto his left knee during his powerful swing. Moreover, he now had to wear an elastic leg stocking and wrap his legs in bandages before playing to aid circulation, combat swelling, and help his endurance while walking the course. After a round he would have to soak his legs in warm water to further aid circulation and reduce swelling in his legs. Hogan went back to his protracted practice routine, but now at a much more pain-filled price.

Less than one year after his accident, Hogan courageously entered the Los Angeles Open. When Hogan called the tournament headquarters to enter the Los Angeles Open, tournament officials tried to be polite and sympathetic, inviting Hogan to be the honorary starter for the tournament, "Honorary starter, hell," Hogan complained to his wife, "If I go out there, I'm gonna play!" Hogan convinced them that he was dead serious and was entered to play. And play he did.

Hogan now had an extensive pre-tournament ritual of a warm soak in the tub to stimulate circulation in his legs followed by wrapping his legs with elastic bandages and special support hose/stockings. This was to try to reduce the swelling in his legs by helping force the blood flow in his legs as he walked. However, the additional time needed to soak, apply liniment and wrap his legs required between three-and-a-half and four-and-a-half hours.

The tournament at Riviera was not without controversy as Hogan wanted no pictures taken of him. It's possible he was fearful of falling down or concerned his knee might buckle during his swing. The photographers there wanted no part of such favoritism and put up a fuss. Hogan relented, but only after getting into an argument with some of the cameramen.

Hogan played well, tying Sam Snead at 280 for first before losing in the playoff. Snead said afterward, "Ben's rehabilitation looked hopeless at times, but that little fellow was a tough character...This was the greatest comeback in the history of sports... Ben's comeback was a great thing, and it showed just what kind of champion's heart he had and what kind of man he was." Hogan lost to Snead in the playoff, but he was back.

The real test for Hogan, however, was whether or not he could compete and win in the major tournaments, namely the U.S. Open and the Masters. The PGA, with its strenuous match play format, that required 36 holes per day for four or five days, was out of the question, and even the U.S. Open with its 36-hole final day would be extremely taxing on Hogan's legs and stamina. Hogan had won the last Open he played in, in 1948 at Riviera in Los Angeles, but had never won the Masters. He tired in the final round on the hilly Augusta course and finished fourth in the 1950 Masters.

In the fourth round of the Open at Merion Golf Club, just outside Philadelphia, needing a par on the very difficult 458-yard par 4 finishing hole to tie co-leaders George Fazio and Lloyd Mangrum, Hogan elected to hit his one-iron on his very long approach shot. The ball settled in the middle of the green about 40 feet from the hole. (The follow through of his swing was photographed from behind Hogan by *Life* magazine's Hy Peskin, and is probably the most recognized photo in golf). Hogan two-putted for par to force a three-way playoff, which he won the following day with a one-under par 69. The man who was never going to be able to play golf again, following a near-fatal car wreck, had now overcome the Open's grueling 36-hole final day format to win the U.S. Open. Hogan had now won the last two U.S. Opens he had entered, 1948 and 1950.

Just a week later that year, Hogan served as a technical advisor in the filming of *Follow the Sun*, a movie about his life. Hogan's contract gave him a great deal of control over the motion picture. While not his normal perfectionist self, he was much more detail-oriented and perfectionistic than the filmmakers ever wanted. At one point Glenn Ford, who played Hogan (and was a terrible golfer) was using clubs that were not the same clubs that Hogan used in that particular situation. Hogan objected, insisting filming stop until the proper clubs were obtained. The director told Hogan that it would cost $100,000 to stop filming to look for those clubs. Hogan said he didn't care. Filming was stopped until the proper clubs were found. And that instance wasn't the only time Hogan stopped the filming.

But Hogan wasn't entirely negative on the film set. He worked with Glenn Ford on his golf grip and swing for some of the close ups. But on some of the close ups and all of the distance shots Hogan made the golf swings himself.

The movie does provide some insight into Hogan's perspective of himself and those who impacted his life. One area in particular is the press, depicted by the character of the antagonistic and sarcastic sports columnist Jay Dexter. The only things missing on this guy are the horns, pitchfork and tail. Another fictional character is Hogan's friend in the movie, Chuck Williams. Williams is a fun-loving guy who is a good golfer but has his personal troubles. Hogan beats his brains out in one match, and then he and Valerie try to help Williams and his wife save their troubled marriage.

There is nothing in *Follow the Sun* about Ben Hogan's difficult boyhood, his family or his father's death, in fact his father isn't even mentioned in the movie. The only comment about his family is that they were poor. As the film starts its conclusion, Hogan, in his first attempt to return to professional golf after his accident, loses the 1950 Los Angeles Open in a playoff to Sam Snead.

The final scene is a dinner being held in his honor. Famed sportswriter Grantland Rice introduces Hogan (Glenn Ford), "And I have the honor, and a very great honor, of introducing a man who the record books will show lost a tournament today. He didn't lose! His legs simply were not strong enough to carry his heart around." Rice looks to the adjoining room, and calls out, "Ben." As Hogan (Ford) enters the audience stands and applauds, then quiets as Hogan struggles to the podium and sits down. Rice turns to Hogan (Ford) and says, "Ben, we've saved a full hour for your eloquent, brilliant and lengthy message." The audience laughs, and as Hogan rises, applauds.

Hogan (Ford) then addresses the crowd. "Thanks" in a barely audible voice reflecting his humble emotion of being so honored. "You know, there was a time when I used to think that once I teed off in a tournament I was all alone out there, completely on my own. Well, this tournament has taught me otherwise. For you see

I wasn't alone out there these past few days. No, I was with the thousands of people who love golf as I do. I was competing against great golfers who play the game as it's always been played, and as it should be played—giving no quarter and asking none. And for that I'm particularly grateful to Sam Snead. I'm very thankful to all of you who've been so, oh so very kind and generous. You've made me very happy. But you've made one other person very happy. Because besides me, she, and she alone, knows how much my playing again has meant to me. Thanks a lot, fellas. See ya around."

Hogan won the 1950 PGA Tour Player of the Year Award, despite Sam Snead having one of his best years ever. Snead won eight official tour tournaments, the Vardon Trophy for the low stroke average, and was the tour money leader. Snead was bitterly disappointed, but had mixed emotions about it. He said, "Of course, 1950 was Ben's comeback year after his near fatal car accident. It was called the 'greatest comeback in sports history,' and I won't argue with that. Heck, they could have given him a six-foot trophy as the best comeback kid, but he just wasn't the best player that year."

In 1951, competing in only four tournaments, Hogan at last won the Masters. He sank the putt on the final hole for a 280 total and a two-stroke victory. Hogan was thrilled to win the Masters. He and tournament founder and all-time amateur great Bobby Jones had enormous respect and admiration for one another, and this was a special event for both of them. Some years later Jones was asked which great player he would choose to make one shot to win a tournament. Jones replied, "That's not hard for me to answer...Hogan. He had the intangible assets, the spiritual."

After finishing fourth in the Colonial National Invitational Tournament in Fort Worth Hogan's next tournament was the U.S. Open at Oakland Hills near Detroit. The course had been redesigned, and every hole altered, making the course longer, narrower and harder with very deep rough and difficult bunkers. The Oakland Hills course was as severe a test as the professionals had seen. The typical U.S. Open standard hard and fast greens in combination with the other course changes made the Oakland Hills track known as "the Monster." Nevertheless Hogan birdied the final hole of his last round for a 67 and a total of 287, to win by two. For the entire tournament there were only two rounds under par, and three rounds of par. The average score for the tournament was 77. Hogan had now won his last three U.S. Opens. ('48, '50 and '51). Given the difficulty of the course, Hogan's final round 67 is regarded as the finest finishing round in Open history. As he accepted the winner's medal from Joe Dey of the U.S. Golf Association, Hogan said, now famously, "I'm glad I brought this monster to its knees."

In his only other tournament that year, Hogan won the World Championship of Golf, an event he disliked because of George S. May, the tournament founder. May was offering a huge purse but wanted to require the players to wear their names on their backs. Hogan refused, and May withdrew the requirement. Hogan, for the third time in four years, was named PGA Player of the Year.

Hogan competed in only three events in 1952, the Masters, the U.S. Open, and the Colonial NIT, winning only the latter. But he made his mark in another way by suggesting to Bobby Jones, the legendary founder of the Augusta National Golf Club and the Masters, and Clifford Roberts, the legendary ruler of the club and its tournament, that they start a "Masters Club" for all the past champions. "The Club" would meet for dinner on the Tuesday prior to that year's Thursday start of the tournament and the winner from the prior year would pick up the tab. Since Hogan had won in 1951, he would host the first meeting, just prior to the '52 Masters. Jones and Roberts liked the idea and the Masters Club was born, a tradition that continues today.

A more ominous development came to the fore in 1952 for Hogan, as his putting began to seriously deteriorate. In the Masters Hogan, tied for the lead after three rounds, three-putted three of the first six holes in the final round and shot a very uncharacteristic finishing round 79. Sam Snead and several other players that were paired with Hogan noticed his putting problems during the tournament. At the U.S. Open on the Northwood Club course in Dallas, Hogan's putting again failed him miserably. He three-putted several times, while the winner, Julius Boros, had only 40 putts in the final 27 holes. Hogan limped home with a 74 to finish third.

While he had had putting problems in the past, costing him an opportunity to win both the Masters and U.S. Open in 1946, now Hogan couldn't even draw the putter back. He would stand over some of his putts for an inordinate length of time before starting the putter back, and at times would even back off the putt rather than starting his stroke. Then when he finally did stroke the ball it frequently looked more like a stab or a jab than a smooth stroke. Rumors began to spread in the press of Hogan's retirement, but with Hogan having a number of lucrative contracts and product endorsements, and a new job at Tamerisk that just required him to make an appearance for a few weeks each year during the winter at the Palm Springs, California club, Hogan had not said anything to that effect.

Hogan worked hard in the off-season at Tamerisk to get his game in shape for the 1953 season. He took a comment made by Valerie seriously when he was complaining about his poor putting. She told him he'd just have to hit his approach shots closer to the hole. While some would have laughed and shrugged the comment off as a joke, Hogan didn't. His practice routine that winter had just that objective. He also shed some 20 pounds that he had gained after the accident to be in better physical condition.

In his first official tournament, he set a new Masters 72-hole scoring record of 274, 14 under par, 5 shots lower than the previous mark. Gene Sarazen and Clifford Roberts said that Hogan's 72-holes of golf were the finest four rounds of golf ever, anywhere!

Amid some controversies regarding his financial demands, tournament choices and charitable donations, plus his intense efforts to play better than he had in 1952, Hogan was also in the process of laying the groundwork to start his own golf equipment company. Over the years Hogan had had an ongoing feud with MacGregor, the equipment company that made his clubs and paid him to use them.

Each time he had a new set of clubs made he went to Cincinnati, Ohio to personally oversee them being made and to inspect the finished product before they left the plant. He always required some rework or modification and at times even had them remake the set before they suited him. Hogan also was angered that he had long been the bridesmaid to Byron Nelson as far as the way MacGregor treated him and the golf clubs bearing his name. "Hogan" clubs made by MacGregor were sold through department stores and sporting goods stores, a lower quality club sold to mass marketers. Hogan refused to promote them. At the time higher quality clubs were sold through golf professional shops at golf courses, and golf professionals "fit" the clubs to the player. Hogan believed he could create a company that could manufacture golf clubs right off the standard production line that would be superior to any clubs that were currently on the market. Now he was in the final stages of putting all the pieces together to try to do just that. In fact, he had looked for a suitable facility in Fort Worth for his company.

On his way to the U.S. Open Hogan decided to stop by the MacGregor corporate headquarters in Cincinnati for a visit. While at the MacGregor factory Hogan was given statistics, test results and the evidence regarding the superiority of the performance of the MacGregor golf ball, which he believed to be inferior and had refused to use in the Masters. The tests had been with a mechanical robot driving machine. At the end of the visit, with pressure still being applied to play the MacGregor ball based on the mechanical robot's results, Hogan was reported to have said, "If you think it's so damned good, why don't you enter that f_ _ _ ing machine in the Open?" before storming out.

Hogan had won three of the previous four U.S. Opens he had entered and had finished third in 1952, but in 1953 everyone except the defending champion, Hogan included, had to qualify for the tournament being played at the Oakmont Country Club, just outside Pittsburgh. Hogan made the field without much trouble, although he was suffering from back spasms and thought he might have pulled a back muscle during the qualifying rounds. Then on a difficult Oakmont course featuring furrowed sand traps and fast, undulating greens Hogan shot a 72-hole total of 283 demolishing the old tournament record at Oakmont by 11 strokes.

With Hogan's record breaking scoring at the Masters and at Oakmont, golf enthusiasts, were starting to call Hogan the greatest player of all time. All-timer Gene Sarazen told UPI's Oscar Fraley, "This settles it, Ben's the best there ever was."

However, there was one blight on such a claim: Hogan had never played in, much less won, the British Open. No record in "The Open" left a hole in Hogan's resume, one he now chose to fill. He headed to Scotland and one of the toughest, if not the toughest, of the British Open courses--Carnoustie. When he first saw Carnoustie, one of the courses dating back to the birth of the game of golf, Hogan understood why no one had won the British Open on his first try. The course was a drab-looking mixture of greens and browns with no trees. It looked to him like the land had been undeveloped since year one. Whereas U.S. courses have boundaries such as trees, fences or hedges, when Hogan stood on the tees at Carnoustie often he could not tell where the fairway ended and the rough began.

Knowing all these factors were against him winning the tournament only made Hogan work harder at learning the course, the keys to playing it well, and acclimating himself to the conditions. To adjust for the tight turf, for example, Hogan worked at catching the ball clean rather than taking his normal swing, which was producing big divots and too much backspin. "Those roughs are like God made them. And they'll be that way when God comes back unless somebody changes them," Hogan exclaimed. Also, the greens were hard, but much slower than they looked.

He was chronically leaving putts short. And the smaller British sized ball would carry farther, particularly into the wind. It also nestled more deeply in the grass. With less air resistance the smaller ball wouldn't curve as easily as the American ball, so Hogan had some major adjustments to make just to be able to use the British sized ball. Given all the changes Hogan had to make, it was almost like reinventing his game all over again.

Like the U.S. Open of 1953 the British Open required two 18-hole qualification rounds. While he easily qualified, he was disappointed in his game. He even apologized to the enthusiastic fans that had followed him for giving them such a poor show. When asked about the playing conditions, Hogan replied that the greens were like putty, and that he would have to have a lawn mower sent over from Texas so they could cut the greens a little closer. When a reporter said he thought the greens had been mowed twice that day, Hogan half-jokingly noted, "It would have been better if they'd put the blades in the mowers." Some took Hogan's remarks as an attempt at humor, others did not.

By the end of the second round, played in wind and rain, Hogan was frequently blowing his nose due to the onset of a head cold. Hogan's head cold grew worse, and that night, before the day he had to play the final 36 holes of the tournament, he had a fever of 103. Nearly 20 years later Hogan recalled that he still shivered when he thought about the weather. It was cold, wet, and windy. Bundled in sweaters, topped off with rain gear, he played through the rain with a raging fever, reportedly 103°. Nevertheless, Hogan finished in dramatic fashion, making a two-putt birdie on the par 5 finishing hole for a final round 4-under par 68, and a four-round total of 282.

The 68 was a new course record for Carnoustie and his 282 total was the lowest ever in a British Open Championship since the tournament went to 72 holes in 1892.

Hogan was totally drained and weary. When he refused to go out and accept the winner's prize right away, many thought it was typical Hogan rudeness to leave the fans, his wife included, out in the rain waiting for him. However, Hogan, with his sense of propriety, was not about to accept the Claret Jug, the British Open trophy, without a sports coat, and his was in the locker room a distance away. Finally, Hogan borrowed one for the ceremony. In fact, Hogan chose to accept his prize dressed in that manner for all tournaments. It was his way of showing respect for an event, its fans and the people who worked to put it on.

Hogan's British Open win climaxed a year that has been talked about since. Despite a balky putter, he won the three major championships he played in, and was unable to play in the PGA Championship because of the schedule conflict with the British Open. No golfer before Hogan had won the Masters, U.S. Open, and British Open in the same year, and no one has done so since. Only Tiger Woods, in 2000, has won three of the four majors in one year since Hogan, capturing the U.S. and British Opens and the PGA Championship.

The Hogans returned to the United States via ocean liner, the U.S.S. United States, rather than another transatlantic flight. Festivities honoring him in New York included a ticker tape parade, a ceremony at City Hall, a luncheon given by the Golf Writers Association, and a dinner hosted by the USGA. President Eisenhower sent a telegram of congratulations that was read by New York Mayor Vincent Impellitteri. Even after the crowd quieted down, Hogan took a few moments to compose himself. His voice cracking with emotion, Hogan told the crowd, "I've got a tough skin but a soft spot in my heart and things like this find that soft spot."

A press conference had taken place aboard ship before it even docked, and Hogan leaked a bit of news: that he was going to start manufacturing golf clubs. He thought he had a revolutionary way of making clubs, had already built some experimental models, and hoped to be in production soon. He wanted a way to stay active in golf after his competitive playing days were over, and making golf clubs was his way to fill that void.

Years later, USGA vice president Ike Grainger remembered the event, in particular

Ben Hogan displays a set of clubs in his office at his new Fort Worth factory, July 1955. (PHOTO COURTESY, *FORT WORTH STAR-TELEGRAM*, SPECIAL COLLECTIONS, THE UNIVERSITY OF TEXAS AT ARLINGTON LIBRARY, ARLINGTON, TEXAS)

Hogan and his demeanor, "It was the kind of night that should have forever laid to rest any of this business about Ben Hogan being a cold and unsociable fellow. I think old Ben laughed and talked with every person in the house, and in some of them two or three times, sharing stories. He couldn't get enough of it."

Hogan had taken on a business partner, Pollard Simons, and the two bought property and equipment to start manufacturing Ben Hogan golf clubs. The first ones were scheduled to come off the West Pafford Street facility production line in 1954. When they did, they were not up to Hogan's standards, and he refused to allow them to go out the door, wanting them to be scrapped. Simons disagreed. He felt that Hogan's strict quality requirements were going to be a costly proposition. At an impasse, the two agreed that one had to buy the other out, but Hogan did not have the financial capital to buy out Simons. However, he could not live with a scenario that did not give him total control over the products bearing his name. Thanks to a loan from Marvin Leonard, Hogan acquired Simons' half of the business.

In 1954, Hogan played in only four tournaments, winning none. Now almost forty-two years old, Hogan's age combined with the damage from the accident was taking its toll. In 1955 Hogan played in just three official tournaments. The 1955 U.S. Open was held at the Olympic Club in San Francisco. Hogan closed with a final round 70 for a 287 total that everyone believed had won him his fifth U.S. Open. The only player with a chance to catch him was the obscure Jack Fleck, who, during the practice rounds, had been rumored to be breaking in a new set of Ben Hogan irons.

Hogan sat quietly, slumped in the locker room as he heard the crowd at 18 roar as Fleck's birdie putt to tie him after 72 holes curled into the cup. He wished that Fleck had made a 2 or a 4, to win it or lose it—he didn't want a playoff. The cool, humid climate at Olympic and the soft turf had exhausted Hogan, both physically and mentally. Since his accident 72 holes was about all his body could take in a four or five-day period. In the 18-hole playoff, Fleck won by three.

Losing in such a fashion was a bitter disappointment for Hogan. An Olympic victory would have been his fifth Open win in his last seven attempts. He is one of four golfers to have won four U.S. Opens; none has won five.

In subsequent years, Hogan tried to compete in every Masters and U.S. Open, and returned to play in the PGA Championship in 1960 after it became a medal play tournament. As time crept by, though, more and more of Hogan's scores were in the 70's and fewer and fewer were in the 60's. But Hogan's focus was on the U.S. Open, where he usually made his best showing, other than at Colonial, in his final years on the tour.

During a cocktail party prior to the 1956 Bing Crosby Pro-Am, Ken Venturi was talking with George Coleman, an oilman from Oklahoma, and Eddie Lowery, a large car dealership owner from San Francisco. When asked what he was doing the next day Venturi blurted out that he and Harvie Ward would love to play Byron Nelson and Ben Hogan, who were also there preparing for the Bing Crosby tournament. Coleman was quick to pick up on the idea and went to Hogan who said he'd love to play and the same was true with Nelson so the match was set up for the following morning at Cypress Point. Hogan, thinking ahead told them to make him a starting time at Pebble Beach. When Venturi objected, that the match was set for Cypress, Hogan responded, "I know that, but I don't want people coming over there and watching me play a couple of amateurs." Hogan turned to Venturi and winked and both got big grins on their faces.

The next morning as they were getting ready to play, Venturi and Ward were keyed up and Venturi particularly wanted to win very badly. Nelson and Hogan were his heroes, and he and Ward were playing very well, well enough that Venturi thought they could win. The four played a $100 Nassau, a lot of money in those days, but the well-heeled Coleman and Lowery, and some Cypress Point members who could obviously afford it, put up considerably more money. The match was a classic, close all the way, with neither team getting more than one-up on the other. Venturi sank a 12-foot putt for birdie on the last hole, and the match came down to Hogan's 10-foot birdie putt. If he made it, the Nelson/Hogan duo won, if he missed they tied. Nelson encouraged Hogan by telling him to sink it and they would win. Hogan responded, "I'm not about to be tied by a couple of amateurs," giving Venturi another wink. Hogan's putt hit the dead center of the cup, to win the phenomenal match. Ward and Nelson shot 67, Venturi a 65 and Hogan had 63, tying his own course record at Cypress. They had 27 birdies and an eagle (Hogan's approach shot at 10 went in the hole.).

Fittingly, Hogan won his final professional tournament at the 1959 Colonial in Fort Worth, beating Fred Hawkins in a playoff. Ironically, Hogan had given Hawkins a set of Hogan clubs earlier that week to use in the tournament. It was Hogan's fifth Colonial title. It was a popular and an emotional victory for both Hogan and tournament host Marvin Leonard, his benefactor in playing professional golf and starting his golf equipment company. After his 1959 victory Leonard gifted the Colonial trophy to Hogan in honor of his achievements at Colonial.

The 1960 U.S. Open, played at Denver's Cherry Hills Country Club, went down in golf lore for many reasons. First, was winner Arnold Palmer's dramatic final-round of 65. Second, was the debut of a young amateur from Ohio named Jack Nicklaus who was paired with Hogan in the final two rounds of the tournament. And lastly, was Hogan's last great chance to win his fifth official Open. Through sixteen holes in the afternoon round of the 36-hole final day, Hogan had hit all 34 greens and had pulled even with the new tournament leader Arnold Palmer. Yet Hogan had made only two putts all day of 10 feet or more, both of them in the afternoon round.

The 17th hole is a difficult par-5 with a green entirely surrounded by water. Figuring he needed a birdie-par finish to win, on his third shot he tried to hit the ball close to the hole and leave himself a makeable putt. The two-level green surrounded by water had a higher back level that severely slopes down to the lower front section in the middle of the green. The pin for the final round was cut on the lower tier dangerously close, just twelve feet from the front edge of the green. He laid his wedge open to cut under the ball to get the maximum backspin he could generate to stop the ball quickly on the firm Open green and pitched a low-flying wedge shot loaded with backspin. Nicklaus thought the shot looked perfect. But after landing on the green, the ball spun back to the edge of the putting surface, then trickled down into the water. After that, according to Nicklaus, Hogan, "just went flat." He was completely drained—of drive, energy, concentration. It was all he could do to finish the round.

During 1960, AMF, formerly the American Machine & Foundry Company, had begun discussions with Hogan to purchase his company. While the Hogan

Company was doing well it was small. Trying to make inroads against much larger competitors such as Wilson, Spalding, Dunlop, Hillrich & Bradsby and Acushnet (Titleist) was challenging. "Hogan was a great little company, but was undercapitalized and consequently didn't have the research and development capabilities it needed to develop new technologies and new products," recalled Ed Corvey, a key member of the AMF team. "Ben realized that, and with AMF's technical capabilities and our committed support it was a good match, particularly since Ben was given a five-year contract that was renewed every year. He remained in control, and that's the way he wanted it."

Corvey would become the Vice President of the AMF Sports Products Group that oversaw Hogan, Voit, Alcort, Wheel Goods and Head, and fiercely guarded the independence of these divisions. Corvey fought to keep their trademarks and brand names, and to keep their trademarks dominant when combined with the AMF mark. "Who would want to buy an AMF golf club?" Corvey would often ask. He had learned from the experience that MacGregor, the name in golf equipment with the likes of Hogan, Nelson, and Demaret playing its equipment had when Brunswick moved it from Cincinnati, Ohio to Albany, Georgia.

Brunswick had made the MacGregor trademark secondary to the Brunswick name and then moved the manufacturing facility leaving many of the craftsmen in Cincinnati. The quality suffered considerably, and Corvey didn't want either of those things to happen to the well-known brands in his stable. Until he left AMF in the early '70s, he fought to keep the divisional people, who knew their products, in control of their operations with as little interference from those well-meaning but lesser market-knowledgeable AMF corporate executives. That enabled the Hogan Company to blossom in the late '60s and become a real force in the golf industry in the late '70s and early '80s. While the AMF Ben Hogan Company had a number of General Managers (later called Presidents), Ben Hogan remained a dominant force in the company until the mid-1980's.

From 1961 through 1966 Hogan played between one and five tournaments a year but was generally out of contention, as his putting continued to deteriorate.

In 1967, Hogan shot 74-73 in the opening two rounds of the Masters. In Saturday's third round, Hogan went out in par 36, but something happened between the ninth green and the tenth tee. It was as if someone had turned the clock back nearly 20 years. Hogan played the back nine like the Hogan of old, rolling up birdies on the first four holes. He made his fifth birdie at fifteen and a large crowd began to follow him as the word spread. At 18, after getting pars at the previous two holes, when Hogan rolled in his fifteen-foot birdie putt for a back-nine score of six-under par 30, a thunderous roar from the crowd resounded across the course. Hogan's 66 matched his lowest round ever at Augusta, when he set the tournament record of 274 in 1953. "I received an ovation at almost every hole," he said. "It made you feel very humble for people to appreciate what you were doing."

Hogan had become embarrassed to putt in front of the public, as it had become his ever growing nemesis, but had managed to beat that demon, if for just nine holes, to highlight the shot making ability he still had in him.

At the Ben Hogan Company he spent a lot of his time on golf club development, testing and trying new things. For example, he worked closely with Dr. Fred Dunkerly, an AMF metallurgist, to develop the first lightweight steel shaft. The shaft was called the Apex shaft, it took the market by storm and made Hogan clubs competitive with the top club makers in the industry. He also oversaw the quality of the products bearing his name. While he didn't manage the day-to-day running of the plant, his indignant disapproval of a shaft or a club head could shut the operation down.

Hogan also took a keen interest in the sales force and the marketing efforts of Hogan Company products. Hogan accepted his trophies in a coat and tie to show his respect for the tournament, so his sales representatives would wear coats and ties to show their respect for the golf professionals and the members/golfers they represented. His salesmen were well groomed, sporting none of the long hair popular then.

Likewise, as Hogan became the elder statesman on the PGA Tour, he let his opinions be known regarding the dress and hairstyles being worn by the younger pros. When Hogan started on the tour, golf professionals were not held in high esteem, but they wore long sleeved shirts and ties when they played. While the game had gained in social status, Hogan still felt that respect should be paid to the people who supported the pros with time and money. That meant proper attire and hair that didn't look like a hippie. To Hogan, hippies showed little respect for authority, and he didn't want that look to tarnish his beloved game. Hogan did not play at all in 1968 or 1969 due to shoulder problems, and in the latter year he underwent his fourth shoulder surgery. No one expected him to play on the tour again, but he played in three events in 1970.

On August 26th of that year, Marvin Leonard, Hogan's beloved friend and mentor, died in his sleep. For Hogan, Leonard's loss was a tough blow. They customarily had lunch together at Shady Oaks Country Club, the course Leonard built so Hogan and other Leonard friends could find some seclusion away from the more heavily trafficked Colonial Country Club.

Following Leonard's death a group of his friends sat around the big round table at Shady Oaks and reminisced about what he had meant to them. When Hogan's turn came, he recalled the time on an early morning over forty years previous that a young Marvin, un-athletic as he was, arrived at Glen Garden Country Club to play golf to relieve his stress. "If he hadn't come along then," Hogan emotionally pondered, "who knows how I might have ended up."

Also that summer, Hogan's sister Princess' husband Dr. Howard Ditto, suffered a heart attack and died. "Doc" Ditto had been Hogan's personal physician. The following year Bobby Jones, the legendary golfer who had won both the British Amateur and Open and the U.S. Amateur and Open all in the same year, and later founded Augusta National Golf Club and the Masters Tournament passed away. That same year Hogan's sister, Princess, died as well. Hogan had named a line of ladies golf clubs after Princess, the only Hogan clubs named for an individual.

Losing Leonard, Jones, Princess and her husband Doc in such a short period was very difficult for Hogan. Moreover, in May of 1971, Hogan's career on the professional golf tour came to an unceremonious end in Houston when he twisted his damaged left knee on the fourth hole. His pronounced limp got progressively worse, and on the twelfth hole his knee buckled so badly on his tee shot that he nearly fell. After whistling his approach shot to the green Hogan told his caddie to go pick up the ball. He then told playing partners, Charles Coody and Dick Lotz, "I'm sorry fellas, I'm through." A golf cart took him back to the clubhouse. Hogan's days on tour were over.

With a little more intensity Hogan continued his off-tour daily routine of going to the office for several hours and then to Shady Oaks to have lunch, hit balls, shower and play cards with his friends. He did continue his regular golf matches with friends, Shelley Mayfield, Gary Laughlin and Eldridge Miles. Hogan often played 18 holes of golf at Shady Oaks with John Grace and others, and occasionally joined other groups for nine holes there. A reflective Hogan once confided to John Grace, the U.S. Amateur runner up to Jerry Pate in 1974, "I never did play well after the accident. I played my best golf in 1948, I could really play."

The circulation in Hogan's legs was so bad later in life that when he contemplated having surgery to repair the torn cartilage in his knee, none of the local orthopedic surgeons wanted any part of it. Steve Cain, an assistant pro at Shady Oaks and later the head professional at Hogan's Trophy Club, said "I heard several doctors talking about it and no one wanted to do the surgery, one surgeon even remarking, 'No way I'll do that surgery. I'm not going to be the one to be known for killing Ben Hogan.'" Apparently they were afraid that due to the poor circulation in Hogan's leg that he would either die during the operation or get gangrene because the extremely poor circulation wouldn't get enough blood to the surgical wound to heal it. Because of that poor circulation, Hogan hated cold weather because he could not keep his legs warm.

While there were now significant holes in his life, Hogan still had his beloved Ben Hogan Company which was thriving. The Company was working hard to develop a superior golf ball and Hogan was key to testing it. The company had not yet purchased a "mechanical man" driving machine to test equipment, so Hogan was the primary source of information and direction on the ball's performance.

As the company gained prominence in the industry and Hogan's efforts were paying off, he enjoyed a close relationship with Hogan Company sales organization, primarily through Lyne Price, the sales vice president. Initially, representatives of the Ernie Saybarac Company had sold Hogan equipment, but in the late 1950s Hogan decided he wanted his own sales organization. Price and five others (Morgan Barofsky, Jack Owens, Tom Martin, Max Baker and Pete Poore) had come from the Saybarac organization to work for Hogan. Saybarac's company also sold a number of other top selling brands to the golf shops. The six were taking a financial risk to leave Saybarac for

Hogan. That was not something Hogan forgot. Years later, in the annual sales-meeting golf tournament Hogan requested to play with the six of them as a reminder that he appreciated what they had done. Hogan continued to play in the Ben Hogan Company golf tournament throughout the 1970s and early '80s. The entire sales organization eagerly looked forward to the event at Shady Oaks as part of the annual company sales meeting.

Throughout the late 1960s and the decade of the 1970s the Hogan Company grew in size and market status, eventually becoming the leading seller of golf clubs in golf professional shops throughout the entire U.S. Riding a wave of new products, new technologies and Hogan's participation in company TV commercials, the company's revenues grew by tenfold from the late '60s until the early '80s.

Drawing sketches of new golf clubs on paper or demonstrating what he wanted changed on a current model, Hogan often had Gene Sheeley, the company's model maker, make a new club for him to test. Sheeley was an experimenter of his own and liked to put things together for Hogan to try. Once a new design was agreed upon, he set about making the master models for each wood or iron in the set. A forging house stamped forgings for iron heads, a wood-turning company made head blanks for woods. Then Sheeley would oversee each operation in the Hogan factory, at various stages running them by Hogan for approval. The final products came out just the way Hogan wanted them.

Striving to make a better club, or a better ball, and participating with the sales organization kept Hogan sharp. The company started making TV commercials in 1976 when it introduced its "Legend" shaft. Asked to participate in the commercials Hogan at first declined, saying, "I don't want to be like one of those damned used car salesmen!" However, when convinced he didn't have to say a word and was shown a story board outlining the commercial and his part in it, he agreed to participate. He reviewed and re-reviewed the boards up until the commercial was being shot, even making last-minute adjustments he thought would better emphasize the idea being depicted. Once the camera was rolling, Hogan hit the ball like it was the U.S. Open, giving the set director exactly what he wanted.

In the early '80s, changes in the company's management and operating philosophy changed the role of Ben Hogan in the company. Since he had sold the company to AMF in 1960 Hogan had not had total control over the day-to-day operations but had significant influence over them. Now in the early 1980s the new management felt that as he aged having Hogan in the TV commercials and actively involved with the sales organization was becoming a liability. It was a good time, the new management decided, to focus on the company rather than the man. Hogan was moved into the background. He was no longer asked to participate in the commercials or to take such an involved role with the sales organization.

In addition, one of the top professionals on the Tour was courted to be Hogan's replacement as the chief designer and quality overseer. The holes in Hogan's life became greater. The Ben Hogan Company was the thing he had personally planned to keep him active and alive after his days of professional tour golf were over. Now he had been pushed aside from that vital attachment, that key role that had kept him involved in the love of his life, the game of golf.

In 1983 Clara Hogan, Ben Hogan's mother fell and broke her hip and was hospitalized. Shortly thereafter she passed away in July that year, but during the final days of her life Ben Hogan was at his mother's bedside constantly.

In 1984 the Hogan Company's parent corporation, AMF, was purchased by Minstar. But, by 1986 the company was losing about two and half million dollars a year, so the president was replaced. The manufacturing vice president, Jerry Austry, was promoted to the top spot. Austry reverted to the previous company strategy of a more active and visible Ben Hogan taking a more prominent position in design and marketing of Hogan equipment. When Austry asked Hogan to assist in the development of a new cavity backed club, a club design concept Hogan did not personally like, he listened. Hogan had an aversion to cavity-backed, investment-cast iron club designs. Hogan played by feel, believing that the feel a player gets from the impact of the club head and the ball is the only information to indicate whether or not the ball was well struck. Hogan insisted the new cavity-backed irons be made of forged steel, not cast from molten metal, because he also believed forged heads provided better feel than did cast club heads.

Forged heads were labor intensive and more expensive to produce than cast iron heads. The new cavity-backed Edge model was developed and made with forged iron heads.

During the design and development of the Edge iron, Hogan Company president Austry commissioned a market study. The results showed that what everybody wanted from the Ben Hogan Company was Ben Hogan. Consequently, Austry asked Hogan to fly to Los Angeles to film a TV commercial for the new clubs. Once again, a TV commercial would feature Ben Hogan, now 75 years old, hitting the golf ball. The commercial hit the airwaves in early 1988, and the sales of the new Edge club pushed Hogan Company revenues up $20 million, a forty percent increase over the previous year, and put the company's bottom line again in the black.

Not long after Hogan returned to Fort Worth from that trip to film the TV commercial, his appendix ruptured. Hogan nearly died. It was also about this time that his memory started to fail him from time to time. His doctor, Jim Murphy, thought the symptoms were the early stages of dementia or Alzheimer's disease. Valerie Hogan, however, refused to believe that. She thought his memory lapses were due to the anesthesia used during his surgery and the medications he took after the surgery.

In mid-1988 Hogan felt well enough to appear at the Waldorf Astoria in New York for a ceremony naming the Player of the Century. Players of the Decade were named for the ten decades leading up to the Centennial event. When initially asked to attend, Hogan declined the invitation. When asked why, he said that Sam Snead, who was not a player of a decade due to the way the decades fell, wasn't being adequately honored. The slight was corrected to Hogan's satisfaction, and he went to New York. Other honorees Jack Nicklaus, Arnold Palmer, Byron Nelson and Snead were all in attendance. All took a turn at the microphone to speak.

When it came Hogan's turn to speak, the room grew quiet. Rarely did he appear in public and even rarer yet did he speak publicly. Hogan proceeded to give what amounted to a 15-minute lesson. He advised the audience to, "Watch good players. That's how I learned. I watched one movement in their swing then couldn't wait to get out by myself and practice that move to find if it would work." That evening, Jack Nicklaus was named the Player of the Century.

43

That same year Minstar sold the Ben Hogan Company to Tokyo-based Cosmo World. Its owner, Moruri Isutani, president of Cosmo World, reportedly paid over $50 million, more than 15 times the earnings for the Hogan Company. At Shady Oaks Country Club, meeting with Mr. Isutani for the first time, Hogan asked the interpreter if Mr. Isutani spoke English. The interpreter said that Mr. Isutani spoke English. Hogan then said, "Mr. Isutani, you just bought the family jewels. Don't f--- it up!!"

Five years later, in 1993, Cosmo World sold the Ben Hogan Company to the AMF Companies of Richmond, Virginia, a remnant of the old AMF. The new owners decided to move the golf-club production line from Fort Worth to Richmond, and the Hogan Company was uprooted for the first time since its doors had opened some 40 years earlier.

Ben Hogan was now near 80 years old and little more than a figurehead in the company. He was bitterly disappointed and angry about the move, depressed at the thought that the Hogan Company would no longer be under his observation. "You could see how this deeply distressed him," said Pat Martin, one of his secretaries at that time. Likewise, his other secretary, Sharon Rea, recalled, "It was like a death in the family. He'd always taken such pride in the work we'd done and the people who worked for him. It was such a personal place to work. That final week he just walked around in kind of a daze, saying goodbye to people in the factory and thanking them, looking as downcast as I'd ever seen him."

Hogan's personal office moved to a two-room suite in west Fort Worth. Sharon Rea said, "It was so sad to see him sitting in that little office with nothing really to do except reply to letters and autograph picture requests and look at clubs he no longer had anything to do with making. He'd turn and stare out the window with this faraway look in his eye, and you'd know he was thinking something."

Hogan had apparently not yet given up though. He scouted around west of Fort Worth for property to build a new factory and rehire all of his laid-off workers. But his efforts ceased after some serious conversations with company lawyers. Hogan finally accepted the fact that he could not legally start a new line of golf equipment. The once proud Ben Hogan Company had now gone the same way the once proud MacGregor Sporting Goods Company had gone two decades previous, its production facility relocated to a different part of the country, and many of its skilled craftsmen and women of high-quality golf equipment were left behind.

As Hogan's memory began to deteriorate, Valerie Hogan began to monitor him much more closely. She hired Elizabeth Hudson, the sister of their cook, Willie Mae Green, to look after Ben full time.

Hudson had heard how difficult Mrs. Hogan could be, and was ready to turn the job down until she met Mr. Hogan. She recalled, "He was so sweet and considerate of me right off. There was this little twinkle in his eye, kind of like a child's. I loved that man right off."

Hudson was given specific instructions as to what Ben could and could not do, which included tapering off his visits to Shady Oaks, the place he'd gone nearly every day of his life since the club opened almost 40 years ago. Elizabeth Hudson regretfully recalled, "He was dying to just go over to Shady Oaks and see his friends and eat some scrambled eggs and bacon, have a cigarette, and ride in that Cadillac he loved so much…'Elizabeth,' she would say to me ten times a day, 'we can't let people see Mr. Hogan like this.' I don't think she intended to hurt him, but she did."

Valerie Hogan was very controlling of Ben Hogan's activities, which apparently included watching golf on TV or even praying. "She also asked me not to pray with him but when she left, we did that too. He told me he loved going to church. One more thing he missed," said Elizabeth Hudson. Hogan must have developed a fondness with Elizabeth Hudson because he asked her to read to him from *Five Lessons*, his book on the golf swing as he had learned it. "He just closed his eyes and just listened, like a baby hearing a lullaby," Hudson said. "Then he opened them and looked at me and smiled and said, 'I practiced a lot, Elizabeth. And when I practiced, I practiced to get it right!'"

Then one day, for no apparent reason, Hogan started talking to her about his father, Chester Hogan: "He said he spent his whole life wondering why his daddy did that because he loved his father very much. He loved his mama too, but it wasn't quite the same. You could tell that he'd spent his whole life tryin' to figure that out, why his father did that. It bothered him terribly, not knowing."

Royal Hogan had been suffering from lung cancer. At that same time Ben Hogan had been suffering with colon cancer and had undergone colon cancer surgery in 1995. Despite the memory problems he went to visit his brother fairly regularly. The two could be very stubborn and tough, but both had a soft spot within, particularly Ben. He sat at numerous bedsides of dying friends, or called regularly on the phone to comfort them. In December 1996 Ben Hogan's brother, Royal, died. "I can't believe Bubba is gone," he said when he learned of Royal's death.

Not long after, Sarah Harriman, Valerie's sister, died of lung cancer also. She had been particularly close to Ben and Valerie. At Sarah's funeral, Ben limped up to the casket in the empty chapel, tapped on it and spoke to her.

Ben Hogan died July 25, 1997, about seven months after his brother Royal's death. Ben Hogan had told attorney, Dee Kelly, that when he died he wanted Valerie to control his estate. "She knows exactly what I want," Hogan had said.

Valerie Hogan's grandniece, Lisa Scott, recalled a conversation with Valerie Hogan concerning a Ben Hogan Foundation after he had died, and stated that Valerie felt that a foundation was too much for her to take on, and that she and Ben were not totally opposed to a foundation, but that he didn't want to be memorialized during his lifetime.

Throughout his career Hogan struggled with the relationship between his wife and his family. Valerie and the Hogan family never hit it off. According to Valerie Harriman, Valerie Fox Hogan's niece (Sarah Fox Harriman's daughter), "What the outside world saw of Valerie Fox Hogan was a terribly shy, beautifully turned out, and loyal wife, the quintessential private woman behind the public man who never had a hair out of place or an ill word to say. What they didn't see was Aunt Val's lifelong struggle to control everything around her, including Uncle Ben. As time went on, that became our family's other little secret."

Two years after Hogan's death, the Ben Hogan Company was sold to Spalding Sporting Goods, who moved the Hogan assembly operations back to Fort Worth. It would have pleased Ben Hogan to have his company back in Fort Worth and to see many of his former employees again making Hogan clubs. A scant five years later the Ben Hogan Company was sold again, this time to Callaway Golf Company in

California, and the assembly operations were moved from Fort Worth to the Callaway facility in California. Callaway discontinued the Ben Hogan line of clubs in 2008.

Ben Hogan could not change his personality. Growing up from the age of nine having to fight for everything, and being totally on your own to achieve success instilled the competitive fighter attitude in Hogan. And unless he stuck to his resolute process, his absolute concentration, he couldn't win. He was shy, an introvert, so he wasn't one to initiate many conversations, particularly to those he did not know well. Hogan was a very private person who did not like to be intruded upon.

As the media became more intrusive, the personal lives of athletes and celebrities were no longer personal, their private lives were no longer private, particularly those at the very top in their respective sports. Professional golf was becoming a different world from the pro tour of the past, and Ben Hogan became increasingly uncomfortable with the new media climate. Sixty years after Hogan's "Triple Crown" season of 1953, you do not have to wonder what he would have thought of playing professional golf today. With remarkable prescience, the man who was so often at odds with the public portrayal he received in the media confessed to Gary Player at the 9th hole at the Westchester Classic in 1970, "I wouldn't like to be a pro in the future. They won't have the privacy we had."

A Closer Glance

"The deepest convictions of our heart are formed by stories and reside in the images and emotions of story… Life is not a list of propositions, it is a series of dramatic scenes… As Eugene Peterson said, 'We live in narrative, we live in story'… Our souls speak not in the naked facts of mathematics or the abstract propositions of systematic theology; they speak the images and emotions of story… So if we're going to find the answer to the riddle of the earth— and of our own existence— we'll find it in story."

TWO:
CONTRIBUTING TO HIS PUBLIC IMAGE

MYTH: *Ben Hogan was an uncooperative, arrogant, indifferent star who rudely snubbed and belittled the press.*

MAN: Ben Hogan was a product of the Depression, of having lived a very difficult life for many years, of living with the dark secret and the horror of his father's suicide. Most people of that difficult period accepted their roles, responsibilities, and shortcomings. They accepted their lot in life, their lack of luck or talent, and made do with it as best they could, and quietly lived their lives. It was an attitude mirrored to the nth degree by Ben Hogan. Hogan developed his talent, worked through his bad luck, and kept quiet. He engendered admiration and respect in the public eye, but acts of love, compassion, and affection were for the quiet of his personal life. "A lot of people don't understand modesty. Not everybody wants publicity, you know." Hogan, like all of us had his flaws, but as a person he was quite a man.

When he was on the practice range or the golf course Ben Hogan felt he was in his "office" and was fully focused on his golf performance. He also at times used anger to drive away fear to aid in his dedication to focus on the objective at hand. Through his competitive years Hogan's apparent "office" routine and his anger-focused mindset landed him the image of a cold fish, a frigid competitor with ice flowing through his veins, and very little, if any, feelings. The combination of several of Hogan's personality traits, to keep to himself, to be critical of those who did not set and adhere to the same high standards for themselves as he had set and strove to adhere to himself, and to be straightforward and blunt, did not endear him to either his peer group on the pro circuit or to the sportswriters and reporters who covered tournament golf.

His public persona, forged primarily in the press, suffered for a number of reasons. Some were Hogan's own doing, others were not. Hogan saw the world one way, through the eyes of a private person striving to be the best in his profession by trying to achieve perfection in his golf swing, and through accuracy and accountability in his daily living.

Hogan, with his private persona coupled with his extraordinary drive to succeed, didn't mesh with the media, and didn't fit with most of the touring professionals; he was the odd man out. It didn't endear him to many of his fellow professionals or the media, and it certainly did not help in developing his public image. To succeed where he had failed previously, then to be the best in his profession, to shoot lower scores, such goals for Ben Hogan just didn't allow time for social pleasantries.

The story goes that Hogan, playing a course he'd never played previously, asked his caddie where to aim his drive on a particular hole that had a blind tee shot. When the caddie responded to "Aim at the church steeple," Hogan immediately asked, "Which side of the steeple?" That story is exemplary of Hogan's perspective on things, very precise and factual. There was no pretense on Hogan's part, he was what he was. And he was as perfectionistic and private in his daily living as he was in developing his golf swing or playing the final holes of a U.S. Open championship.

Sportswriters, for the most part, had their own perspective. Each article didn't have to be perfect, but it had to be good—interesting, informative, entertaining, and timely to meet deadlines. Compromise, however, was not an active word in Hogan's vocabulary, and press deadlines meant nothing to him. If the press wrote something about Ben Hogan, particularly if they quoted him, he wanted it to be exactly right, period! His perfectionism manifested itself in super critical responses to articles about him that he found to be inaccurate, and he delivered the criticism to the writers in his very straightforward and forthright manner—bluntly. Hence, the feud ensued.

Once Hogan made it to the top of the professional golf circuit the run-ins came more often, and Hogan became more cautious about making responses to questions. There were writers he trusted and those he did not.

Gene Gregston, in his book on Hogan, relates the following story: "One year at the Masters, Hogan was sitting talking with reporters when one he was wary of asked a question. Ben could almost fuse the discs of the writer's spine with his cold gaze, and after glaring at the writer for a moment, he dropped his head and studied the floor. The other writers shifted from one foot to another in the awkward silence."

Gardner Dickinson Jr, then a Hogan protégé, witnessed the scene and afterward asked Hogan, 'That was a very simple question-- why did you embarrass the guy?' 'Well, I know him,' replied Hogan, 'and I was just trying to visualize what kind of headline the guy's paper would get out of what I would answer.'"

Ken Venturi, a close friend of Hogan's, experienced an example of Hogan's fear after the 1956 Masters, the tournament Venturi almost won as an amateur. After a first round 66, the lowest round ever recorded by an amateur in the Masters, Venturi held a 4-shot lead over the field going into the final round, and a 5 stroke lead with nine holes to play. However, a back nine 42 caused Venturi to lose to Jackie Burke by a stroke. After having said the right things during the award ceremonies, Venturi flew back to his hometown of San Francisco. He was feeling down, and replayed that final round over and over in his head. Friends and members of the press welcomed him home, but he felt that the press came looking for a story too. Venturi was comfortable with them, he knew how the game was played, at least he thought he did. Venturi recalled that he got along with Snead just fine in the final round, but that he was nervous, so Snead pretty much left him alone. He explained that he was fine with the change in the final round pairings. At that time the final round leader each year was paired with Byron Nelson, but since Nelson was close to Venturi and had tutored him in the past, they asked Ken if it was OK to change the pairing to avoid the appearance of helping Venturi win the Masters.

At the end of the conference he attempted to comfort his mother, who was crying, telling her not to worry, that he would show them, he'd win the Open. There were no more questions. Venturi figured he did well, but he figured wrong.

The next day the headlines said it all:

'Sam Snead gave Venturi the silent treatment.'

'Venturi says they didn't want an amateur to win, so they changed the pairings.'

'Venturi vows to get revenge. Says he'll win the Open.'

As Venturi recalled in his book, "I was incensed. The reporters had gotten the story all wrong, and now I was going to pay the price. I had tried to explain what happened, but the quotes were taken out of context. The account circulated throughout the country, making me come off like a sore, arrogant loser. The power of the pen had struck another victory."

Ben Hogan could be outspoken, even quick with a quip, but it all depended on the situation. He would rather have been thought of as rude than having his words twisted to mean something he did not say or intend to say.

After his playing days ended, Hogan let his secretary fend off requests from the media when he didn't want to respond. Although, sometimes he had to do it himself, and he could do it bluntly. During the week of the Colonial golf tournament one year, a man showed up at the doorway of the men's grill at Shady Oaks Country Club. He got the attention of Charles Hudson, the headwaiter, pointed in the direction of Hogan, and handed Charles a business card. Charles walked over to Hogan's table, handed him the card, and whispered something into his ear. Hogan took the card, tore it in half, and handed it back to Charles, and said something to him. Charles then returned the torn-up card with Hogan's verbal message to the man waiting at the door.

Roger Williams, a Shady Oaks member, witnessed all this. He hadn't recognized the man at the doorway, so he later asked Charles what that was all about. The stranger was a member of the British press who had just shown up and wanted to interview Hogan. Hogan had given him his answer.

In 1970, after spending a week with Hogan in Fort Worth during the Colonial NIT, in which Hogan played, Nick Seitz, of *Golf Digest*, wrote a personal article on Hogan. Noted Seitz, "I asked him if his popular reputation as a grim, machine-like person bothers him. 'I could care less,' he said caustically. 'I get along with everybody I know... Too many people hear or read something written from uneducated preconceptions, and it takes off. There's a great difference between intelligence and wisdom. You might have a college sheepskin, but that doesn't make you educated. Life's too short for me to go around explaining myself. A lot of people don't understand modesty. Not everybody wants publicity, you know.'"

In the Publisher's Comment column of that issue of the magazine, when asked about Hogan's reputation for two-word answers to questions and incredulous stares accompanied by no words at all, Seitz commented to publisher Howard Gill, "He usually has been interviewed in a locker-room, before or after a competitive round, when he's practically in a trance of concentration. He's a different personality away from a tournament. If you stay away from the obvious questions and give him time to formulate carefully his chain of thought, he is an exciting talker. I doubt anyone has thought about golf as much or as incisively as Ben. I was a little nervous at first, but as it turned out, my major problem was reading all the notes I had scribbled across soiled cocktail napkins, phone message sheets, and scorecards, after I had used up three notepads."

Hogan might also remain silent when a response or explanation seemed appropriate. When benefit golf matches were set up for Skip Alexander, a popular golf professional who had been badly burned, Hogan was scheduled to play but did not show up. Considerable outrage was expressed in the press, but Hogan made no response and issued no statement. Later, a Fort Worth golf writer wrote about the circumstances, explaining that Hogan's plane had circled Charlotte, North Carolina, for two hours, but had been unable to land due to bad weather and had to return to Augusta, Georgia.

Hogan's dislike for flying also contributed to Hogan's image problem. John McMackin, Hogan's attorney, flew with Hogan numerous times, and John put it bluntly, "Ben didn't like to fly. He was a white-knuckle flier. He didn't go a lot of places because of it. There were instances he was criticized for not attending events, but it was because he didn't like to fly."

Gene Smyers, a close personal friend of Hogan's agreed and added, "Hogan was never very comfortable with flying. He even missed some award ceremonies because he didn't like to fly. He took some severe criticism about not being at some of these ceremonies, but the fact of the matter was that Hogan was afraid to fly. As wealthy as he became late in life, and the many things he liked to do, fish, hunt, play golf at Seminole, Hogan flew about once a year."

Smyers recalled a private plane incident he, Hogan and four others had on a fishing trip to Montana. The plane was apparently overloaded and because of the excess weight, the plane had trouble taking off. It appeared the plane would not clear the grove of trees that were just beyond the end of the runway. Everyone could see what was in front of them, and watching the trees become larger and closer without gaining much altitude became a horrific site. Somehow the plane managed to barely clear the trees, but Smyers somberly noted, "We all thought we were gone, and I'm sure that didn't help alleviate Hogan's reluctance to fly one bit."

During the prime of his career Ben Hogan was in demand, and he used that popularity to escalate his fees for exhibitions and appearances. Some tournament officials reportedly even paid him money just to show up and play in their tournament. This raised the ire of some fellow competitors who felt Hogan was being shown favoritism.

Following Hogan's 1953 Masters victory, the Pan American Open in Mexico City supposedly offered Hogan an estimated $5,000 appearance fee without offering the defending champion, Lloyd Mangrum, anything. For several weeks the sports pages in Mexico and the United States wrote about the alleged selfishness of golf's best player, using unnamed sources. Pan American officials denied Hogan was receiving $5,000, but some major players, including the defending champion Mangrum (who by that time had been offered a $1,000 guarantee), withdrew from the event.

The issue was compounded by a story out of Las Vegas criticizing Hogan for not playing in the Las Vegas Tournament of Champions. The article quoted, anonymously, a tournament official and a PGA official commenting that Hogan had requested appearance money and was refused, so he refused to play. Mangrum was interviewed about his role in the issue and was quoted as saying, "Any argument between a sponsor and Hogan or any other players isn't my business, but I do know that Ben's never done anything to help his fellow pros. But that's all right. Maybe we've never asked him. Still, he hasn't gone out of his way, either."

Hogan, a couple of weeks later, talked to a writer and indicated the whole thing was idiotic, "I'd have been delighted to play there, especially since it was in aid of the Damon Runyon Cancer fund. Apart from that I'm a free man living in a free country. I don't like being told where I have to play and where I can't play. If I have to take orders as to where I can or can't play, I suppose I might as well go to Russia."

While Hogan didn't like criticism, for the most part, he didn't publicly defend himself. Rather, he turned those things inward, but, when it

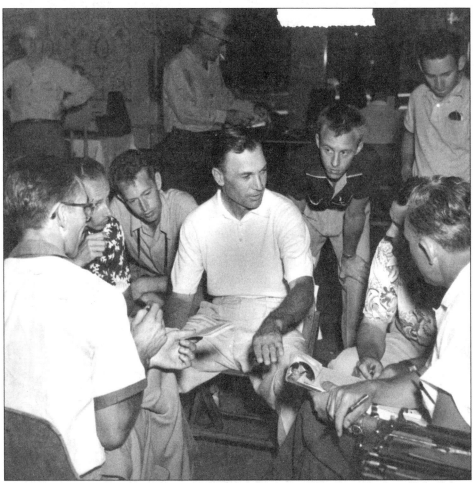

Ben Hogan explains his round to the Press. (PHOTO COURTESY OF COLONIAL COUNTRY CLUB)

came to the exhibition fees he charged and accepting any appearance money he might have been offered, he knew exactly what he was doing.

Tournament prize money was not enough to provide a viable living during almost all of Hogan's playing days, even for the top money winners. By pushing up the fee structure up for his appearances and exhibitions, Hogan was a major impetus in making the profession better for the other players, and for those who were to follow. He knew that raising his fees would cause the appearance and exhibition fees for the other golf professionals to rise as well. As the leading figure in golf at the time Hogan felt this was his part in growing the game, helping professional golfers to earn a better living. If he, as the number one draw in golf, didn't do it, who would? "I've been criticized for not playing in this tournament or that, or for demanding appearance money or guarantees, by the same fellows I'm helping," he said. "They don't realize that every time I raise my exhibition fee or the amount of appearance money, it's helping all professional golfers. An exhibition fee of $1,000 was unheard-of until I got it. But you'll notice that when I raise mine, others do the same, and the young fellows coming up in the future will be able to demand more because we raised the level."

Jim Murray, the great sports columnist of the *Los Angeles Times* thought Hogan the greatest golfer of all time until August 1980, when he wrote an article titled, "Sorry, Ben, Jack's the best." Murray writes, "I'm going to have to force my lips to say this, and I'm going to say it only once...Jack Nicklaus is the greatest golfer of all the ages of all that sport. Jack Nicklaus, not Ben Hogan. There, I've said it. I'm going to hate myself in the morning, but as Paul said to the Corinthians, you sometimes have to put aside the face of your childhood."

The Rev. Granville Walker, then retired minister from University Christian Church in Fort Worth (Hogan's Church) took umbrage with the Murray article in his church bulletin in Oregon the following Sunday, Dr. Walker wrote:

"TO ALL WHO GATHER IN THE FIRST CHRISTIAN CHURCH OF PORTLAND OF A SUNDAY MORNING TO WORSHIP, WHETHER ANGELS OR DEVILS, SAINTS OR SINNERS, GOOD OR BAD, SMILING OR FROWNING, AND EVERYBODY GOTTA BE SOMETHIN'....

Last Tuesday's *Oregonian* carried an article by one Jim Murray who writes a syndicated sports column in which he uses a passage from *I Corinthians 13* to justify his shift of loyalty from Ben Hogan to Jack Nicklaus as the greatest golfer of all time which causeth my blood to boil. Ben Hogan, all things considered is STILL the greatest, for if Nicklaus, great as he is and nobody questions his greatness, had to overcome all that Ben did following his brush with death in a terrible automobile accident right outside El Paso some years ago, when even his doctors, Dr. Oschner in particular, thought he probably would never be able to walk again, it is doubtful whether even Nicklaus, great as he is, would have been able to rise up, overcome almost impossible physical wreckage, and then go out and win tournament after tournament including the Masters and the British Open. It was a marvelous demonstration of Christian fortitude and determination, as admirable an accomplishment as his, as of then, unparalleled golf career!"

I'm sure Reverend Walker meant no disparagement to either Jim Murray or Jack Nicklaus, but rather shows here his intense feelings for his friend, the man Ben Hogan. The immense admiration this respected man of the cloth had for Ben Hogan can be summed up in his statement, "If there is anything more remarkable than Ben Hogan the golfer, it is Ben Hogan the man." Reverend Walker understood another side of Ben Hogan that very few did, that Hogan was a man of deep faith.

Jim Murray had a great deal of respect for Ben Hogan. Hogan had a great deal of respect for Murray. The two were legends in their fields, but I suspect that the attraction between the two was as much from their personal character as from their abilities in their chosen vocations. The fact that Murray had decided that Nicklaus was the greatest golfer of all time didn't diminish Hogan's opinion of Murray in the least. And it wouldn't surprise me if it even enhanced Hogan's respect for Murray. That's how Ben Hogan lived, by his principles, and he respected those who lived by theirs. Jim Murray was a pallbearer at Ben Hogan's funeral.

In his July 26, 1997 article written the day after Ben Hogan died, Murray eulogized him in the *Los Angeles Times*, "Hogan was quite simply, with apologies to Jack Nicklaus, Arnold Palmer, and even Tiger Woods, the best striker of the ball who ever played. It didn't come naturally to him; he mastered it, subdued it, as he did every challenge in his life. Hogan was grim, stubborn, stable, and relentless. He practiced till his hands bled… I worshiped him, revered him… He was a man of uncompromising integrity."

On the TV side, there was Jim McKay, the renowned ABC Sports anchor. McKay was in Fort Worth for the broadcast of the 1980 World Gymnastics Championships. Our paths crossed, and I set up a golf game at Shady Oaks with two of the Hogan Company executives, Hank Rojas and Dennis Iden.

After they finished their round, they went to the men's grill that overlooks the 9th and 18th holes to have lunch. As they were eating, McKay felt a tap on his shoulder, and a voice close to his ear said, "I've always wanted to tell you that I think you are the very best at what you do."

McKay recalled, "Turning around, I was shocked to see the hawk eyes and the slow smile of Ben Hogan, my golf idol and a man not known for giving fulsome praise. We talked only for a minute or two, but that was enough. It was the best compliment I've ever gotten."

Dennis Iden recalled Hogan stating, "I admire you, Jim. You did more at what you do than I ever did in golf," as he looked directly into McKay's eyes. Hogan didn't lavish such praise very often, and those nearby were struck by Hogan's words. McKay graciously called me a few days later to thank me for arranging the golf game at Shady Oaks, and to tell me that he had met Ben Hogan. I acknowledged that I had heard that Mr. Hogan was very complimentary of him. McKay replied, "Yes, he certainly was. That was the nicest compliment I ever got."

Jim McKay was one of a kind, a man who brought warmth, sincerity and humanity to sports in a very spontaneous way. Several years later Darryl Fisher, a graduate school friend, and I bumped into Mr. McKay in an airport. I introduced myself adding that I used to be with the Ben Hogan Company, and then introduced Darryl. McKay again thanked me for the golf game and once again commenting, "That was the nicest compliment I ever got." Hogan's sincere, heartfelt words obviously made quite an impression on him that day at Shady Oaks.

LPGA professional Kris Tschetter got to know Ben Hogan well in the 1980s as she practiced at Shady Oaks. Hogan tutored her and became a good friend. She wrote in her

2010 book, *Mr. Hogan, The Man I Knew,* "The idea of putting on a mask for the public is nothing new. Celebrities have been doing it for as long as there have been fans. The character Mr. Hogan created helped perpetuate the mystique that still surrounds him today. But the real Mr. Hogan was the man who cut his banana in half for me every Monday, the man who would toss me a Snickers bar as he rode past in his cart, the man who would press his nose against the window to make faces at small children, and the man who generously and quietly gave to those whom he saw were in need."

THREE:
Hogan's Character

MYTH: *Ben Hogan was an uncooperative, unbending, uncaring superstar who thought only of himself.*

MAN: Ben Hogan was a man of his word, with impeccable integrity, who was rigidly ethical and believed others should value those same qualities just as he did. Hogan didn't attack or demean others in the media, even though others treated him that way. He felt such things should be treated as private issues to be resolved between the individuals involved.

"His [Ben Hogan] name alone defined concentration, determination, even perfection. The Little Man had no yardage book, no golf glove, no self-congratulation, no logo, no bullshit, and no pretence. Everything he accomplished, he dug out of the ground. Ben Hogan was an imperfect but honorable man, a champion and a gentleman." – Curt Sampson, *Hogan*

The dictionary defines *character* as "The combined moral or ethical structure of a person; moral or ethical strength; integrity; fortitude."

Integrity, being a man of your word, and loyalty were important virtues to Ben Hogan. They were the basis of the values he lived by, and he expected others to live by lofty principles. While he was no *Bible* thumper, he lived by values consistent with The Good Book, so his expectations of other people's character were not unrealistic or self-serving; he just thought people should live by high principles. To Hogan, a man's word was his bond. If he told you he would do something for you, he did it. It may take a while to get done, but it got done, without any prompting or reminding. Hogan believed in that principle, and he measured people by their commitment to their word.

For most, it was his golf accomplishments, and they are enormous, that earned him their respect, but for those who knew him, it was his high values, strong principles, and lifelong determination that were the reasons they called him "Mr. Hogan."

Gene Smyers, who handled Ben Hogan's personal insurance, and who sat and visited with Hogan nearly every day for some thirty years at "the table" at Shady Oaks Country Club acknowledged, "I can tell you who the man liked, but I can't tell you who the man didn't like. Ben Hogan didn't speak ill of people."

While Ben Hogan was unabashedly honest, he was not one to publicly badmouth others. This was possibly a reaction to his own sensitivity to being publicly criticized, or having his personality or character questioned publicly.

John McMackin, Hogan's attorney for the development of the Trophy Club, spent a lot of time with Hogan during the years Hogan was negotiating with and working with the land developers in designing the golf course and laying out the overall Trophy Club development. In reflecting on those days McMackin said, "I'll tell you this about the man, if Hogan told you something, you could take it to the bank. He took a long time to answer. He thought about it before he spoke. He didn't change anything he ever said. I don't really remember Ben ever saying anything bad, no derogatory comments, about any individual."

Bob Brumby, a New York columnist got to know Hogan, and in fact, came up with a business venture idea that centered around Hogan. Brumby and Hogan were driving between Phoenix and Tucson one day when he proposed the venture to Hogan. Jimmy Demaret detailed the Brumby/Hogan discussion of the proposition:

"'Ben,' Brumby said, 'how would you like to start a chain of golf schools all across the country, the same thing Arthur Murray has done with dance studios. We'd call it 'The Ben Hogan School of Golf.' We could hire professionals for each school, train them in your technique, and then find space in a big department store in every large city in the country.'"

Ben listened carefully. 'It sounds good,' he said finally. 'But it's impossible, Bob. It would take too much of my time. I wouldn't be able to do anything but teach in those schools. And I don't know about the money. I'd only be able to teach in one at a time.'

'It wouldn't take much time,' Brumby answered. 'All you'd have to do is train the pros for a month or so, and then take a tour of your schools maybe once a year. You'd have all the time in the world to play.'

Hogan turned to the writer in surprise, 'Oh, no! I couldn't let people pay for a lesson under my name unless I was there to give it myself. I couldn't ask anybody to take a Ben Hogan lesson unless I was the teacher.'

'When Ben said that, I saw about a half million dollars going out the car window,' Brumby told me [Demaret]. 'But, you know, I didn't even mind. I felt good. I was with a man who was honest right down to the core.'"

Frank Mackey, one of the marketing executives at the Ben Hogan Company, was at Shady Oaks Country Club one day with a dozen or so club professionals who were on the Hogan Company Club Professional Advisory Staff. These staff professionals had come to Fort Worth for a meeting with the Hogan Company marketing group to review the product line, discuss the current trends in the industry and to play golf. The staff pros spotted Hogan at his usual table at Shady Oaks and wanted to go over and visit with Hogan. Frank went over to Hogan and asked if the pros could come over.

Hogan responded that now was not the time, and told Frank to tell them, "I'll see them tomorrow." Frank relayed the message, and they all went about their business, some undoubtedly thinking Hogan had kissed them off. The next morning when Frank went over to check with Hogan about meeting with them, Hogan already had chairs set up in his office so the staff pros could come in, sit down and visit. Frank said the pros came in, that Hogan was charming, and they all had a wonderful visit.

One of Hogan's Shady Oaks cronies once accidentally overpaid a young man $400. The young man, realizing the mistake, returned the money. The Shady Oaks member remarked to Hogan how nice it was that the young man had returned the money, to which Hogan responded, "He was supposed to, wasn't he?"

Shelley Mayfield, former touring professional and head golf professional at Brookhollow Country Club in Dallas, related another example of Hogan's commitment to his word. During one of their frequent rounds of golf together, Shelley complained that he was having trouble with his wedge shots, and complained to Hogan that he needed a new wedge. Shelley was on the Ben Hogan Company Advisory Board and played Hogan equipment. Hogan said he would look for a wedge for Shelley.

Months passed. The two played golf together numerous times, but the wedge hadn't arrived. Shelley said he wasn't going to ask Hogan about it, and Hogan never brought the subject up either. More than six months later, Shelley received a letter from Hogan, saying he hadn't forgotten the wedge, but he was working on a new model, the dies were now being made. Several months later, Shelley got another letter saying two wedges were on their way, and that they would need a lot of work. That was Hogan's way of telling Shelley to take them to the practice tee and "work" with them frequently. The practice notation in the message tickled Mayfield. He said that Hogan liked to needle him when the opportunity arose, and if Hogan ever stressed anything, he stressed practicing. Sure enough, several days later the two wedges showed up at Shelley's Brookhollow pro shop.

Similarly, when Bill and Kathy Cornelius, the 1956 U.S. Women's Open Champion were visiting Hogan's office one day on the way to Waco for an LPGA event, Kathy asked Hogan to sign her copy of his book, *Five Lessons the Modern Fundamentals of Golf*. Hogan started signing, then abruptly stopped exclaiming "dammit." He scratched through what he had written. He called Claribel Kelly, his secretary, and asked her to bring him another copy because he'd made a mistake on Kathy's book. Claribel said she didn't have any, but should have some more copies in a day or two. Hogan promised Bill and Kathy that he would sign a book for them when more books came in.

Several days later a gentleman approached Kathy on the golf course in Waco and handed her the signed copy of the book. The man told Kathy and Bill that Hogan had sent him to deliver it to her. Now they had two copies. Before they left Hogan's office Kathy had asked for and received the copy with the error on it.

Al Barkow in his book, *Golf's Golden Grind the History of the Tour*, discusses a situation where a pro on the tour had asked Hogan for some swing help. Hogan told him that he'd be better off going back to Chicago and getting a club job. "Hogan promised that he would help the fellow out in one way or another. The pro later got a small interest in a new public golf course and, some two years later after his conversation on the practice tee with Hogan, asked Ben if he would dedicate the opening by playing an exhibition. Hogan made a trip to Chicago to cut eighteen ribbons. His word was his bond—once given, no other insurance was necessary."

Shortly after she came to the states from Australia to play on the LPGA Tour, Jan Stephenson came to the Ben Hogan Company to inquire about becoming a Hogan Staff player. She began using the clubs and ball, and even modeled the Hogan ladies sportswear for photos in the catalog. Jan developed a relationship with Mr. Hogan, and they discussed the golf swing, and he occasionally gave her advice after watching her swing. At one point Jan decided she needed to try the new experimental metal woods that were being developed. After trying several, Jan bought one, and used it in a tournament. Sometime later the manufacturer offered Jan a $25,000 contract, plus bonuses, to use their metal woods, a significant contract for an LPGA player in the early 1980's. Jan went to Hogan with her situation. She told him of the contract that she had been offered.

Hogan looked at her and said incredulously, "They want to pay you $25,000?"

"Yes, sir, they do," Jan acknowledged.

"Well, then you take it.. Go ahead with it," was Hogan's response.

"I still want to play Hogan irons, can I still come by the plant and have my irons worked on?" Jan asked.

"Certainly," Hogan replied, "Without question."

When Jan recalled the incident she laughed as she repeated Hogan's words, with a little extra emphasis on the way Hogan intoned "YOU" in his question, "They want to pay you $25,000?"

Two other stories, very similar, yet very different portray both sides of this character trait that Hogan so highly valued. One that has been often told and retold was Gary Player's call to Ben Hogan requesting help with his golf swing, and Hogan's negative response to the request. On occasion, Hogan himself told the story. The story appeared in print under Player's name in the sports section of the *New York Times* on January 19, 1975. When he called, Player was competing in the 1973 Brazilian Open in South America.

The story said, "When the overseas operator got the call through, and Mr. Hogan answered, I said, 'Mr. Hogan, this is Gary Player. Outside of you, I figure I have practiced harder than anyone else in the history of golf. I will understand if you do not care to answer, but I must ask if you'll allow me this one question about a golf swing.'" Everything was quiet for a moment or two, and then Mr. Hogan said, "'Gary, who do you work for?' When I told him Dunlop, he replied, 'Well, call Mr. Dunlop.' And without another word, he slammed the receiver down in my ear.'"

Hogan claimed he did not slam the receiver down or hang up on Player, but that he was irritated because it was late at night, and the conversation simply ended after "Mr. Dunlop."

The way the story has been told and retold over the years, Hogan was made to look like the bad guy. He has never publicly articulated what went into his decision.

Early in Player's career, at the 1958 U.S. Open at Southern Hills C.C. in Tulsa, Oklahoma, he played 36 holes with Ben Hogan and Charlie Coe. Afterward, Player was at his locker when Hogan tapped him on the shoulder. As Gary "turned round" his face was about a foot from Hogan's. "'Son, you're going to be a great player someday,'" Player recalled. As Hogan was getting ready to leave, he asked Player, "You practice hard?" "Yes, very hard," said Player. "Well, double it," Hogan instructed, as he walked into the dining room. Player thought Hogan's words and the tone of his voice were extremely encouraging.

Right after the Open, Hogan had Ernie Saybarac, head of the rep firm that marketed Hogan's golf equipment then, track down Player. Hogan offered Player a $2,000 contract to play Ben Hogan equipment. At that time Hogan paid no pro to play Hogan equipment on the tour, so Player would have been the first. The very same week, Jack Harkins of First Flight offered Player $9,000 to use that firm's clubs. So Player signed with First Flight without telling Hogan.

"Back in 1958 that $9,000 was considerably more than the $2,000", reflected Player, "I had no money, just enough to scrape by, but I didn't have enough to play the whole year. So, I went ahead and signed with First Flight. If I made a mistake, a major mistake, in my golf career—that was probably the biggest mistake I ever made. Hogan took a liking to me, and I probably would have learned a lot. I believe I would have won more majors if I had gone with Hogan."

While signing with First Flight might have been a major mistake, not telling

Hogan before he signed the First Flight contract was an even bigger mistake. Hogan was not pleased. As a man who felt very strongly that a man's word was his bond, Hogan believed that the agreement had been made. Hogan thought Player was at least obligated to respond to him before agreeing to another contract. Hogan took Player's signing with First Flight without telling him as a slap in the face, a lack of respect.

When asked if he thought his signing the First Flight contract had anything to do with Hogan's declining to answer his question years later, Player commented, "I think he was disappointed that I didn't sign with him. Deep down, I think that was the main factor for his not wanting to talk to me about my question. But, I knew he wouldn't want to say anything. I was asking about something about the backswing, and it wasn't the kind of thing he would discuss like that."

Hogan truly believed that Player would become a great professional golfer. Practicing alongside Hogan at Greenbrier one year, Gardner Dickinson remarked that he didn't think "the recently arrived Mr. Player would be able to 'cut the mustard' with that slicey swing of his." Hogan disagreed, noted Dickinson, "Oh, yes he will," said Hogan. "You see, when all those other players have gone to their rooms or to the bar, Mr. Player will be out there practicing. He'll outwork everybody."

Perhaps if Player had informed Hogan of the First Flight offer, and told him of his difficult financial circumstances, Hogan may have offered him a greater amount, or offered some personal financial support like he later did to Gardner Dickinson. That, however, will never be known.

Player called Valerie Hogan shortly before she passed away in 1999. He complimented Mrs. Hogan on how encouraging he felt she had been to Mr. Hogan during his career. Mrs. Hogan responded, "Gary, my husband admired you."

An episode very similar to the Player story, yet one of great contrast, took place between Hogan and Ken Venturi. In the late 1970's, Venturi, then retired as a player and working as a golf announcer for CBS, came by my office at the Hogan Company to visit during the week of the Colonial Tournament in Fort Worth. When he played golf for recreation, he used the Hogan golf ball. He wanted to visit and pick up a few items he needed.

As we talked, Ken mentioned that he would like to talk to "Mr. Hogan," so I picked up the phone and called Claribel Kelly. She said that she would check to see if he was available and would call me back.

Several minutes later, Hogan walked into my office and greeted Venturi. Ken and I stood up, and Hogan and Venturi shook hands. I fully expected Hogan to escort Ken over to his office, but he sat down right there. For 15-20 minutes the two discussed family, Ken's wife Beau (a Fort Worth lady) mutual friends, Ken's golf game, various aspects of golf broadcasting, and Hogan's practice schedule. I was thrilled to be there to hear it all.

When Hogan got up and went back across the lobby to his office, I told Ken that what just happened was very rare, that I didn't recall ever seeing Hogan do that, and that he usually confined himself to the privacy of his office unless he was on his way back to the factory or to Gene Sheeley's model shop.

Ken said that he thought he knew the reason Hogan did what he did, and he told me why. Here is a shortened version of what Ken said:

"In '58-- I had turned pro in '56, I still hadn't signed with a company.... MacGregor wanted to sign me, but that meant I would have to play their ball and I didn't like the ball.... Ben made me an offer to sign with his company. He didn't have anybody on his staff. And he offered me a price. It wasn't very much at all, but they didn't have any money. And I said, 'Let me think about it,' and he said, 'Before you do anything, will you give me a call before you make a decision?' And I said, 'Ben, you've got my word on it.'

Months went by, and I got approached by U.S. Royal.... they offered me five times what Hogan had offered me. Not that it was that much, but it was quite a bit in those days....Well, the head of U.S. Royal, John Sproul, came to San Francisco to Venturi's advisor, Eddie Lowery's office, and he brought the contract to sign...

I said, 'I've got to call Ben Hogan first and tell him what I'm going to do and give him a shot.' So we called Ben's office. I talked to his secretary, and she said he was not in....I said, 'Well, could you track him down?' I said [to

Sproul], 'I can't sign because I haven't gotten a hold of Hogan.'

Sproul said, 'What's the difference? Sign here, and then tell him tomorrow, because he can't match this price. So just sign, 'cause I gotta leave.'

"John, I can't find him. I gave Ben my word."

'Well, you could lose this contract.'

"John, if I lose it, I lose it, but I'm not breaking my word to Ben Hogan."

He stayed overnight, and the next morning we called Ben's office and he was there. I told him what the price was, and he said, 'Ken, I can't match it, but thank you for calling.' I then told him, 'I didn't want to sign the contract until I spoke to you.' And he said, 'Is John Sproul there?' And I said, 'Yeah.' He said, 'Let me speak to him.'

So John takes the phone and says to Hogan, 'Let me tell you what this dummy guy did. He said he wouldn't sign the contract until he spoke to you first, and he could have blown the contract. I was going to leave town, and I was going to say the heck with it, you don't have a contract, and he said, 'Fine, go.' So he is talking, and I don't hear Hogan, of course, and Sproul said, 'No, I'm not kidding you. This guy was adamant. He was ready to blow the contract because he gave you his word.'"

"I get back on the phone, and he says, 'Ken, that means a lot to me. That is really something. Your loyalty and dedication and your word has meant a lot. I want you to know something: If there is anything you ever need or ever want in this world for golf or anything else I can do, you call me first.' That's where we cemented our bond."

As Ken finished his version of the above story in my office, he added, "He [Hogan] advised me to accept their offer, and wished me well—and I don't think he's ever forgotten that I kept my word to him about that contract. I think that's why he came over here. He's a man of convictions, and being a man of your word, and loyalty is very important to him."

Many years later, after reading the whole manuscript of the story I had written to be sure it was correct, Venturi became very contemplative and commented,

"Ben was a man of his word. My father was a man of his word, too. My father said you can break any contract in the world, but you can't break your handshake or your word. When it was spoken, you could never break that. And that was true of Ben Hogan. I mean his handshake or his word was his bond."

The relationship between Hogan and Venturi went well beyond my understanding. As we stood there, Venturi, in a reflective mood, related several other stories regarding Hogan. He told me of the great match in 1956 at Cypress Point Golf Club between the team of Byron Nelson and Ben Hogan playing against Harvie Ward and himself, both amateurs at the time. Venturi dubbed it, "The greatest golf match I've ever seen."

One week after Venturi's dramatic 1964 U.S. Open win at Congressional, Venturi, Hogan, and Chi Chi Rodriguez were paired at the Carling Open at Oakland Hills in Michigan. At the par 3 ninth-hole, all three players were walking up to the green, Rodriguez ahead of Hogan, winner of the 1951 U.S. Open on that very course, and Venturi, the new Open champ, who had just won the Open. As Chi Chi neared the green a thunderous roar erupted from the crowd, and Chi Chi started bowing and then took off his hat and went into his popular toreador/bullfighting routine.

Hogan and Venturi were walking closely together but considerably behind Rodriguez. Hogan turned his head to Venturi, who was a step or so behind him, and with one eyebrow raised, said, "I wonder who he thinks the applause is for?" Venturi, sensing Hogan's mood, shot back at Hogan, "Him?" Hogan snapped his head again back toward Venturi, cocked his head and panned, "Are you crazy?" Venturi chuckled at Hogan's lighthearted humor, particularly on the golf course, but was struck by the "Are you crazy?" remark because it was the identical words and mannerisms his own father used to use—the very same words in the very same manner. Venturi would have erupted in full laughter had he not been so taken aback at the moment by the striking similarity between Hogan's words and mannerisms and those of his own father.

A story Venturi wrote in his book, *Getting Up & Down*, took place when he and Hogan were paired together at the 1966 U.S. Open at San Francisco's Olympic Club. On the morning of the first round, when Venturi appeared on the first tee, Hogan looked down at Venturi's hands and asked, "What the hell is the matter with you?"

69

Venturi's hands were white and cold from a disorder that eventually drove him from the tour. Venturi replied, "My hands are not doing very good, Ben, but don't worry about it. I'll get by." Venturi could see the genuine concern in Hogan's eyes and hear it in his voice. He noted in his book, "He [Hogan] was the toughest, meanest competitor I've ever encountered, but there was a tremendous amount of warmth in that man. The experts complain about how Hogan was a heartless individual. To those 'experts,' I have only one thing to say: you didn't know him."

Later, on the second hole, Hogan was standing over a 15-foot putt and suddenly began to shake. Venturi couldn't believe it. It got worse, and Hogan froze. Then he stopped and walked over to where Venturi was standing. Venturi said Hogan's eyes "were dead." He told Venturi he couldn't draw the putter back. Venturi didn't know what to do, but felt compelled to respond. Initially at a loss for words, but feeling the truth was the only solution, Venturi then said, "Who gives a shit, you've beaten people long enough." Hogan's eyes came to life and he was able to hit the putt, almost making it.

Going down the fifth fairway Hogan thanked Venturi for what he'd done. "For what?" Venturi asked. "You know what for," Hogan replied.

After the round Hogan asked Venturi to come with him to the locker room, and as they entered, Hogan told the attendant, "I don't want anybody to be with us right now. Nobody." Hogan looked at Venturi and told him, "You're the only person who could have said that to me. I'll never forget that as long as I live."

Ken Venturi wasn't the only player on the PGA Tour who found Hogan warm and friendly. At a 2011 Ben Hogan Foundation breakfast Bruce Devlin also described how he bonded with Hogan during his early years of the tour during the 1960s. "He was a very warm person, really. When he was out socially with me, he was totally different than on the golf course, and if he had something to say, he'd talk a lot."

Devlin talked to Hogan just before the Ben Hogan Tour started. He said it wasn't right that the PGA was charging a $300 entry fee for his son Kel to play the Hogan Tour, but only $100 for him to play senior events. And the Hogan Tour players did not get air fare discounts or insurance. Hogan just said that didn't seem right, but little else. However, the next day he called Deane Beman, the PGA

Tour Commissioner and passed that information along. Hogan didn't attend the first Ben Hogan Tour event because the changes hadn't been made. It wasn't long before the changes were made. Devlin concluded his talk by saying, "A lot has been said about Ben Hogan that wasn't true. He was one of the nicest men I ever met."

In 1983, several years after their visit in my office, Ben Hogan made himself available for a lengthy TV interview about his life with Ken Venturi. Ken got to do the interview because he was a man Hogan completely trusted, a man who would respect Hogan's principles, who would interview Hogan to reveal more about the man, but would not try to sensationalize anything Hogan might say. Hogan knew Venturi would not try to drum up something controversial just to gain publicity. Venturi and Hogan had a bond of mutually strong trust and respect for one another. Consequently, Hogan allowed himself to be as vulnerable as he would have felt in front of those television cameras as they taped his every word in that lengthy, very personal interview. Hogan openly talked about how he almost didn't make it on the tour, and that his biggest check (in terms of importance to him) was for less than $400 at Oakland in 1938. And Hogan expressed the anguish he felt on the 71st hole in the 1960 U.S. Open at Cherry Hills that tormented him still to the day of the interview. The interview reminded me of the personal chat they had in my office years earlier, just two men casually chatting.

When Hogan passed away, Valerie Hogan called Venturi to ask if he would be a pallbearer. Mrs. Hogan graciously acknowledged that Venturi's wife, Beau, had passed away just two weeks previous, and said she would understand if he couldn't attend. Venturi said he would be there no matter. Mrs. Hogan then said to Venturi words that he said he will never forget: "Ken, you were always Ben's first choice."

Ben Hogan and Jim Murray, the great sports columnist of the *Los Angeles Times* had a mutual respect for one another, despite some trying times. In 1949, Murray was working for *Time* magazine and was sent to Los Angeles to verify information on the *Time* cover article on Hogan, which Murray thought was the first time a golfer ever graced the cover of *Time*. With the printing presses on hold and an East Coast deadline looming, Hogan finally finished practicing. "It was getting on into the night in New York and Chicago. It didn't matter to Hogan. He checked each statement as if it were a ten-foot putt for the championship." Finally after a long discussion on a question Murray asked Hogan about the "average" distance he hit each club. (Hogan insistently refused to OK an "average" distance, because he felt there was no such animal, that it would depend on a whole lot of variables—atmospheric conditions, the time of day, the velocity and direction of the wind, maybe even the curvature of the earth." Hogan finally compromised, but Murray noted, "Hogan was not a good compromiser but the presses were waiting, at several thousand dollars a minute in lost time. Hogan didn't care he was meticulous."

In his 1993 autobiography, *Jim Murray the Autobiography of the Pulitzer Prize Winning Sports Columnist*, he wrote, "I guess I revered Ben Hogan as much as any athlete I ever knew in any sport…. Hogan was one of a kind. Purposeful, totally devoid of hype, demanding of respect…. I always felt I was in the presence of royalty. He was a man of unassailable integrity."

FOUR:
THE MIND OF BEN HOGAN

MYTH: *Ben Hogan was a mechanical ball-hitting machine that only needed to be wound up before teeing up a golf ball.*

MAN: "It would not be amiss to add that the superlative game he ultimately developed depended at least as much on the tireless thinking he put in over the years as it did on his tireless practicing… Ben has a truly remarkable mind. At its core, it is the mind of a scientist. " - Author Herbert Warren Wind.

Ben Hogan was a perfectionist, factually minded, and exacting. He put himself 100% into any task or project, and in so doing, analyzed, calculated, evaluated, and theorized "what if." He was not given to "gut feel" without understanding the logic and reasoning behind such instincts, and theory had to be substantiated by performance results.

He did not have the benefit of a college education or technical training. Nonetheless, he had a technical mind that could focus on a problem, develop a theory to solve that problem, and then set about proving his theory correct or incorrect. He would take his results and move on from there. He demanded proof, in the form of hard data, to substantiate that changes were for the better. He did it in his work at the Ben Hogan Company, his oil business investments, and his other personal business as much as he did out on the practice range.

If it was golf equipment, he carefully reviewed engineering drawings and listened to physics theory, but the real proof came in the results that he achieved on the practice tee or, later, in observing the Hogan Company mechanical-man hitting machine. If a drilling company or a geologist suggested that he consider a financial participation in the drilling of an oil well, he studied the various geological maps, the seismic test results and any other data he could acquire to appropriately analyze his investment opportunity.

And if it was a TV commercial in which Hogan was to be the focus, he would study the storyboards, ask the reasons regarding camera angles, question the purpose of various shots, and how they conveyed the right meaning/communicated the correct message to the viewer.

Ben Hogan had learned his golf swing the old fashioned way—he earned it through trial and error on the range. He called it "digging it out of the dirt." He did this by hitting more practice balls every month than most people hit in a decade. He tinkered, he experimented, adjusted, and re-adjusted. He exhaustively tried things, throwing out the techniques that didn't work, keeping the ones that did, and then refining those successful methods to a higher level. He learned the best way for him to swing at a golf ball and then trained his body to do it that way.

Hogan's search for the perfect swing was a lifelong journey, so not only did he learn how to better hit the ball, he learned how he learned to better hit the ball. An exercise he tacitly implied in his suggestions to aspiring golfers to "become better acquainted with their equipment" or by asking "Do you know where the practice range is?" "How well acquainted with that club are you?" or "Do you have a practice bag?"

Hogan's books *Power Golf*, and *Five Lessons the Modern Fundamentals of Golf*, are good examples of his methodical, technical approach to the golf swing. The books contain detailed suggestions on how to develop a correct golf swing. To help the golfer better grasp the concepts, Hogan's *Five Lessons* narrative is illustrated by detailed drawings to better enable the reader to visualize the techniques of Hogan's text.

Herbert Warren Wind, after working tirelessly with Hogan to write *Five Lessons the Modern Fundamentals of Golf*, said of Hogan, "Ben has a truly remarkable mind. At its core, it is the mind of a scientist. In testing the efficacy of a theory or an idea, for example, he can, upon reaching a junction in the road where two alternatives present themselves, start down one fork and make his way patiently along as he probes the many secondary and tertiary side roads, reach definite conclusions about the soundness of what he discovers at the end of the road, and, finally, either incorporate those new facts into his previous knowledge, or, rejecting the whole journey as impractical, retrace his steps without confusion back to the original junction in his investigations and set out calmly down another fork to see what that offers."

Likewise, when Hogan and Dr. Fred Dunkerly invented the APEX lightweight steel shaft in the late 1960s, Hogan found that Apex-shafted clubs enabled the golfer to swing faster and hit the ball farther with the same effort expended with heavier shafted clubs. Not being totally satisfied with just one success, Hogan pushed on. Since they were easier to swing, Hogan tried making the clubs longer. Longer clubs would hit the ball even farther, and if the control was just as good with the longer club, another game improvement would result. Consequently, with the introduction of the APEX shaft to the golf market in 1968, Hogan extended the standard length of all Hogan Company irons by half an inch, making the standard 2-iron, 39¼ inches versus the industry standard of 38¾ inches. On his personal clubs, Hogan made his driver longer and cut off from one-half to one inch from the bottom of the shaft to make the shaft stiffer because he had also discovered that he could better control the ball with an even stiffer shaft in the lighter weight clubs. So Hogan's mindset was to push the advancements just one more step to see what that might bring. He did this the same way in his club design as he did in his swing development, a never-ending search for the next improvement.

Gardner Dickinson was an assistant pro for Hogan at Tamarisk in Palm Springs in 1954. Dickinson had a degree in clinical psychology and was a qualified tester in psychometrics (mental testing). He thought it would be fascinating to test Hogan's I.Q. Hogan wouldn't agree to the testing so Dickinson slipped a few verbal I.Q. questions into the conversation every few days.

Dickinson concluded, "I was unable to administer the manual dexterity portions of the test, but I think we can concede that Hogan was far above normal in that department. Even so, I calculated that Ben's I.Q. was in excess of 180, a score that would place him in the high genius category."

Whether it was through his life experiences or whether he was born with it, Hogan had the personality and mindset of a scientist or an engineer, or both. From the difficulties of his youth to his problems with a hook, the distraction of the crowds, and a near fatal auto accident, Hogan had learned how to compensate in order to remove the obstacles that stood in his way. He learned from his experiences, and in so doing became a very methodical person, adopting an almost scientific methodology. His disciplined, analytical personality helped him master golf's mental side as well as the swing. Before a tournament he would often walk the course in reverse, starting at the 18th green and walking to the 18th tee, then from the 17th green to the 17th tee, etc., to get a better feel for the demands of the course. Hogan's course management demanded that he perfect the techniques to move the ball from left to right and from right to left as the situation demanded. It also included whether such movement should have a high or a low trajectory. Then he would map out a shot-by-shot plan that he would set into motion when the tournament began: a low draw here, a high fade there, for the most advantageous position for his next shot. He is reported to have left his 7-iron out of his bag during his famous 1950 US Open victory at Merion because "there was no 7-iron shot on the course."

When a tournament began, Hogan, to put his plan into action, locked himself totally into his "office" as if encapsulated into a personal cocoon. "I would take longer on that first tee than I would any other place on the golf course. I was gearing my brain, taking a look at that fairway, taking three or four practice swings. A lot of people wondered what I was doing up there, why I didn't tee the ball up and hit it. I was organizing myself to play this round. I thought harder about that first shot than any shot I played. It set the tone for the day."

Then on the course, for each shot, he would, in computer-like fashion, input all the information that would affect the outcome of his effort before hitting the ball. The process required total concentration. Once he hit the shot, he immediately moved to the demands of the next one. He used a combination of emotional control and inner anger to block other, less helpful emotions: fear, anxiety, stress, tenseness. Head down, eyes straight ahead to keep distractions minimal. Hogan stalked the course like a tracker in pursuit of his quarry, which for him was success. This focus left little for peripheral activities, such as fraternizing with the players or the crowd, or clever showmanship. What the spectators came to see, he thought, was superior golf, and to deliver that Hogan had to lock himself into his cocoon and stay oblivious to everything, and everyone, else.

Players use various techniques to relax themselves and to give themselves the best mental edge they can to aid their performance. Some use humor, others talk, some are quiet. Sam Snead noted about Hogan, "I used humor to relax me and to have fun. Byron's approach was different from mine, and, of course, Ben's was a different game altogether. His response to people who asked him if he had fun and why he never seemed to smile on the course was 'There's nothing funny out there!' I think Ben learned from his earlier career when breaks in his concentration cost him. So he taught himself just to look down and block out all that was going on around him. He'd hardly ever say a word while you were playing with him, and that was just Ben Hogan's way of playing."

Such concentration, focus, and emotional control over a 5 to 6-hour period is not easy, and doesn't happen at the flick of a switch. Hogan meticulously hit practice balls before a round. His focus and concentration were totally on the task at hand. In his later years, his preparation included carefully wrapping his injured legs and his damaged left knee to contain the swelling in his legs and keep his knee from buckling under the stress of shots demanding his weight being strongly shifted to his left side.

Hogan was rarely, if ever, satisfied with his entire round, and he was unusually tough on himself about the mistakes he made on the golf course. Sam Snead noted about the differences between Hogan, Byron Nelson, and himself regarding mistakes, "One of the most obvious differences between Ben and Byron and me was in the manner we handled mistakes. Ben, Byron, and I were all fierce competitors, none of us liked losing. Byron seemed to accept that he was human and that he would miss a shot here or there, and I think I was much the same way. You got the feeling that Ben hated, I mean hated, the mistakes he made. The manner in which he talked about his performance when it was poor was so angry and unforgiving that you found yourself feeling sorry for him."

Craig Harmon related playing with Hogan in Palm Springs one day when Craig was just 18 years old. Hogan popped up his drive on one hole, and as he was walking down the fairway to his ball, a fair distance from Craig, Hogan mumbled emotionally under his breath to keep anyone from hearing, "I hate that f_ _ _ing shot!" It surprised Craig because he didn't know the man cursed, but it illustrated that Hogan's emotions were strongly in play when he made a mistake, even during a "friendly" game of golf.

Angrily brooding over a troublesome shot, he might look directly at people, even those he knew well, and never see them. His attention focused on working out a particular problem with his swing or with a particular club; Hogan was still as intensely focused as he left the golf course to head for the practice tee or the locker room as he had been on the golf course. To him he was still at work until he had quieted the concerns that preoccupied him, but sportscasters and spectators expected all of that to have been put aside, and a friendly, congenial conversation mode to now be in its place for him to answer questions or sign autographs. Immediately after a competitive round of golf, if Hogan were upset by a shot or two he deemed less than acceptable or was in an analytical mode and had his train of thought broken by a request for an autograph or a question from the media, Hogan most probably would not give them the response they desired. Such conflict undoubtedly helped elevate the feeling to both the media and the public that Hogan was brusque, cold and aloof, thus adding to his image as a sour, arrogant, even rude individual.

During Hogan's final appearance in the U.S. Open in 1967 at Baltusrol in Springfield, New Jersey, Claude Harmon, his friend and fellow pro, and Claude's son Dick went to watch him play. Hogan was on the putting green practicing when the Harmons saw him. Hogan, after stroking a few putts, stood and took several puffs on his cigarette while staring directly at them. Claude said, "Hello, Ben." Hogan never said a word or acknowledged their presence. He just turned and continued with his practice.

After the round, Hogan spotted the Harmons and called out to Claude, "Hey, what are you doing here? It's good to see you."

"We just came over from Winged Foot to watch you play," Harmon responded. "We've been following you all day. We saw you over on the putting green and said hello to you."

Hogan, startled, responded, "The hell you did. I didn't see you. Well, let's go have lunch." So the three of them went inside and had lunch together.

In 1970 Jack Owens, a regional sales manager for the Ben Hogan Company, and I followed Hogan for two days during the Colonial NIT. I went with a vested interest to watch the boss compete in a PGA Tour event. Hogan was then 57 years old, but tee to green was still better than most, if not almost all, the players out there.

As Hogan exited the putting green going to the first tee, he spotted the two of us as he walked by. "Hi, fellas, good to see ya," he said as he passed us on his way to the first tee.

"Well I'll be damned," Jack said. "I'll bet I've watched him play twenty rounds of tournament golf, and that's the first time he's ever spoken. Normally he just tunes everybody out. I remember walking with Valerie once, and he walked by us just like that, and I don't think he even recognized her."

Gary Player, an admirer of Hogan, observed him on and off the course. Regarding Hogan's manner on the golf course, Player recalled an incident that illustrates the point, "The golf course was his office. He was different off the golf course, but you just can't walk into people's offices and interrupt them....To Hogan an interruption on the golf course was the same as being intruded upon during a board meeting, a sales call or operating a precise tool or instrument. Rightly or wrongly Hogan felt his space violated if someone disrupted his focus and concentration."

When Hogan locked onto something he needed to analyze that issue before moving on. Gary Player noted that "Procrastination is the biggest thief of time," and Hogan certainly agreed. Even away from the golf course, Hogan would sometimes lock onto an item and have to solve it or take care of it immediately, blocking everything else from his mind.

The Ben Hogan Company purchased paint for its wood clubs in the 1970's from the Ford Paint Company in Grand Rapids, Michigan. The company was owned and operated by Dick Ford, brother of Gerald Ford, U.S. President following the resignation of Richard Nixon. Dick Ford was a friendly, congenial man who always had a smile on his face. On his trips to Fort Worth, Ford would usually go to Hogan's office to visit for fifteen or twenty minutes about the latest developments on the paints we were using and to occasionally discuss politics.

Ford recalled that on one occasion, the day after his usual visit with Hogan, he was in the plant looking at the finish on wood clubs to be sure the paints and polyurethane coatings were coming out as planned. He was discussing the process and finishes with a plant supervisor. As they were talking, Hogan walked by on his way to model maker Gene Sheeley's office. Dick said, "Hello, Mr. Hogan." Hogan never broke stride, didn't say a word, and didn't look to one side or the other. He just kept going straight to Sheeley's workshop. Dick noted, "I was always amazed at the intensity of Hogan's focus. He had the ability to shut out the world. I know he meant no disrespect to me because I could see he was intent on something, but a lot of people thought he was aloof, cold or very unfriendly because he didn't always exchange pleasantries or stop to visit. But I don't think that was the case. He could just block everything out except what he was focused on. His exceptional ability to focus was one of his very important keys to success in golf."

Hogan typically would pause and reflect over a question before offering an answer, or he might give a short quick response and then pause. Too often, however, people couldn't stand the silence and would start the conversation moving and Hogan's response would be missed.

Fundamental to Hogan's entire mental makeup was the basic set of moral values that he believed in and lived by; the principles that guided him through life. He believed in right and wrong, in good and bad, in decency, hard work, perseverance, loyalty, dedication, commitment, being honest and trustworthy, a man of your word and respecting the rights of others. Having integrity, respecting women, being a gentleman were an integral part of his makeup, and he expected it of others. Growing up under the difficult circumstances of helping his widowed mother with household expenses in the 1920s and 30s had to influence Hogan's sense of values. She was the one in his early childhood who instilled in him that he was just as good as the other kids. Whether he learned his values from his mother or with the help of his brother, Royal, or Valerie, or through his arduous journey from a difficult childhood to golf stardom, these characteristics defined the man, Ben Hogan.

FIVE:
HOGAN'S METICULOUSNESS

Ben Hogan's credo might have been something close to the saying attributed to Michelangelo, "Trifles make perfection, and perfection is no trifle." Hogan was meticulous in everything he did, whether it was his daily routine, building his house, working on his golf swing, building a golf club, building a golf course, looking over advertising for the Hogan Company, the clothes he wore, the food he ate, or the inquiring of athletes in other sports about ways to improve performance. Ben Hogan was dutifully meticulous and fastidious at every undertaking. He believed in high quality so everything he bought, undertook or worked on was very high quality. Even his daily routine was meticulously structured from morning to evening.

You could practically set your watch by the comings and goings of Hogan's daily routine. He would arrive at the Ben Hogan Company at 9:00 am and leave at noon. He would go to Shady Oaks and park in the same parking space every time he arrived at the club, but as a safety precaution he had five different routes he would use to drive to the club. He would eat lunch at the club, even though the dining room was closed every Monday. On those days he stopped by Roy Pope's grocery store and picked up a sandwich that he took to Shady Oaks to eat. After finishing lunch he would hit golf balls. When he was hitting practice balls he showered immediately after he finished practicing, which was usually about 2:30 in the afternoon. After he quit hitting balls daily, due to his failing health, he'd take a shower at 4:00. He would leave Shady Oaks at 6:00 to go home and have dinner between 6:30 and 7:00.

When Hogan's house was being built, he closely monitored every aspect of its construction. He had the fireplace torn down and rebuilt several times until it finally met his approval. The bricks used to build the house were made right there on the job site. The builders mixed the materials and fired the bricks on the spot so that each brick could be made with a slight irregularity because Hogan wanted a "texture" to the outside wall of his house!

When Hogan practiced, he didn't "beat" balls. He was very deliberate, and took a considerable amount of time between shots to mull something over in his mind. He would look up into the sky or trees, and you could tell he was evaluating something. And then with the club in his hands he would roll another ball over to his hitting area and go through his swing routine to strike the ball. Having watched him from a distance on numerous occasions, I often wondered, "What in the world is he thinking about all that time between his shots?" He once told John Grace, the 1974 US Amateur runner-up to Jerry Pate and Shady Oaks member who played many rounds of golf with Hogan, "The most important shot you hit is your next shot." So he most likely was dutifully reviewing his last shot, and then preparing for his next shot. Before, during and after his prime Hogan would hit balls for hours upon hours.

Gene Smyers, Hogan's insurance man and friend, recalled a time when a friend of his observed Hogan as he started to practice at 10:00 am. The observer asked if he could watch him practice. Hogan said sure. Hogan practiced with the 4-wood until noon. He went to the snack shop and got a Hershey bar and a Coke, and smoked a cigarette, no doubt mulling over the two-hour session. He then went back to his practice area and hit 4-woods until 4:00 that afternoon, six straight hours of hitting nothing but one club. Smyers' friend sat through the whole session, and afterwards asked Hogan if he always practiced like that. Hogan replied, "I'm going to hit this 4-wood until I know exactly what it will do every time I hit it."

John McMackin, Hogan's attorney, was eating lunch at Shady Oaks one day when Hogan stopped by his table and asked John if he would to come out to Hogan's practice spot when he finished eating lunch. Hogan said he wanted to talk to him. John was handling the legal matters regarding the Trophy Club Golf Course that Hogan was developing. When he finished lunch John dutifully got a golf cart and drove out to see Hogan. John watched Hogan hit several balls and then asked him what club he was hitting.

"I'm hitting a 4-iron," Hogan's responded.

"How far are you hitting them?" John asked.

"I'm hitting them between 174 yards and 176 yards," Hogan replied.

"You mean you're hitting them 175 yards?"

Hogan bent down and picked up his cigarette, straightened up and answered, "No, John, I'm hitting them between 174 yards and 176 yards, so that means I'm hitting them 174 yards, 175 yards or 176 yards." His tone of voice was one of irritation, so when he went back to hitting balls John drove off and went on about his business, and left Hogan to his practicing.

Ben Hogan was very meticulous about the golf balls he used. While most PGA Tour professionals carried a metal ring gauge to check the size and roundness of their golf balls, Hogan's ring gauge was much thicker. USGA rules specify the minimum diameter of a golf ball (1.680 inches), so the hole in the ring gauge was right at the minimum diameter. If a ball dropped through the ring gauge without hanging up in the ring gauge it was illegal. Hogan's ring gauge, being thicker, would hang up more balls and gave him a better idea of their roundness. But, in addition Hogan would put his golf balls in a solution that would allow them to barely float. Once they were floating and not moving, he would take a pen and mark a dot on the top of the ball, gently submerge it and spin it very slightly. If the dot on the ball again came to the top and stayed there he would discard the ball as not being perfectly symmetrical, that the center of mass was not in the center of the ball, causing the ball to not spin perfectly.

While filming an episode of the TV show "Shell's Wonderful World of Golf", Hogan looked at the scorecard on a par-3 hole. The card said it was 152 yards to the middle of the green. Hogan remarked, "The yardage on the card is wrong. It's 148 to the middle." Later the hole was again measured and determined that Hogan was right. It was 148 yards to the middle of the green. Hogan hadn't measured the hole, he was just uncanny in his ability to read and determine distances.

Sometimes Hogan's meticulousness ended up being humorous as well. Lawyer John McMackin flew with Hogan to Houston numerous times to meet with the real estate company involved with Hogan in developing the Trophy Club. John noted, "Hogan couldn't stand the way I played golf. On one flight coming back from Houston he was trying to show me something about the golf swing and was having a difficult time trying to get his message across. So in frustration, he told me to stand up in the aisle of the plane. We were on a commercial flight, on Braniff Airlines. Needless to say, I was more than a little hesitant to stand up in the middle of a plane full of people and practice my golf swing, but Hogan insisted, so I finally agreed. I stood up in the aisle, and Hogan got behind me and gave me a golf lesson right there on the plane. I felt a little foolish, particularly when people started recognizing Hogan and started paying attention to what he was saying, watching our every move. I don't know that it helped me much…. but it's an episode with Hogan I'll never forget."

Tom Stites, a club designer at the Hogan Company, was meeting with Hogan about building a prototype shaft with a bend in it. As Hogan was explaining very specifically how he wanted it made, Tom told Mr. Hogan that he didn't understand exactly what he wanted. Hogan reached into his desk and pulled out a flyswatter that had a wire shaft and handle, bent it the way he wanted it and said, "This is what I meant." He handed the flyswatter to Tom and told him to grip it and take a stance like he was going to address the ball. Tom gripped the flyswatter and took his stance. "No, no," Hogan said, "Come over here."

Tom moved around the desk, and took his stance. Hogan reached over and adjusted Tom's grip, evidently he didn't like the way Tom was gripping the flyswatter. Hogan then started working on the flyswatter some more. After a few adjustments, Hogan looked at Tom and said, "There, that's what I want." Tom felt he understood, but just to make sure he walked out of Hogan's office still holding the flyswatter in front of him just as Hogan had instructed. Luckily for the club designer nobody saw him holding that flyswatter out in front of him, gripping it with both hands like his life depended on it, marching across the Hogan Company lobby! (Tom still has that flyswatter!)

When Phil Romaine was assembling wedges in the custom-club department, and a couple of the heads snapped as he tried to bend them, he complained that the heads hadn't been cured properly. A short time later Hogan walked into the department; he had apparently heard about Phil's complaint. He took one of the heads and tried to bend the hosel slightly. It snapped. Hogan said, "Phil's right. Send 'em back," and walked off. No further testing was needed. They went back to the manufacturer who supplied them.

As early as the 1950's Hogan had expressed a serious interest in building a golf course to Shelley Mayfield. Shelley spent the winters in Florida working for Dick Wilson the famous golf course architect. While he was on one of his Florida trips Hogan called Shelley aside and asked him if he would have a professional photographer take pictures of every hole on the Pine Tree golf course using an 8-10 foot stepladder for each shot. Standing on top of the ladder, he wanted shots from behind every tee towards the landing area in the fairway, then from the landing area towards the green. Finally, he wanted a picture from behind each green shooting back toward the landing area in the fairway. Hogan also wanted to get all the bunkers surrounding the greens in the pictures.

Shelley agreed and the pictures along with the bill were sent to Hogan. Hogan sent Shelley a thank you note and the reimbursement check for the pictures, but beyond that Shelley never heard anything more about Hogan's "golf course."

In 1974, just after I had been promoted to Vice President of Sales & Marketing, Mr. Hogan called me into his office. He had just started designing the Trophy Club golf course, north of Fort Worth, and I was about to learn how Ben Hogan worked with people at the Ben Hogan Company. He didn't phone them or use memos. He relied on direct communications. He had us come to his office, or on occasion he would come to our office, but he talked to us directly, face-to-face. Hogan told me to come in and asked if I would do him a favor. He said that he had been watching the Inverrary golf tournament on TV and noticed during the telecast that the sand in the sand traps looked different to him, so he thought they were using a special type of sand. He asked me to get in touch with the greens keeper at Inverrary, and while I was at it, to ask him about the grass they used on the fairways and greens, and what grasses they used to over seed during the winter months. (Hogan was now deeply involved in designing the Trophy Club golf course near Roanoke, Texas, now in the town of Trophy Club, Texas.)

I made the calls and got the information. They used Tifton 419 Bermuda grass on the fairways, and 328 Tifton Bermuda on the greens. They over seeded with a combination of Manhattan Rye grass and Pencross bent. Because the two seeds were very different in size he put them on separately rather than mixing them together. And the sand was a special grade of sand that they imported from Ortona,

Florida. They used the more expensive #70 sand trap sand because it would not compact and remained fluffy. I wrote a memo with the information and gave it to Claribel.

During the course construction, Hogan went to the site daily to inspect, work and rework the layout. He even bought a Jeep 4-wheel drive vehicle so he could drive all over the property. One day Hogan asked his friend Earl Baldridge to go out to the course with him. On one of the holes, a bridge across a creek was being built and Hogan, meticulous as ever, wanted to be sure it was in the right place. After spending well over an hour moving stakes around to show Earl where the bridge should go, Hogan was finally satisfied. In all that time he had moved the stakes maybe a foot.

When Trophy Club was built, the Ben Hogan Company was owned by AMF, and at that time AMF also owned Harley-Davidson. When Ben Hogan was ready to buy golf carts for his course, he wanted to buy Harley-Davidsons. Steve Cain, the head professional at Trophy Club, worked out a deal whereby the Trophy Club could be the test course for the new Harley electric golf carts. The Trophy Club would not have to buy the carts, just use them and let the Harley-Davidson people monitor and maintain them. Harley-Davidson had been making high quality gasoline-powered carts for a long time, but electric-powered carts were new to them, and their models were still of unproven quality.

Hogan, however, insisted on buying the carts. So the club bought 60. But, before long the electric carts began having problems. It was hard to keep half of them operational. Hogan called Ray Tritten, a former president of the Ben Hogan Company who was now an AMF vice president. Tritten came to the club with the Harley-Davidson national sales manager, the regional sales manager and the local salesman.

The Harley people decided to replace all the electric sub-assemblies on the carts. Hogan asked who was going to do the replacements. The Harley managers concluded, "We'll let our local sales representative do it. That's the best way to straighten this out."

To which Hogan retorted, "I have no faith in your sales representative to do anything! The best way to straighten this out is to give me my money back and I'll go buy EZ-Go carts!"

Two weeks later, Hogan got his money back and Steve Cain bought 30 EZ-Go golf carts.

On numerous occasions Mr. Hogan or Claribel Kelly would give me progress reports on the either the golf course or the temporary clubhouse at Trophy Cub. It was usually Claribel. Claribel knew both Shirley (Givant), my secretary, and I liked her Hogan stories, and she liked to tell them, so it was a great arrangement. One day Claribel came into my office straight across the lobby from Mr. Hogan's with a strange look on her face. She asked me what size I was, looking at my waist. I didn't know what to make of the question, so I stammered "size 32."

"Well, gimme your belt," she continued, and noting my surprise, howled in laughter. "Mista-ogn forgot his belt today, and he's goin' out to the course, and he needs a belt to keep his pants up."

Claribel started towards me like she was going to take the belt right off me, but I got the belt off first. I was 30 years old, a size 32 and in good physical condition. Hogan was 62 years old. I couldn't imagine he could wear that belt. Half an hour later Claribel re-appeared, her big grin beaming. "The belt fit fine, so Mista-ogn will bring it back to you tomorrow," she said, and then laughed again as she turned and left my office. I saved the belt. At age 52 I had only gained 10 pounds in those 22 years, so pulled it out of the drawer where I had it tucked away, and tried it, it didn't fit, not even close. Hogan at 62 must have been in pretty good physical condition.

On another occasion Claribel came to my office muttering to herself. I asked what was going on. "Oh, Ben's been in his office for an hour with some salesman showin' him plates and silverware," she said.

"He's doing what?" I asked, not sure I understood her correctly.

"Hell, Ben's in there a pickin' out plates and silverware for the clubhouse. What does he know about flatware and china?"

Sure enough, Hogan chose the silverware and china for the clubhouse. If he was going to do a country club, he was going to do it all.

Several months later Claribel again summoned me to "Mista-ogn's" office. I sat down in one of the two green leather chairs opposite Hogan's. Hogan handed me several pieces of paper. "*The New Yorker* magazine is going to do an article on the Trophy Club golf course. Would you take a look at this, and tell me what you think?" Hogan asked.

The request caught me blindsided as I didn't fancy myself a critic. "Sure," I commented, "When do you need it back?"

"I need it tomorrow," Hogan said as I noted the several pages of double spaced text.

I nodded and said "Okay, be glad to," and exited for my office. I took my assignment from Mr. Hogan very seriously and pored over that manuscript in fervent detail. My knowledge of the history of golf and the many people who made up that community was quite limited, but I was familiar with *The New Yorker* magazine, so I went over that text nine or ten times each time finding an item or two to comment on or change, all of it minor. Knowing how meticulous Hogan was I didn't want him to think I hadn't carefully and exhaustively examined every word, phrase or sentence.

Near the end of the article, the 18th hole at Trophy Club was described in detail. While I had never seen the hole, Hogan had described it to me in detail on several occasions. I took exception to this guy Wind's description because Hogan had described the hole to me, and the article, in my opinion, hadn't adequately portrayed the risk/reward tradeoffs or the difficulties the hole offered. In short, it was a tough hole offering a pressure-packed finishing hole if you needed a par or birdie to win or tie a match.

I noted my concerns and offered a few suggestions, rewriting some of the copy regarding the 18th hole. Early the next morning, I returned the text with a goodly number of red-marked suggestions to Mr. Hogan who glanced down at it and got a somewhat puzzled look on his face. He said thank you, he would look over my suggestions later, and I left. What happened from there I haven't a clue, except later, I realized the author of that article was the famous golf writer Herbert Warren Wind who, among other things, authored with Hogan, Hogan's instruction book, *Five Lessons the Modern Fundamentals of Golf*. I don't recall seeing any of my "suggestions" in print.

With the introduction of the Legend shaft we convinced Hogan to participate in the TV commercial. Once he agreed, he was in 100%. He looked at the storyboards, reviewing each shot with its accompanying commentary. He didn't like the way the camera moved from the clubs in the bag to the shaft band and made a good suggestion to revise the camera movement, so the storyboard was revised.

On the set he got into the very specific details. For instance, he changed the way they had depicted him pulling an iron club out of the bag, because he didn't pull an iron out of the bag like that. He also wanted to know which side of the flag the director wanted him to hit the ball.

In 1983 Ray Coleman, the Ben Hogan Company National Sales Manager, suggested to Mr. Hogan to create a Ben Hogan Company ring to commemorate the 1953 founding of the Hogan Company. The ring would be an incentive award for sales performance. Hogan liked the idea of the ring, but wanted the final approval of the ring design. A special ring was to be made for Mr. Hogan that had 10 diamond chips and a ruby, with the initials WBH inside the ring so that all the salesmen, if they made their annual quotas, could one day have a ring like Hogan's. On one side, the ring design had "BEN HOGAN" in block letters at the top and the year 1953 at the bottom. In between was to be a raised, side view of Ben Hogan's head wearing his signature white cap. Mr. Hogan requested that his watchword phrase "In Pursuit of Excellence" be added in very small letters on the top of the ring.

They called Chuck Scherer at Diamond H to have a sketch made of Hogan's face for the left shank of the ring. Using a recent picture of Hogan, Chuck's artist made the first drawing. Chuck, a golfer and somewhat intimidated by Hogan, brought the sketch to Hogan's office for Hogan to approve. "Do you think this looks like me?" Hogan asked. Chuck looked at the sketch and then at Hogan, "Yes, sir, I do," Chuck responded. Hogan merely shook his head no, that he didn't agree, and sent a bit of a disgusted look in Chuck's direction. Chuck then left to have the sketch redrawn. He returned several times with revisions and similar results. Finally, a more than somewhat frustrated Scherer asked, "Mr. Hogan, I think that ring looks exactly like you, what don't you like about it?" Hogan's response was immediate, "Look," he said looking directly into Scherer's eyes, "This is a ring commemorating 1953, your sketch looks like me now, I want it to look like I was back then."

Changes were made using a 1953 Ben Hogan photo and the sketch taken to Hogan. He nodded his approval and the rings were made. To Hogan's way of thinking, if the rings were to commemorate the 1953 founding of the Hogan Company, then Hogan's likeness in between his name and the year 1953 should be a 1953 Ben Hogan likeness.

At the annual sales meeting Hogan, wearing his ring, presented each of the rings to the achieving salesmen, personally placing each ring on the finger of the salesman—

with dramatic impact.

Ben Hogan's golf shoes were unique, custom made, some in New York City and some in London. Hogan's shoes had two extra spikes in them, one in the heel and one under the ball of his foot. These gave him stronger footing for his forceful swing. Gene Smyers liked the appearance of Hogan's shoes, so he asked him where he got his shoes. Hogan told Gene to call Claribel Kelly, his secretary, for the name and number. Gene called, said he was coming to New York and would like to have a pair of golf shoes made just like Ben Hogan's. The man at the other end asked, "Did Mr. Hogan tell you what the shoes cost?"

"Yes," Smyers said, "He said they were $450, isn't that right?" (This was in the '70s.)

"Well," came the answer from the other end, "It's been some time since Mr. Hogan had some shoes made. They're now $650 a pair, and you'll need to have the lasts made for your feet and they're $650." Thirteen hundred bucks for the first pair, but after that only $650! Gene decided to pass on the shoes.

Hogan wore felt dress hats in the winter and straw dress hats in the summer, hats that he kept in immaculate condition. One day Jim Moore finished showering at Shady Oaks, and as he started walking to the men's grill from the locker room, he spied Hogan's hat sitting on top of Hogan's locker. Jim's a big man: six feet five with weight appropriate to match his height, and a hat size much larger than Hogan's. He had a full head of hair that he'd just washed and dried so he felt he wouldn't be getting the hat dirty, if he perched Hogan's smaller sized hat way atop his hair. He thought it would be a humorous thing to do. He looked in the mirror and thought it looked pretty funny, so he proceeded out to the men's grill with Hogan's hat on and a big grin on his face.

Hogan, when he saw Moore enter the room, froze. Jim recalled, "It was as if I'd thrown a piece of dirt at him. I knew instantly that I'd made a mistake, and Hogan let me know in no uncertain terms that I had. He wasn't rude, just matter of fact. The incident, however, never affected our relationship."

Hogan was meticulous about maintaining his weight. He was very strong physically, with the wrists and forearms of a blacksmith (his father was a blacksmith) and hands that were calloused from the hours of practice and the extremely hard cord-line grips on his clubs. He rarely ate heavy foods, preferring chicken breast and fish. Though not much of a pasta eater, for he liked meat sauce on his spaghetti. Hogan liked his scrambled eggs made with cream, not milk, so if they were made with milk, they immediately went back. There are reports of him sending back scrambled eggs three times at Shady Oaks before the cooks got it right. When asked if Hogan ever sent back one of his meals, Walter Kaufman, the owner and chef at the upscale Old Swiss House in Fort Worth, a favorite restaurant of Hogan's, proudly replied, "Only once, and that wasn't because of the food, it was because the plate wasn't hot enough! When we served a group that included Ben Hogan, I personally brought his meal to the table. I would place it in front of him and stand there until he nodded slightly. That was my signal that everything met his expectations. No one else would notice, but his slight gesture to me was like him clapping his hands that everything was fine."

Willie Mae Green was the Hogans' cook for more than 20 years. Willie Mae was an excellent cook. She had her own restaurant for a period of time. On one occasion Hogan came into the kitchen when Willie Mae was having trouble with the gravy for chicken fried steak. He picked up a spatula and stirred until the gravy was just right. Other than that one occasion, the only cooking he ever did was steaks outside on the grill.

Hogan did allow himself one self-indulgence nearly every day, and that was ice cream. Willie Mae said his favorite flavors were vanilla and butter pecan. There is a notable exception to that though. When Hogan's brother, Royal, made homemade ice cream, Hogan's favorite flavor was whatever "Bubba" (Royal) was making.

Hogan was as observant and inquisitive as he was meticulous, and his attention to detail impressed athletes from other sports. During the 1970's, Colonial Country Club hosted a tennis tournament and the tennis professionals playing Head equipment (Head was also owned by AMF) would come by the factory to get golf equipment. Arthur Ashe, Bob Lutz, Dennis Ralston, and Charles Passarel were the most frequent visitors and Hogan occasionally watched them play. When he saw them at the factory or at Shady Oaks Country Club, he frequently asked questions. How did they generate such power in their stroke or serve? Hogan might have also asked something about their daily routine when they were playing. He observed that a person's muscles, even a person's eyes, change from day to day, causing the person to act or react differently. Even a mechanical driving machine will operate slightly differently on a cold day versus a hot day. The relative "size" of his fingers each day was something he was cognizant of, as he noted in Chapter 1 of his 1948 book *Power Golf*.

"Personally, I like my hands to be thin. When they feel puffy I can't grip the club the way I like to. I can't explain why, but some mornings my hands will feel fat and puffy. When they feel that way I know that I am not going to play my best that day, which should give you an idea of the relation of the condition of your hands to successful golf."

Tommy John, the famed baseball pitcher, came by the Hogan factory each time his team came to play the Texas Rangers. Tommy had a golf tournament fund-raiser in Southern California, and the Hogan Company donated prizes for the event. Tommy, ever the gracious person, would come by each time to personally say thank you for our support.

On one occasion Tommy went to Shady Oaks Country Club and ended up in a conversation with Hogan. Since Tommy depended more on curveballs and change ups than on sheer speed, he and Hogan got into a conversation regarding his grip on the baseball and its impact on the flight of the ball. Hogan asked if the baseball ever felt differently from game to game. He acknowledged that it did, that at times the ball felt more comfortable in his hand that at others. Tommy said one of the issues was that the circumference of the baseball could be plus or minus one-quarter inch. That meant the circumference difference between the largest ball and the smallest ball could be one-half inch. Hogan was appalled that the professional baseball standards would allow such inconsistency. He checked golf balls to be within several one-hundredths of an inch in diameter. Hogan said he drank ginger ale to relieve any puffiness in his fingers, so the grip on his clubs would feel better to him. He suggested that Tommy might try it to see if it might make the ball feel slightly smaller, easier to grip and control. Hogan also noted that alcohol tended to make him retain water in his hands and made the grip on his clubs feel slightly bigger, so he was careful in his alcohol intake during golf tournaments. Tommy said he was amazed at Hogan's meticulousness.

Tommy said he had purchased a set of Hogan Junior clubs for his daughter and noticed that the iron heads were pinned to the shafts, and that he hadn't seen that in other companies clubs.

Hogan said, "There's only one way to make a golf club, the right way. Pinning irons is the right way."

"That in itself told me exactly who Ben Hogan was, and what his operation standards were, that you don't just glue a shaft in because it's a kids club," Tommy said.

Hogan asked Tommy to come out and watch him hit practice balls. Tommy said he was flattered that he was given that privilege. Bob Gibson, a Shady Oaks member, told Tommy, "He must really like you because he doesn't ask anybody to come out and watch because he doesn't hit it that well anymore."

He could have fooled Tommy because that day "Hogan 'pured' it every time!" Then Tommy added, "The thing that impressed me about Mr. Hogan was the kind of man he was. He was a quality kind of person."

[When Dr. Frank Jobe, the famed orthopedic surgeon performed the first experimental elbow surgery procedure on the pitching arm of Tommy John, it was the first time it had ever been done to a major league pitcher. The procedure, in which the damaged pitching elbow tendon was replaced with the tendon in the non-pitching arm, was very successful and is now called "Tommy John" surgery. Tommy was never known for his fastball, in fact, he tells the story that he told Dr. Jobe before the surgery, that after the surgery he wanted to be able to throw the ball hard like Sandy Koufax. After the successful surgery, the rehab process and getting back to his top pitching form Tommy complained that he should have been more explicit in his instructions to Dr. Jobe, that he wanted to throw it hard like Sandy Koufax, the Hall of Fame pitcher for the Dodgers, not like Mrs. Koufax. Perhaps the good doctor didn't recall that "Sandy" Koufax was a man.]

Claribel Kelly was Ben Hogan's secretary from the day he started the Ben Hogan Company in 1953 until she retired in 1984. She stood less than five feet tall, and had a raspy voice. She said that she could usually tell what kind of day it would be by the way Mr. Hogan said hello each morning. When he was "having a bad day" or "in one of his moods" she'd come strolling across the lobby, look into my office, put her hand up by her mouth and "whisper" in a not too quiet voice that "Ben's bein' a real pain today" or some such comment. If I would ask her first how things were going, and it was a tough day, she'd grimace, throw her hands up, or make some expressive motion to let you know. Some of the time I think she did that just for the sport of it and to add a little excitement for the day.

Claribel loved jokes, funny stories. She also loved Ben Hogan. She protected him like a brother, regarding it as her duty to guard his privacy. Occasionally, however, she told a few Hogan stories of her own. She recalled the time that "Mista-ogn" was working on something for the local cemetery in Dublin, Texas, where his father was buried. Claribel said, "Ben was just a workin' over what he should do to help the cemetery. He was right in the middle of all that, when the phone rang. I put my hand over the mouthpiece and yelled into M'sta Hogan, 'Ben, President Eisenhower is on the phone.' Ben said, 'Tell him I'm busy right now and I'll call him back.' I said, 'No, Ben it's not his secretary, President Eisenhower is actually on the phone.' 'Well, tell him I'll call him back. Tell him I'm right in the middle of something now, and I'll call back shortly.' So I told the President that, and he said that he wanted Mr. Hogan to meet him at Augusta to play golf. So I asked him to hold on a moment, and I shouted in to Ben about the golf game, and he again told me to tell the President that we'd call him right back. So, I told the President of the United States that M'sta Hogan was too busy right now, and he'd call him back shortly.

"A few minutes later, after he'd finished and decided what to do about the cemetery, he asked me to call President Eisenhower, and they had their conversation about meeting at Augusta to play golf. And M'sta Hogan did meet the President at Augusta a short time later and played golf with him."

Hogan meant no disrespect to President Eisenhower. He liked President Eisenhower very much, and had a great deal of respect for the man. He also appreciated Eisenhower's love for golf. In fact, after Hogan won the 1953 Masters, he stayed at Augusta to meet President Eisenhower, and they played golf on the Tuesday after the tournament with Byron Nelson and Clifford Roberts, the Masters Tournament director. Hogan had a large framed photo of the four of them sitting on a bench at Augusta National hanging in his office.

Hogan's meticulous manner of tackling something, focusing on it until he had completed it, solved it or resolved it and moved on to something else was just the way he was, even if it meant putting off his friend, the President of the United States, for a few minutes.

SIX:
HOGAN TURNED INWARD – RESPECT

MYTH: *Ben Hogan was a cold, selfish, self-centered man who did not respect others.*

MAN: Ben Hogan was a shy man; turned inward from his experiences early in life. He overcame his failures by developing his ability to completely focus and concentrate on his task at hand, even using anger to drive away fear, to keep his mind totally focused. Ben Hogan was given no respect, none, until he earned it through his success in golf. He respected the privacy of others, and demanded respect for his own privacy, which offended those who wanted something from him or who didn't try to understand him.

While most men are hindered from strong, close male friendships, Ben Hogan was much more so because of his early experiences in life. Loyalty, faithfulness, and encouragement are necessary to form a strong close bond with others, but throughout most of his career, other than family and maybe three or four friends, Hogan was offered little of such keys to close relationships. Consequently, Hogan withdrew to his inner person, trusting in his own values, abilities, and strengths.

Rejection and harassment marked Hogan's early years, first as a nine-year old, by the tragic death of his father. Selling newspapers late into the night, and having to fight to sell them, causes a fatherless nine-year old, to read a lot more into "no" than declining to buy a nickel newspaper. That's a rejection. Later in life, after he became successful, whenever Hogan saw a boy selling newspapers he would buy all the newspapers the boy had, and tell him to go home and go to bed.

When caddying, he endured hazing, being picked on by bigger caddies, even being hit with belts. As he started to play golf, he was forced to go it alone through the subtle, and not so subtle treatment given to him by others in and out of the golf community. Not being afforded playing and practicing privileges, renting a golf shop, but no "friends" coming to support you, all etched indelible, bitter marks on

Hogan. Such treatment may have slowed Hogan's development in golf, but it also may have only enflamed his passions to prove himself on the golf course.

Hogan learned to turn inward to improve his lot in life, calling upon his own driving force, whatever or wherever that ultimate source of strength came from. He was by himself, strictly on his own. Hogan learned that his outward reaching was almost always met with the inner pain of rejection. Consequently, he became a very private, self-reliant, and self-dependent person.

Jim Murray, the revered sportswriter, described it in a February 4, 1990 column:

"Few ever had a tougher time breaking into golf than Ben Hogan. It is a story almost Dickensian. Or, at least, Horatio Alger....

"It was a hard time. Veterans on the tour did not help the newcomers the way they do today. They even hazed them. You never spoke to a rookie. He was after your money, and there wasn't enough to go around.

"Hogan didn't mind. I once asked him if his peers ever offered any advice on his game when he first came on tour. 'I never asked them,' said Hogan, coldly. 'I didn't belong to the lodge.'

"In a way, he never did. There was always something about Hogan that set him apart... there was a purposefulness about Ben Hogan on the course that made you shudder. It was almost as if he were extracting some frightful revenge from it. He didn't play a course, he stalked it....

"There are more myths about Hogan than there are about Lincoln....He's half-man, half-myth. He was a cult. The funny part is, it was all true."

As he attempted to play professional golf he struggled financially, going broke numerous times. While Byron Nelson had the offer of others to financially back his attempt to make it on the tour, Hogan did not. Playing on a financial shoestring as he started his professional golf career, a dreadful hook kept him from success. He gradually overcame that problem by countless hours of grinding practice sessions, but several times in the process Hogan used up his entire savings trying to make it on the pro tour without success, and on a couple of occasions he even had to sell his golf clubs to pay his way back home.

However, this aloneness caused him to be considered aloof and anti-social. He was silent and intense. While walking to the first tee for his playoff with Sam Snead in the 1950 Los Angeles Open, Hogan's first tournament after his accident, an irritated Hogan growled at friend Bob William and *Sports Illustrated* correspondent Jack Tobin. William asked him about it later. "I had to get mad at something," Hogan said. "I use anger to drive away fear." To keep other emotions from creeping in, to control his nerves, he used anger to totally focus his immediate attention on the task at hand. Golf writer Al Barkow described it this way:

"Focus has become a big buzzword in sports psychology. Ben Hogan practically invented it 40 years ago. In the second round of the 1948 United States Open, George Fazio, paired with Hogan, holed out a four-iron second shot on a par-four hole. There was a huge gallery, and it responded with a roar, but Hogan apparently missed the moment.

"At the end of the round, Fazio's eagle was not recorded on his card, which Hogan was keeping. Hogan would not put down the two. He said he didn't see it. Obviously, he didn't hear it either. It took an hour to persuade Hogan to sign off on the score, else his friend Fazio would be disqualified. I asked Hogan once if as a tournament golfer he ever considered himself an entertainer. His response was immediate, unequivocal, and, of course, terse: 'No.'"

To more effectively focus to compete to the best of his ability, Hogan used anger to drive away his fears during competition. For this Hogan was labeled cold, ruthless, and impenetrable. To many, perhaps even most, such actions by Hogan to compete as best he could came across as a man with a chip on his shoulder. Hogan most likely did have a chip on his shoulder, but in looking back at the first 25 years of Ben Hogan's life that's not too difficult to understand.

Respect, esteem, and veneration are feelings, expressions, or traits that Ben Hogan missed out on as he grew up. He was given no respect as a poor-boy runt who had no outstanding talent that would cause others to look up to him. He was shown no respectful regard or appreciation as a young boy or teenager. Other caddies treated him like dirt, the country club turned him out when he turned sixteen and was too old to caddie, and no local fatherly types, other than Marvin Leonard, were around in his early years when Hogan needed help, assistance or encouragement. Mr. Leonard, a Fort Worth businessman, for whom Hogan caddied, was the only one who offered and provided financial help and encouragement in his early years on the tour. That lack of respect was to be a driving force that not only compelled Hogan toward success, but it also marked his treatment of others. Even after he became the biggest name in golf, his personal letters of encouragement or sympathy would include the phrase "with your permission" or something similar to show his respect for them and not wanting to intrude on their privacy.

Hogan earned respect on the golf course through his dedication to the sport and his ability to command the ball. Many people called him "Mr. Hogan," but he didn't believe that fellow competitors should necessarily address him that way. Tom Weiskopf said, "I'm glad I had the opportunity to meet Ben Hogan, to talk with him and to play with him. I called him 'Ben,' not 'Mr. Hogan,' because at the time he was a fellow competitor despite our age difference. Ben Hogan didn't think fellow competitors should call him "Mr. Hogan" either.

Another younger pro was Dave Marr. In his early years, Marr was an assistant to Claude Harmon at Seminole Golf Club in Florida, where Hogan frequently practiced and played during his annual tune-up for the Masters. Consequently, Marr played a lot of golf with Hogan at Seminole. Every day when Hogan would walk by, Dave, then a 20 year old assistant pro, would respectfully say, "Good morning, Mr. Hogan," and Hogan would nod and continue on his way. One day, however, Hogan turned around, came back to Marr and, looking him in the eye, said, "Dave, don't ever call anybody Mister that you may one day have to play." Hogan then turned and went to the practice tee. "I've never forgotten that," Marr said years later "from that morning it was 'Good morning, Ben.'" Obviously Hogan was a pretty good judge of talent as years later Marr and Hogan were paired together in the Masters and Marr was in contention to win.

Dave Marr was a very congenial man, one of the nicest golf commentators on television after his days on the tour. At the 1981 U.S. Open at Merion Golf Club, Dave took me, then the Ben Hogan Company Vice President of Sales and Marketing, on a short tour of the course. Marr pointed out where the network had their cameras stationed for their expanded coverage that year. He showed me the "production truck" and introduced me to the production crew that would be doing the telecast. And, of course, he showed me the location where Hogan hit his famous one-iron shot to the 18th green, the 72nd hole of the 1950 U.S. Open. Ironically, Dave, a truly nice man and a true Hogan fan, died within months of Mr. Hogan in 1997.

A definition of "respect" given in the dictionary is, "to refrain from intruding upon or interfering with: to respect a person's privacy." On one occasion, I was asked by Mr. Hogan to join he and Lanny Wadkins for a round of golf at Shady Oaks, just the three of us. As we approached the 2nd green, an individual greeted Hogan and Lanny. We were all riding in separate carts, and while I didn't know the person, it appeared that either Lanny or Hogan might have. However, nothing was said as we putted out and went to the tee of the 3rd hole. The three of us hit our tee shots and drove to our balls.

After I hit my approach shot to the 3rd green, and as Hogan and Wadkins prepared to hit their second shots, this person dropped down a ball and proceeded to hit a shot to the green, apparently planning to join the group. Nothing was said, although I was aghast. Lanny later remarked that he, too, was astounded that anyone would do that. We finished out the hole, and as we started toward our carts to go to the 4th tee, Hogan got in his cart and said, "Thanks, fellas, I've enjoyed it, but I've had enough for today." Then he headed for the clubhouse. The individual had violated Hogan's privacy, and ours, and Hogan would have none of that. Lanny and I were extremely disappointed, but we certainly could understand Hogan's feelings. On a couple of occasions Mr. Hogan joined a foursome that I was playing in at Shady Oaks, but he always asked, "Mind if I join you?" before becoming part of the group.

Several days later Lanny received a check in the mail from Hogan, paying off a bet they had going when he decided to call it a day.

However, gracious was not always Hogan's reaction when his privacy was invaded or he was shown a lack of respect, and he reacted negatively when it was. On one occasion Ben Hogan was seated at a table in the men's grill at Shady Oaks when a successful Fort Worth businessman sat down next to him at the table. The two didn't speak, but the man picked up one of the white cloth napkins laying on the table, blew his nose on it and laid it back down on the table right next to Hogan. Hogan said nothing. He took out his cigarette lighter and lit the napkin on fire. The businessman looked back, and seeing the burning napkin quickly picked it up, put out the fire, and discarded it into the trash. Never a word was spoken between the two.

While confronting Hogan took considerable internal fortitude, it didn't necessarily negatively impact the relationship. In fact, if he was wrong, more than likely Hogan gained respect for the person for calling him on the error of his ways.

One example is a run-in that Jack Williams had with Ben Hogan at Shady Oaks Country Club not long after Jack had become president of the club. Several members had taken it upon themselves to make changes in the golf course. Hogan wanted it stopped. So Hogan went over to Williams as he was eating lunch with his son Roger. Hogan bent over and said to Williams, "Jackson, if you don't straighten up this club, I'm going to kick your country ass," and walked back to his table.

Several minutes later Hogan got up from his table and headed toward the locker room. Williams, not a small man, got up from his table and headed after Hogan. After waiting a minute or two Roger decided he should go check on his father. When Roger walked into the locker room, there stood Williams and Hogan face to face with Hogan back against his locker. "You may be a golfing great, but to me you're just an ass, and if you want to kick my country ass, I'm good and ready!" Jack Williams was saying.

From that day forward, Jack Williams and Ben Hogan had the best of relationships. In fact, Hogan bought half a dozen automobiles for his employees from Williams. He never asked the price, or specified the color. He just said, "Make sure it has a spare tire in it."

In his column the day after Ben Hogan's death, Pulitzer Prize winner Jim Murray said of Hogan, "What kind of man was he? Well, they said he was cold, aloof and a loner. A boy whose father shot and killed himself in front of his family when the boy was nine years old is not apt to be a cutup. He kept the world at bay. But he could be fun-loving, a wonderful dinner companion to share a pre-meal martini with. Hogan didn't care whether you liked him or not, just whether you respected him."

As much as anything, Hogan respected the job of being a golf professional. After Shady Oaks was built, he would usually practice at a selected spot on the "little nine" located inside the regular 18-hole course. He used a golf cart to drive out there and the trip back. The trip didn't drain much of the charge from the batteries that powered the cart, so Art Hall, the Shady Oaks club pro, offered to let Hogan use a cart for free. Hogan's response to Art's offer was pure Hogan. "Art, you're a professional, you sell your services, so I'm going to pay for the use of this golf cart, whenever I use it." And he did. Every day that Hogan drove a golf cart to practice, he paid $10.

SEVEN:
THE BEN HOGAN COMPANY

Ben Hogan started the Ben Hogan Company in his hometown of Fort Worth in 1953. He believed the standard clubs made for the golfing public could be made to much more rigid and exacting standards. He believed he could do just that, make golf equipment to such high quality standards that every set would be the most precise in the industry. Hogan felt if he could do that, his company would flourish.

From the beginning the philosophy and tone of the Ben Hogan Company was quality, selling to the "carriage trade," wealthy, discerning customers who wanted the finest equipment money could buy. Those principles remained consistent under the constant monitoring of Hogan as long as he was active in the company. He felt his mission was to set new standards of performance and quality in the golf equipment business, just as he had set new standards of practice and play when he was active on the professional tour.

When the first batch of wood clubs produced by his new company were not up to his standards, Hogan cut the heads off with a band saw to keep them from being sold as rejects. It was estimated that he destroyed about $100,000 worth of inventory, and that ended the partnership he started with Pollard Simons, a Dallas businessman. By cutting the heads off those woods Hogan had drawn a line in the sand, and his partner, Pollard Simons, decided he did not want to cross it. It was agreed that one of them would have to buy the other's interest for the company to continue. Hogan didn't have the money to buy Simons out, but neither did he want to let any equipment be made with his name on it and shipped without his approval of the quality of the merchandise. Hogan felt strongly that equipment with his name on it had to be the best equipment made in the industry. Now in a tremendous bind, Hogan did not know what to do, but he knew he had to do something. (More later on the rest of this story.)

Hogan's little company struggled during the late 1950's. It was undercapitalized and needed more research and development (R&D) capabilities. Consequently, he sold his company to AMF in 1960 to give it the financial and technological resources it needed.

As part of the sale, Hogan negotiated a personal five-year contract that was to be renewed every year, giving him a minimum of four years at any point in time to exercise his authority should something not be done to his liking. While he did not personally control the day-to-day operations, which he left to a professional management team, through his oversight as chairman of the board, he exercised great influence over the way the company was run, primarily in the R&D, quality and sales & marketing areas.

The company general managers worked closely with Hogan to utilize his vast golf and equipment knowledge, and to motivate company employees both in the factory and the sales and marketing department.

During his trips through the factory, Hogan would almost always look at the golf equipment to be sure the quality was up to his standards. He wanted the clubs and balls made a certain way and he did not want any deviation from it. He had an unbelievable eye for picking out even minor flaws. His trips through the plant usually made the factory production and quality managers nervous. It didn't take long for word to get around that Hogan was on the factory floor.

On one such trip Hogan stopped at a rack of wood clubs that were nearly ready to be matched into sets and packed into boxes. He pulled a wood off the rack and inspected it. Then, holding it by the grip in his right hand and extending it high above his head, he swung the club downward, slamming the club head hard onto the concrete factory floor. The club made a loud crash as the metal sole plate hit the concrete and the wooden head shattered, sending pieces flying in every direction. The noise was unmistakable.

Once they realized what had transpired, everyone went back to work, with increased intensity, paying closer attention to the details of their jobs.

After such walks through the plant, Hogan would call a meeting of the quality control inspectors. Holding up a club not to his liking, his charge to them would be, "I don't care if we only make one club a day, I don't want anything like this getting out of this plant." He would then ask if everyone understood, then adjourn the meeting.

Archie Allison started working for the Ben Hogan Company in the early 1960's, and he knew there were two sides to Hogan's motivation, the carrot and the stick. Archie recalled an instance when he had taken a local pro, Bart Haltom, into the plant to get him a set of clubs. "Since Bart was a particularly good player we thought we'd pull his set off the production line and match them the way he wanted."

"I pulled a club from the rack, and as I was checking the specifications I noticed a little black mark on my hand," he said. After pulling several more clubs he realized that there was a very slight gap between the hosel of the iron head and the black plastic ferrule that is supposed to fit tightly against the iron head, and that someone had filled in the gap with a black waxy type material to hide it."

"I got Bart a set of irons that didn't have the waxy fill, and was able to do it without Bart's knowledge of it," he continued, "but while I figured they were using the wax in less than 20% of the clubs I'd seen, I knew Hogan would be furious. After I went back to my desk I was sitting there mumbling to myself, trying to figure out what to do and how to tell Hogan, or whether or not I should even be the one to tell him, I mumbled out loud 'What would Hogan do if he found out?'

"The words had no sooner left my mouth when a deep voice behind me asked, 'Found out what, Archie?' Startled, I immediately snapped my head around to make doubly sure it was who I thought it was. Of course, it was Hogan! There he was, big as life, and the lump in my throat felt the size of a baseball. As I turned my chair around to face him, my brain was going crazy. Those steely blues locked right onto mine like they were looking right into my brain for the answer to his question. I jumped to my feet, but Hogan's stare never left my face. It's very hard to adequately describe Hogan's stern demeanor, but with his strong voice and the way he could set his jaw, furrow his brow just so and fix those steely blue eyes on you, it was almost scary...This was not a time to beat around the bush, no time to try to be diplomatic. Man, I confessed on the spot like a sinner at confession after being caught right in the middle of a sin. I felt like the six-year old with his hand in the cookie jar, I couldn't get those words out fast enough. I told Hogan what I had just found, and he demanded to see the clubs, turning and heading out the door before he finished his sentence. We went directly to the iron assembly area where I had found the irons. He looked at the irons, ran his fingers along the area in question on a few of them, saw the black, waxy stuff, and he was fuming. He immediately headed for the plant supervisor's office to call a meeting with the manufacturing and quality people."

Archie continued, "I heard there was one ass chewin' like none other in that meeting, one that I'm damned glad I wasn't on the receiving end. Later some people who were apparently involved in putting that stuff in the irons did some nasty things to my car in retaliation for telling Mr. Hogan, but there was no way I wasn't going to come 100% clean when Hogan confronted me like that! No way!

"But," Allison noted, "that's one thing I always thought about Mr. Hogan's management style that in my mind made him a great manager, you always knew where he stood. You always knew exactly what he wanted, and what he expected from you. I like that in a boss."

While the company grew in the early 1960s, it made relatively small inroads against its much bigger competitors that for decades had dominated the golf industry: Wilson, Spalding, MacGregor, Dunlop, Acushnet (Titleist golf balls) and Hillrich & Bradsby.

That changed when Hogan met Dr. Fred Dunkerly, an AMF metallurgical engineer with a Ph.D. from Carnegie Tech (now Carnegie Mellon) in Pittsburgh. Together they designed and developed the Apex shaft, the industry's first successful lightweight steel shaft. Dunkerly's scientific bent and technical knowledge coupled with Hogan's knowledge of the golf club, and his own scientific mind made the two a great innovative team.

Hogan's acute sense of feel and keen insight into the golf swing, golf mechanics and golf equipment, outlining what he wanted in shaft stiffness, flex characteristics, balance points, and feel coupled with Dunkerly's metallurgical expertise and knowledge of physics and mechanics enabled them to significantly reduce the weight of the shaft and the club. The shaft design resulted in a significant reduction of the overall weight of the clubs, particularly the longest club, the driver. Together, they developed a truly remarkable product.

Recognizing the lighter clubs were easier to swing and easier to control, Hogan added ½ inch to the length of each iron. He knew a longer club would hit the ball further, so he tested the combination of the lighter club and longer length. It worked. Consequently, when Apex was introduced, in addition to being lighter in weight, Hogan irons were made ½ inch longer, which enabled them to hit the ball even farther.

The Apex shaft was a genuine breakthrough in the golf industry, the most significant technological change in golf shafts since the transition from hickory to steel. It became the most dominant shaft in golf for over a decade, until improved graphite shafts began to be developed. Response to the shaft, a proprietary product, was overwhelming. For several years, despite the continuous rapid expansion of production capacity, club production could not keep up with demand. A growing backlog kept deliveries continually three to six months behind. The Apex shaft put the Ben Hogan Company on the golf club industry map.

Hogan had an uncanny ability to see and feel minute changes and differences in golf clubs. The ability to do so totally amazed even those of us who were exposed to it, including the club model maker, Gene Sheeley. Gene joined the Hogan Company in the early 1960's, a position he held for more than 30 years.

Gene was a decorated ex-Navy and ex-Marine who was very mild mannered, humble, and soft-spoken. Even his brothers were not aware of all the military medals he had won in World War II and in Korea. Gene was very knowledgeable of golf clubs and club design, having worked for the Kenneth Smith Golf Company for over 20 years before joining Hogan, and he greatly respected Hogan's capabilities when it came to designing clubs.

One day Gene stopped by my office and asked me to join him in showing Mr. Hogan a new prototype driver. We stood at Hogan's office door until Hogan acknowledged us and invited us in to his office. Hogan stood up from his chair behind his desk, and Gene handed him the driver. Hogan rested the head of the club on the plastic mat that was under his chair and gripped the club. He then raised it slightly off the floor for a couple of moments, then set it back down.

"Gene, this driver's a little too long," Hogan commented.

"I don't think so, Ben," Gene responded.

"Yes, Gene, this club's a little too long. Take it back and recheck it before we go any further."

Hogan wouldn't evaluate a club that he thought was not exactly right, so Gene and I left his office, Gene taking the driver with him. After we rounded the corner of the short hall from Hogan's office and started into the main lobby in the front of the building, well out of earshot from Hogan, Gene exclaimed, "I'll be damned." I asked him what was wrong. Gene looked at me and said, "This driver is one thirty-second of an inch too long, and Hogan could tell it. I never thought he could tell that slight of a difference. Well, I'll shorten it a

Ben Hogan has golfers trying his new Ben Hogan clubs. (PHOTO COURTESY LEE ANGLE COLLEC-TION)

thirty-second and come get you when I'm ready," and he headed back to his model shop.

I stood there at the door to my office flabbergasted. I went to my desk and pulled out a ruler to see how long a thirty-second of an inch was. That driver was 43 9/32 inches long instead of 43 8/32 inches long (the standard length of a Hogan driver was 43¼ inches long). How could anyone tell the difference? Well, apparently Ben Hogan could, immediately.

Later that morning when Gene returned and we took the driver back into Hogan's office, Hogan's first question was on the length, and Gene admitted, "You were right, Ben, that driver was one thirty-second of an inch long. So I shortened it, and it's right on the money now." Hogan just nodded in satisfactory agreement, and went back to examining the club.

Gene recounted a similar instance when he had taken Hogan the 2-iron of a new iron model in for Hogan to approve. The club now had the grooves stamped into the face and the head had been plated and finished. The 2-iron was shafted and gripped and ready for use. Hogan, still sitting in his chair, gripped the club, but left the heel of the club head resting on the plastic mat that surrounded the back of his desk. He then lifted the club slightly, raising it just up off the floor. He looked at the head very carefully, and then lowered the head again to the floor. "Gene, this club's loft is a half of a degree or so weak" (meaning that it had one half a degree too much loft.) Gene took the club back to the loft and lie machine in his model shop and checked the loft. Sure enough the loft was exactly what Hogan said it was, one-half degree weak from the Hogan standard 2-iron loft.

Ray Coleman was the Hogan Company quality control manager in the late 1960s and early 1970s. He usually arrived at the plant about 6:30 each morning to make his rounds through the plant. In the early 1970s the Hogan Company was running three shifts, around the clock, in the ball plant, the iron-head grinding room, and club assembly area to keep up with the growing demands for its products. As Ray pulled into his parking spot one morning he noticed Hogan's black Cadillac parked outside Gene Sheeley's building. Ray figured that Hogan was having Gene make something for him or was getting some new clubs to test that day.

Near the end of his rounds as he approached the grinding room, Ray noticed Hogan standing behind someone, watching as the person ground and polished the iron heads. Ray thought he could have been getting some special grinding done on some heads for his personal clubs, so he went back to his office.

A few minutes later Ray's office door opened, and in walked Hogan. In his hand were three iron heads he'd brought from the grinding room. "Dammit, these clubs are gawd-awful!" Hogan exclaimed. (Gawd-awful was the worst something could be to Hogan. If Hogan called something "gawd-awful," you knew immediately they were totally unacceptable.) "You shut this plant down until they can do it right," Hogan said in a raised voice. With that, he threw the iron heads he had in his hand against the wall and stormed out of Ray's office.

Ray, more than a little shocked, hurried over to pick up the heads to examine them. He picked up the first head, and immediately dropped it. It was much too hot for him to hold without burning his hand. He put on a work glove so he could pick up the heads to examine them. Even with the work glove, Ray could feel the heat of the heads in his hand as he hustled the twenty-five yards or so back to the grinding room to stop the process, then headed to Hogan's office to see what was bothering Hogan about the grinding of these heads.

When he arrived at Hogan's office, Hogan waved him to come in, and Ray sat down across the desk from Hogan, holding the heads in the glove in his hand. Hogan pointed out that he wanted a distinct line ground on the iron heads, where the iron face joined the hosel, that would help the golfer more easily align the club to the target. Hogan used that line himself as an alignment aid, and he felt it would help all golfers, if ground correctly.

Upon leaving Hogan's office and relieved that the problem could be easily remedied, Ray wondered: How the hell could Hogan carry those heads from the grinding room to Ray's office in his bare hand when Ray couldn't even pick one of them up without a glove on after Hogan had carried them from the grinding room to his office?

One year Hogan's final approval of the models came much later than usual, and it was looking bleak that clubs would be ready for the national sales meeting. This was a major problem. Hogan, sensing the urgency of the situation, in a meeting one day simply stated, "If someone would get up off his butt, and get these things finished like he should, these clubs would be ready on time." That's all it took for Gene Sheeley. He worked around the clock to get those model prototypes done in less than three weeks, not the six that they would normally take. He personally carried the models to the forging house located in Illinois and got the whole process speeded up. Not only were the photo samples were ready on time for the sales meeting, but so were numerous sets of sample clubs. Hogan commanded that type of loyalty and dedication because everyone knew his level of loyalty and dedication was greater than ours.

Sometimes Hogan used humor to get his point across. Gene Sheeley liked Hogan's sense of humor, particularly when it was the dry, deadpan type. Gene described it as, "Hogan liked to give me a 'shot' every once in a while." One year Gene had just spent an exhausting week on modeling prototypes. Hogan, knowing that two more weeks of hard work lie ahead, wanted to lighten up the moment and rejuvenate the group involved in the design work. So he asked Gene, "What are you going to do next week, Gene?"

Gene, turning around noticed a slight grin on Hogan's face, responded, "Now that the prototypes have been approved, I think I'll be mowing the yard."

Hogan, in a matter-of-fact facial expression, shot back, "Well, if those finished clubs aren't ready for the sales meeting, you'll have plenty of time to mow your yard."

Gene, knowing Hogan was needling him, broke into a big grin, and said, "Well, if I don't get that yard mowed, Marge [Gene's wife] will be on my butt, and she's just as tough as you are!"

With that Hogan and the whole group burst out laughing.

Hogan was totally consistent about his stance on quality. If a set of clubs came back to the plant from a dissatisfied customer and found its way to his office, Hogan would look at the clubs, and if he agreed with the customer, he would send him or her a new set, with no questions asked. On one occasion Hogan sent the customer a new set, and somehow the old set went to the repair department, where it was fixed at no-charge, and then returned to the customer. When we discovered the mistake, we notified Hogan. His reply was, "Let them keep both sets."

While designing clubs and balls and overseeing quality and performance were Hogan's major areas of involvement, he also exercised his authority in other areas. He took a personal interest in the company's sales and marketing department for several reasons. He believed the salesmen represented him personally as well as the company and the products we sold. Hogan salesmen were required to wear

The Ben Hogan sales organization at the 1971 National Sales meeting.

coats and ties when they called on customers. He wanted the company image to be one of high quality and prestige, that its products were the best money could buy. He wanted clean-shaven, well-dressed, articulate sales people who, if the situation arose, could talk to the president or chairman of some major corporation about Hogan golf equipment and make a positive impression. Indeed, many top corporate executives were golfers, and on numerous occasions our salesmen had discussions with corporate CEOs and company presidents. Hogan also reviewed the print advertising, participated in the development of TV commercials and the annual equipment catalog, and was kept apprised of the marketing policy and plans.

Throughout the '70s the Ben Hogan Company flourished. A succession of Ben Hogan Company Presidents, Neal Crane, Ray Tritten and Bill Sovey, who all had manufacturing backgrounds, helped to keep Hogan club production expanding while maintaining highest levels of quality and keeping the company's bottom line growing.

A major research firm, via inventory and purchase audits as a representative sample of golf shops across the country gave quarterly reports of club sales and market shares. Over a period of several years the audits showed that Ben Hogan clubs gained market share during the mid and late 1970s to become the top sellers in the country in golf course professional shops. The Hogan golf ball became the top money-winning ball on the PGA Tour in the mid to late '70s too, even though it struggled to substantially expand sales against the Titleist and Top Flite balls. Ben Hogan's little golf company grew tenfold from a four million dollar business in the late 1960's to over forty million dollars in sales by 1980.

For most of his career, particularly in his later years, Hogan had been a terrible putter and Hogan Company putter sales were lackluster too. In the late 1970s, without Hogan's input, a radical-looking line of wooden-shafted putters was developed with the grip consisting of a thin leather strip on the top and bottom of the flattened grip end of the wood shaft. While he didn't call them "gawd-awful" in front of the salesmen, there was no question how he felt about them. The putters didn't sell well at all, and at the end of the year we were stuck with approximately $125,000 (at wholesale cost) of useless inventory.

I had come across a company that would barter spot TV advertising time for such products. The only catch was there was no guarantee where the putters

Ben Hogan inspects Hogan golf balls as they go through the painting process. (PHOTO COURTESY DOUG MCGRATH COLLECTION)

would be retailed, and at that time Hogan sold its equipment almost exclusively through golf professional shops at public golf courses and country clubs.

After checking with several salesmen, and with several golf professionals whose business opinions I respected, I decided it was a go for the TV commercial spots. I also decided I had to discuss it with Mr. Hogan first. No way did I want one of his friends telling him K-Mart was selling Hogan clubs, even if it was these "gawd-awful" putters.

Hogan knew that I knew that he had personally cut the heads off of somewhere around $100,000 worth of unsatisfactory wood clubs when he first started the company, to keep them from going into the marketplace. I anticipated Hogan would want a similar demise for these putters.

I carefully presented my arguments for the barter to Mr. Hogan. The pros wouldn't buy them at any price. We could get our full wholesale price through the spot TV commercial time on golf tournaments in markets we selected, etc., etc. It would save us $125,000 and give us valuable TV air time for our golf ball commercials. The only catch was they couldn't guarantee where the putters would be sold. But, neither the salesmen nor the golf professionals I had talked to cared where the putters ended up, because in their opinions, the putters weren't worth even our cost, let alone the wholesale price.

He listened, then without hesitation stated that we should destroy the putters. When he finished I countered, saying that we were the most loyal manufacturer to the pro shops and planned to stay that way, but that the $125,000 would come right off the bottom line if we destroyed them, whereas the TV commercial barter would help us improve our golf ball market share.

Hogan listened, then again said, "Tim, you can do what you want, but I think we ought to destroy them, I'd burn 'em." I took Hogan at his word that I could do as I thought best. When I completed the deal, I went to Hogan's office and told him that we had gone ahead with the barter. I never heard any complaints from our salesmen or any of our golf-professional customers, and Mr. Hogan never mentioned the subject to me. While that discussion with him was one of the toughest conversations I've ever had with anyone, I think because I had shown him the respect of discussing it with him ahead of time, he did not take offense with my actions despite his strong disagreement with them. Reflecting back, I found Hogan's "Burn 'em" comment, particularly amusing; with their wooden shafts, those putters definitely would burn.

Ben Hogan's personal influence on the company and its employees was enormous, and his business philosophy and opinions were greatly respected by those who had been there long enough to appreciate them. Hogan was short on words, but long on influence and it was easy to tell on which side of an issue Hogan stood. However, dealing with Mr. Hogan required persuasion, patience, and on occasion, confrontations with top management. Hogan didn't shoot from the hip, make changes quickly, or go with the current market fads.

In late 1979 AMF brought in a new president from outside AMF to run the Hogan Company. The new president had a packaged-goods marketing background. Within a couple of years the new president moved Ben Hogan aside, removing him from his active marketing role, no longer featuring him in TV commercials or print advertising, and downplaying his importance in club design work and quality oversight. The rationale was that Hogan was getting older, he was now nearing 70 and his image for precision, quality, and high performance golf equipment had to be transferred to the Company management and employees.

Almost all of the vice-presidents either left or were replaced, and the new management changed the company policy of marketing its products primarily through golf shops at golf courses by developing marketing programs attractive to the off-course golf discount stores. This success was short lived and the company struggled financially.

In 1984 Minstar, a conglomerate headed by Irwin Jacobs, bought AMF, dismantled it, and sold it off division by division. By then the Hogan Company was losing money, and the new owners cited problems, including distribution and manufacturing inefficiencies, that needed correcting to make the company profitable again. "Everything was messed up… Bad managements stand out like red lights, and this one certainly did. Jacobs principal move was to replace [the] Hogan president."

The new owner made changes in the Hogan Company top management, bringing in a new Hogan president, Jerry Austry, who brought Ben Hogan back into the active role he once enjoyed, and again featured Ben Hogan in the TV commercials.

However, the Hogan Company was sold and resold several times, and in 1993 its manufacturing was moved to Virginia. This was a particularly sad time for Ben Hogan, seeing all his manufacturing, customer service and corporate people let go. Some were transferred to Virginia, but most of the office personnel and skilled club makers, many of them craftsmen, were terminated. It also meant Mr. Hogan would be moving to new office space in Fort Worth, leaving the 2912 West Pafford Street office he'd occupied since he started the Ben Hogan Company forty years earlier. In 1999, after Mr. Hogan had passed away, the company was sold again, this time to Spalding Sporting Goods, and the Hogan club assembly, a mere shadow of its former manufacturing capability, was moved back to Fort Worth. Eventually the company became part of Callaway Golf, who bought it from a bankrupt Spalding Sporting Goods.

Hogan Company employees, particularly those of the 1960s through the 1980s era, look back with pride to have been associated with the man who made his name so meaningful in golf, and the company that was an industry leader, one that made the finest products in the golf business. During its peak years the AMF Ben Hogan Company had a company culture that insisted upon highest quality, product integrity, and taking care of the customer. Satisfying the customer with the best products, backed by a quality guarantee and a philosophy that loyal customers bring other customers, the Ben Hogan Company grew and prospered.

The source of that company culture was the man, Ben Hogan, and the principles he lived by. As long as Ben Hogan was actively involved, encouraging everyone to be the best at what we did, the company culture was well understood and appreciated by all. While the company was driven to grow, it was never by selling products that didn't meet Ben Hogan's performance standards, or that were at the expense of being the best. Company integrity was important. He instilled the high ideals and goals that stimulated the employees to do the best they could, to work as a team, to care about each other, and most importantly, to satisfy the customer.

Unfortunately, the numerous sales of the company, the changes in management, locations, and personnel eroded that strong company culture and eventually sucked the vitality and life out of the company.

EIGHT:
HOGAN SPEECHES/HONESTY

MYTH: *Ben Hogan was a man without feelings or wit, a hollow, empty man.*

MAN: Ben Hogan was a man of deep feelings, humor, and charisma, and his speeches reflected the inner man that was not evident on the golf course, and not often on display in public.

In the midst of Ben Hogan's planning to develop the Trophy Club golf course and country club, he needed to get the approval of the town of Westlake, Texas for a particular jurisdiction. John McMackin, Hogan's attorney on the club, went with him to the Westlake City Council meeting to discuss their proposal. John recalled, "Hogan was concerned that either of the cities of Fort Worth or Denton might try to annex the land into their jurisdiction, so he went to request that the Trophy Club be an 'extra-territorial jurisdiction' of Westlake, which would prohibit any surrounding city from annexing the Trophy Club property."

Hogan went to the City Council meeting to discuss the situation. McMackin continued, "Ben was a great speaker, particularly when he was passionate about something, and Trophy Club was important to him....Hogan spoke passionately about the situation, and the need for the jurisdiction. I was so moved by his presentation that I thought the city council would just hand it to him....They approved his request." Today, nearly 40 years later, the town of Trophy Club remains free from annexation.

Hogan would almost always compose his own speeches, and he usually spoke without notes unless he was specifically referencing certain items. He was very articulate and took speech making seriously. He spoke from the heart, and his style of taking deep breaths and sighing occasionally during his talk made the listeners feel he was drawing his thoughts from his innermost being.

Even if he was asked to speak on the spur of the moment, he could mesmerize his audience. Ben Matheson, a member of the Board of Governors at Colonial Country Club recalled the time that the Board decided to recognize Lee Trevino, Ben Crenshaw and Tom Kite with Honorary Colonial memberships. To commemorate the occasion a small cocktail reception was held that included the board, the honorees and an invitation was extended to Valerie and Ben Hogan. The Hogans accepted and attended the festivities. Each of the honorees, after he had received his honorary membership card, spoke for a few minutes. Then Ben Hogan was asked if he would like to say a few words, and he said he would. Matheson said Hogan spoke to a spellbound audience for more than twenty minutes as Hogan recalled his career, complimented each of the honorees for their superior golf abilities and accomplishments, and extolled the Colonial golf course. He had a way of connecting with his audience.

But, Ben Hogan didn't spin things that he didn't believe in, and if things weren't quite to his liking, he just might say so publicly, and possibly, very bluntly. Consequently, there was always a little concern about what he would say when he rose to speak. Every time during my eight years as Vice President of Sales and Marketing, I awaited his remarks with fear and trepidation as I hurriedly reviewed recent events to be sure we were as buttoned up as possible.

At the Hogan Company, Ben Hogan spoke at various company functions. Three such speeches each year were particularly important: at the dinner for the PGA Tour players during the Colonial tournament in May; at the club professional staff visit in the fall; and most important was at the company's national sales meeting in August.

During the Colonial each year the company hosted a cocktail party and dinner for the professionals on the PGA Tour who played Ben Hogan golf clubs and/or the Hogan golf ball. At the conclusion of the meal, Hogan would get up and say a few words. He had a sincere interest on how things were going on the tour. He watched the tournaments on TV, read about them in the newspaper and golf magazines, and frequently discussed developments regarding the tour players with the Hogan Company PGA/LPGA tour director. And he liked chatting with the twenty to thirty players who attended annually. The tour players considered it a privilege to spend time with "Mr. Hogan."

Another important Hogan speech was each fall, following the dinner on the final evening of the Advisory Staff professionals' visit. The company had approximately 500 golf professionals on the Advisory Staff, and each year thirty to forty were invited from country clubs and public golf courses around the country. They would tour the factory, critique the Hogan product line, offer ideas for the product line, solicit ideas from the Hogan people, and play golf. They also got to meet and visit with Ben Hogan.

Wednesday evening was the special occasion. Following the coat-and-tie dinner, Mr. Hogan spoke. One of my tasks was to double check with Hogan that he was willing to talk after dinner. His usual response was, "These guys didn't come down here to hear me talk." Hogan knew better, and in my thirteen years at the Hogan Company, he never let Lyne Price or me down.

On occasion, one or more of the professionals asked Hogan about the golf swing, which he usually parried with a response that they ought to give him a lesson. When they persisted, he was known to take off his jacket, loosen his necktie and give a lesson on the golf swing. He might even ask one of the staff professionals to come up and be his student to help illustrate his swing philosophy. In several instances, he gave a real lesson, not just a demonstration. You talk about a focused, mesmerized audience!

During my tenure Hogan did a marvelous job, each and every time, sending his audience off on their white horses to slay the competitive dragons. However, that was not always the case.

Prior to and during my tenure, the Hogan Company had followed the "Pro only" policy of selling its equipment through green-grass/golf pro shop facilities, golf shops at country clubs, golf courses and driving ranges. Traditionally "pro line" golf equipment was a higher quality, more precise golf instrument than the golf equipment sold in sporting goods stores or department stores. Ben Hogan started the Ben Hogan Company because he felt he could make higher quality equipment and wanted to market it through the green-grass/golf pro shops that fit golf clubs to the players. The logic is that if the clubs are fitted to the golfer, he or she will be able to play better than just taking a set off the shelf or rack. As such, most of the golf manufacturers' policies supported having their golf clubs "fitted" to the golfer by a golf professional, as opposed to being sold by a clerk at a sporting goods store or a department store.

But in the early 1970s off-course golf discount stores appeared and a lawsuit challenging the "pro only" sales policy was filed against the golf equipment manu-facturers, including the Ben Hogan Company. Most of the companies started to sell pro line equipment to these "off-course/golf discount" stores, but Hogan and Ping stuck to their "green-grass" policy, deviating only in a selected few geographic areas where the golf professionals had basically thrown in the towel on selling golf equipment. Hogan club sales continued to rise, and by the late 1970s, Hogan golf clubs moved into the #1 sales position in the green-grass/golf pro shops, and Ping club sales were on the rise. In the late 1970s it became apparent that among the leading golf club manufacturers only Hogan and Ping were serious about keep-ing the green-grass/golf pro shops as their predominant channel of distribution.

In late 1979, AMF replaced the Hogan Company president with a man who was not from the golf industry. The new president began to implement his marketing approach, and things began to change. The new man wanted to phase Mr. Hogan totally out of the marketing picture. He reasoned that Hogan's stature needed to be transferred to the people in the company. I protested that we had something no other golf company had... Ben Hogan, and we needed to make the most of him. I had seen PGA Tour professionals stop their conversations in the locker rooms to watch Hogan Company TV commercials featuring Ben Hogan's golf swing. They also went out on the golf course to watch him play on the tour, and each year when we had a dinner for the PGA Tour profession-als during the Colonial NIT, those invited came to see Ben Hogan. Similarly in the fall when we invited some of our club professional staff members to Fort Worth, they wanted to see Ben Hogan. That persona was not something to abandon. Serious ama-teur golfers respected Mr. Hogan's quality image and our high quality clubs, and average players looked to the better players' equipment when making their own choices. Hogan could be difficult to work with, and it was widely suspected the new president's style and personality clashed with Hogan's, but Hogan's presence was very meaningful to the Ben Hogan Company, both internally and externally. And to the Hogan Company sales force, Ben Hogan was their spiritual leader, being able to motivate the men like no other.

However, I was feeling the growing pressure that such a move would take place with or without my consent, or maybe even without my presence. Pressure was also mounting to move away from the Hogan Company "green-grass" pro shop policy, another significant change I strongly opposed. At that point Hogan and Ping were the envy of every other manufacturer in the industry when it came to relations with the golf professionals at country clubs, golf courses, and driving ranges. Not only were the golf professionals, then the opinion leaders, when it came to golf equipment, but the green grass pro shops also were, by far, the most profitable equipment segment for most of the manufacturers. Hogan could always make that move to the golf discount stores later if the market went in that direction, but not when our clubs were #1 in sales in the on-course pro shops according to a quarterly nationwide pro shop audit. Momentum in that segment was still strong for Hogan and Ping, but was slipping for those manufacturers who chose to focus more on the golf discount stores.

Hogan and Ping were doing well in the pro shops in the late 1970s, and a study confirmed the green-grass/golf pro shop policy was helping Hogan and Ping. Comments and opinions from companies and golf discount stores cited the strengths and weaknesses, and future prospects of the various companies. Comments from retail golf discount stores that Hogan was not freely selling at the time, indicated that Hogan was doing well, noting that the company made very good clubs, was doing excellent research and dominated the good player segment, so they needed to carry them. But, they complained that they were experiencing delivery problems getting Hogan equipment, and that Hogan was trying to control the bootleg activity where legitimate buyers were fronting for, or passing clubs along to the golf discount stores.

Comments regarding some competitors, however, were not very complimentary, complaining about the marketing strategies, the lack of industry knowledge in the top management, and that they were losing market share in the golf discount stores. They admonished that there was considerable room for improvement in their marketing approaches.

Underlying all this was the sense that if Hogan and Ping changed their marketing and distribution strategy away from its green-grass/golf pro shop policy and focused more on the retail golf discount stores, the change would weaken Hogan in the green-grass/golf pro shop outlets and help those competitors' whose future strategies and plans had already focused their marketing efforts more towards the golf discount stores. Thus, maintaining its green-grass pro shop marketing strategy/policy would help Hogan, and also Ping, to maintain their strengths in the green-grass/golf pro shop accounts, and would make marketing strategy more difficult for competitors who had not stayed with green/grass pro shop only policies. Comments were noted regarding the issues at Hogan and AMF, Hogan's parent company, that the recent top management changes may cause other personnel changes, which may precipitate change in the 'Pro Only' policy due to AMF pressure. One person noted that Ping's pro-only policy would pay off for Ping in the long term, and Ping is the only manufacturer of those discussed that today remains as a top club manufacturer and competitor.

In the early 1980s, the entire top management team of the Hogan Company did change. Some chose to leave, others were sent packing, and in February 1982, I was fired. Mr. Hogan was then pushed aside, and out of his more engaged role, with no public exposure in the marketing and advertising areas.

When Hogan was moved to the background, the company culture began to change. He resisted change to the new company marketing strategy of opening up the off-course golf discount store sales channel.

At the sales meeting that August a new sales channel philosophy was implemented as the company introduced its new product line, and the retail golf discount stores were now in play. Heretofore, Hogan had been very involved with the sales force and was not only fully informed of what the plans were, but he also had a say in determining the marketing policies and advertising plans. Now, he was definitely out of the loop, and he began to realize it.

That fall, on the final evening of the 1982 Advisory Staff visit, Hogan indicated to the sales manager that he was not in the mood to make a speech to the group. But when he was introduced to speak anyway, he reluctantly rose. Then, he immediately launched into his feelings regarding the new marketing policies. He began a tirade regarding the way the company was being run. He did not like the direction it was headed and, "By God, we're not going to sell to the golf discount stores!" he thundered, beating his fist on the dinner table to add an exclamation point to his outrage. As he concluded his brief talk, Hogan pointed to the company president, and to that crowd, that was like Moses pointing to Pharaoh. He looked right at him with those "steely-blues" and exclaimed, "This man, here, is the one responsible for what's happening. He's in charge, and he's the one responsible for these decisions, for the change in direction of the company." Hogan then abruptly sat down, obviously upset.

The group was stunned. The Hogan Company people sat in a hushed silence. Some staff professionals looked down, while others fumbled with their napkins or conversed quietly with the persons seated next to them, still not believing what they had just heard. The president rose and tried to regain the group as best he could, and under the circumstances did quite well. However, there was no mistaking where Ben Hogan stood. He believed that knowledgeable golf professionals should fit golf clubs to players, and now his merchandise was being sold in off-course golf discount stores, locations he considered to be mass merchandisers, and in the late 1970s and early 1980s many of those facilities were mere discount stores, offering little or no club fitting. However, without the day-to-day control over the company or its policies, and getting no support from AMF executives, Hogan could do very little to reverse the changes in the marketing policy or the direction of the company.

The most important speech Ben Hogan made each year was to the sales force on the last evening of the Hogan Company National Sales Meeting. That speech was meant to be a stem-winder to motivate the salesmen to hit the road full-bore to sell the new Hogan product line. He mostly talked about the new club or new shaft the company had designed that year, and the resulting performance improvements. He knew each product inside and out. To our sales organization, "if Ben said it" then it was true! John Ferries, Benton & Bowles Advertising Agency VP in charge of the AMF parent-company account during the mid-1970s attended several Hogan Company sales meetings and was amazed at Hogan's effect on the audience. Years later Ferries confessed, "I had never seen an individual have an audience so spellbound, and have not seen anything like it since. It was incredible how Hogan had the audience mesmerized as he described the iron head in incredibly precise detail, even though he didn't have the club in his hand. He just moved his hands around like the club was there in his hands, drawing a picture for everyone to see."

Undoubtedly, Ben Hogan's most memorable sales meeting speech came at the

1973 sales meeting. That year the iron club market was beginning to segment into the traditional forged-blade style irons and the new cavity-back, investment-cast irons first developed by Ping. Both the Hogan marketing and engineering groups wanted to expand the line by adding a modified cavity-backed club. Ben Hogan had designed the Apex model in 1972 and had revised it only slightly for the 1973 model. He was not yet convinced the cavity-backed iron was a good idea, and he strongly preferred the steel forging method of iron making to the investment-cast process used in making cavity-backed clubs. Hogan believed that both cavity-backed clubs and the investment-casting process reduced the feel that was transmitted up the shaft to the players' hands, and to Hogan—feel was critical to the player being able to know if he struck the ball properly.

Since the early cavity-backed clubs utilized a hard metal in the investment cast process, Hogan did not like the new concept at all.

Each year Lyne Price in his letter inviting the salesmen to the sales meeting included a strong reminder for them to get their hair cut before coming to Fort Worth, and he was dead serious about it.

That year (1973), the day before the meeting started several members at Shady Oaks were giving Hogan a hard time about the length of hair on some of the Hogan salesmen who played golf there on the weekend before the meeting began. The intensity of the hair situation was pushed up several levels when the sales vice president's son, Jeff Price, who had been a Hogan salesman several years previous, was standing on the first tee with a friend of his, who had long hair, talking with several Hogan salesmen that he knew. Hogan's Shady Oaks buddies were throwing barbs about this long haired individual that they said was one of Hogan's salesmen with a hippie haircut.

Mike Sieverson, one of the salesmen, was playing golf later that Sunday afternoon at Shady Oaks. Mike had pitched in the minor leagues and had kept his hair short while playing baseball, so keeping his hair short was no big deal. He had gotten his hair cut the day prior to arriving.

As Mike's foursome was about to hit their approach shots to the par-4 second hole, salesman Joe Oppenheimer, in the cart with Mike, turned to him and offered him his cap. "Nah," Sieverson said, "no need for that."

"Are you sure?" Joe asked again.

"I don't need it," Mike replied, "I just had my hair cut yesterday."

Oppenheimer pressed the issue one last time, "Well, there's Hogan putting on the back of number two green (Shady Oaks cut two holes about 20 feet apart in the back of the very large #2 green so Hogan could practice his putting in private), and with the wind blowin' your hair all over your head, I thought it might be a good idea." Mike again declined.

A few minutes later, as Mike was lining up his putt, he could overhear conversation between Hogan and the other salesmen.

"Who the hell is that?" Hogan inquired. "That's Mike Sieverson from Atlanta," Oppenheimer responded.

"Oh, I didn't recognize him with all that damned hair!" Hogan growled.

After putting out, Mike walked over to greet Mr. Hogan. "Hi, Mr. Hogan, I'm Mike Sieverson from Atlanta," Mike cheerfully intoned with his typical big smile, but his stomach a little knotted. Hogan responded, but never took his eyes off Mike's forehead and hair.

As they rode over to the 3rd tee, Joe, never one to pass up a good barb, turned to Mike and said, "Yeah, I see what you mean, you didn't need the hat. Sorry I even mentioned it."

That evening, at the opening cocktail party of the sales meeting, Hogan called Lyne Price aside and began bending his ear. When the conversation ended, Lyne promptly found me and said, "Look, Tim, Hogan's not going to show up at the meeting tomorrow until six or seven of these guys get their damned haircut. Here's the list. You need to get them together, I know a place downtown that opens at 7:00 am, take them down there to get their hair cut. And make damn sure they cut off enough so that Hogan won't be pissed off when he sees them again. Now I'm countin' on you to get this done, because we can't start the meeting until you take care of it. You go tell 'em you'll pick 'em up about a quarter to seven. And when you're done tellin' 'em, report back to me, and tell me what they said, because I need to reassure Hogan so he'll show up at 8:30.

125

At 6:45 the next morning, I drove Mike Sieverson and five others to downtown Fort Worth so they could get their hair cut.

After unsuccessfully trying all week to catch Hogan alone to ask him to sign a picture for one of his staff professionals, Mike, in exasperation, on the last afternoon of the meeting before the dinner at which Hogan was to speak, followed Hogan into the men's room to ask him to sign the photograph. Mike prefaced his request by saying, "Mr. Hogan, I hope I'm not out of line asking this in here, but I have a picture from Bob Ledbetter, a good staff pro of mine in Alabama, that I'd like to get autographed. Would you sign it for him?"

"No, Mike," Hogan responded, "You're not out of line. Sure, I'll be glad to sign it, just take it to Claribel, and I'll sign the picture, and I'll send him a letter with it."

"Thanks, Mr. Hogan, I really appreciate that," Mike sincerely replied as he felt the weight of the world had just been lifted from his shoulders.

By the time Hogan was supposed to address the sales force that evening, word was his temperature was hotter than the August sun, and in August, Texas is very hot. Lyne Price told me that several salesmen got Hogan cornered after their golf round and were givin' him a hard time about the new iron. They were bitchin' about needin' a cavity back club like that new Ping club, and I think Hogan is really pissed off. I don't know if he's even going to give his speech after dinner, and you know how important that is. And to top that off, one of those guys got into an argument about Hogan's third shot on the 17th hole in the 1960 Open at Cherry Hills."

"What?" I asked incredulously.

"Yeah," Lyne continued, "Now Hogan's pissed off about that too, cuz that idiot all but called Hogan a liar to his face."

Jack Owens had been standing next to Hogan earlier, and he confirmed the story on the discussion of the 17th hole at Cherry Hills. He'd been standing there during the whole episode and tried to diffuse it, but the salesman wouldn't back down. Chip Bridges, then a salesman in South Florida, confirmed it as well.

"Yep," Chip noted. "I was standing there with my back to the conversation, and I couldn't believe what I was hearing. I didn't dare look around, but I sure wasn't going to miss this one, so I just kept backing up a little to be sure I heard the whole thing. Hogan just matter of factly said he hit it a foot or two short of where he wanted to, and got really good bite on the ball because he had a tight lie. Then this guy says 'Naw, you hit it fat, and it landed short in the water,' and started arguing with Hogan. If this guy has a job in the morning it will be a miracle."

We sat down for dinner in the Shady Oaks dining room, and Jack and I, both Regional Sales Managers at the time, sat next to each other in case Hogan did leave.

Sure enough, a little while later as dessert was being served, Hogan got up from his seat and headed straight out the exit from the dining room. He didn't say "Hi," "Bye," or anything else. Most of the group was eating dessert, so Hogan's exit hadn't been that noticeable to the group, and those that saw him leave probably thought he went to the men's room.

About fifteen or twenty minutes passed when Jack exclaimed, "Who the hell is that?" Some guy with long hair, a loud, bright blue sport jacket, no tie, and a handful of golf clubs strode right by us on his way to the head table. Jack and I started figuring that Lyne had developed a backup plan, and had hired a comedian who was going to break the tension if Hogan bolted. Lyne could be pretty resourceful, and Jack and I started to smart a little, figuring that Lyne, being the prankster he was, had set us up for his gag.

We didn't have to wait long until we found out. When he reached the head table he tossed that set of irons down on the table, knocking over several water glasses and breaking several others. The commotion caused the room to hush to a dead silence as all heads now snapped around to the head table. Everyone was wondering what was going on. No one had ever barged into a Hogan meeting like this, let alone some longhaired hippie type, carrying cavity backed, cast clubs.

The guy picked up one of the clubs in his right hand, pointed to the club head with his left hand, and started his spiel. "I'm the local sales rep, and I'm here to sell you a goff club with a hoewul in the back. Ya' can't play goff unless you got clubs with a hoewul in the back. If ya lookee here we got little hoewuls, big hoewuls, fat hoewuls, skinny hoewuls, and if ya don't have hoewuls, ya can't play goff.

"With these clubs with hoewuls, ya don't even have ta practice, cuz the hoewuls take care of all that. Jus' stick 'em in your bag and you're ready to shoot par. Now ya can't feel a damned thing but that doesn't matter, cuz with hoewuls ya don't need feel, cuz the hoewuls do it all...

"We c'n make lots of 'em too, cuz we just pour the stuff in a mold and bingo, ya got another club with a hoewul right smack in the back, another par shooter comin' up. We c'n pour 'em fast so we got lots of 'em to sayale."

This routine went on like that for a good ten minutes. The guy had some older woman's wig on, as it had a lot of gray in it, making him look like some 60-year old hippie, and he emphasized almost every word he spoke, particularly the "hoewuls." He hung onto that "o" each and every time he used the word, almost like a dog's howl. It was hilarious as hell, and the guy apparently knew a little about golf and golf clubs.

The guy was into the routine for a minute or so before Jack Owens and I looked at each other, we figured it out about the same time. The guy doing the routine was The Man himself, Ben Hogan. When Jack realized it, he started laughing so hard he literally fell off his chair.

No one would ever believe this one. The one everyone thought was so serious, even dour, was doing a stand-up comedy routine that Johnny Carson would have been proud of. He never missed a lick; it just rolled off his tongue, one sentence right after the other, like he'd been doing it all his life.

After Hogan finished his routine, he took off the wig and smoothed his hair. He took off the bright blue jacket, put on his tie, straightened it, put on his suit coat and went over to a bag of Hogan clubs standing near the head table. He pulled out the new Hogan iron and gave a serious, technical talk on the new club.

The salesmen were awestruck. They were glued to every comment, every technical fact. Hogan even emphasized the fact that he put his tie and suit coat on before talking about the new iron because it was a jewel, as good a club as could be manufactured. He also said he was proud of his sales force because they represented him personally, and he believed they conducted themselves as gentlemen. He was on a roll. He was doing his magic, showing that he could motivate that sales organization like no one or nothing else.

Later, as everyone was leaving Shady Oaks, Hogan walked up behind salesmen Archie Allison and Larry Reed in the parking lot as they were on their way

Lyne Price shows his amazement as Ben Hogan starts to take off his wig after his Hoe-wul presentation at the conclusion of the 1973 annual sales meeting. (PHOTO COURTESY HOGAN ESTATE)

to their cars. Walking between the two Hogan salesmen, Hogan put a hand on each of their shoulders and said to them, "I'm really not an old fuddy-duddy, but you boys represent me, and I want that done in a certain way." Then he put his arms around the two of them and added, "And you boys are doing a very fine job."

Archie said later, "You know, I would have run through the wall for that man right then. He was a terrific motivator, because he always spoke directly from his heart in situations like that. No BS, no posturing, just straight Hogan talk."

A day or two later, I tried to get a copy of a photo from Hogan's wig presentation, but apparently Hogan had taken the film right then and there after the meeting. No one was getting a copy of those photos unless Ben Hogan gave it to them.

LYNE PRICE'S RETIREMENT TOAST

Lyne Price had been with the Ben Hogan Company since Ben Hogan started selling golf equipment in 1954. Lyne was a unique individual, born in Kentucky, strong in his beliefs and actions, a fast-talking salesman who would not take no for an answer. A finicky eater, he drank only Coca-Cola from the small 6-oz. green bottles, never from cans (plastic bottles hadn't been invented yet). When they stopped selling Coca-Cola in the green 6-oz. bottles in the grocery store, he would buy it by the case from a local gas station owner who put them in his "Coke" machine.

Lyne's affiliation with Hogan started when he was a sales representative for the Ernie Saybarac sales organization, a sales rep company that initially sold the Hogan line of golf equipment. He then joined the Hogan Company when Ben Hogan decided to start his own sales department. Lyne became the Hogan Company's first sales manager, then Vice President of Sales. He developed a close relationship with Ben Hogan.

When Lyne officially retired from the Hogan Company, he worked as a consultant to run Hogan's newly-developed PGA and LPGA tour programs. He used Ben Hogan in his sales presentations as God's apostle for golf, comparing Hogan's statements on golf to Billy Graham's commentary on the Bible.

On the tour, he didn't take any foolishness from the pros. Lyne was a man who believed your word was your bond. At the Masters, he once told a European pro playing on the U.S. tour that when he had taken the Hogan balls from Lyne, he on several occasions had promised Lyne that he would go through the official ball count with Hogan, but had not done so. Consequently, Lyne removed the balls from the player's locker and told him he would never give him Hogan balls again. And as he departed, Lyne added, if he was that kind of individual, "he ought to get his lyin' ass back across the Atlantic Ocean."

Lyne was also one who gave you a shirt and told you exactly how to wear it, and if Hogan was involved, he'd probably do it at least two or three times.

Once, four Hogan salesmen had been invited to play at Seminole Golf Club in Florida during the PGA Golf Merchandise Show in West Palm Beach. Since Hogan had been a frequent guest there during his playing days, before they left for the course, Lyne laid down the do's and don'ts at least twice, including where to park their rental car and how much to tip the boys that toted their golf bags from the car to their golf carts, etc., etc.

When they returned that afternoon after playing golf they were relaxing in their motel room when Lyne's wife, Bea, walked by. Knowing how uptight Lyne had been about their Seminole trip, they conned Bea, a complete straight arrow, into telling Lyne that she had overhead these guys discussing winning a couple thousand dollars in a gin rummy card game from several Seminole members.

Bea told Lyne as soon as she got back to the room. Lyne, in preparation for the coat and tie dinner that night, was in the middle of his unique manner of preparation. After his shower he would fix his hair, put on his hat, then his boxer shorts, shoes, and socks. Then, he would shave. When Lyne heard about the gin rummy game, and members of Seminole losing several thousand dollars, he was extremely irritated and immediately went out the door, down the outside walkway to their room to confront them. After being greeted at the door Lyne, trying to play it cool, calmly asked, "Well, how'd it go at Seminole?" Lyne said.

"Fine, Lyne," came the group answer.

"Well, what'd ya shoot?" Lyne inquired.

"Well, Lyne, we got rained out about the 14th hole, so we just went back to the clubhouse for a beer," one of them answered.

"What'd ya do then?" Lyne further inquired.

"Aw, nothing" they responded, and they could hold it back no longer as they all burst out in laughter.

"What's so funny?" Lyne asked.

"We got ya, Lyne. We jerked your chain on this one, big time," they roared.

"Whadda ya mean? I was just comin' down to see how you boys played Seminole," Lyne retorted, faking innocence.

"Well, do you always walk outside and clear round the motel to a person's room with just your boxer shorts and your hat on, just to see how well they played golf?" they howled.

Lyne looked down to see he had gone clear around on the outside perimeter of the motel to their room wearing just his boxer shorts, shoes, and socks, and naturally, his hat. He stalked off without further comment.

Lyne was a first-class story teller and a practical joker. His favorite practical joke was his "pet mongoose" that he kept in a box in a closet nearby his office. Lyne had been the victim of golf professional Morgan Fottrell's prank when he was in Hawaii, and he thought the gag was so terrific that he offered to buy it, but Fottrell insisted on giving it to him.

From that point on, at the Hogan Company with new employees or with visitors, Lyne would set them up by casually mentioning that he had a pet mongoose that he had brought back from Hawaii, and that he allowed the Fort Worth zoo to keep it on display. When the person expressed an interest in seeing the mongoose, Lyne would bait the trap and promise to try to get it from the zoo. Lyne would drag this out to build up interest, then, when the unsuspecting person was set up and eager to see the critter, he would set the mongoose cage on his desk. The cage was half covered with screen and the other half was an enclosed wooden box with a small hole "to allow the mongoose to go in and out of the wooden box portion of the cage." Sitting on the floor of the screened part of the cage, Lyne always had a jar lid with a piece of lettuce on it "for the mongoose to nibble on." Lyne, of course, would start to show off his prized pet, but the uncooperative mongoose was almost totally hidden in the wooden box part of the cage, with only the mongoose's tail visibly sticking out into the screened part of the cage. Lyne would tap on the wooden box to try to get the mongoose to come out, which it naturally would not.

Lyne had a temper, so it would not seem unusual for him to get upset, so in keeping with his reputation, he would get very angry at the mongoose, and after banging on the box part of the cage with no success, he would get a wire to poke it through the little hole to make the mongoose come out of the covered box area. As he became more furious at the disobedient mongoose after poking it with the wire and shaking the box, he would trip a small hidden latch that caused the top of the box to flip open, and all of a sudden the tail that was visible came flying out of the box. Naturally, Lyne would station the one being duped into the position where the tail would be flung, so the poor soul immediately thought he had been attacked by the angry mongoose when that agitated animal came flying out of the box. Any nearby observers, and this prank usually drew a crowd, were strictly on their own to get out of the way of the fleeing fall guy (or gal).

Keeping a straight face during Lyne's antics was difficult, but it was rewarded with some of the most hilarious actions one can imagine as that tail came flying out of the box. Women would scream, men would yell as they all jumped, leaped, dodged, or ran to avoid the varmint. After the victims recovered from their initial fright, and were assured there was no rabid mongoose running amuck, they too joined in the laughter, relieved that it was a joke and not the real thing.

So when it came time for Lyne's retirement party, it seemed sinful not to give Lyne his due. Roasting his feisty butt in front of the Hogan sales and marketing organization seemed the only appropriate thing to do at his retirement dinner. There wasn't an individual in that group, with the possible exception of Hogan (and I'm not too sure about that), who hadn't been on the butt end of one of Lyne's practical jokes or pranks.

The vice president of the J. Osawa Company, the Hogan Company distributor in Japan, gave a deadpan testimony to Lyne totally in Japanese, with no interpreter. No one had a clue as to what the man was saying, but the other Japanese there were laughing hysterically. The combination of the deadpan speech that almost looked like he was giving Lyne's eulogy, and the other Japanese sales people uncontrollably laughing caused the rest of us to roar in laughter. The evening was filled with one individual roaster after another, culminating with Ben Hogan.

Everyone thought Hogan would give a serious speech, and it started out that way. Hogan talked about Lyne's tough early years and his first job in Youngstown, Ohio, as a collector of repossessed automobiles. The job was fraught with danger, and Hogan recounted Lyne's fist fights, getting shot at, and more, all in the line of duty, until the company went broke, and Lyne had to find another job. His next job was a siding salesman. Unfortunately, Hogan said, the company also failed. Hogan continued in that manner, stating that during every job that Lyne had in the past, the company went belly up, and Lyne had to go find another job. While several of the stories were in fact true, Hogan did embellished them quite a bit to spice them up, and Lyne started to get irritated. He had been the top dog in this sales department, a department that to this point had been very successful, and Hogan was telling everyone present that every company Lyne had worked for had gone bankrupt.

Lyne sensed that we all believed every word that Hogan was relating, and he wasn't used to being at the butt end of the joke, not in front of his sales department, and certainly not by Ben Hogan. Hogan's episodes were realistic and believable which made everyone laugh when the punch line came as the business went bust. With each episode, the crowd laughed harder and louder, and Lyne got more and more agitated. Finally, Hogan got to the punch line that he was damned glad Lyne was retiring before the Hogan Company went broke. The place exploded in laughter. Lyne was toast, and burnt toast at that. His face was red from heat. That just made us red-faced with laughter, laughing harder because he had it coming, and he knew he had it coming.

Ben Hogan really cared for Lyne Price, and all that he had done for the company, so Hogan turned serious to finish his speech. He concluded his presentation. "I have known Lyne Price for many, many years. He was one of the first people to come out to the plant after we opened up for business in 1954. And we have worked together in this business of golf ever since…. Lyne's contribution to the Ben Hogan Company goes far beyond his work in sales. His influence and interest reaches out to every part of our operation…. And believe me, he pushes us all, even me. But Lyne's influence at the Ben Hogan Company is only part of the picture. His influence in the golf industry is tremendous. You'd be amazed at the respect and esteem shown this man by players and golf people alike…. And, Lyne, you and I don't always agree on

Lyne Price, Hogan Company Sales & Marketing VP, rubs his eyes as Ben Hogan roasts him at Lyne's retirement party. (PHOTO COURTESY OF JEFF PRICE COLLECTION)

Ben Hogan laughs as Lyne Price, Hogan Company Sales & Marketing VP, gives him a golf swing tip. (PHOTO COURTESY OF JEFF PRICE COLLECTION)

everything, and we've had our moments of irritation with one another, but I wouldn't trade you for anyone else I know of in the business... and if I had a son, I would have wanted him to be just like you. Again, Lyne, my congratulations to you on these awards tonight, and my sincere best wishes to you for many more good years."

Hogan's close turned Lyne's irritation to tears.

NINE:
THE KINDER, GENTLER BEN HOGAN

MYTH: *Ben Hogan had no feelings. His grim determination on the golf course was the external manifestation of his hollow, uncaring emptiness that kept him from relating on a human feelings level to other individuals. "There's Ben Hogan sitting with all his friends."- Jimmy Roberts quote of Jimmy Demaret's humorous comment about Hogan sitting by himself at a table in the Champions Clubhouse in Houston, TX.*

MAN: Ben Hogan had feelings and friends. He enjoyed time with his friends and had a very warm, kind, caring, and compassionate side to his personality. While Ben Hogan was never one to wear his feelings on his sleeve, or even show his feelings in public, he had sensitivities and feelings that he showed and shared, but they were not necessarily for public consumption.

Despite his reputation to the contrary Ben Hogan liked to participate in life with his friends. From casual conversations to fishing or hunting trips, Hogan enjoyed time with friends. When asked about Hogan's reputation as an aging, solitary sourpuss, Mike Wright, Shady Oaks Director of Golf, from 1986 until after Hogan's death in 1997, responded, "That's a totally untrue characterization of the man. Ben Hogan was older when I was at Shady Oaks, and he was a grandfatherly type. He had a welcoming side towards guests and friends. In his later years, he was a softie."

William White, a friend of Louisiana touring professionals Jay and Lionel Hebert had several friendly encounters with Hogan, including at a tournament in which Hogan was playing. One year in the early 1950s at Colonial, White watched Hogan practicing in private just off the side of a fairway. Hogan was hitting a fairway wood. At first he just watched Hogan's swing, but then he started to follow the ball and realized that he was hitting the balls through a "V" shaped gap between two tall trees about 175 yards down the fairway. The trees were about 60 -70 feet tall, and the gap between the two tallest trees at the widest point was about 20 feet. White stood there amazed as Hogan hit about 25 balls between those two tall trees, "with the identical trajectory and not one touched a leaf."

When Hogan finished practicing he noticed White standing there, so White walked over and introduced himself and told Hogan he was a friend of Jay and Lionel Hebert. The two visited for what White described as 30 minutes, and then the two walked back to the clubhouse talking most of the way.

White noted another congenial moment when he and Sam Schneider were watching Hogan practice at the Masters. A crowd about 10 rows deep had collected around Hogan watching him practice, and White and Schneider were on the very outer fringe of the crowd. Hogan, never one to quickly beat balls, in pausing between shots turned around and spotted Schneider. He dropped his club and waded through the crowd, approaching Sam with, "Sam, you old S.O.B. where in the hell have you been?" The three visited for several minutes before Hogan went back to practicing. Schneider had known Hogan since his caddying days at Glen Garden Country Club where Sam was the caddy master.

White's commentary on his moments with Hogan, "Don't give me that crap about Hogan being one you can't talk with. I never found a nicer person nor a more pleasant one than the gentleman who showed me great courtesy to sit there and answer my questions. I only wish I could have spent hours with him."

Gene Smyers, Hogan, and four others took a fishing trip on a private plane heading to Livingston, Montana. The group floated down the Yellowstone River for two days, the six of them fishing in two boats, each with a guide. At one point on the river, Smyers looked over and saw "Hogan just keeled right over. He just went down." They got the boat in to the shore, and carried Hogan on to the bank of the river. He was white as a sheet, and looked terrible. He had a leg cramp and you could tell he was in great pain."

The guide asked Hogan if he wanted them to take him to the pickup point. "No," Hogan responded, "Let's continue on." Hogan wanted no special attention, no prima donna treatment. The group was having a good fishing trip, and Hogan didn't want to detract from it. After his friends massaged the cramp out of his leg,

Hogan and everyone else got back into the boats and they continued on. That night they had a fish fry in the city park. "Hogan enjoyed it immensely," Smyers said.

While Hogan was not very outgoing with strangers, he would give and take with people he knew. One day he was supposed to play at Shady Oaks with John Griffith, I.L. Taggert, John Howell, and Kelly Shannon, but Hogan hadn't shown up when they were ready to tee off. There was a telephone next to the No.1 tee box, so one of the group called into the pro shop and said, "Tell Hogan to get his ass out here if he wants to play with us."

Hogan could sit and talk with the ladies as well as banter back and forth with men. Shay Cates was sitting with friends in the mixed grill at Shady Oaks early one afternoon after finishing lunch when Hogan approached through the entrance to the men's grill. Hogan knew Shay well because they both smoked. At social functions, they often sat next to one another for that reason. He looked at her and asked, "Do you ladies mind if I sit with you for a while? I'm tired of listening to those know-it-alls over there," motioning with his head to the other room. The ladies all laughed, and Hogan sat down and talked with them, exchanging stories for a couple of hours.

Hogan, however, was not one to talk about himself much. On one occasion, Dr. Wym Van Wyk wished he had. Valerie Hogan's niece, also named Valerie, was interested in learning fashion design. Wym's wife, Chris, had a successful dress design business in Fort Worth, so Ben and Valerie Hogan asked if they might take Chris and Wym to dinner so their niece could visit with Chris about becoming a designer. Wym expressed his discussion with Hogan that evening this way, "We had a very nice conversation, and Hogan was articulate on the subjects we discussed, but I didn't want to ask him golf questions fearing he might think I was intruding or wanting him to recount stories he's told many times. And he apparently didn't want to bring up golf fearing it might give me the impression that golf is all he could talk about. I wish I had asked about golf because he was a good conversationalist, and I know it would have been interesting."

In the early 1990s Roger Williams had set up a Major League ex-players golf tournament at Shady Oaks Country Club. Roger was seated next to the Milwaukee Braves pitching ace, Lou Burdett, and Hall of Famer Early Wynn of the Cleveland Indians. Wynn, a 300 game winner with the Indians who ranks 20th on the all-time career victories list, had a camera around his neck and was taking pictures, when he leaned over and asked Roger, "Isn't this where Ben Hogan plays golf?" Roger acknowledged that yes this was where Hogan played golf. "Well, I want to see him," Wynn demanded as he got up and headed out of the dining room. Roger and Burdett got up to follow Wynn, and the group headed down the flight of stairs to the men's grill, Hogan's standard location when he was at the club.

As they rounded the corner from the hall into the men's grill they ran face to face into Hogan. Roger, taking the initiative, started to introduce the two famous players so that Hogan would know who he was talking with. "Mr. Hogan this is my friend Early Wynn…"

But before he could finish his introduction, Hogan interrupted, "Early, how are you doing, my boy? Good to see you," and he put his arms around the portly Wynn and gave him a hug. Roger was taken aback by the whole thing, because he had no idea that Hogan even knew who Early Wynn was, let alone that he would embrace him in such a friendly manner. Wynn started fumbling with his camera, so Roger quickly introduced Burdett. Then Wynn had his camera ready and said he wanted a picture with Hogan. Hogan agreed, and they got another person there to take a picture of the trio with Hogan. The group exchanged pleasantries for a few moments, and then headed back upstairs.

Ben Dickson was the head golf professional at the Muskogee Country Club in Oklahoma, and a member of the Hogan Company Club Professional Advisory Staff for nearly 30 years. In the mid-1960s, he came to Fort Worth at the invitation of the Hogan Company for one of the Advisory Staff sessions. After a round of golf with the staff group at Preston Trail Country Club, Dickson was driving a car full of staff pros back to the inn where the group was staying when the engine stalled on the exit ramp to the hotel. Dickson pulled to the side to the road and was trying to restart the engine when another car pulled over behind him. It was Hogan. After asking about the problem, he told Dickson to pop the hood on his car. Hogan took off his sport jacket and looked under the hood. He tinkered with something, and then told Dickson to try the engine again. It started right up, Hogan closed the hood, smiled at Dickson, and said he would see them later at the staff dinner. Dickson, as he recalled the incident, added, "I have the utmost respect for Ben Hogan."

Just as Hogan's career on the tour was hitting full stride in 1942 (he had been the leading money winner on the tour in 1940, 1941 and 1942) he joined the military service. He entered the army as a lieutenant attached to the Personnel Distribution Command in Atlantic City, and part of his duty was to visit hospitals to help raise the morale of the wounded. As he toured from hospital to hospital, he noticed wounded men using crutches and discarded casts to hit battered golf balls around. Hogan was moved to go beyond helping with morale, he persuaded friends and golf equipment manufacturers to donate clubs and balls, and they helped the hospitals requisition other equipment to help with the physical rehabilitation of the servicemen. No fanfare, Hogan just did what he could behind the scenes to help those in their recovery process. "Those men were such an inspiration," Hogan was quoted as saying.

He would also visit the surgery wards and watch the surgeons operate. He found himself fascinated by the surgeons' ability to make the body compensate. Years later he said, "I am convinced that the knowledge and inspiration I gained from those wartime hospitals made my recovery from the accident possible."

Hogan took his tour of military duty seriously, and it obviously made a profound impact on him. The emotions he felt for those wounded men and his efforts to help in both their physical and mental rehabilitation undoubtedly helped them. He got some of the golf equipment manufacturers to contribute their golf equipment to the hospitals so the wounded men could use them in their rehabilitation.

In the mid 1980's the Thunderbirds, the Air Force precision flying team, came to Fort Worth for an air show. While here they visited the General Dynamics facility that made the F-16's that they flew. Robert Stennett, one of the General Dynamics hosts, took them to Shady Oaks to play golf. After the round they were in the men's grill and spied Mr. Hogan across the room. After twenty to thirty minutes of conversation, they decided that they wanted to have their picture taken with him, so they pestered Robert, who tried to caution them that you just didn't walk up uninvited and ask to have your picture taken with him. They persisted and finally convinced Robert to at least ask, so Robert, who did not know Hogan well went over and posed the question. Robert

Ben Hogan gives a clinic for fellow soldiers, during his military service in the early 1940's. (PHOTO COURTESY HOGAN ESTATE)

said, "Mr. Hogan couldn't have been more hospitable as he replied, 'I'd be honored to have a picture taken with them.' And so they had their pictures taken with Mr. Hogan." Hogan, in fact, had a photo of the Thunderbirds in flight formation that hung over his secretary's desk that was signed by the pilots, and below the photo was a note in calligraphy, "To Ben Hogan, who is also pretty good with a stick in his hand."

Ben Hogan has often been portrayed as a man without emotions, a man without feelings. In the fall of 1977, Hogan invited me to his office, asked me to sit down, and handed me a Christmas message by Charles Hanson Towne. He said he wanted to send a letter to the golf professionals with this Christmas message on it in appreciation for their efforts on behalf of our company. As I read the message I was touched by its warmth and by Hogan's heartfelt desire to share it with our golf professional customers:

"Christmas would mean nothing if it were not shared
with someone. It is a festival which cannot be indulged
in alone. The gaudy red ribbon about the simplest gift
causes the gift to take on a merit which it did not
possess before; and just as a single rose may light up
a room, so one word on a card, written in sincerity,
may brighten the dimmest winter day."

Hogan ended the letter with "All of us at the AMF Ben Hogan Company would like to extend our appreciation of the friendly association we have enjoyed with you and to take this moment to remember you with our sincere thanks and our very best wishes for your enjoyable Holiday Season.
Sincerely,
Ben Hogan

I was truly moved, not only by the gesture, but also by the feeling embodied in the message and Hogan's desire to share it with golf professionals across the country.

The "Wee Ice Mon" probably aptly fit the man in his "office" in competition on the golf course, but it hardly fit the man who Grantland Rice, the famous sportswriter, described as he introduced Hogan at the end of the movie "Follow the Sun" by saying, "His legs simply were not strong enough to carry his heart around."

During the 1953 British Open CBS radio broadcaster John Derr and Hogan got to know one another. Derr helped Hogan in booking his practice times, and the two ate lunch together daily the week before the tournament, so they became friendly. Because he wasn't feeling well, reportedly with a temperature of 103, Hogan didn't hit many practice balls before the final 36 holes on the last day of the tournament. He didn't take any medication either, fearing it might impair his judgment on the course. On the final round Hogan made a birdie two on the par-3 13th that helped to seal Hogan's victory. After the tournament was over, Hogan asked his caddie, Cecil Timms to give Derr something. Timms reached into one of his coat pockets and pulled out a ball, and said, "When we had our only deuce of the last round, Mr. Hogan gave me this ball and said, 'Put it aside. Mr. Derr might want it as a souvenir.'"

"Here's a guy who has never competed over there, winning the British Open, supposed to have ice in his blood, and yet he's thoughtful enough to tell his caddie a friend might want it as a souvenir," Derr said, adding, "My daughter, Cricket, has it in her safe."

For the most part, Hogan's compassion and empathy for others was done on a one-on-one basis. His letters to the sick or injured were always short and personal. And on numerous occasions, he offered consolation, encouragement, or money.

Hogan wrote letters to accident victims or individuals who were seriously ill. His letters were gracious, compassionate, and always offered encouragement. While I had drafted numerous letters for Mr. Hogan on business matters, these personal letters of encouragement were always done by him. These were letters that came from the man's heart, and he put them in his own words.

On two separate instances when I mentioned that friends of mine, Fordyce Gayton and Treadway Charles, were battling cancer, Mr. Hogan graciously sent both letters. I caddied for Fordy (he gave me my first pair of golf shoes), and Mr. Charles was my high school golf coach. In his letters to them, after asking their permission to allow him to offer a word of encouragement, Hogan commented on the shocks that the human body can absorb and that recovery is possible with faith, hope, and determination—three qualities I believe Hogan felt very strongly about. In his letters of encouragement Hogan always asked the individual's permission to offer encouragement, a reflection, I believe, of his own honoring the privacy of others. He sent similar letters to many others, golfers and non-golfers alike. One letter went to a boy from nearby Weatherford who lost a limb in an accident. The boy was not a golfer but Hogan had heard about it and wanted to offer his encouragement.

Archie Allison recalled: "In the early 1960's, when the company was small, on numerous occasions, I was asked to take envelopes, and one of Mr. Hogan's caps, to a children's hospital in Dallas. Although I never knew what was in those envelopes, I suspected it was checks for donations to the hospital. I always had to take them to the same lady in the hospital in North Dallas." On one of these occasions, Hogan asked Archie to pick up a quart of paint in Dallas. Archie did and when he gave the paint to Hogan, Hogan gave him a check to pay for the paint. Archie put the check in a frame and hung it on the wall at home. Later Archie got a note in the mail that simply said, "Cash that damn check!" Signed, BH. Archie took the check off the wall and cashed it.

Likewise, Hogan had another young man, Ernie Horn, help him with his philanthropic projects. Ernie had met Ben Hogan through Marvin Leonard who had helped Ernie's family following the 1949 flood in Fort Worth.

Ernie recalled, "Hogan had a tenderness, a compassion for people who had come upon hard times because of a serious illness or an accident. He would anonymously help people in their time of need. Several times Valerie & Ben Hogan found out about people needing help, clothing, food, etc. The Hogans would help people in various ways. They offered their help by paying hospital bills, buying clothing, or even buying or repairing cars. On numerous occasions, I was called upon to assist in their efforts. In agreeing to participate, I was sworn to secrecy as long as the Hogans were alive. They wanted no one to know that they were doing this," and Ernie added, "You know Hogan had a mean streak, so when he made me promise, he really made me promise. I knew that he would be big time unhappy if I crossed him, and their secret wasn't kept. I respected and understood that. Mr. Hogan was absolutely one of the most private gentlemen I have ever known."

Claribel Kelly would also give Ernie a routing envelope, for sending interoffice mail that was filled with cash. Ernie would usually take it to the Cook Children's Hospital. Less frequently, he would be asked to take the envelope to an address and to deliver it directly to a family. At Christmas Ernie would be asked to take boxes or bags of canned goods to families homes. To remain anonymous, he would place the box or bag on the doorstep, ring the doorbell or knock on the door and run. Ernie would deliver money, clothes, or boxes and bags of canned goods to the families. He said such charitable giving, being able to help people anonymously, brought Ben Hogan a lot of joy.

Hogan, on numerous occasions, would collect money for people who had been in an accident of some misfortune. On one such occasion, Gene Smyers walked into the Shady Oaks men's grill one afternoon and as he approached the "round table" greeted Ben Hogan. "Hi, Mr. Hoag," as Gene called him.

"Smyersie," Hogan responded barely looking up, "gimmie $200!" Smyers, puzzling over Hogan's request, stood there fishing through his pockets for some money as Hogan spied Eddie Chiles, Chairman of the Western Company.

"Eddie, gimmie $500!"

Then came Monty and Tex Moncrief from Moncrief Oil Company, and Hogan hit each of them up for $500.

One after another Hogan badgered everyone for money as they entered. Smyers was feeling pretty good that he got off with a $200 touch, but still wondered what Hogan was up to. Once he'd made sure that he'd committed everyone who had walked through the door, Hogan explained that he was taking up a collection for Rosalinda, one of the waitresses there at Shady Oaks. She had been shot coming home from the grocery store the night before, and he was collecting money to give to her family to help take care of her medical and family expenses. He collected nearly $7,000 for the family.

One afternoon Gene came into Shady Oaks about 5:00 and saw Charles Hudson, the headwaiter in the Shady Oaks men's grill. "Mr. Smyers, Mr. Hogan left this afternoon about 3:30 and about 4:15 he came back," Charles said. "He asked me to drive him to

John L. Ash to see the Oxxford representative who was going to be there for a showing of swatches so that Mr. Hogan could buy some suits. So I drove Mr. Hogan down there, and they showed him the material swatches, and then after they fitted Mr. Hogan for his suits, Mr. Hogan turned around and told the salesman, 'That young man over there, fit him for one too.' At first I said no, he didn't need to do that, but he insisted, so he fitted me for a suit, I got one too." That was a suit Charles Hudson was very proud of. When he passed away Charles was buried in his light chocolate Oxxford suit. Jimmie Hudson, Charles' widow said, "No one else was going to wear that suit. I wasn't going to give that suit to anyone." Obviously it was a special gift to both of them.

When I had to replace an employee that both Hogan and I liked, I went in to Mr. Hogan's office and explained what I was going to do. He said it was my decision to make, and that he didn't have any advice to offer. I thanked him for listening to my dilemma. Several weeks later Claribel called and asked me to come to Mr. Hogan's office. He asked me to sit down, and then commented to me. "Tim, I know you had to make a tough decision several weeks ago about letting someone go. I just want you to know that you made the right decision." Hogan knew that I was bothered by the decision. He was empathetic enough to call me in and give me support for a decision that he knew I wished I didn't have to make. I left his office with a lump in my throat, greatly appreciating his gesture and support.

In February 1982, I was fired from my position. Before I left, I went in to see Mr. Hogan. Such a thing had never happened to me, so I was very upset and embarrassed for being fired. Again, Mr. Hogan was very reassuring and offered encouragement. "Tim, you did the best you could, and I appreciate your efforts here. You'll do fine wherever you go."

I wasn't so sure. I was going through a divorce, so I didn't want to leave Texas, or Fort Worth, since that would mean leaving my stepdaughter, Heather, and my son, Jordan. There were no golf or sporting goods companies locally, so I was really torn.

I said, "Thank you, Mr. Hogan, those words mean a lot to me. This place is so much a part of me, and I believe so strongly in what we've done here that I don't think I could work for another golf company. Because of you, this has been more than a job to me. It has been a very rewarding experience.

Ben Hogan with the author when he became the Sales and Marketing VP.

"I believe I've grown as an individual, having worked with you, seeing how you stand by your principles, making tough decisions, regardless of the consequences." Hogan leaned forward in his chair, resting his forearms on his desk, and looking me directly in the eyes, now with softness in his eyes that at times could be his steely blues, said, "Tim, you have a family to take care of, so do what you have to do. If you're offered a good job with another golf company, go ahead and take it. Don't worry about anything here. You take care of yourself and your family. And you'll do just fine."

I thanked him and went out to Claribel's desk to say good-bye to her. She handed me the large poster-size cover of the April 1978 issue of Golf Magazine that two of my friends at the magazine, Mac Moore and Ron Reimer, had given to me, and Mr. Hogan had signed—"To Tim Scott, with kindest personal regards, Ben Hogan." Several years earlier Claribel had given me one of Mr. Hogan's personal golf bags that she said he wanted me to have.

Bernie Coyle was the Hogan Company computer department manager. He was working late one night. Bernie remembered, "Around 10:00, my office door was open and Hogan stuck his head in and asked, 'How's the computer project coming?' I said, 'Swell,' to which Hogan responded, 'I don't like that word swell, it reminds me of hippies.'

"Well, how does 'pretty darn good grab you,' I blurted back. I was tired, and it probably wasn't that respectful a response.

"'Better than swell,' Hogan retorted."

Fifteen years later when he left the company, Bernie went to Mr. Hogan's office to say good bye. Bernie recalled, "Hogan said to me, 'By the way I want to apologize about that evening. I know I caught you off guard, and you were working late and deep in thought. I should have accepted your response of "swell." That Hogan would remember that—and apologize to me about it 15 years later, really impressed me."

Hogan had a golf club with a weighted handle that he swung inside the Shady Oaks clubhouse to strengthen his "swing muscles". In 1988, just two years after he had become the Shady Oaks' head golf professional, Mike Wright broke his right elbow and had his arm in a sling. As he was going through the healing process, Hogan appeared with another weighted club, just like his own, that he gave to Mike. By using the weighted club, Wright was able to strengthen his elbow and regain the power that he previously had in his swing. Wright recalled, "Nothing was ever said. Hogan just showed up with the club one day and gave it to me…. That was just the kind of man he was."

Rosemary Godwin, one of Hogan's assistants, recalled a personal example of Hogan's caring side. "I will never forget looking up, at my father's funeral, and seeing Mr. Hogan walking down the aisle at the end of the service. As you know, he went nowhere in public, particularly in his later years. But he came to that funeral with 400 people there, and he didn't sit in the back either."

In 1960 Claribel's husband died. Hogan told her to take as much time off as she needed, and he would take care of it. Money wouldn't be a problem. She just needed to do what she needed to do to take care of her two children. Shortly after she retired in 1984, Claribel developed cancer of the vocal chords. Claribel's daughter, Colleen Sowden, recalled, "Mr. Hogan was wonderful when mother was sick. He told me not to worry about the finances, that he would take care of them. He told her that she should get the very best care possible, that he would take care of it, regardless of what treatment or facilities were required. He was very generous. When they told him that she wouldn't last much longer, he got very upset."

One day a call came in to the River Oaks Country Club in Houston for Dick Harmon, the head golf professional. He was told that the caller was Ben Hogan. Dick, who was out giving a lesson, came to the phone, expecting some friend of his to tell him he knew that using Hogan's name would get him to answer the phone, but Dick immediately recognized Hogan's voice as he said, "Dick, I tried to call Lochinvar to talk to your dad, but he wasn't there. Where is he? I'd like to talk to him." Dick responded that his dad was in the hospital. "The hell he is," Hogan responded, "How can I get hold of him?" Dick gave Hogan the hospital phone number, the two of them chatted a few minutes, and then hung up.

Dick reminisced about Hogan calling his dad, Claude Harmon, "He asked him what was wrong with him and how was he doing. Dad told him he had serious heart problems and was not doing well….the doctors and nurses were trying to get him to walk every day…. It was difficult. It was tiring. And it was too much. 'Ben,' he said, 'I don't know how you did it. I just can't do this,' his voice trailing off as if he was giving up."

"Mr. Hogan sensed dad was being overwhelmed by the enormity of the task, so he went over his own difficult time....in detail day-by-day, beginning from day one. 'Claude,' he said, 'the first day I just tried to walk around the bed. That was all I could do, and it wasn't easy. I had to push myself to do that. Then the second day, I tried to walk around that bed two times....Then, after I got along with that fairly well, and started to gain just a little strength; I tried to walk down the hall, then I tried to walk twice down the hall.... Claude, I just tried to concentrate on the day in front of me, just that one single day because thinking about more than just that one day seemed to make the task overwhelming, so I had to take it just one day at a time. And you can too.'"

Dick wistfully added, "For the last month of dad's life, Ben Hogan called him each and every day—every day."

Ben Hogan may not have congratulated his friend, Claude Harmon, for his hole in one on the 12th hole at Augusta that day in the 1947 Masters, but he didn't miss a day of talking to him when Claude Harmon needed it most.

Similarly, when Hogan's good friend Earl Baldridge was gravely ill and in the hospital, Hogan went to see him daily. During his last days, when Baldridge was in a coma, Hogan went to the hospital every day and just sat there with him for at least an hour or more each day, just the two of them. One such day John McMackin, Baldridge's son-in-law, came by, and saw Hogan as he started to enter the room. Hogan hadn't noticed John, so John decided not to interrupt their time together and left. Years later there was a softness in McMackin's voice as he recalled Hogan's thoughtfulness in spending time with his friend, even though Earl probably never even knew he was there.

In 1993, after calling his 2912 West Pafford Street Hogan Company office home for 40 years, Hogan, at the age of 81, left that office for the last time when the company had once again been sold, and this time the factory was being moved to Virginia. Doxie Williams, his personal administrative assistant for thirteen years, accompanied him out the door that day:

"It was the Friday preceding the Memorial Day weekend, and we were the last ones there to turn off the lights and leave the building. I walked him to his private entrance as I had always done…. This time, as I was seeing him out. He stepped out the door and then he turned around, touched an index finger to his mouth, and put his finger on the door handle like he was kissing it good-bye. That nearly brought me to tears…. It really broke his heart to be moving out of it." Several years later, Spalding Sports Worldwide purchased the Ben Hogan Company, and in 1999 moved the Hogan club facilities, then an assembly operation, back to Fort Worth. It was a very welcome homecoming, but also very sad that Mr. Hogan wasn't still here to enjoy it too.

In his will Ben Hogan left money to non-family members and around a million dollars each to two local charities: Cook Children's Hospital and University Christian Church. Harris Hospital later sought approval, which was granted by grandniece Lisa Scott, to name their Harris Hospital rehabilitation centers "Texas Health Ben Hogan Sports Medicine." Hogan's kindness, compassion, and his physical struggles after his accident, for the most part unseen in his public life while he was alive, continue even after he was gone.

The Gentleman

Ben Hogan was a gentleman. While in private conversations, he could use locker room vocabulary. The several times I had heard such language in his office, he spoke in a muted voice level that even his secretary in her office next door couldn't hear. If Hogan used a vulgarity, you could rest assured that no women were present, and he had better not get wind of one of his employees getting foul-mouthed in front of women either.

In the mid-1970s, AMF decided to use one advertising agency—Benton & Bowles, for all of its consumer products businesses, including the Ben Hogan Company. Until then, the Hogan Company had used a local Fort Worth agency, Jack T. Holmes & Associates, for as long as the company had used an ad agency. Jack Holmes, who owned and headed the agency, was very mindful of Mr. Hogan and his way of doing things and personally oversaw the Hogan account. No one from AMF had bothered to notify us at Hogan of the change. John Cantwell, the Hogan Company ad manager, found out by reading *Advertising Age* magazine. That AMF blunder prompted immediate phone calls, including calls from Ben Hogan himself to AMF's chairman of the board, Rodney Gott, to voice his displeasure. It was all to no avail; Benton & Bowles, a big New York ad agency, was now our ad agency.

The Hogan Company held its annual National Sales Meeting each August. It was the company's big event each year to introduce the new product line with much fanfare. The new agency wanted to show the outtakes from some of their TV commercials at the opening dinner, which followed the first day of the meeting. Since few people in the Hogan Company had never seen outtakes, we all agreed it would be a novel addition to the meeting, but several of us who had seen these outtakes at a previous AMF function questioned the propriety of one commercial in mixed company. We knew it would infuriate Mr. Hogan if it were shown when women were present, so we insisted that it be removed. The agency said it didn't have time to edit it out the offending piece of 16mm film, but they did say that they could simply stop the outtakes before the offensive ad came on because it was close to the end of the reel. We finally acquiesced. I was concerned about it, but apparently not concerned enough.

As the outtakes were shown after dinner the laughter from the audience grew louder and louder with each humorous outtake. I was holding my breath. Then, Ricardo Montalban was doing a coffee commercial. He raised the cup to his mouth to take a drink as the camera panned in for a close-up shot. Then Montalban quickly jerked the cup away and gasped, "Aahhh, too f___ing hot."

The reaction in the audience was mixed, some laughed, some snickered, and some gasped. I was angry that they had shown it, but I was especially mad because I knew Hogan would be absolutely livid, and Hogan's positive participation in the sales meeting was always crucial. After the outtakes film ended, the lights came up and Bill Sovey, the president of the company, made a few closing remarks. I strained to look for Hogan. He was white hot, as if all the blood had drained from his face. When Sovey finished, Hogan made for the exit, his eyes fixed on the door. He spoke to no one, and he never broke stride. He was gone in a matter of moments.

The next morning I got the expected call from Claribel Kelly. Shirley Givant, my secretary, took the call and came into my office. "Mr. Hogan wants to see you," she said, with a look of dread on her face. I headed straight to Hogan's office. He wasted no time, exchanged no pleasantries, and minced no words. "Tim, who the hell's in charge of advertising at AMF?" I told him and in a few moments Claribel appeared at the door and indicated that Don Fox, the AMF Advertising VP, was on the line.

Hogan was not pleasant, and the conversation was very direct. "Fire that advertising agency," Hogan demanded in no uncertain terms, and, no he didn't care if they were the agency for all of AMF's consumer products, he wanted them off the Hogan account beginning today. If he was unwilling to make that decision, Hogan said he wanted to speak to Rodney Gott, the AMF Chairman of the Board. He said we didn't run the Ben Hogan Company that way and Fox should be embarrassed that his ad agency had greatly offended a mixed crowd of Hogan employees with their crude outtake on the film. Getting no satisfaction from Fox, Hogan ended the conversation and tried to call Rodney Gott, AMF's chairman, but Fox must have gotten to Gott first because Gott was "unavailable" to take Hogan's call. I went back to my office and called John Ferries, the B&B executive responsible for the entire AMF account. I had met John several years previous, when I was a second year MBA student at the Amos Tuck School of Business at Dartmouth. Professor Ken Davis suggested that I invite John to participate in a Tuck marketing/advertising career panel, and John graciously came to Hanover, New Hampshire to participate. Consequently, I felt comfortable in calling him directly, and since he had not been at the meeting, laying out the whole scenario, from our not being informed of the agency change to the commercial outtakes and Hogan's reaction.

B&B wasn't fired that day, and relations with it were quickly smoothed out when Ferries immediately came to Fort Worth to personally assure Hogan that such a *faux pas* would not happen again. In fact, despite the outtakes incident, Hogan later cooperated fully with the agency in making the first Hogan Company TV commercials. He was the main attraction of all the commercials that followed.

One Hogan Company president had a particularly foul mouth. One day Hogan came out to Rosemary Russell's desk to ask her about something. Rosemary had been hired to help Claribel Kelly who was growing older. The Hogan Company president was on a tear about something. Although his door was closed, the vent over his office was apparently connected to the one over Rosemary's desk. The torrent of foul language coming from the next office was almost like it coming from a muffled speakerphone on her desk. Hogan left Rosemary and marched straight into the president's office and told him he had better clean up his language because women all over the office could hear him. Hogan raised his voice loud enough that all the women in the vicinity could hear what he was saying.

Rosemary noted, "The interesting thing to me was that Mr. Hogan did like the man, and never seemed to hold a grudge. It was as if he needed to admonish him for his lack of manners in mixed company, almost like a parent. Later Mr. Hogan was very caring and compassionate toward him when his daughter became seriously ill while away at college. Mr. Hogan continued to check on her condition and encouraged the president to take time off and to go get her if he needed to."

Mike Wright, the Shady Oaks Director of Golf, one day asked Mr. Hogan how he would like to be remembered. After a long pause, Hogan, one of the greatest golfers of all time, looked at Mike with his blue eyes locked on Mike's, and said, "Mike, I want to be remembered as a gentleman."

Max, Duffer and Buster

Ben Hogan had affection for animals, particularly dogs. At a point when the ASPCA (American Society for Prevention of Cruelty to Animals) was running out of money and would have to shut down its Fort Worth dog shelter, he gave it money to stay open, with the understanding that there would be no publicity, not a mention of the contribution.

Ben and Valerie Hogan for many years had a small poodle named Duffer. As Duffer grew old and ailing, Hogan would sometimes sit up all night taking care of him. Duffer was buried near the Hogan house and a tombstone was placed next to his grave.

A diabetic schnauzer named Buster had been adopted by the members of Shady Oaks. They fed him kitchen scraps, gave him daily insulin shots, and playful pats. After Buster died in 1993, Hogan walked into the pro shop and asked Mike Wright, Director of Golf, where Buster had been buried. Wright led Hogan to the spot near the putting green. Hogan removed his hat and placed it over his heart. Then he dropped to one knee, not easy for 81 year old Hogan, particularly because of his auto accident injuries. He kissed his fingertips, and lightly touched them to the grave. When he returned to the pro shop tears trickled from Hogan's eyes.

During one of the rounds of the 1961 U.S. Open at Oakland Hills, John Grace, a Michigan native who later moved to Fort Worth and played many rounds of golf with Hogan, remembered that a dog ran across the fairway when Hogan was about to hit. While the dog was not in the immediate area where Hogan was intending to hit his tee shot, he refused to tee off until the dog was removed from the course. He told the tournament officials, "That might be some little kid's dog, and I don't want to possibly injure it."

Given Hogan's feelings towards dogs, it's not too hard to understand the relationship that had developed between him and a mutt named Max.

Max was a black and white mutt that looked like a large border collie, but might have been part shepherd. Max became a legend around Shady Oaks in the late 1970s and early 1980s because of his affinity for watching Hogan practice. When Hogan got into his golf cart to go hit balls, Max would climb right up onto the passenger seat next to Hogan and sit there, head up, and body erect, almost like he was at "attention." It was as if he were the caddie going out with Hogan to retrieve balls. Upon arrival at the designated practice spot, Max would climb down, lie beside the golf cart with his head between his front paws, and watch Hogan hit his shots.

When practice was over, Max would climb back up onto the seat of the cart and ride back to the clubhouse with Hogan. It was uncanny. Max would not watch anyone else hit balls, just Ben Hogan. That dog probably saw more Hogan swings than any one person, and it probably spoiled him because of his apparent disinterest toward all other golfers. Max might occasionally watch another golfer hit a couple of practice shots, but after one or two swings, Max lost interest and off he'd go. Not with Ben Hogan, he'd lie there the entire time, and only get up to leave when Hogan was ready to head back to the clubhouse.

Gene Smyers had a firsthand experience with Max's discerning eye. Max rode out to the practice range with him one day, laid down as Gene took a few warm up swings, and then watched Gene hit a couple of shots. Then Max got up and left. While Gene was a pretty decent player, he wasn't Ben Hogan, so Max wasn't interested.

Ben Hogan and his best galleryite, Max. (PHOTO COURTESY OF SHADY OAKS COUNTRY CLUB)

To Ben Hogan, Max was more than a dog that watched him hit golf balls. Hogan really liked him. One particularly cold, windy day, Hogan led Max into the men's grill and invited him to sit at his table for lunch. Hogan ordered a hamburger and shared it with Max. A Shady Oaks member saw Max seated next to Hogan enjoying his portion of Hogan's sandwich. The member found the club manager, and dragging the manager into the men's grill, asked, "Are you going to let that go on?" The manager, after gazing at the two enjoying lunch and knowing full well that Marvin Leonard had built Shady Oaks initially so he, Ben Hogan, and some of their friends could enjoy a more private setting, responded, "Well, you're more than welcome to voice your displeasure to Mr. Hogan, but I've got more important matters to attend to at the moment," and walked off.

One year, Hogan went to Florida to practice and play at Seminole Golf Club near Palm Beach. Gary Laughlin, one of Hogan's golfing buddies and a partner in some of Hogan's oil exploration efforts, typed up a letter from Max telling Hogan how lonely and mistreated he felt because Hogan was in Florida and far away from Shady Oaks. Max said he missed Ben and wasn't eating right, and the members weren't taking care of him like Ben did. Gary then inked Max's paw print at the bottom of the letter and mailed it to Hogan at Seminole. Hogan got such a kick out of the letter that he carried it with him to show everyone during his Florida stay. Gary even claimed that Hogan took it with him to a black-tie event and showed the letter to everyone he met at the party.

Max was a very bright dog. Every Saturday night at Shady Oaks the club had a buffet that was served in the dining room that overlooked the 1st and 10th tees, the only time such a meal was served in that room. Max parked outside the big glass double doors and waited for Hogan. If Hogan wasn't there, Gene Smyers or Gary Laughlin, or another round table friend, would let Max have his buffet dinner too. Every Saturday night there was Max, lying dutifully outside the door waiting for his Saturday night special, and sure enough, Hogan or one of his friends would oblige with a sampling from the buffet.

In 1980, a sports writer for the Dallas Morning News wrote a column about Hogan that included a comment about Max, "the club dog, sitting obediently while Hogan strikes ball after ball after ball."

Hogan wrote the columnist a letter complimenting him about the article, but in the letter Hogan also cautioned:

"There is a problem however, stemming from your article in that Max is suing me for contributory negligence. You recall that you called Max 'the club dog.' Everyone, including Max, knows he is not a dog but that he is President, Chairman of the Board, and protector of the club's membership.

I have explained to Max that this article was written unbeknown to me, but he will not accept that. Our relationship is rather strained in that when I speak to him now he wags his tail very slightly, whereas in the past he would give me a vigorous waggle. Also, he has stopped watching me practice. This, of course, really puts me down since he was my last gallerite (sic).

I will try to settle this suit out of court for a few quarter pounders, but if Max refuses and requests a jury trial, I am positive I will lose this case and he will be awarded the whole herd of Santa Gertrudis from the King Ranch."

"TOOFIES" – THE GRANDFATHERLY BEN

The film crew and Mr. Hogan had returned from the TV commercial shoot on the Shady Oaks course and pulled up to the pro shop entrance of the club. As our golf carts came to a stop, my little boy, Jordan, spotted me as he was coming up the walkway and came running up to say hello. He was almost three at the time, very energetic, and never met a stranger. I bent down and gave him a big hug, then held his hand as I straightened up to talk to Mr. Hogan and the others as we discussed the commercial we'd just finished shooting.

A few minutes into the conversation Jordan gave my hand a tug and quietly, but audibly whispered "Dad." I looked down at him and shook my head, indicating "Not now, Jordan." A few minutes later came an impatient tug and a little louder he whispered, "Dad." I again looked down, raised my eyebrows and shook my head a little more emphatically and mouthed "No, Jordan, not now." He again decided that the response was not to his liking and then came in a slightly louder tone. "Dad, I'm thirsty, I want drink."

"Just a minute Jordan. Not now." I was also growing impatient, "We'll get one in a minute, but I can't do it right now," furrowing my forehead to emphasize to my point.

Not to be denied came, "Dad, I'm thirsty. Will you get me a drink?" I looked down, and growing irritated, and asked him one more time to wait a minute. After about exactly one minute came the familiar "Dad." As I started to bend down and negatively respond to the little guy in a more forceful manner, Mr. Hogan intervened, "Come on, Jordan, I'll get you a drink." Hogan held out his hand for Jordan to grab hold, and as the little tyke grabbed his hand, the un-flapped Hogan pointed to his golf cart and off they went. Hogan helped the little guy scramble up on the seat, and they rode off around the putting green to the men's grill on the opposite side of the clubhouse.

A few minutes later they returned, Jordan with the small green glass Coca-Cola bottle clutched tightly in both hands. Hogan helped Jordan climb down from the cart, and they rejoined the group, Hogan with a smile of satisfaction that he had helped the little tyke out, and Jordan contently drinking his Coca-Cola, not really knowing (or caring) who his benefactor was.

We had scarcely resumed our conversation when Jordan, again tugged on my trouser leg. "Dad," he whispered. When I didn't respond he upped the audio a little, "Dad," he again said, with another tug on my leg. This time I looked down, and as I did he motioned for me to bend down, he wanted to whisper something to me. I half bent down, and as I did Jordan asked, "Dad, what are my toofies?"

"What?" I asked, not understanding what he was saying.

"What are my li'l toofies?" he said audibly louder. "Mr. Hogan said I couldn't drink the Coke while I was riding on the cart because I might hurt my li'l toofies," Jordan said it loud enough that all of us could hear. I hesitated a second, then looked toward Hogan.

Hogan grinned. "I told him he better not drink the Coke while we were riding in the cart because we might hit a bump, and he might crack that glass bottle against his mouth and hurt his li'l toofies," Hogan said with a broad smile as he tapped his own teeth with his index finger. The grin on his face got bigger, and he started to chuckle. When the rest of us started to laugh, then Hogan broke into one of his full laughs and the whole group burst out laughing.

Jordan Scott wishes Ben Hogan happy birthday with a box of chocolate golf balls.

A few weeks later at the office Hogan pulled me aside. He had a grin on his face.

"I saw your little boy at the club yesterday."

"Oh," I said, a little apprehensively. Jordan was an active little kid and liked to run around the Shady Oaks pool area with a towel tied around his neck, playing Superman. Sometimes he strayed from the pool area. Shady was a genteel, conservative club, with a predominantly older membership, some not too favorably disposed to noisy, rambunctious children. The younger kids weren't supposed to run unsupervised in the clubhouse, but if Jordan saw a familiar face off he'd go.

Hogan continued, "I was walking down the hall and the little fella' came up the other way. He came right up to me and said, 'Hey, aren't you Mr. Hogan?' I didn't recognize him right away, so I answered "Why yes, young man, and who are you?"

Jordan responded without the slightest hesitation, he said, "Aw, Mr. Hogan, you know me. I'm Jordan." (Since the Coke incident Jordan must have thought he was one of Hogan's drinking buddies.)

Hogan said, "Ah, yes, now I recognize you." Jordan added, "Well, it's nice to see you, Mr. Hogan, but I gotta' go, I'm supposed to be out at the pool. I'm not supposed to be in here, and I don't want to get in trouble, but I saw you come in and wanted to say, 'Hi.'"

Hogan chuckled to me and said, "He's a nice little boy." As he turned to go about his business, I said thank you. I'm sure he realized how much that meant to me, and that I very much appreciated his gesture. On several other occasions when Jordan was with me, and Hogan saw us, he came over to say hello. Once, a couple years later, we were playing golf on the "Little Nine" at Shady Oaks, and he came over as Jordan, then five years old, was about to putt. "Let me see you make one, Jordan," Hogan encouraged as the little guy got ready to putt. Jordan picked up his ball and moved it closer to the hole so he had a better chance of not disappointing his drinking buddy—but missed the putt anyway. I was taken aback with Hogan's ease and understanding in the way he related to Jordan. I hadn't expected that.

Rosemary (Russell) Godwin, who worked for Mr. Hogan, expressed how good he was with her children when they came to his office. He would have them sit on his lap,

Ben Hogan's little helper gathers "Easter eggs" as he watches in amusement. (PHOTO COURTESY HOGAN ESTATE)

talk to them, play with them, and give them gifts, sometimes colored golf balls that he kept in his desk for such occasions.

A local Fort Worth doctor related to me that once a father, who was a neighbor of Hogan's, had played with his daughter in a man/woman golf tournament at Shady Oaks. As soon as they finished their round, the father left to play in another tournament at a different country club. That father/daughter team ended up tied for first place and had to play in a sudden-death playoff, but with the father gone, the daughter had to play the other couple by herself. So Hogan rode in the cart with his neighbor's daughter to give her some moral support during the playoff. Later, when Hogan saw the father, he gave the father hell for leaving, telling him his first commitment should have been to his daughter.

When the little girl, Jessica McClure, fell into a well in west Texas and the rescue efforts took several days, Doug McGrath, Hogan Company sales vice president recalled, "Mr. Hogan was so concerned about her that he had a TV brought into his office to follow the story, and even sent a check to the family to help offset some of the costs of getting her out of the well."

Mike Wright, Shady Oaks Director of Golf, commented, "Ben Hogan had a caring attitude toward young people and children. If Hogan saw someone working hard on his or her golf game up on the practice tee, usually young people, Hogan would go up to the practice tee and watch them. After observing for a short period, Hogan would offer suggestions to help them with their swing." On numerous occasions after observing one of these sessions, Mike would ask the boy or girl about the session when he or she returned to the pro shop. Wright observed, "Most of them were very nervous and so preoccupied with Hogan talking to them that they didn't necessarily comprehend what he was telling them, but they were all excited that Hogan had taken the time to watch them, and then to make some suggestions to help with their swing."

Similarly, Dr. Wym Van Wyk, a Fort Worth orthopedic surgeon was at Shady Oaks when two boys about 13 or 14 years old came into the grill area with their golf clubs and began talking about playing golf. Hogan called them over and said to one of them, "Get me one of your clubs, and I'll show you a few things." Hogan got up and went over near Dr. Van Wyk and his friend's table, so right away the

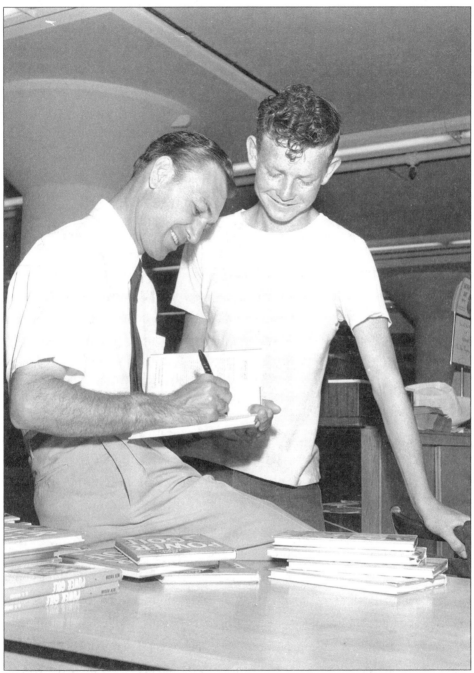

Ben Hogan signs a copy of his book, Power Golf for a young boy at Leonard's Department Store, May 1949. (PHOTO COURTESY, FORT WORTH STAR-TELEGRAM, SPECIAL COLLECTIONS, THE UNIVERSITY OF TEXAS AT ARLINGTON LIBRARY, ARLINGTON, TEXAS)

two adjusted their chairs so they could take it all in without being too obvious, and paid rapt attention as Hogan gave the boys a series of tips. "It was just the five of us in there. I couldn't remember them all," Wym commented, "but he told them how to hold the club, to keep their lower body still, and to swing through the ball. I should have taken some notes, but I didn't want to be too obvious about it, after all, he was doing it for those boys. But, he gave those kids some very good pointers, and I don't know if those boys even knew who was giving them the advice."

Brian Hull, a Shady Oaks member, was escorting his two young daughters in wet bathing suits from the swimming pool. Not wanting to walk through the clubhouse with the wet swim suits, Brian led the girls, holding each girl's hand, around the clubhouse on the cart path. As they passed the men's grill they heard a "thump, thump," from the large plate glass window. They looked around to see a man with his thumbs in his ears and wiggling his fingers at the girls who immediately dropped their dad's hand and responded in a similar fashion. Brian did a double take when he saw that it was Ben Hogan initiating the funny gestures for the girls.

After raising my son as a single parent, and remembering Hogan's care and concern for him that day, and after hearing numerous other instances of Hogan's relating to kids, I wondered why Hogan didn't have any children of his own. From my experience and from what others have told me, Hogan related well to children. One theory was that Ben wanted children, but Valerie didn't, so they had no children. Another was that because of the accident, they were unable to have children.

Later I read what Al Barkow had written: "His [Hogan's] life was defined by the game. It was his decision not to have children because, he said, it would be unfair to them. He would not give them enough of his time. He had to practice, you see."

That comment did not surprise me. I had never heard Hogan say anything about children, but that comment fit with my experience, and the experience of others I'd talked to about the subject. I had been surprised by Hogan's "toofies" comments with Jordan, because I never expected Hogan to be able to get down to a child's level in relating to the little tyke, but that day he certainly related better to him than I did.

TEN:
PIC & MARVIN

MYTH: *Ben Hogan was a selfish little man who cared nothing about anyone else, particularly his fellow competitors, and gave little back to golf.*

MAN: Ben Hogan was invited to attend and receive an award at the "Celebration of the 100th Anniversary of Golf in America" at the Waldorf Astoria in New York. A panel of 25 or so officials, media, and representatives from the sponsoring groups decided on the award winners. Hogan was named the Player of the Decade for the 1948 - 1958 period, Robert Jones for the 1928 - 1938 decade, and Byron Nelson for the decade 1938 - 1948. Hogan was also one of four golfers nominated for the Player of the Century Award, with that winner to be named at the ceremony. When he was contacted about appearing, he courteously declined, saying he felt honored, but that he would not attend. When asked why, he said, "Because Sam Snead is not being duly recognized." The way the decades had been broken down Jones, Nelson and Hogan had won the decades of the Snead era, and Hogan felt that Snead, with his outstanding record including having won more tournaments than any other professional, should have been recognized at that level. Hogan felt strongly enough about it not to attend an award ceremony where he might be named the Golfer of the Century. The committee reconsidered, recognized Snead for his significant stature in golf and included Snead speaking like the other decade winners. Hogan agreed to attend. Hogan showed up at the ceremony and was given thunderous applause by the 1,000 plus attendees as he walked into the ballroom. Appropriately enough, Hogan spoke right after Snead.

Other than his father, there were two men in Hogan's life who had a tremendous impact on the man, Henry Picard and Marvin Leonard. While no one else saw anything in Ben Hogan or cared enough about Hogan to offer him assistance or support, these two men of different professions invested time, encouragement, and offered or gave

Ben Hogan and Sam Snead pose for pictures for spectators after finishing their round in the 1950 Colonial NIT. (PHOTO COURTESY OF COLONIAL COUNTRY CLUB)

financial support to Hogan as he struggled on the professional golf tour. Hogan greatly appreciated both men for their impact on his life, and publicly stated so and showed his deep respect and gratitude for them.

HENRY PICARD

Henry Picard was a golf professional, a friendly gentleman with a warm, winsome smile. I met Mr. Picard in the late 1950s as my early interest in golf, like Ben Hogan's, came from caddying as a young boy. I was caddying in the Squaw Creek Country Club (Vienna, Ohio) pro-am. After the caddies had been assigned their bags for the tournament, we all gathered by the putting green to wait for our players to arrive. We gathered beside the putting green, introduced ourselves, and asked each other who the players were in our group. A tall, slim, elderly gentleman, maybe 50 years old (I was 13 or 14 years old, and 50 then seemed elderly) walked up, pulled a putter out of the pro's bag in our foursome, took out a sleeve of balls, and walked over to practice his putting. He wore a long-sleeved white shirt, complete with cuff links and a necktie. "Who in the world is that?" I asked. "Some guy named Picard, from Cleveland, and Henry Picard, Canterbury Country Club, the bag tag read." We ambled to the first tee as our foursome was called. Someday this would be with our pro wearing a long sleeved white shirt and a necktie. No extra tips from prize money in this tournament!

A few minutes later, Mr. Picard came over to us and pulled out his driver. "How are you boys today?" he asked with a warm smile on his face. We all gave the standard response, "Fine, sir, and you?" Then the announcer on the first tee introduced Mr. Picard, and we got our first idea who this guy was. "Now of the first tee, Henry Picard, golf professional at the Canterbury Country Club, winner of the 1938 Masters and the 1939 PGA Championship..." After that I didn't hear a word. I was too awestruck and impressed to listen any further. I was new to golf, but I'd heard of the PGA and the Masters. But a guy playing golf wearing a white dress shirt and a necktie? I'd never seen that before (or since) on a golf course. Well, white shirt, cuff links, necktie, and all, Mr. Picard shot par on the difficult Squaw Creek course that day, making a few crucial birdies to help our team finish 2nd or 3rd. So each of us caddies got nice tips--Mr. Picard was our kinda guy.

When I went to work for the Ben Hogan Company, my first assignment was to return to New England (Dartmouth is in New Hampshire), to sell golf equipment. While selling Hogan equipment wasn't particularly easy in northern New England then, winding your way through Maine, New Hampshire, and finally Vermont in the fall is not a particularly bad assignment, especially if you like beautiful fall foliage. I finally arrived in Montpelier, Vermont, where the golf professional was none other than Mr. Henry Picard. I introduced myself to Lennie Bourne, the assistant pro, and told him why I was there. Lennie explained that Mr. Picard was about to leave for Seminole Golf Club in West Palm Beach, Florida, where he usually ordered his golf merchandise. I said that was fine, but since I was here, I asked if Mr. Picard would like to look at the new Hogan line. We had a new iron model that featured the new Apex shaft. Lennie checked with Mr. Picard who said sure, he'd like to see the new line.

I brought in my samples, set them up, and when Mr. Picard came out, I introduced myself. I went through the whole spiel about the new line. When I finished, Lennie asked if he could take the 5-iron of the new left-handed model out to hit a few balls. Lennie was excited to try the first left-handed club Hogan had made. It was my last stop of the day so I said sure, and off he went. That left Mr. Picard and me alone to visit for a few minutes. I knew, of course, that he would not remember that Squaw Creek tournament, but I recalled the event to him, and the fact that he had played in a long-sleeved white dress shirt and necktie. As I started, "Mr. Picard, you won't remember, but..." He stopped me in mid-sentence, and with his warm, friendly smile said, "Son, just call me, Pic." He recounted that when he was playing on the tour all the pros wore dress shirts and ties. We reminisced for a few minutes. He asked how long I had been with the company, and if I had met Mr. Hogan yet. I amusedly recanted my recent episode of meeting him on the golf course, and the terror I felt when I realized he was about to watch me hit a golf ball. Pic good-naturedly reassured me that I was not alone in those ranks, and that even among the pros on the tour, Hogan struck fear in the hearts of many, if not most.

After Lennie returned a few minutes later, I thanked "Pic" for the visit and for taking time to see me, collected my samples, and said good-bye.

I saw Mr. Picard several times at Seminole. After he retired to South Carolina, we kept in touch, and I continued to send him his Hogan Advisory Staff golf equipment there. When he came to Fort Worth in 1991, and his picture with Mr. Hogan was in the local paper, I cut it out and sent it to him, along with a note, in which I expressed my desire to convince Mr. Hogan to let someone write his autobiography. Although I had been gone from the company for almost ten years, I occasionally dropped by to see friends and to say hello to Mr. Hogan. Pic, in his soft humor, sent me a note back that included, "Your idea of having Hogan write his autobiography is great, but I doubt if I'll ever read it. I also had a great idea years ago. I did not win." Henry Picard was a warm, friendly human being and a very special man, much more special to Ben Hogan than I knew at the time.

In 1937 Ben Hogan was almost broke again and ready to give up the golf tour, possibly for the last time. Henry Picard overheard a conversation Ben and Valerie Hogan were having about his being unable to continue on the tour due to financial difficulties. Picard walked over and offered Hogan financial support if he ever needed it, which gave Hogan enough encouragement to continue on the tour. While Picard never had to give Hogan any money, knowing the offer was there enabled Hogan to continue.

The following year Picard recommended Hogan for an assistant professional job at the Century Country Club in Purchase, New York, which would help provide the means he needed to keep playing on the tour. Later that same year, Picard had Hogan invited to the Hershey Round Robin Four Ball tournament in Hershey, Pennsylvania, where Picard was the head professional. Unexpectedly, newcomers to the invitational, Hogan and Vic Ghezzi, won the tournament. While at the tournament, Picard introduced Hogan to Milton Hershey. Several years later, when Picard moved to the Canterbury Country Club in Cleveland, he recommended Hogan as his replacement as the head professional at Hershey, and Hogan became the head golf professional representing the Hershey Country Club on tour. With his professional jobs at Century and Hershey, Hogan was able to work on his golf swing and make enough money that he could continue playing on the professional circuit.

Henry Picard works with Hogan's grip to eliminate his hooking problem by trying to slice the ball.
(A/P WORLDWIDE)

Late in the year 1939, Hogan was still struggling with his dreaded hook, and hadn't won a tournament on his own. Prior to the PGA Championship that year Picard recommended that to eliminate his hook Hogan should learn to "slice" the ball. He told Hogan to lift the ball and slice it, and once he could do that, to begin slamming it hard, with the same slicing motion. He said it would straighten out and that he would be unbeatable. Picard took Hogan to the practice range and showed him exactly what he was recommending. Hogan took Picard's advice and began to reinvent his swing. Hogan was a fast learner. During the fall/winter off season, Hogan practiced particularly hard to learn and perfect the new technique. The improvement in results was almost immediate. In mid-1940 Hogan won his first tournament, the North and South Open at Pinehurst, and then three of the next four tournaments he entered. In 1946 Hogan won his first "major", the PGA Championship. And, as they say, the rest is history.

Ben Hogan was so grateful for Henry Picard's friendship, his encouragement, his offer of financial support, his recommendations for the golf professional jobs at Century and Hershey, and for his advice to help Hogan with his golf swing that 20 years later when Ben Hogan wrote his first book, *Power Golf,* he dedicated it to Henry Picard—

DEDICATION

To: HENRY PICARD

Champion, Professional Golfers Association, 1939

One of the best friends I have in professional golf is Henry Picard, an outstanding player, an outstanding teacher and an outstanding man. As most of you know, when I first started playing tournament golf I didn't do too well. It was a long time before I won enough money to pay my expenses. Although Picard was probably unaware of it at the time, I can truthfully say now the encouragement and an offer of financial assistance that I received from Henry at one very important period in my golfing career gave me the courage to keep going.

This story will probably embarrass Henry, but it is so typical of him that I would like to tell it anyway, and I hope he will forgive me. At one time during those early days before I had ever won a tournament my finances were low, and I was a long way from home. In fact, I had no idea of where the money to get my wife and me home was going to come from in case I didn't win any in the particular tournament I was playing in at the time. Henry must have sensed my predicament, because he came to me before that tournament and said, "Look, Ben I don't know what your financial situation is and it is none of my business, but I want you to know that if you ever need any help to stay on the tour you can always come to me."

Fortunately, I never did have to call on Picard for financial assistance. But knowing that help was there if I needed it enabled me to forget about my troubles. I went out and won enough money in that tournament to keep going. I've been going ever since.

Again, when he decided that he wanted to play tournament golf only occasionally, Henry recommended me for the job that he held as the playing professional for the Hershey, Pennsylvania, Country Club. Thanks to Henry's recommendation, I got the job. I still represent Hershey on the tournament tour and it has been a very pleasant association for me.

To sum it all up, Picard by his offers of financial assistance, his recommendation, words of encouragement, and golfing hints has helped me more than I can ever repay. Never in all the years that I have known him have I ever been able to repay him for his interest in me.

Therefore, as a small measure of gratitude and appreciation, I would like to dedicate this book to Henry Picard. He has been a real friend and an inspiration to me at all times.

Gardner Dickinson turned professional in 1952, and described the first time he played with Ben Hogan, which was in the 3rd round of the 1953 Pan American Open—

"Choking like a dog, and generally playing like someone who'd never held a club before, I proceeded to three-putt the first four greens. On the narrow sixth hole, I knocked an iron into the woods, then stormed off the tee and flew up the fairway. Hogan grabbed me by the shoulder, suggested I slow down, and advised me to move up to the ball more quickly and let instinct have a chance. I was genuinely startled even to be addressed by the 'Wee Ice Mon' on the golf course, let alone given advice...I settled down, limiting myself to only six three-putt greens, and posted a 78 to Ben's rather easy 68. After we finished, Ben stopped by my locker and encouraged me to keep playing, expressing his belief that I would become a good player.

Hogan the following week offered Dickinson his financial assistance. Gardner Dickinson wrote a book, *Let 'er Rip Gardner Dickinson on Golf* in 1994, and the book was "To Ben Hogan."

Obviously, Ben Hogan was deeply grateful for the kindly acts his friend, Henry Picard, displayed for his friend, Ben Hogan. Hogan returned Picard's kindly favor to Gardner Dickinson, and Dickinson likewise dedicated his book "To Ben Hogan."

Hogan's words were often like his golf shots in a tournament—he may not hit as many as others, but he made them count.

MARVIN LEONARD

On a cold, dreary looking day late in the fall of 1977, the advertising agency and camera crew prepared to shoot another Hogan Legend shaft TV commercial. New film of Hogan hitting the ball would give the commercial new life and more visibility.

Because of the dark overcast sky and the limited light, Doug Keeney, the Benton & Bowles account executive for the Hogan Company, and the film crew had selected the middle of the Shady Oaks 8th fairway for this shot, because it was the highest, most open spot on the golf course. The very high-speed camera we were using needed as much light as possible, and this spot was it, wide-open and at the highest elevation on the golf course. It was also one of the farthest points from the clubhouse. To provide Mr. Hogan a place to keep warm and sit down during downtime, Keeney had leased a small trailer and parked it on the edge of the fairway near the shoot sight. Considerable time passed as the crew tried to get the balky high-speed camera, necessary for the slow motion shot of Hogan's swing, whirring correctly. During the wait the three of us retreated to the trailer to keep warm. Keeney, never one to be bashful, asked Hogan about the beginnings of the Hogan Company: why he got into the golf equipment business, and how he got the company started. Hogan was in a particularly good mood, despite the lousy weather, and obligingly recounted his reason for starting the company. He wanted to have something to do when he retired from the professional golf tour. Never one to really enjoy just sitting around, Hogan knew retirement from competitive play would leave a void in his life, a void that a golf equipment company could help fill.

Hogan told about his desire to build such high-quality equipment that good players could take a set, any set, with the correct specifications, off the shelf in a pro shop, and feel confident they had the best clubs in their hands. Hogan knew that while most of the golf manufacturers could make precise custom equipment for the touring pros or top amateur players. The stock merchandise shipped to pro shops were not so precisely made. His desire was to fill that void with precise, high quality equipment.

Hogan continued to recall some of the early problems he had in getting started: "I had a partner when I first got started, and when we made our first batch of wood clubs, I was not satisfied with the quality. Since it was our first batch, I felt it had to be the finest quality, but my partner wanted to "X" them out and sell them as rejects. I told him that I did not want to get started that way. These clubs had to be just right so that we came onto the market with the best from the very beginning. But he was persistent in wanting to sell them as rejects so the company could get some money out of them. I was just as persistent, and totally convinced that selling that equipment was wrong, and that selling that first batch of woods as rejects would badly tarnish the high quality image that I wanted for our equipment. So, I went over to the plant one night and cut the heads off all those clubs with a band saw, turning all the woods into scrap. That way they couldn't be sold as rejects.

"Naturally, my partner was not pleased. In fact, he was so upset he insisted that the partnership couldn't continue, either I had to buy him out or he wanted to buy me out.

"I was in a real spot. I didn't have the money to buy him out, and I didn't want my name on golf equipment I didn't have control over, either design or quality. I didn't know what to do or how to go about doing it.

"I remember shortly after that sitting at the bar at Colonial [Country Club], very depressed, and not sure at all about what I was going to do. I was just sitting there, dejected, looking down and trying to figure out what I was going to do. Marvin Leonard, the man who built Colonial Country Club and later on, Shady Oaks, and a very successful businessman, walked over. He and I had become good friends over the years because of our love for golf. He asked me what was wrong, why I looked so dejected, so I told him about the situation at the company. I described what had happened regarding the woods, and that I didn't feel they were good enough for top line woods, and my partner insisted on selling them as rejects to get some money out of them. I told Marvin that the woods weren't good enough, and that I didn't want to start out that way, because I wanted to make the best clubs, so I'd gone over to the factory and cut the woods into scrap. Then I told him that my partner obviously didn't agree with what I'd done and had given me an ultimatum that one of us had to go—either I had to buy him out or he would buy me out, but that we couldn't continue as partners. I reluctantly told Marvin that I didn't have the money to buy my partner out, but I sure didn't want to sell the company to him, so I was just sitting here trying to figure out what I was going to do. I looked back down at the bar, trying to sort all this out and figure out what to do.

"Marvin didn't say anything, he just pushed his hand over toward mine, and I turned to look. He was sliding something over to me, and then I saw what it was. It was a check. A check that he had made out to me and signed, but he'd left the rest, including the amount, blank. I couldn't believe it. I tried to refuse it by starting to push it back to him, but he insisted, by saying, 'Now make sure to take enough to get you started, not just the amount you need to buy the company.' I asked him if he wanted to know how much I needed or what I was going to do with it. 'No, just take what you need, and make sure you have enough to get the company up and going.' That was the kind of man Marvin was. I didn't know what to say, except 'Thank you, Marvin.' So with that I bought out my partner and got the company started the way I wanted to get it started."

While Mr. Hogan didn't mention a dollar figure, speculation had it that the clubs he destroyed were worth in the neighborhood of $100,000 (in 1954 dollars).

About that time the camera crew came into the trailer and indicated that the camera was now working, and they were ready for Mr. Hogan to hit some balls for the shoot. Hogan did a few twists and turns to limber up his body before going out into the cold. Once outside, he took a few warm-up swings, and then proceeded to hit the ball as requested for the commercial.

Marvin Leonard was probably the closest person Ben Hogan ever had to a father figure. Their relationship began in 1927 when as a 14-year old caddie, Ben met Mr. Leonard, a very successful 32-year old businessman whom doctors had instructed to take up golf for his health. Marvin Leonard and his brother Obie had developed the thriving Leonard Brothers department stores that had grown out of their initial buying and reselling anything they could to pay the family bills. But as the business had grown Marvin had been spending so much time and mental energy on the business that it was causing serious health problems. His doctor suggested he try golf to get him away from the office. Leonard took the doctor's advice, bought some clubs, and rising early each morning, he tried to get in nine-holes of golf before work. Young Ben, to get a head start on the older caddies, made the trek to the golf course before the sun came up and was there to greet Mr. Leonard.

The two spent the early morning hours together, one trying to play the game to relax from his business stress, the other seriously investing himself in it to learn how to play it well. Perhaps Mr. Leonard, who had four daughters and no sons, saw some of himself in Ben Hogan. Hogan's difficult childhood reminded Leonard of his own tough upbringing, and the boy's determination to walk five miles to the golf course early each morning as the sun came up to carry his golf bag most likely engendered thoughts of his own daylight-to-dark business drive.

Seeing a successful businessman who invested himself in the community and charitable organizations, and who was greatly admired by those in the Fort Worth/Dallas area, Ben undoubtedly looked up to the man that he worked for on an almost daily basis. That most assuredly influenced Hogan's perspectives as he too became successful and also philanthropic in the Fort Worth area. The two were a lot alike in many respects. Both worked hard, enjoyed golf, and did not care for publicity. Both were quiet, humble individuals who believed in loyalty, respect, and integrity. Having such an influential person take an interest in his life, Hogan naturally developed an affection for the man and gravitated to the things that Mr. Leonard espoused—hard work, community service, donating to hospitals, churches, and local charities, just to name a few.

That relationship was only strengthened when Mr. Leonard was the only person to help Ben financially when he was first trying to play on the pro golf tour in the early 1930's. Hogan borrowed money from Mr. Leonard on several occasions, and when Hogan ran out of that money he returned home flat broke. Years later, when Hogan began making money on the pro tour, he tried to pay back Marvin Leonard the money he had borrowed from him. "Forget it, Ben," said Marvin. "I'm just glad you're doing well."

Mr. Leonard's daughter, Marty, recalled the evening they dedicated the Leonard Room at Colonial Country Club, the club that Marvin Leonard had built and later sold to the members at a fraction of its worth. "When they dedicated the Leonard Room at Colonial Country Club, there were a bunch of us from the family and a few close friends sitting around just talking, and Ben told the story how daddy had loaned him money when he was first starting out on the pro golf tour. Years later after he had started to make some money of his own, he offered to pay daddy back, but daddy said he didn't have to pay him back, just hearing Ben offer to pay the money back was all the payment he needed. I noticed that as he told that story, Ben had tears in his eyes."

Mr. Leonard was a very community-minded individual and had come to love golf. He not only developed Colonial Country Club, and later Shady Oaks Country Club, but also brought the U.S. Open to Colonial in 1941 and started a ladies golf tournament at Rivercrest Country Club (also in Fort Worth).

In April of 1969, Marvin Leonard was honored at a very special dinner held in his honor that Ben Hogan helped put together. Hogan liked to "ride" or kid the people he liked, and his dry sense of humor and great charming smile made such efforts an endearing event, so when Hogan was one of the speakers at the dinner honoring Marvin Leonard, he wasted no time in going straight at the honoree, as detailed in the Colonial Country Club history published in 1986:

"'For the edification of you out-of-towners, we here in Fort Worth like to honor people who have never made a success of anything,' Hogan said dryly.

Ben Hogan jokingly shows what he thinks of Marty Leonard's shot. Marty was a top amateur player in North Texas. (PHOTO COURTESY OF MARTY LEONARD COLLECTION)

'We pick out people who have never contributed one thing to this city's success. We only honor complete parasites.' He paused, then added: 'Our honoree tonight goes beyond that.' The crowd erupted with laughter at the clever irony."

"Hogan described Marvin Leonard's career as being a series of "mistakes" from which his younger brother, Obadiah (Obie) had to bail him out. Hogan explained that Obie had come to the rescue by visiting the Leonard's store shortly after his older brother had opened it and discovered that Marvin was "giving away" the merchandise. So said Hogan, 'While Marvin was home sleeping, Obie was down at the store changing the prices.' The audience roared."

"According to Hogan, Obie continued to cover his brother's mistakes until Marvin Leonard decided to sell his Colonial Country Club to the members. 'Marvin had spent years getting the club out of the red and into the black and then he sells it for his original cost,' said Hogan. 'Well, that's when Obie quit him.'"

"Hogan, who was celebrating his 34th wedding anniversary that evening and whose wife, Valerie, was seated with him on the dais, reported that Marvin Leonard's father had once asked him what he planned to be when he grew up. 'A philanthropist,' replied Marvin. 'Why a philanthropist?' asked the father. 'Because they're all rich,' said his son, showing wisdom beyond his years. When Obie Leonard was asked the same question, he answered, 'I want to be my brother's partner.'"

"Ben Hogan turned serious before concluding his remarks. 'Marvin Leonard,' he said, his voice softening with emotion, 'has done more for golf with his time and his knowledge and his money than anyone I know. I don't know that anyone else would have had the nerve and the foresight to do the things he did. I doubt if Colonial would exist. I doubt if Shady Oaks would exist. I doubt if the U.S. Open would have come here. Marvin, I salute you.'"

So sincere, funny, and well delivered were Hogan's remarks, that when Herb Graffis, the noted golf writer, got up to speak later in the evening, before turning

Marvin Leonard presents Ben Hogan with the 1952 Colonial NIT trophy, May 1952. (PHOTO COURTESY OF COLONIAL COUNTRY CLUB)

his attention to Marvin Leonard said to Hogan, "Ben, your performance here tonight would have made Abraham Lincoln at Gettysburg seem tongue-tied."

Ben Hogan wrote the "Foreword" to the history of the Colonial Country Club, *The Legacy Continues A 50-year history of Colonial Country Club 1936 - 1986,* and said this about his friend Marvin Leonard--

"As I once said at an appreciation dinner for Marvin Leonard, I don't believe the success of the club or the NIT [Colonial National Invitation Tournament] would have been possible without him. He was a pal to people of all walks of life, not just to those of us who played golf with him. He made the city of Fort Worth a better place to work and live. He was my very good friend, the sort of friend a man is lucky to have—loyal, trusting, honest, and caring—and I miss him."

–Ben Hogan, July 1986.

[Marvin Leonard had passed away in August 1970.]

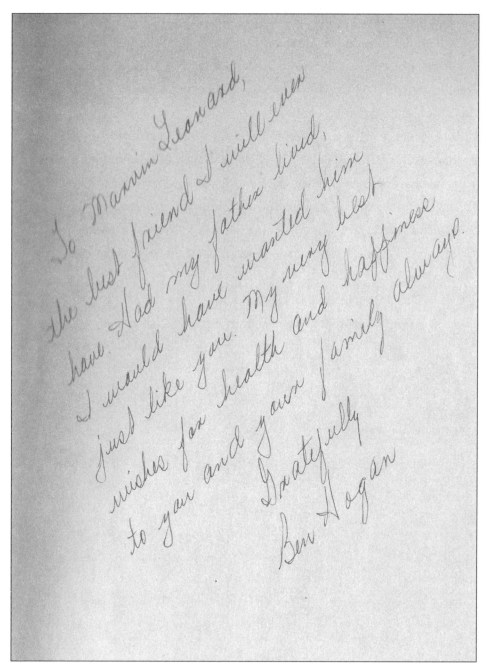

Ben Hogan's inscription to Marvin Leonard in Hogan's first book, *Power Golf.* (PHOTO COURTESY OF MARTY LEONARD COLLECTION)

ELEVEN:
SENSE OF HUMOR AND NOTABLE ONE-LINERS

MYTH: *Ben Hogan was a sullen, dour, unfriendly man who disliked people, had no sense of humor and was totally oblivious to all others on or off the golf course.*

MAN: While Ben Hogan wasn't affable, he wasn't necessarily unfriendly. He had a dry sense of humor, and could be quite witty and funny, and very creative in his humor. While to most, Hogan was very stand-offish, with those he developed a camaraderie with, he liked to kid, or "ride," them, and most of the time, realizing that most of his friends were reluctant to initiate such play with him, he initiated the fun with them.

In 1970, Hogan had planned to play in the PGA Championship at Southern Hills Country Club in Tulsa. On Sunday afternoon before the tournament, Eldridge Miles, who played a lot of golf with Hogan, was taking his clubs out of his car just as Hogan was putting his in his car.

"How's the course?" Eldridge asked Hogan.

"They've sprayed it with some growth chemical and the rough is knee-deep, so I've withdrawn, and I'm heading back to Fort Worth," Hogan replied. Then, after he closed the trunk he looked at Eldridge, and with a big smile on his face added, "And as crooked as you hit it, you ought to go back to Dallas."

Eldridge laughed as he reflected on the occasion. "He was right. On the 9th hole, I sprained both my wrists, and I couldn't hit a ball for a week."

Golf writer Nick Seitz spent a week with Hogan in 1970 in preparation of a *Golf Digest* article when he was introduced to Hogan's sense of humor. Seitz wrote,

> "The thing that surprised me the most about Hogan was his sense of humor: droll, flavored with earthy southwestern spice, [that was] often evident. I remember my unsuspecting introduction to it. I accompanied him

Ben Hogan playfully shows what he thinks about putters and putting. (A/P WORLDWIDE)

to Shady Oaks for lunch—he lunches there regularly, and he introduced me to the manager, who personally attends him. 'This guy has 15 kids,' Hogan said. Expressionless, he added: 'Screwed himself right out of a seat in the car.' I had heard dozens of stories about Hogan's dourness, and [I,] in no way was prepared for this. I nodded innocuously. After a lengthy silence, I suddenly became aware of what he had said, and burst out laughing. Hogan, who had been watching me closely, joined in the laughter. He was amused not at his own line but at my delayed response. His probing blue-grey eyes suggested: 'Didn't expect that from the austere Ben Hogan, eh?'"

Hogan, with his conservative philosophy, really never liked loud flashy clothing or jewelry on men. Jim Moore, a member at Shady Oaks, and a regular in our Saturday morning golf group, decided to start wearing what Jim described as "a string with some cylindrical pucca shell beadlike ornaments on it that a lady friend had talked him into wearing." Jim's a big man, 6' 5" or so, with an athletic build at about 230 pounds or so, and he knew Hogan well, as both played gin rummy in the men's grill at Shady Oaks. Before long Hogan noticed his neck chain, and one day as Hogan and his friend Earl Baldridge approached him. Hogan asked Jim, "Tell me, Jim, what do you think about when you look into the mirror each morning to put on your necklace?"

Hogan's comment caught Moore completely off-guard, and he said all he could do was to force one of those big, toothy grins that cartoon characters got when they were caught doing something they shouldn't be doing. Later when he told us the story, he commented, "The forced smile on my face was bigger than the one on the Cheshire Cat in *Alice in Wonderland*. But looking back on it, it was pretty funny, and Hogan didn't say it in front of a group, so he didn't try to humiliate me." We all did notice that Jim was no longer wearing his pucca shell "necklace."

A frequent straight man on the golf course was Hogan's friend and fellow pro, Tommy Bolt. Bolt was a perfect example of a man who did things differently than Hogan—Bolt had a thunderous temper, and occasionally let it all out, even by throwing his clubs. But, he and Hogan got along very well together. "You have to give Ben a chance," said Bolt, "that's all he wants. He's the friendliest guy in the world, but most of these guys either don't want to believe it, or they're scared to approach him.'"

During a practice round Tom Weiskopf, as he and Hogan were walking down the fairway, took the opportunity to ask Hogan who, in his opinion, were the best players. As they walked, Hogan named Byron Nelson, Sam Snead, Jimmy Demaret, and then Jack Nicklaus whom Hogan thought was something special. Hogan then looked right at Weiskopf to emphasize his point, and added, "To tell you the truth, you see that guy standing over there," pointing to Bolt, "I want to tell you if we could have screwed another head on his shoulders you could have forgotten these others." Hogan obviously thought Tommy Bolt had a great deal of golfing talent. Then Weiskopf noted, "After he said that, he added, 'He's a phenomenal individual.'" Weiskopf was struck by the fact that Hogan made the distinction between Bolt the golfer, and Bolt the person, and offered strong praise and respect for Bolt, both as a golfer and as a person. Later, when I talked with Weiskopf about that episode, Weiskopf added, "Tommy Bolt is a friend of mine. Tommy is a very special person—a giving, caring, sensitive person." Hogan was obviously looking way below Bolt's surface bluster and comments to see the real Tommy Bolt, a man he respected as a golfer and as a person.

On one occasion, when Hogan and Bolt were playing at Colonial, they started calling their shots—what club the particular shot required, and how it should be struck. As they approached the par-3 16th, Hogan claimed it was a 4-iron shot that day, Bolt insisted it was a 5-iron.

Hogan hit first, and hit his 4-iron. It landed near the hole and ended just several feet away from the flag. Hogan turned to Bolt, and with a look of vindication on his face, blurted, "See, I told you it was a 4."

"Yeah," Bolt shot back, "but you hit it fat."

"Well, it called for a fat 4-iron," Hogan replied.

Bolt had a penchant for calling everyone male, "Son." One of the last exhibitions, if not the very last, that Hogan gave, was with Tommy Bolt at the Bardmore Club in St. Petersburg, Florida. As luck would have it, Bolt's caddy was Randy Reifers, a former teammate of mine from the DePauw University golf team, who was having Bolt help him with his golf swing. Randy recalled, "I had on light blue slacks, a yellow Ban-Lon shirt and sunglasses, and apparently my hair was quite a bit longer than Hogan would have liked. Hogan wore gray slacks and a white cotton golf shirt, and he started needling Bolt by commenting, 'Tommy, you see him?' looking over at me, Bolt grunted a 'Yeah.' 'Well,' Hogan continued, 'when's your caddy going to get a damned haircut?'" Bolt just laughed and Randy gets a kick out of the story every time he tells it to me. He recalled the exhibition as, "the two trading barbs amid some serious golf. On the back nine, Bolt hit a particularly good drive. Hogan asked, 'Is that the place to be?'

'Son, that's the spot. It's perfect,' responded Bolt.

'Well, then, I'll be right there,' Hogan countered. Hogan moved his feet in his customary waggle fashion, then set himself, and drew back his driver. He nailed the ball dead on the screws. The group watched the flight of the ball, and then saw it land about three feet from Bolt's ball and roll several yards past. 'How's that,' Hogan asked? Bolt just looked over at his friend and smiled."

Tommy told the story of the time that he went to Australia to play in the Australian Seniors Open. While he wasn't under contract, he was playing Hogan clubs, using a Hogan staff bag, and playing the Hogan ball.

When he returned to the United States, he called Hogan to tell him of his victory, and that he'd won using all Hogan equipment—clubs, balls, golf bag, and even a Hogan putter. Bolt knew the company gave a small bonus to tour staff players when they won a tournament, and he called Hogan to ask how much he would get. Bolt said Hogan just responded, "Aw, Tommy, you don't need the money."

Several days later, Bolt received a letter in the mail from Ben Hogan. In the letter, Hogan commented, "I knew you would win that tournament because you were using our equipment, and everyone else in the tournament was using hickory-shafted clubs and gutta percha balls." Bolt roared. His friend had stuck the needle to him one more time, but as I recall, Hogan included a check for $1,000.

Ben Crenshaw noted about Hogan's conservative bent, and his sense of humor: "A few years ago, this conservative state of mind made him a trifle impatient with the fashion of longer hair among the younger set of golfers. Nathaniel Crosby tells the story of staying with Mr. and Mrs. Hogan as houseguests of Mr. and Mrs. George

Coleman. One day, Nathaniel got up early, took a shower, dressed, and was returning down the hall to his bedroom when he ran into Hogan. Nathaniel had a towel in one hand and a hair dryer in an [the] other. Hogan took one look at the hair dryer and looked incredulously at Nathaniel and said, 'What the hell are you going to do with that?'"

Ben Crenshaw was having problems with his driving and was out on the Shady Oaks practice range. Gary Laughlin, a mutual friend, asked Hogan if he'd go out and take a look at Crenshaw's swing and help him out. Hogan agreed and walked out to the practice tee to observe Crenshaw's swing. After watching Crenshaw spray a few tee shots, Hogan told him to wait a minute, and he would go get his own driver for Crenshaw to try. Hogan went to the bag room by the golf shop, pulled out his driver from his bag and walked out to the practice tee. [Hogan's clubs are extremely difficult to hit, if not impossible, except for Ben Hogan, might be more accurate. They have ultra-stiff shafts, coarse cordline grips with a reminder set way over in the "slice" position, and his driver was open faced with 9-10 degree loft, and curvature on the face different from standard clubs.] He handed Crenshaw the driver, and Crenshaw hit his first tee shot with it. Like everyone else who hit Hogan's club the first time, the ball started out to the right and sliced further to the right, landing in the 10th fairway to the right of the practice range. Sensing what he had in his hands, Crenshaw decided on the necessary corrections, but over corrected, and the ball shot left, a low screaming hook that landed in the first fairway to the left of the practice range. Hogan, observing that and realizing that Crenshaw really needed some time alone on the practice range to work things out, walked off. Laughlin, seeing all this, went over to Hogan as he approached the golf shop and said that it was rude of him to just walk off like that. Hogan responded, "Hell, Gary, I can't help him. He can't even hit the practice range."

A frequent subject of Hogan's barbs was the fashion of young golfers. He was not a fan of long hair, loud clothes, or jewelry such as neck chains on men. Once when asked about the younger players on the tour, Hogan replied, "Some of them seem to be off balance when they swing—too much hair."

Hogan invited Bruce Devlin to play a practice round with him before the 1966 U.S. Open at the Olympic Club in San Francisco. Devlin had never seen the course and back then Olympic had just one fairway bunker on the left side of the sixth fairway. Not having seen any fairway bunkers on the previous holes, Devlin asked Hogan if he thought the fairway bunker came into play. "No, Hogan responded, "You just hit to the right of it."

Young Joe Matthews had just bought a brand spanking new golf glove in the Rivercrest Country Club pro shop in preparation for his lesson that Marvin Leonard had arranged with Ben Hogan. He wanted to be totally ready when Hogan arrived at the practice tee for this lesson. After brief introductions, Joe hit a few balls, and Hogan's first comment was, "First thing you need to do, Joe, is to get rid of that golf glove. It interferes with your contact with the grip." Joe later became a superior amateur player, but after that day never wore a glove again.

Several years later, when Joe was about to take Valerie Harriman, Valerie Hogan's niece, to a formal dance, and the handsome, well-dressed couple was about to have their picture taken in the Harriman living room, Ben Hogan commented, "You're a mighty fine looking couple, but Joe, you'd look a lot better with your fly zipped up." Joe turned red, turned around and checked his fly. He turned around with a big smile on his face: it had been zipped up. Hogan was just pulling his leg.

Hogan, with a big grin, was discussing his round with Lee Trevino in Houston: "He tried to talk to me. He tried to talk to my caddie when he was around. Then he tried to talk to his caddie. If none of us would listen, he tried to talk to the crowd, and if no one there would listen, he started talking to himself." Hogan then turned serious and noted, "But the man can play. He can move the ball around the golf course. He can play."

Ben Hogan's good friend Jimmy Demaret was also a talker and a fun loving guy. Thinking about his own very private, shy personality Hogan joked, "If I had my game and Demaret's personality I'd really be something." That really would have been something!

When Phil Romaine first went to work for the Ben Hogan Company, he had Ping long irons (2, 3 & 4 irons), and Hogan short irons (5-PW) in his bag. After talking to a few people at the company, Phil decided he'd better get some Hogan long irons if he was going to work for Ben Hogan and hit golf balls for the man, so he got some new Hogan long irons. As Phil arrived at Shady Oaks with a couple

Jimmy Demaret pulls a gag on Ben Hogan; one Hogan later used on others. (A/P WORLDWIDE)

other Hogan employees to hit balls for Mr. Hogan, Hogan in his typical meticulous manner noticed the shiny, long irons in Phil's bag that obviously had considerably less use than the short irons. He looked at Phil, squinting his eyes a little, and quipped, "Son, you're either one hell of a long hitter, or you play very short golf courses!"

Famous for his humor, the veteran golf writer and author Dan Jenkins, himself a Fort Worth native and an accomplished player as a young man, knows a good line when he hears it. He has written often of playing a charity exhibition round with Ben Hogan, Raymond Gafford and Royal Hogan. Jenkins had topped nearly every shot on the first two holes as they started the round. After watching this, Hogan came alongside Jenkins on the third hole, and with a glint in his eye gave him a tip: "You can probably swing a little faster if you try hard enough."

Hogan also had some very notable, philosophical, inspirational quotes—

Dan Jenkins began his career as a Fort Worth newspaperman covering Hogan, who remains his golf hero. Another quote of Hogan's he's cited shows that Hogan knew where to draw the line: "I've never forgotten what my mother told me when I was a boy. She said we might not be well off, but I was as good a person as anybody else in the world. Your name is the most important thing you own. Don't ever do anything to disgrace it or cheapen it." What a different world it would be today if everyone tried to live by that credo.

"There's a great difference between intelligence and wisdom," Hogan said to *Golf Digest* Feature Editor Nick Seitz in explaining his relationship with some in the press.

"I have never achieved what I thought was success. Golf to me is a business, a livelihood in doing the thing that I like to do. I don't like the glamour. I just like the game."

"I never took a day off, and I enjoyed the search." – Hogan to Nick Seitz during an interview for the "Forward" to *Golf Digest's* Classics Book printing of Hogan's book, *Ben Hogan's Five Lessons   The Modern Fundamentals of Golf.*

"There are no shortcuts in the quest for perfection. People have always been telling me what I can't do. I guess I wanted to show them. That's been one of the driving forces all my life."

"You only hit a straight ball by accident. The ball is going to move right or left every time you hit it, so you had better make it go one way or the other."

TWELVE:
WHEN FIRST MEETING BEN HOGAN

First meetings with Ben Hogan were almost always difficult. Hogan's legendary status as a golfer and the public descriptions of him they had heard or read, depicting him as an aloof, cold person put people very ill at ease. When first meeting him, even employees of the Ben Hogan Company felt a little uncomfortable.

When Tom Stites joined the Hogan club-design staff, his first meeting with Mr. Hogan was at Shady Oaks—almost in the men's room. When Tom saw Mr. Hogan in the men's room, he remembered that his dad had told him never to meet anyone for the first time in the men's room, so he walked outside and waited. When Hogan came out, Tom acted as if the meeting was incidental and introduced himself, "Hello, Mr. Hogan, I'm Tom Stites, and I just came to work for your company."

Hogan ignored Tom's outstretched hand, bent slightly forward, and looked Tom directly in the eyes with the "Hogan stare." After looking at Tom for what Tom thought was an eternity, Hogan grabbed his hand with both of his hands, shook it, and said, "Well, sonny, don't screw anything up."

Tom said he didn't go near Hogan for several weeks after that. Hogan's stare made him feel that Hogan was looking directly into his brain, if not his soul. It spooked him.

My college golf coach at DePauw University, Ted Katula, affectionately known as the "Katman," had played college golf and football at Ohio State. He played football for the legendary Buckeye head football coach, Woody Hayes, and golf for the well-known Ohio State golf coach, Bob Kepler. The Kat was a senior and captain of the Buckeye golf team when a young kid named Nicklaus was an incoming freshman. Kat was a talker, and when we were riding to our college golf matches, he would tell us story after story about Woody Hayes and Jack Nicklaus. One of our favorite needles was to ask the Kat to tell us some stories about when he played on Nicklaus' Ohio State team. Quickly—I mean instantly, the Kat would bark back, "I was the captain of that team. Nicklaus played on my team."

The Coach was a good looking guy with a winsome personality, an expressive face and a big, warm, friendly smile. And apparently, both at Ohio State and at DePauw, in his bachelor days the Kat was quite a ladies' man. In fact, he had a car, a Studebaker Golden Hawk that was known as the "Bird of Prey." He was always quick with witty quips and got away with things that other people could not. He taught a women's physical education golf class at DePauw giving group golf lessons on the golf swing and on how to use woods and irons. He would tell his female students with a straight face, "Iron selection is very important, and for women, I usually recommend General Electric, Sunbeam, or Westinghouse." When he got the blank or irritated look he expected from the young women, he would break out laughing and tell them he was only kidding, but with a twinkle in his eye that made most of them wonder. Kat was just that kind of guy.

When I was with the Hogan Company, I met Jack Nicklaus here in Fort Worth in the early 1970s. I was playing in the Colonial pro-am and Nicklaus and I were on the putting green prior to our tee times. I decided I had to find out, once and for all, if all the Kat stories about his relationship with Nicklaus were true. I putted over to the cup where Nicklaus was putting. When our eyes met I introduced myself and told him I had played college golf for Ted Katula at DePauw. "Oh, yea? What's the 'Kat' up to these days?" Nicklaus inquired. When he called the Coach "Kat," I knew that Nicklaus at least knew who he was. I replied that the Coach was some kind of administrator or something, in charge of the university student union and responsible for all the campus-wide social activities at DePauw. Hearing that, Nicklaus tossed the three golf balls in his hand up into the air and leaning back looking at the balls as they rose, he followed them up with his eyes. But as the balls started back down, Nicklaus' gaze went heavenward as if asking the good Lord for a favor, and a big smile appeared on his face as he said, "Good Lord! Heaven help them." I knew right then and there that Nicklaus really knew the Katman.

Kat knew and occasionally conversed with some well-known people, so celebrities were not new to the Coach. Famed golfer Tom Weiskopf is also a friend of Ted's, and Katula was one of the finest amateur golfers in Indiana so he traveled among an elite group in that regard as well.

In the late 1970s, the Coach spoke to the Dallas/Fort Worth DePauw Alumni group on a Friday evening. The next morning he, Charles Harris, the Hogan Company sales representative in Indiana, and I played golf at Shady Oaks. We teed off about 8:30, and after finishing the front nine, stopped by the men's grill for a soft drink. I saw Hogan standing near his corner table on the other side of the room, so I walked over with Kat and Charles Harris a few steps behind. Kat knew Hogan spent a lot of time at Shady Oaks, so this was not an unexpected meeting that we were about to have. As we approached, I said, "'G'morning, Mr. Hogan. How are you today?" Hogan smiled, nodded his head, and we shook hands. Then I continued, "Mr. Hogan, this is Ted Katula, and you know Charles Harris, our salesman in Indiana. Ted was my college golf coach at DePauw University. He played football at Ohio State for Woody Hayes, and was on the golf team at Ohio State with Jack Nicklaus."

Hogan walked over to the Katman, extended his hand to shake and said, "Nice to meet you, Ted." Then Hogan put his hand on Ted's shoulder, and with a big grin continued, "Tim's game still needs a hell of a lot of work." When Hogan put his hand on Ted's shoulder as part of his friendly response, the Kat absolutely flat choked. His entire response was, "Nice to meet you, Mr. Hogan" and a flash of that big Katula smile. I waited for Kat to say something, anything, but nothing was forthcoming. Kat had changed to Hogan clubs and absolutely loved them, so he had plenty to chitchat about, but, he had cottonmouth, flat dried up, so I commented that Ted was now playing Hogan clubs to give him an opening—he nodded, but nothing came out, and apparently nothing was about to come out. So I tried a couple of more times— bringing up the Hogan 2 wood and 1 iron that Kat loved. Nothing! It's the only time in the 45 years or so that I knew Ted Katula that he was at a total loss for words. The Kat and I have laughed many times about his meeting Ben Hogan. As the Kat later reflected, "Scotty, when 'The Man' walked over to me and put his anointed hand on my shoulder, I just lost it. I couldn't talk. I was speechless."

Difficulties in first meetings with Ben Hogan, however, were far more the rule than the exception. It was very rare for individuals to break into fluid conversation with Hogan, even when Hogan started the conversation with a very friendly, warm greeting or offering his hand for a handshake. Perhaps that's what threw them off; the preconceived image they had of Hogan was that of a distant cold, unapproachable, or disconnected person. So when he greeted them with a warm, friendly smile and an outstretched hand, there was disconnect from anticipation to reality that could have put them at a loss. Hogan, or someone who knew him, would frequently have to help the conversation along for a while until the new person regained his or her ability to converse. This was true even of first meetings with many of the tour players who came to the annual Hogan dinner party the week of the Colonial. Hogan would ask about their golf games, how they were playing, etc. to get the conversation rolling.

However, when first meetings were part of a scheduled encounter, the outcome could go either way. Before Phil Romaine went to work for the Ben Hogan Company, Bobby Morris, the golf professional at the Great Southwest Golf Club and a longtime friend of Hogan's, arranged for Romaine to talk to Mr. Hogan. Romaine said that Hogan's secretary, Claribel Kelly said that he could see Mr. Hogan for 20 minutes. Romaine had two tablet pages of questions he wanted to ask Hogan about the golf swing, so he went into Hogan's office for his 20-minute session to try to get as many of his questions answered as possible. He emerged two-and-a-half hours later with an answer to every question he had on his pad. One question was how Hogan could focus so intently.

Hogan said that he had to "get bored with the target."

Romaine asked, "You mean like getting totally hypnotized into the target, [and] that your eyes had to be like radar?"

Hogan said, "Yes, I like that idea."

Tour player and golf commentator Bobby Clampett had a similar experience. In a meeting with Hogan, after gathering a little nerve, Clampett, who had studied Hogan's golf swing extensively while trying to incorporate some of Hogan's techniques, asked Hogan a rather insightful question about Hogan's golf swing. The discussion lasted well over an hour.

You couldn't rush Hogan. Often he needed time to reflect on the question and collect his thoughts before he would answer. Many first-timers couldn't stand the silence in the room, so they would have to try to keep the conversation moving by saying something else. Doing so usually short-circuited Hogan's process and negated his responses. I often wondered if Hogan wasn't laughing inside when these people nervously ended the silence.

Hogan might appear totally oblivious to the conversation, only to comment or raise a question on a point made several minutes prior. This would totally fluster many newcomers as their minds were focused on the current topic and would have to think back about that part of the conversation. Such disconnects were very common with people meeting him for the first time.

PRESENCE ON THE GOLF COURSE

While meeting Ben Hogan in social or business gatherings had a definite effect on people, his presence at or on a golf course elevated the impact of fear to an entirely different level. It had to have been the most intimidating imaginable. Much of it had to do with the respect people have for Hogan's vast technical knowledge about the golf swing, and his ability to control a golf ball better than anyone else ever had. It's almost like having the apostle Paul watching you give an oral report on the New Testament book of Romans (and believe me, it's a tough book). Consider this episode early in the career of Tom Weiskopf, who would later become an outstanding player on the tour and British Open Champion.

Tom Weiskopf played with Hogan five times—all within a year's time. The first was in the final round of the 1967 Houston Champions tournament. After the third round a group of players were having a cookout. Weiskopf's wife, Jeane, offered to call to get their starting times for the next day. When reading off the list to them, she came to Tom's name: she said his "starting time was 1:00, and he was paired with, who in the heck is Ben Hogan?" Jeane, new to the tour, didn't know who Ben Hogan was. Weiskopf, also new to the tour, was totally terrified.

The next day other players came out to watch them play. Weiskopf later recalled in a self-deprecating manner, "They came to watch Hogan; they sure weren't coming out to see me. Hogan talked infrequently but was very courteous. He didn't try to avoid conversation, but he just wasn't talkative. Hogan was the epitome of shot-making. His ball control was sheer amazement.... Both Hogan and I had shot 68, but if I had putted for him his score would have been a lot lower." [As a spry 54 year old in 1967, Hogan shot 69-69-72-68 to finish tied for third in the tournament.]

After the round Weiskopf went through it in detail for a group of fellow pros noting that he was in the woods on this hole, while Hogan was in the fairway. On another hole he was in the water and Hogan was in the fairway, on yet another he was in the rough, Hogan in the fairway.

Finally, Jeane broke in, "Tom, you shouldn't be so hard on yourself. Hogan was boring. You were more exciting to watch. You were in the trees, the water, the sand, and he was just in the fairway all the time. He was just boring—in the fairway all the time."

If a major champion-in-waiting like Weiskopf could be so flustered by Hogan, imagine his effect on club pros. Gardner Dickinson recalled a practice round prior to the 1965 PGA Championship at Laurel Valley in Pennsylvania. He and Hogan arrived at the first tee as a number of teaching pro foursomes were in line to tee off.

"I know this is going to be fun," Dickinson wrote in his book. "Each group insisted that Hogan and his foursome tee off in front of them, but Ben waved them on, saying, 'Oh, no. Go right ahead. I'll wait my turn.'

"I have never seen golf pros make swings like I saw that day. Ben laid those steely blues of his on those poor fellas, then kept on staring at each one as he drove off. Pretty soon their hands began to tremble, their throats to clog, and their waggles reduced themselves to wiggles. As each addressed the ball, Ben would turn to me, close his eyes and silently shake his head. Sure enough, here came the sky balls and duck hooks. Balls fell everywhere—right rough, left rough, sometimes not even a hundred yards from the tee. It was pathetic. For twenty minutes no one, as I recall, hit a decent drive. Finally one of the club pros came up to Ben and said, 'Mr. Hogan, you just stopped this practice round. If you don't tee off in front of me, nobody else will play today.' So off we finally went. Although I never asked him about it, I could tell Ben enjoyed intimidating those fellows. But he affected all of us that way, even when he wasn't trying."

I went to work at the AMF Ben Hogan Company in July of 1969, a week or two prior to the national sales meeting which concluded with a golf tournament. While I'd only played two or three times in the past several months, I had been playing fairly well (for me back then, mid/upper 70s). Having moved to Fort Worth from Stamford,

Connecticut, I was not very familiar with the Shady Oaks golf course, having played it only once or twice. The Hogan salesmen, sensing they had a naive, northern rookie there, were laying it on thick. During lunch they were offering me some "friendly" advice regarding golf in Texas. They told me that since Shady Oaks had lots of trees and brush outside the fairways and rough, there were lots of rattlesnakes around the course, big rattlers, and they explained how painful death by rattlesnake bite could be. Go into the rough after a ball and you were toast. Being from Ohio, I had never seen a rattlesnake, let alone come across one on a golf course. My hamburger stuck in my throat.

After hitting a few practice balls and a few putts, I felt confident that my game was in pretty fair shape. While I started a little shaky, not hitting the ball particularly solid, I managed to scramble for pars each of the first three holes. On the fourth hole, as I straightened up from teeing up my ball to take my stance with my driver, I noticed the tire of a golf cart about a foot from the tee marker, it was no farther than five feet from my ball. I looked up and saw a very familiar white cap. There he was, sitting in his golf cart, arms folded across his chest with a serious expression on his face, looking right at me with those steely blues, waiting for me to hit a golf ball. My eyes made contact with those of Ben Hogan. Now if Jack Nicklaus was intimidated to ask Ben Hogan to check a ball mark in the line of his short putt during the 1960 U.S. Open at Cherry Hills, and Tom Weiskopf was terrified, you can imagine my thoughts.

Hogan wasn't playing in the tournament that year, because he recently had shoulder surgery. We had been forewarned, though, that he was going to come out to watch the tournament. But I was totally unprepared for this. Why wasn't he there when the other three guys in the foursome teed off so I could have gathered myself a little? Why did he have to show up just as I was teeing off? Couldn't he have announced himself before he showed up, instead of a cold turkey deal like this?

Imagine getting ready to hit a golf ball and finding Ben Hogan, the acknowledged best striker of the golf ball—ever—less than ten feet away from you, staring at you, watching you hit a golf ball, or should I say attempt to hit it? Choke would hardly describe the sensation. My mouth went totally dry, tightness went down from my neck through the pit of my stomach, and my legs felt wobbly. If I hadn't been 25 years old and in good physical condition, I might have thought I was having a heart attack. I do not know what happened next, I really don't, but somehow my ball ended up in the boondocks among some trees and brush left of the fairway. I was a slicer, a "fader" as I became more sophisticated in my golf jargon, but I had hit an ugly duck hook the first time Ben Hogan ever saw me swing a club. Ughh! He had spent years trying to eliminate that ugly hook from his game, and my first shot in his presence was a duck hook. What an introduction. Nice to see you, Mr. Hogan.

I found my ball. While I had a decent lie, my swing and line of flight were not obstructed by the trees or brush, there was brush on both sides and quite a bit directly behind me. The dread of rattlesnakes now was my main concern. My feet never stopped moving from the time I got out of the cart. I whacked that ball out of the rough and kept right on moving. If those rattlers were going to get me, they were going to have to hit a moving target. I was still alive, still breathing after Hogan's stare and treading into rattler territory.

Some friendly banter from my playing partners, particularly Billy Phillips, the salesman from Jackson, Mississippi, an excellent player who commented, "I'm just glad it was you and not me who had to hit that tee shot in front of Hogan. That seemed to settle me down as I played well the remainder of the round—almost. I was four over par heading down the 18th fairway and feeling pretty good about my round at Shady Oaks. But, after a good tee shot, I hit my second shot just beyond the trap to the back right side of the green. The eighteenth green at Shady Oaks is just outside the men's grill, Hogan's hangout. As I walked over to my ball, my worst fears were realized. There stood Ben Hogan, outside the grill on the small patio just behind the green, smoking a cigarette, and watching. You guessed it; I chunked my chip shot into the trap. Then on my fourth shot, I left the ball in the trap, finally, I 3-putted for an 8.

On those two holes, 4 and 18, I was seven over par, but I was one over par for the other 16 holes, for a 79 on Shady's par 71 layout. With the 8-handicap, I was given, as a newcomer, I finished second in the management division of the tournament? Can you imagine Mr. Hogan's surprise as he shook my hand during the presentation and humorously asked, "How in the hell did you win second place?"

One year at the sales meeting, Hogan decided he wanted to play with the original six salesmen that joined him when the company decided to have its own sales force. Lyne Price, in no uncertain terms, told the other five that under no circumstances were they to spend a lot of time looking for lost balls or slow up play. Rumor has it that he said "I'll fire your asses if you make Hogan look for lost balls or it takes us five hours to play." Pete Poore was so nervous before the round, he constantly had two cigarettes going, lighting a second from the first, even before he finished the first one. On the sixth hole, Max Baker's tee shot hit the sloping fairway and rolled about six inches into the left rough. He wouldn't even look for it. While Jack Owens quickly found the ball, Max wouldn't even go over and hit it, "Don't worry about it, I'll pick up on this hole," Max said to a dumbfounded Jack Owens. No way was Hogan's group going to be delayed 30 seconds for Max. He wasn't losing his job over a lost golf ball.

When Dennis Iden, a Hogan Company soft goods salesman, had his first opportunity to play with Hogan, Chip Bridges, the Hogan Company PGA/LPGA Tour Representative, gave Dennis the Lyne Price briefing. Both Chip and Dennis were very good amateur golfers. Chip had played quite a bit with Hogan and said his greatest thrill in golf was shooting 30, six-under par on the back nine of a round at Shady Oaks while playing with Hogan. For this occasion Chip even cautioned Dennis that Hogan's short putting was so bad that it might even give them the "yips" if they watched it for a full round, so they needed to concede Hogan's second putts. Neither Hogan nor the group would have to endure that spectacle. Dennis got it down, maybe a bit too well. On their first hole, Hogan left his first putt about 8-feet short of the hole, much too long to concede. Iden, however, remembered his briefing and charged the ball like a linebacker going after a fumble, picked it up and tossed it back to Hogan. The ball hit Hogan, who wasn't looking that direction, squarely in the chest, and it startled him so much he dropped his putter right out of his hand. Dennis was so horrified that from that point on, any time he conceded a putt to Hogan, he handed him the ball.

Even in "friendly" rounds of golf at Shady Oaks, Hogan was a competitor and a presence. Dennis recalled one day when he and John Miles were playing Hogan and John Grace. All were very strong players and strong competitors (Grace was the 1974 U.S. Amateur runner-up to Jerry Pate). The Iden/Miles team was up on the match as it reached the 15th tee. The 15th is a relatively short par 5, dogleg left, with trees closely along the right hand side of the fairway and a creek running diagonally across the fairway in the area where tee shots are likely to land. Iden liked to start his tee shot down the right side, just inside the tree line, and draw it back to the left side of the fairway to have a shorter shot to the green. As he straightened up from teeing his ball, Hogan commented to the group, "You know, they've gotta get a guy out here with a cherry picker to remove that branch that hangs out from that tree down there on the right side of the fairway." The prick of the needle duly noted, Iden grinned at Hogan, who smiled back to acknowledge the mental gamesmanship, and then Dennis proceeded to hit his tee shot.

Later, as Iden and Miles were collecting on their bet, Dennis asked Hogan, "Can you sign that twenty dollar bill for me?" Knowing Dennis' intention was to frame that bill with his signature on it and retell the story how he had beaten Hogan out of twenty bucks, Hogan retorted with a smile, "Sure, but if I sign that twenty dollar bill, it's the last thing I'll sign for you, including your paycheck."

Dennis' immediate response was, "On second thought, maybe I'd rather not have it signed."

The spring after I went to work at the Hogan Company, I joined Shady Oaks Country Club as a junior member (under 35 years of age). Soon I was playing with a regular Saturday morning group, a very competitive bunch.

One morning we had finished the front nine and the match was close. On the back tee on the 10th hole a voice said, "Mind if I join you?" It was Ben Hogan. With Hogan there the memories of that first company golf tournament flashed through my brain, like a train signal with accompanying bells at a dangerous crossing, and again, the gates were down, the lights were flashing, the bells were ringing, but there was no train coming, and a quick accounting of my pocket money and the status of the match told me I could be in serious trouble. Choke city!

Naturally, all four of us responded in unison, "Oh no, come join us."

Well, I thought that at least I had some experience with this type situation so maybe this time it wouldn't be so bad, uh, uh. Wrong. I was determined I wasn't going to duck hook another tee shot in front of the man, but I really didn't intend to block my tee shot to the far side of the 9th fairway, to the right of our fairway. At least this time despite the tightening in my chest, I was still able to fake breathing normally. Progress!

Our golf carts headed in all different directions off that tee, going after errant tee shots both left and right. Only one of the five of us ended up on the fairway, but it wasn't any of our foursome. Gary Laughlin laughingly commented, "I guess Hogan was just lucky again."

Hogan joked with us and put us at ease on that first hole, enough that we were soon back to needling each other about ugly shots or misdirected putts. He even joined in on some of the banter.

When we got on Buzz Kemble for blowing a birdie attempt and causing his team to tie the 15th hole, Hogan asked, "Buzz, why the hell do you play with these guys if they treat you so badly?"

As we stood on the par 3, 16th tee, we discussed what club to hit. The green is shallow from front to back with a 10-15 foot drop down in front and in back of the green, making club selection very important. The flag atop the flagstick was limp, indicating the wind was still, so we were all selecting 7-irons when Hogan commented that 7 was not enough club.

Buzz went ahead and hit his 7. His shot hit just short of the green and rolled back into a sand trap at the bottom of the embankment, saving it from rolling down into the water. Hogan shook his head and commented, "I told you seven wasn't enough. Just look at the top of those trees over there to the right, and back here to the left of the green."

If we had looked very carefully at the top of the trees which were a good way from the green, we would have seen wind up there, and it was in our face. But down at the tee and up by the green, the flag wasn't even waving. There was no evidence of wind at all, none. Walter Williams then quipped: "Now you know, we play with him cuz no one else will."

Amid the laughter, the rest of us switched to 6-irons, trying to do so without Hogan noticing.

One year at the Hogan Company dinner during the Colonial NIT, a young professional, Bill Calfee, got up enough courage to ask Hogan if he'd like to play golf the next afternoon. Hogan, to Calfee's complete amazement, said yes, that Calfee should meet him at Shady Oaks for lunch, and they'd play. The next morning, Claribel called me to Mr. Hogan's office. Hogan explained that he was playing with this young man and asked if I would like to have lunch and play with them. After a long one-second review of my schedule, I said I'd love to and practically ran out of his office.

Calfee was a young pro from the Tampa area who hit the ball long, but had a tendency to turn it right to left—a hook, the ugly word in Ben Hogan's vocabulary. After lunch we hit a few balls then headed to the first tee.

Calfee and I rode together in a golf cart, so among the chitchat I asked him how he ever ended up getting to play with Hogan. "Well," he explained, "I just blurted it out. I said I'm not playing in the Pro-Am, would you like to play golf tomorrow? He kind of paused and looked right at me, and I think I went pale, but then he said, 'I don't have any appointments, so yes, meet me at the Shady Oaks clubhouse at noon. We'll have lunch and then play.' I was kind of stunned, and when I went back to my table and told everyone, he said yes, they went nuts. So here I am."

Calfee started out well making two birdies in the first four holes. The 5th hole at Shady Oaks is a long par 3, cut into the side of a hill with trouble on both sides of the green—particularly the left, and in back of it. Just beyond the trap that guards the right side of the green, a steep hill rises up, and to the left of the green is a steep valley with deep weeds and a creek at the bottom. Trees guard both the left side and the back of the green, so the left is definitely the worst place to be. Calfee asked Hogan what club to hit.

Hogan said, "4-iron."

Calfee rolled over on the four iron and hit a big, high, ugly hook. While we did find his ball, Calfee struggled to make a double bogey 5.

Several holes later, on the long, dogleg right, par 5, 8th-hole, Calfee hit a huge drive over the corner of the dogleg, giving him an opportunity to reach the green in two. He asked me what club to use. He said that he was afraid to ask Hogan since he had asked him on the 5th hole and had hit that ugly hook. After looking over the shot, I suggested that he go ahead and ask Hogan, so Calfee asked him what to hit.

We both thought Hogan would just respond back from his cart on what club to use, but no, Hogan drove his cart over to Calfee's ball, got out and walked over to the ball. He stood over the ball as though he were going to hit the shot, studied the lie and looked at the trees beside the green and those to our right to see if any wind was blowing He looked again at the lie downhill, with the ball slightly higher than his feet—perfect for a snipe (a screaming low hook). Hogan pondered the situation, thought a moment, and then told Calfee "Take your 2 iron, and aim it at the left-hand corner of the second bunker by the green, get it up in the air, and don't hook the gawddamned thing."

Calfee absolutely crushed the 2-iron. He also blocked it a little to the right, sending it into the trees to the right side of the green. I chuckled to myself that Hogan must have that effect on every player. Calfee got into the cart, and as we drove toward the green, proudly asked, "Did you see that?" "Yea," I said dryly, "You hit it in the trees." Calfee's response was immediate, "Well, at least I didn't hook the damned thing." He later said that Hogan's remark almost cracked him up, for he didn't expect that kind of humor from Hogan on the golf course.

After our round we went to the men's grill and had a drink with Mr. Hogan. While we were there, Hogan gave Calfee some advice. He told him, "A golf swing is only 25 % of the game. Good swings don't win tournaments, good management on the golf course does. Decide how you play certain holes. You must know when to be aggressive and when not to be." After a short visit, Calfee then excused himself to go to Colonial and hit balls.

The *Tampa Tribune-Times* newspaper did an article on the round and Calfee is quoted as saying, "When I went into the locker room on Thursday, those guys were on me like animals ravaging after a piece of raw meat. There they all were—Tom Watson, Hubert Green, and Tom Weiskopf, all of 'em. They fired questions, how did he hit it? Did he talk to you? What was he like?" Calfee said he described in detail his exciting experience with Hogan, and the Tampa sportswriter also described the 5th and 8th holes and Calfee's caution around Hogan. "I was afraid to talk much. I didn't say a whole lot unless he spoke to me. He said very little. I told him I was having a set of Hogan clubs made, and he said he'd look at them personally and have a couple of things done to them that might help me out. He couldn't have been nicer... It was very enlightening. It's an experience I'll never forget."

However, not everybody folded the first time he played in Ben Hogan's presence. In 1995 Texas Governor George W. Bush was playing golf at Shady Oaks Country Club with Tom Schieffer, President of the Texas Rangers Baseball Club and Shady Oaks member, Roger Williams. The Governor's eight-iron approach shot hit the cart path behind the ninth green and took one more, big hop before banging against the big plate glass window of the men's grill. Hogan, sitting inside at his table that overlooked the ninth and eighteenth greens, was startled by the noise. Seeing it was Governor Bush walking towards the ball, Hogan went to the window to watch the Governor play his next shot. The ball had come to rest about eighteen inches to two feet from the building wall and the window. With no room for a normal backswing it was nearly an impossible shot to hit any length, and a likely result would be to "chilly-dip" or hit the ball "fat", especially with the distinctive figure of Ben Hogan standing right at the window, looking down at the ball. As the Governor approached the ball he noticed Hogan positioned on the other side of the glass, barely three or four feet from his ball.

In a friendly game most people would take a penalty stroke and move the ball away to allow a clear shot, but with Ben Hogan watching, Governor Bush wasn't about to do any such thing. After nervously testing out several possible ways to strike the ball, the Governor took a half swing hack at it and caught the ball flush. It flew about thirty feet, bounced a couple of times, rolled across the cart path, down the little slope and up onto the green. The Governor started walking toward the green, but he couldn't help but look back to see Hogan's reaction. Hogan smiled and gave the Governor a "thumbs up" sign indicating his approval. Later as the Governor discussed the shot, he commented, "I've never had that much pressure before. I still don't know how I did that."

Hogan asked John Grace, a Shady Oaks member, to play nine holes late one day in the fall of 1974, shortly after Hogan had watched John's entire U.S. Amateur finals match on TV, when John finished runner-up to Jerry Pate. Naturally, Grace accepted as Hogan had been his golf idol since he was a kid. John thought, "This is it. This is great. I get to play with my idol." Obviously John was playing well at that point, and that day shot 31, to Hogan's 34.

After the round, Hogan, his competitive juices flowing, said to John, "Next year, we're gonna play some, and I'm gonna kick your butt. John played a lot of golf, very competitive golf, with Hogan in the following years.

John recalled, "Hogan loved to compete. He loved a good match. When they threw up 4 golf balls to determine who would play on teams, if Hogan's ball ended up closest to mine, Hogan would re-throw the balls until he and I were on opposite teams." This was because Hogan and Grace were usually the two best players in the group, and Hogan truly wanted a good match, one that would challenge him to win.

Once when playing in a group with Grace, Hogan, on a long par 3, put too much stress on his left knee, and it couldn't handle it. He fell down as he completed his swing. The group asked Hogan if he wanted to quit, but Hogan said no, he was O.K. and wanted to finish. They kept on playing and finished, but Hogan didn't play again for several weeks after that until his knee felt better, and the swelling had gone down.

On June 5, 1977, Hogan and Joe Cates played a match against John Miles and Bill Flynn at Shady Oaks. Hogan played extremely well that day, hitting the ball close to the flag on nearly every hole. Despite his exceptional ball striking and accuracy that day, Hogan could only manage a one-under par 34 on the front side, with 8 pars and a birdie. Hogan parred the difficult 10th. He birdied the 11th hole, parred the long par-3 12th, and then ran a string of 3 birdies in a row on 13, 14 and 15 before parring the par-3 16th. After birdieing the most difficult hole on the back nine, the uphill par-4 17th, Hogan was 6 under par for the day. Another birdie on the 18th would give Hogan a 6 under par back nine score or 30, and a 7 under par total of 64 on the par 71 Shady Oaks course.

Joe Cates recalled, "As we were going down the 18th fairway, the three of us who were playing with Hogan, all knew he needed a birdie on the last hole to shoot 64, which would be the first time Hogan ever shot his age. We didn't know if Hogan was aware of it, but we sure weren't about to mention it. Hogan hit his second shot to the elevated green on the par-4 18th hole and stopped it about four feet from the pin, but none of us would dare say anything to him about the significance of the putt. He had hit it so close all day long that a decent putter would have shot 59. As it came to Hogan's turn to putt, we were holding our breath because of his erratic putting. We wanted to be part of Hogan shooting his age probably more than he did, so we were all dying inside as he studied the putt and then stood over it longer than any of us wanted him to. Finally, he drew his putter back and stroked the ball. As the ball rolled toward the cup our hearts were in our throats. Thankfully, thankfully, it was only 4 feet and we didn't have to watch very long before we got our answer as the putt rolled into the cup for the 64."

After the round Hogan asked Bill Flynn to ask Joe Cates for the scorecard, so Bill walked into the locker room and asked Joe for the card to give to Hogan. Joe said, "No." Taken aback, Bill repeated the request emphasizing that it was Hogan who wanted the card. Cates responded, "No, I kept score, it's my scorecard!" Flynn, hesitatingly, went back out to the grill room and explained to Hogan that Joe said "no." Hogan grinned, and said, "I don't blame him. Have him make a copy for me." After some thought, they made four copies.

Cates recalled, "As we were copying and signing the scorecards, so we could all have a copy signed by Hogan, we could tell that Hogan too was thrilled as he asked for a copy to give his secretary, Claribel Kelly."

With good players, Hogan could be very subtle about offering advice on the course. He had a regular group that he frequently played with during the 1960s and '70s that included former PGA tour pros and now club pros Shelly Mayfield and Eldridge Miles, and oilman Gary Laughlin. Shelly knew Hogan on the tour and later became the head golf professional at Brookhollow Country Club. Eldridge was the head golf professional at Dallas Country Club (later at Bent Tree and Glen Eagles), after coming off the PGA tour in the late '60s. Gary Laughlin was the final member of the foursome, and Gary was in the oil business with Hogan, and a very good golfer.

Matches for this group were typically a $5 Nassau, with two-down automatic presses, and while they weren't playing for much money, Eldridge couldn't remember if they ever settled up after the matches, he said they played like it was the National Open. They took caddies, teed it up, and played hard.

Eldridge recalled an occasion when they were on the long par-5 15th hole at Preston Trail. They all had hit good drives, but Eldridge had out driven the rest, so he took out a driver and hit his second shot about a yard short of the green. It really was a terrific shot from the fairway. As he started walking proudly toward the green, he was waiting for Hogan to congratulate him for such a terrific shot. After they had walked 10 or 15 yards, Hogan confided, "You know, Eldridge, I was never good enough to hit a driver off the fairway." Eldridge didn't know what to make of the remark, but over time and numerous such comments, he understood that Hogan was giving him a pointer on how to play. Eldridge, a long hitter, said he never hit a driver from the fairway again.

A similar occasion occurred on the par-3 4th hole at Brookhollow Country Club. The wind was blowing from right to left; Eldridge, first on the tee, stepped up and hit his ball about four feet from the hole. "Whadya hit, E?" Gary Laughlin asked. "Eight iron," Eldridge responded.

Finally, Hogan hit his shot, obviously with a longer club that flew the ball at a much lower trajectory, and nestled it about 2 feet from the hole. As they walked to their cars after the round Hogan asked, "By the way, Eldridge, do you ever hit a soft shot?" Again, Eldridge realized that Hogan was giving him a tip. Hogan had hit a 5-iron on that par 3, keeping the ball down, out of the wind, and he cozied it to two feet when Eldridge had hit an 8-iron up in that wind, leaving the results more to chance.

Eldridge also learned how observant and meticulous Ben Hogan was. One day on the 18th tee Hogan pressed the bet. Eldridge, like all good golfers followed his standard procedure as he set to hit his tee shot. Then he hit a bad tee shot. As they were walking down the fairway, Hogan walked up beside him and said, "You know, Eldridge, a fella should hit that last shot the same way he hits the rest of 'em," and then walked over to his ball. Eldridge was dumbfounded. He knew that he had taken that one extra waggle before the tee shot, and the "hawk-like" Hogan had also noticed, and then let him know he noticed it.

Hogan, on a rare occasion, was very direct when giving instructions. AMF executives had asked Hogan to play golf with Mr. C. Itoh, chairman of one of the largest trading companies in the world, headquartered in Japan. Frank Mackey, another Hogan employee and a former TCU golf team member and I were asked to join them to make a foursome. Mr. Itoh was a novice golfer and asked Mr. Hogan to please give him instructions to help him improve his game while we played. Hogan noted the usual beginner mistakes and offered his advice frequently, but not with every shot or two, perhaps once or twice a hole. Mr. Itoh had the typical beginner's tendency to raise his head rather than keeping it down until after the club had impacted the ball.

After several of the same reminders to no effect, on one hole where Frank and I had hit our balls considerably further than Mr. Itoh and down the oppo-site side of the fairway, Hogan finally blurted out, "Dammit, I told you to keep your head down!" Frank and I were far enough away that we acted like we hadn't heard a thing and were preparing to hit our next shots, so Mr. Itoh wouldn't feel embarrassed, but we had a hard time keeping from snickering or laughing. Hogan didn't want to embarrass the man, but he definitely wanted to get his message across. Mr. Itoh did improve as we progressed, and when we finished Hogan auto-graphed the new hat Mr. Itoh had bought in the pro shop just prior to our round.

Eldridge Miles came off the PGA tour late in the summer of 1968 to take the head golf professional job at Dallas Country Club. The club wanted Eldridge to own the merchandise in the golf shop, stock it, merchandise it, pay for it, and profit from it. Eldridge called Al Channel, the Hogan Company credit manager, and asked Al if he could help him out. Al told him that he would not only allow Eldridge to defer payment until April 10th of the following year, but he would also still allow him a 2% discount when he paid the bill on or before April 10th. Eldridge jumped on that and loaded the shop with $50,000 of Hogan merchandise.

That following spring Hogan called Eldridge and asked if he wanted to play at Preston Trail. Eldridge said sure and the game was arranged with Eldridge, Hogan, Shelly Mayfield, and Gary Laughlin. When they came to the 14th hole, Hogan and Laughlin were 2-down, Hogan wanted to press and said that Gary (Gary was playing to a 2-handicap and got 1 stroke a side) should get his stroke on this hole, the 14th. Shelly objected saying that the #1 handicap hole on the scorecard (although none of them had a scorecard with them) was the 15th and Gary should get his stroke there. Hogan contended the 14th was the more difficult hole, and usually played into the wind, so it was really the more difficult hole, and Gary should get his stroke there. Shelly wasn't about to cave, so he tossed that hot potato to Eldridge with the retort, "Tell 'em 'E' you're a member here. Tell 'em where Gary gets that stroke, it's on the 15th hole, not here." Eldridge replied. "Hell, Shelly, in 8 days I owe the Ben Hogan Company $50,000, and I don't have the money right now, so Mr. Hogan can have that shot wherever-the-hell he—wants it." Eldridge has a great sense of humor, and the way he drawled that drawn out "wherever-the-hell he wants it" absolutely cracked Hogan up. He tossed his driver into the air, and bent over in laughter, one of his full body laughs. Eldridge bemused, "We all got a good laugh out of it, but, when the laughter subsided, Gary got his shot on the 14th hole, where he made par, giving him a net birdie, and he and Hogan won the hole."

On another "friendly golf" occasion at Preston Trail, the same group teed off the 15th hole, and Shelly and Eldridge had Gary and Hogan two-down. After the group teed off and started walking to their tee shots, Gary started to tell a joke, a long joke. Just as they approached their balls, Gary was about to give the punch line to the joke. Remembering they were two-down, Hogan scolded, "Gary, quit telling jokes and play golf!" Eldridge said he never did learn the punch line to that joke.

The same group played at Shady Oaks one day, and after hitting their tee shots on the tenth hole, Eldridge wasn't sure of the yardage to the hole, so he called over to Ben Hogan. He expected Hogan to just shout back the approximate yardage and continue on. Nope. Hogan got out of his cart (they were riding on this occasion), found a distance marker and stepped off the distance. "It's 134 yards to the pin," Hogan intoned to a flabbergasted Eldridge. Eldridge had just wanted an approximate distance, but Hogan didn't do approximate, so he stepped off the exact yardage to the pin.

Stuart Fitts related a couple of instances that his father, Grant, had told him when he had played with the Eldridge, Shelly, Laughlin, and the Hogan group. The first time Ben Hogan ever played Preston Trail Country Club was shortly after it was built in 1965. As the group was standing on the back tees of the long par-3 4th hole, Hogan, arms folded across his chest, surveyed the hole and exclaimed, "You know, this is the first time I've ever seen a dogleg par 3." There, extended over top of the regular tees was a large limb that would present no problem for the regular tee box, but from the back tees, the players had to either play over it, under it, or around it. The group played shots over it or under it, but Hogan faded his ball around it and went on. Grant Fitts, playing in the group that day, however thought that it wasn't a very good idea to have an obstruction like that for those playing from the back tee, so he called the course superintendent and had that limb cut off the following Monday when the club was closed. One of the owners, however, didn't care for Mr. Fitts redo of the 4th hole, so the two of them went nose-to-nose over the change. But the change had been made, the par 3 was no longer a dogleg.

Hogan, Gene Smyers, Gary Laughlin and Gus Layton (more than a legend at the gin rummy table) were playing golf at Shady Oaks one day. As they were about to tee off on the first hole, Gus, first to hit, went to the men's regular tee markers to tee off. After he'd plugged his ball into the turf and straightened up to hit it, Hogan called out, "Gus, what in the hell are you doing?" "Why, I'm getting ready to hit," an astonished Gus retorted. "Not if you're going to play me, you're not," Hogan shot back. "You mean I have to go back there with you?" Gus appealed. "Well, let me ask you this, what do you give me at the gin rummy table?" Hogan responded. Gus meekly pulled his tee out of the ground and went back to the back tee to join a smiling Hogan, Smyers, and Laughlin.

Ben Hogan was a competitor whenever he played golf, even if it was a friendly match or the Ben Hogan Company golf tournament. The annual Ben Hogan Company sales meeting had a golf tournament on the final day of the meeting, and concluded with dinner at the country club where the tournament was played. In 1960, however, the meeting schedule had an unprecedented change. After the golf tournament, Hogan overheard several of the salesmen commenting that Morgan Barofsky, the salesman from the San Francisco area had hit an 8-iron for his second shot on the 8th hole, a 575-yard, dogleg-right, par-five. (The tournament was played from the regular men's tee markers.) Hogan couldn't believe it, but the salesmen stuck to their story.

At dinner that night Hogan got up and announced that Barofsky and two other salesmen were to meet him at Shady Oaks the next morning to play golf. As imagined the change in events caused quite a stir, and the salesmen Hogan named off were all real good players: Morgan Barofsky, Bob Moser, and Owen Chapman, so interest was very high.

Hogan shot a 1-under par 34 on the front side and was even with two salesmen and three shots behind Bob Moser, who carded a 4-under par 31 on the front side. Hogan promptly shot a 6-under par 30 on the backside, finishing 5-under on the last six holes for a total of 64, besting Moser by 2, Barofsky by 4, and Chapman by 7. Moser, however, made the point that he was all even with Hogan in match play as Hogan had birdied #10 to Moser's bogey and eagled #15 to Moser's par. All four had shot par 71 or better, and the group had 19 birdies and an eagle among them.

Barofsky hit a 6-iron or 7-iron on his second shot to the 575-yard par-five 8th hole, so Hogan was still not convinced Barofsky had hit an 8-iron the day before.

A final example of Hogan's on-course presence involves Paul Richards, former Manager and General Manager of the Baltimore Orioles. Richards was an avid, excellent golfer, and very, very competitive. He wanted nothing more than to beat Hogan whenever the two of them played together. One day Richards and his friend, Buck Jordan, went to Shady Oaks to play with Hogan. Richards was very meticulous about his golf swing, his equipment, and he practiced and played as much golf as his schedule allowed. So when he got to play with Hogan his competitive juices were really flowing. This match was competitor versus competitor.

While Hogan's swing was quick and aggressive, Richard's Oriole clean-up hitters couldn't swing harder at a baseball than he did at the golf ball. On the 18th hole Hogan's tee shot ended up about 15 yards in front of Richards' drive. As Richards was selecting his iron for his approach shot to the green, he asked Hogan which club he should use. Hogan replied, "Six." Richards laced it to the front part of the unusually large 18th green. Hogan drove up to his ball, pulled out a club and drilled it to about 10 feet from the hole.

As Hogan started back to his cart Richards asked him what club he had used. Hogan answered, "Six." "Six!" an irritated Richards roared in disbelief. "You were nearly 20 yards in front of me and told me to use a six?"

"Yea, but I don't swing from my ass," Hogan replied, with a widening smile on his face as he put his club back in his bag, got in his cart, and started off for the green. Richards stood there red-faced, not at all appreciating the joke at his expense, and the needle about his golf swing, but Buck Jordan was doubled over in laughter.

THIRTEEN:
BEN HOGAN WITH A GOLF CLUB
I WOULDN'T HAVE BELIEVED IT MYSELF

MYTH: *Ben Hogan's swing, sound of the impact, and the shot's trajectory, were, well, just different, and the authority with which he struck the ball was unmistakable.*

MAN: There's not much myth about Ben Hogan's ability to strike and control a golf ball.

Ben Hogan's feats with a golf club are legendary, but it's still hard to imagine how good he really was. Those who played with him or saw him play acknowledged there was something different about the way Hogan struck a golf ball—his solid, strong swing with perfect balance, the sound of the impact when he struck the ball, even the flight pattern of a Hogan-struck ball.

Gary Player said, "I never saw a man who could swing like Ben Hogan. Sam Snead had a great fluid, natural swing, but Hogan had the best mechanics. I admire Tiger Woods and Ernie Els, but Hogan was different. I would love to see Hogan play under the conditions of today. Today it's much different, the conditions. Today there are no spike marks on the greens; the courses are so well groomed; the traps are exquisite, smooth; the best brand new practice balls that you don't have to pick up yourself; flying your own jet rather than driving everywhere; improved finances and the great medical improvements. It's mind boggling on the differences, and what he could have done. But, you really can't compare one era with another—they're just too different."

Jack Nicklaus, in his book *The Greatest Game of All: My Life in Golf,* wrote, "During the time I have played golf, the best technician, by far, has been Ben Hogan. No other modern player, as I see it, has approached his control of the swing, and I wonder if any player in any era has approached his control of the golf ball. Ben has probably hit more good shots and fewer poor shots than any man in history. He is the best shot maker I've ever seen."

Ben Hogan in top Hogan form at Colonial during his outstanding 1948 season. (PHOTO COUR-TESY, *FORT WORTH STAR-TELEGRAM*, SPECIAL COLLECTIONS, THE UNIVERSITY OF TEXAS AT ARLINGTON LIBRARY, ARLINGTON, TEXAS)

Consequently, Nicklaus made it a point to play practice rounds with Hogan whenever possible after he was paired with him in the 1960 U.S. Open at Cherry Hills in Denver. Nicklaus noted, "I have had the pleasure of playing quite a number of rounds with Ben Hogan since that day in Denver. At the Masters, for example, we always play at least one practice round together. He names the day, and we go out and play. I always learn something from watching Hogan. Of all the golfers I know, he's the best positioned throughout his swing, and he's so strong through the ball. The tempo of his swing is superb, all the time."

Author Al Barkow described it this way, "Yet Hogan was matchless. If nothing else, no one has ever hit a golf ball quite as he has. The sound of the club against the ball and turf was strangely different. There is no adequate descriptive word or non-word for it. It wasn't a thwock or clack or zunk. It was… different. So, too, was the flight of the ball, generally described as a controlled fade—the famous Hogan fade…. He was not a man who played golf, he was absolute golf, the ultimate corporeal manifestation of an idea."

You didn't have to be around people who have played with or watched Ben Hogan hit a golf ball very long before the "Hogan stories" start to roll.

Nick Seitz of *Golf Digest* wrote in the *New York Times* "The Golf Clinic" about an experience when Hogan was practicing at Shady Oaks. "He was hitting a long iron at a caddie stationed in the distance, and shot after shot soared high, landed softly, bounced once and found the caddie. The young man barely had to move. After 30 minutes of this marksmanship, I was moved to compliment Hogan. He shook his head negatively. 'There's way too much difference in the trajectory of those shots,'" he said. Seitz added, "That is when I came to appreciate that there is practice and then there is practice. When Hogan complained about the differences in the trajectories, he was talking about a few feet. That's all—just a few foot difference."

John Grace, the 1974 U.S. Amateur runner-up, while never far from the center of the fairway, was never a long hitter. He noticed one day when he played with Hogan at Shady Oaks that Hogan's tee shots had been right beside his for the first seven holes. Then on the long par-5 eighth Hogan hit his tee shot 40 yards past John. The next few holes Hogan again was near even with Grace's tee shots. However, on 14, again a par-5, Hogan was 30 or 40 yards in front of him. On both occasions John had hit the ball very solidly off the tee.

The second time was too much for Grace. He wanted to know what Hogan was doing, so he asked him, "What's going on here? You're right with me on nearly every hole and now you're 30 or 40 yards ahead of me, like you were on the 8th hole. How did you do that?"

Hogan replied, "Well, I just got tired of being back there with you, so I just swung a little faster." John was amazed. He knew that Hogan had slowed down his swing to shorten his drives. "But I don't understand," John said, "how he could hit it shorter like that and be so accurate."

Similarly, George Archer reported a round at the Masters that he played with Hogan and Arnold Palmer. Archer recalled:

"I'll never forget the third hole, where Palmer hit one of those low drives and the crowd roared like crazy. Hogan took the cigarette out of his mouth and threw it down on the ground. He threw it so hard it bounced off my shoe. I was stunned. He then hit this little low fade and people clapped because it was down the middle. I then hit a three-wood down the left side. When we got down there, there was one ball about even with me and then the third ball was about eighty yards ahead."

I got down there first to my ball. Meanwhile, Hogan and Palmer were walking and talking, and their caddies were with them, and all four walked right by the first ball near me, and they all went to the long ball up ahead. So I'm thinking, 'Who's going to be the one to have to turn around and walk back to his?' Hogan got down there and never looked at the ball. He just puffed on his cigarette and looked at the green. Palmer had to bend over and look at the ball, and then turn around and walk back to his ball. And the crowd was like 'Wooooooooooo.' Hogan sent a message there that was unreal, and that was, 'There would be no more screaming for those Arnold Palmer drives.' And there wasn't. He has a sand wedge to the green, and the hole was about 400 yards long, so he had hit his drive about 310. Hogan was long when he wanted to be long. He could really rip it."

Pine Valley Golf Club in New Jersey is one of the most difficult golf courses in the country. It is a series of small island patches of green stuck in a massive sand desert. There is little or no rough, with shots that miss the fairway ending up in the sand. Yard for yard, it is one of the toughest, if not the toughest track in the United States.

In his early years, when he was the golf professional at Hershey Country Club in nearby Pennsylvania, Hogan went to Pine Valley to play one day. Apparently there was no one to play with, so he went out by himself. Now, if there was ever a course that was designed for the accuracy of a Ben Hogan, it is Pine Valley. When he came in, he was asked what he shot. He answered and the responses he received from those in the room were frowns and funny looks. The score Hogan reported broke the course record by a couple of strokes, but no one in that clubhouse that day would believe him. They didn't know who Ben Hogan was and couldn't believe that this stranger could shoot such a score on that course— but he did.

Legend Shaft Commercial

Roughly 35 years had passed since Ben Hogan was at Hershey Country Club and played that day at Pine Valley, when we asked him to shoot TV commercials. During those commercial shoots, I learned never to doubt my confidence in the boss.

Ben Hogan did not want to do a TV commercial. "I don't want to be like one of those damned car salesmen in those TV commercials," he protested when we discussed producing the first Ben Hogan Company commercial. The marketing group was convinced that having Hogan swing a golf club in a television ad would generate great impact on our audience, and over time would increase the audience that watched the ad. After showing him the storyboard detailing the commercial, we finally convinced him that he wouldn't have to say a word, just swing the club and hit the golf ball. Once Hogan reluctantly concurred, he put heart and soul into it. He studiously reviewed the storyboards at several stages, asked relevant questions and made suggestions regarding the way the commercial was to be shot, and was meticulous all along the way. Once he was involved, he was involved 100 percent.

The day of the commercial shoot was textbook perfect at Shady Oaks Country Club—bright but not glaring sun, and blue skies with small wispy traces of clouds.

Hogan arrived shortly after the rest of us had assembled in a small room adjacent to the men's grill. As he strode into the room, the group rose to meet him, and he introduced himself. Hogan, while very cordial, usually received a somewhat stiff and forced response to his initial "Hi, I'm Ben Hogan" as he offered his right hand and went right on with "Pleased to meet you."

Hogan ordered a cup of coffee and sat down at the end of the conference table to look over the task at hand. The director sat down next to Hogan and reviewed the storyboards with him, picture by picture, and Hogan meticulously again studied them. After asking numerous questions, Hogan understood exactly what he was being asked to do, what the objective of each shot was, and what commentary would accompany each portion of the commercial.

Since I had been over the storyboard numerous times previously, I paid as much attention to Hogan as I did the Director's information. I watched him as he pictured the idea in his mind, then he would look back at the storyboard and, if satisfied with the plan, he let the discussion proceed. If something was unclear, he asked for clarification. If he didn't like the camera angle or the way a shot was to be taken, or had an idea that he thought would improve it, he suggested a change.

At one point, Hogan suggested to change the way for the camera to move from the club head to the shaft band in a natural way to make the visual look more authentic. As Hogan and the director went through the last few shots and the general flow of the commercial, the camera crew went out to the selected spot near the 18th green to set up the camera.

The 18th green had been selected because the camera could be positioned on a rise slightly behind and to the right of the green. This gave an excellent view of the ball as it landed near the hole. The large elevated green was some 15-20 feet above the level of the fairway. It had a ridge running diagonally from left front to right rear, giving it a two-tier effect. We had asked the greens keeper to cut the hole on the upper level in the right rear just behind the ridge. That was a tough pin placement, but would allow the camera shot to clearly show the ball hitting near the pin and stopping close to the hole, thus depicting the improved control and accuracy of the shaft, the main thrust of the commercial.

Hogan drove up in his golf cart, stopped near the camera placement, got out, and walked over to the camera. In a semi squat position, putting his hands on his upper legs for support, he peered through the camera eyepiece to see the field of focus of the camera, then straightened up to survey the same area with his eyes. He peered through the camera again then walked over to the director and me.

"Now what is it you want me to do?" he asked, looking directly into the eyes of the director.

"Just hit it up there close to the flagstick, so we can get a shot of the ball stopping by the hole," came the reply.

Hogan turned and surveyed the position of the flag on the green and asked, "Which side of the pin do you want me to hit it on?" The startled director's eyes made immediate contact with mine, searching for some indication if Hogan was serious or if he was joking. He was caught totally off-guard and the poor man was dying, searching for some sign. I gave a slight nod to indicate the question's legitimacy.

"This side here, between the flag pole and the camera," the director said as he pointed to the near side of the flag.

"OK," Hogan responded. He got in his cart and drove down the fairway about 125 yards from the flag.

As the director walked over to the camera, he looked at me and asked, "Was he shittin' or was he serious? Does he actually think he can hit that ball right there?"

"Dead serious," I responded. "He wanted to know exactly where you wanted him to hit it, and he plans to hit it there."

The director looked at me as if to say, "Yea, right. I've gotta' see this."

The director moved behind the camera. Down the fairway Hogan pulled his 9-iron out of his bag and took a few warm up swings. "Looks good right there, Mr. Hogan," he shouted. Hogan dropped a few balls down beside his cart and hit two practice shots. He then waved to us that he was ready.

The cameraman motioned that he was ready. The director yelled, "Action!" The camera whirred as Hogan lofted a shot at the flag. It landed about a foot to the right of the flag, dead even with the pin, bounced about four or five feet, and spun back to within 18 inches of the hole. If the lighting was correct and the camera in focus, we could call it a take and go home. (As it turned out, that was the shot we ended up using in the commercial.)

"Great, that's it," roared the director. "Now a few more just like that just to be safe, and we'll have it."

Hogan hit another fifteen to twenty shots and all, except one, landed to the right of the pin and came to rest within five feet of the hole. The director yelled down to Hogan that we had enough footage, then turned to me with a look of astonishment and admitted, "I never would have believed that. Even after you told me he wasn't kidding, I thought you were putting me on, too…. That's damned amazing." The poor man still couldn't believe what he had witnessed. It was good he had it all on film.

"Not bad for a 65-year-old, ay?" I said.

Apex Ball Commercial

In the 1970's, the Hogan Company was growing rapidly as the quality and performance capabilities of its clubs, particularly the irons, were second to none. Further, the company made clubs to the exact specifications golfers requested. Bob Moser, a Hogan staff professional at the Everglades Club in Palm Beach, Florida, got his clubs custom made every year. At one point, though, he was so frustrated with his game that he just pulled a stock set of irons off the rack in his pro shop—and promptly went out and shot 29 on the first nine-holes he used them!

Touring professionals, on the other hand, had financial contracts and monetary considerations that entered into which manufacturer's equipment they would use. The Hogan Company had one of the smallest tour budgets of any of the golf manufacturers, but the quality of the equipment and the exactness to our specifications lead some players to turn down more lucrative contracts. They felt that they could play significantly better playing Hogan equipment and win more prize money than they could with the equipment of our competitors including the contract money they offered.

We were, however, still struggling with our golf ball, the Hogan Apex ball. The reputation of the Titleist ball, the large tour program of Acushnet, its manufacturer, and strong advertising campaigns were difficult to overcome. We were making significant inroads with the Apex ball on both the LPGA and PGA Tours, but the Titleist ball was well established with a loyal customer base.

In the heat of the struggle, Acushnet changed the dimple pattern on the Titleist ball, a change not well received on the tour. The Hogan Apex ball then became the hot commodity on the tours, particularly the PGA Tour where it was winning more and more money, and many tournaments. Mr. Hogan sent a personal letter to each winner, and with the letter included a little bonus check for $1,000. More and more players, either under contract to other manufacturers who did not have a ball or who did not have a ball that met the tour player's requirements, began using the Hogan ball. Tom Watson won so many tournaments with the Hogan ball that Mr. Hogan, in one of his letters, told Watson that he was almost becoming a pen pal, and that Watson was getting more correspondence from him than any of Hogan's closest friends or business acquaintances.

During the five-year period from 1973 through 1977, players using the Apex ball won more money on the PGA Tour than any other golf ball, including the Titleist. Nevertheless, Titleist had much greater brand recognition and market share among recreational golfers. The Hogan Company needed to make some noise about our ball's success on the tour. By doing so, we felt that we would substantially increase Hogan golf ball sales, particularly to the better players. Our biggest weapon, obviously, was Ben Hogan hitting the golf ball. We decided to do another TV commercial, this one for the Hogan Apex ball.

The "little 9" at Shady Oaks Country Club, a 9-hole, par-3 course surrounded by the regular Shady Oaks 18-hole golf course was selected as the shoot location. The chosen site allowed the film crew total freedom with no interruption or delay. In addition, there were several small oak trees in the background of the teeing area which offered a good backdrop behind Mr. Hogan, and would also help make the small white golf ball, which we were trying to film in flight, more visible.

The plan was to film the ball coming directly at the camera from Hogan's tee shot, and then to mechanically freeze it so the ball filled the entire TV screen at the conclusion of the commercial. Thus, Hogan planned to hit the ball with a driver directly over the top of the camera, as close to it as he could, without actually hitting the camera. The camera was positioned about 15 to 20 yards down the fairway. A thick Plexiglas plate was positioned to protect the camera, and the two-man crew, should Hogan hit a ball lower than planned.

Chip Bridges, the Hogan PGA/LPGA Tour representative, had stopped by the model shop that morning to pick up a new set of irons that Gene Sheeley, the Hogan Company model maker, had made for Mr. Hogan. The clubs still had the little plastic protective bags over each iron head, as all new Hogan irons did when they were shipped from the Hogan factory.

Chip and Hogan arrived shortly after we had begun our final planning discussion. Hogan was dressed in his gray business suit, and he walked in he introduced himself to everyone. After he had a complete understanding of the shots planned and felt good about the flow of the commercial, Hogan was satisfied. He went to the locker room to put on his golf clothes as the rest of us headed for the shoot location. Chip remained behind to show Hogan to the filming site.

When Hogan arrived, he methodically inspected the entire set up. After receiving satisfactory answers to his questions, everyone took their places. Hogan moved to the tee and found the spot where he was to tee up the ball. Chip and I walked over to our golf carts to the right side of the tee to a choice spot to watch Hogan in action as the director told everyone to take their places. The two cameramen hunkered down behind the thick, clear Plexiglas protective shield. Hogan took a couple of practice swings and teed up a ball. He straightened up and stared down the fairway beyond the camera. The director announced "Action." Hogan took his stance. The high-speed camera started whirring, building to a higher pitch, and whined when fully up to speed.

Hogan drew back his driver then brought the swing forward, nailing a screaming liner about a foot or so over the top of the camera and the Plexiglas shield. He repeated the shot six or eight times. Each time he drilled a squarely struck ball no more than 18 inches directly over the camera set up behind the Plexiglas plate.

The crew asked for a short break to reload film, recheck the lighting, and make some adjustments. I hopped in my golf cart to go retrieve the balls Hogan had just hit. As I started off I noticed Hogan and Chip looking at Hogan's new irons. Once I picked up the balls down on the fairway, I started back toward the teeing area when I noticed Hogan hitting a few practice shots with one of his new irons. I was about 175 yards down the fairway from where he was hitting the balls and about 30 feet from where they were landing.

I stopped my cart at the side of the area where the balls were dropping, figuring I would pick them up when he finished. I watched one ball drop and was relaxing in the cart when all of a sudden I noticed a ball coming directly at me. As the ball approached, I tried to judge whether it was going to hit the roof of the cart or come underneath it. I couldn't tell. I started moving my feet and leaning my body so I could dive out of the cart if the ball came under the top of the cart. As the ball came closer I still wasn't sure whether the ball would hit the top of the cart or come under it. At the last moment, I lunged horizontally to my left, abandoning the cart with a desperate dive. As I landed on the ground, I heard a loud bang. The ball careened off the top of the cart and bounced down the fairway.

Rolling on my side, I saw the ball rolling down the fairway, and as I stood up to brush the dewy grass and dirt off my pants and shirt, and to check my tie, I heard laughter coming from the filming area. I turned around to look at the tee and could see Bridges nearly rolling on the ground in uncontrolled laughter and Hogan laughing heartily as well.

I figured Chip must have asked Hogan to try to land a ball on top of my cart with his new 5-iron. That's the kind of thing a prankster like Chip would do. He'd get a kick out of it—as most of us would. But, Hogan was pretty amused by it himself, so I wasn't so sure who initiated the joke. Chip later told me it was Hogan's idea. Regardless, Hogan too was greatly amused at my hasty, undignified exit from the cart, as both he and Chip were still laughing loudly.

The whole thing caught me totally off guard, but I couldn't help but laugh myself. Then I stepped on the floor of the cart, so I could peer down at the top of the cart. There it was, a small smudge nearly in the dead center of the roof. The top on that cart could have only been about 3 feet by 4 feet, and I was 175 yards from the tee, yet Hogan, now 65 years old, and using a club he'd hit only two or three times, had landed the ball right in the middle of the roof of the cart with one shot. I stepped down and went to retrieve the ball. That one, I stuck in my pocket so I could show it to others when I recounted the story. I figured that I'd get a "yeah, yeah, right" response of disbelief, so I wanted proof.

I arrived back at the tee to some good-natured ribbing about my lack of confidence in Hogan's ability. "What's the matter, Tim, no confidence in the boss?" mused Chip. Bridges, a fun sort of a guy, was still so particularly amused, I again thought the whole thing was his idea, and he once again began laughing uncontrollably.

Hogan was grinning too, and his eyes had their accompanying look of amusement as he examined my facial response between puffs on his cigarette. His grinning facial expression and the twinkle in his narrowed eyes, characteristic of when he had said something funny or was mulling something over in his mind, caused me to wonder what the hell was he thinking behind that grin? I imagined it was something like, "Well, what do you think of them apples, sonny boy?" But right then I had to admit the episode did liven things up quite a bit, and the three of us were enjoying the fun the thing had caused. Later, when Chip told me it was Hogan's idea, I remembered the twinkle in Hogan's eye and the amused grin on his face, and it caused me to believe that Hogan really had initiated the prank.

Once again, the director's called for "places" and our little group visit broke up and returned us to the task at hand. After Hogan's driver sent several more, well-spanked tee shots zooming closely over the top of the protective shield, one of the cameramen asked him if he could bring it down a little closer to the shield.

"Sure, I can, but I was being careful not to hit that Plexiglas," Hogan cautioned.

The cameraman confidently replied, "Oh, there's nothing to worry about. This Plexiglas is so thick it won't be a problem." Hogan was convinced otherwise, and he again warned the cameraman that the golf ball would most likely shatter the Plexiglas. The cameraman's response was again not to worry. The Plexiglas was much too thick for a golf ball to shatter.

Hogan agreed to hit the ball a little lower, but only after the cameramen moved the camera to the right edge of the Plexiglas, started it running, and then huddled at the far left side of the shield. After starting the camera,

Ben Hogan in a playful moment with the author.

they quickly scurried to the left side of the shield. Hogan took dead aim at the upper right hand corner of the shield, directly above the camera. He then uncoiled his characteristically forceful swing and again struck the ball solidly.

The smack of the ball off his club was quickly followed by a loud crash of the explosion of shattering Plexiglas. Pieces went flying in all directions. The force of the ball as it struck the upper right corner of the shield had completely ripped away that corner, strewing shards fifteen yards down the fairway.

Disbelief showed in the widened eyes of the cameramen. All morning long, they had felt so safe behind that Plexiglas shield. Now they realized they hadn't been safe at all. For the remainder of the shoot, which thankfully was only two or three more takes, they fearfully started the camera running, then quickly moved to the far end of the Plexiglas.

When we finished, I drove down to pick up the golf balls that remained on the fairway, looking particularly for the one that had shattered the Plexiglas shield. I put it in my pocket with the other ball that had struck the top of my cart—another souvenir.

HOGAN & HIS SHAG BOYS

Standing by the flagstick is usually one of the safest places to avoid being hit by a golf ball when most golfers, including most professional golfers, are hitting the ball. Not so with Ben Hogan. One of the most dangerous jobs in Fort Worth, Texas, was shagging balls for Ben Hogan.

Art Hall, the golf professional at Shady Oaks during the 1960s, '70s and early '80s had trouble keeping kids around the pro shop during the school year. Hogan liked to hit balls every day at about 1:00 and needed a boy to shag balls, so Art was continually recruiting new shop boys who could shag balls for Hogan.

One of those boys was Jimmy Burch, who later became a sportswriter for the *Fort Worth Star-Telegram*. In a 1995 commentary Burch wrote:

"On quiet afternoons in the golf shop at Shady Oaks Country Club, nothing stirred activity among the bag boys faster than a seven-word announcement from the club pro: 'We need someone to shag for Hogan!'

Suddenly, clean clubs needed rewashing. Non deadline club repairs became priority items. To a bunch of teenagers from west Fort Worth, this was a task best left to the next guy, especially on a bright, sunny day....

Shagging for Ben Hogan-- who always hit with Ol' Sol behind him so he could better follow the flight path-- could be a death-defying task on Shady Oaks' nine-hole practice area.

Lose one in the sun and you might end up wearing a bruise the size of a golf ball for a week. The man, even at 66, was that accurate. My thighs, shins and shoulders still shudder at the memory. But, almost two decades later, I'm thrilled that I got to trade a few bumps and bruises for some cherished memories I'll pass along to my children and grandchildren....

The normal procedure involved Hogan dropping off his helper at an appointed spot, wet towel, and shag bag in hand, then driving back 100 yards or so to begin working on his short game. With you as the flagstick....

Suffice to say, during an hour's worth of shagging, the toughest choice was deciding whether to field short-iron shots on one hop or two. Believe me, these plays were so routine that even a Rangers shortstop could not boot them. Never in the 30-odd times I shagged for Hogan did he fail to deposit at least one ball into his bag on the fly. Usually, the total was three or four. Once it reached six. As the years passed, I'm more amazed by that performance each time I reflect on it. I remember every shot I watched him hit on the practice range. And, in retrospect, I relish every bruise."

Art Hall told another boy, Fred Reynolds, that Hogan was coming to hit balls and for him to get ready. "Why do I always have to shag for him?" Fred asked.

"Because you don't say much, and Hogan likes you," Art replied.

"Hogan wouldn't talk much," Fred admitted. "When we pulled up to the spot where he wanted to practice, he would just point to the spot where he wanted the shag balls dumped."

But this particular day, while Fred was getting the items he needed to shag balls, Art told Hogan that Fred was in a bad mood, that "You'd better watch it today 'cause Fred's having a bad day."

So when Fred and Hogan started out to the golf cart, Hogan turned to Fred and asked, "You doing OK?" Fred said yes, that he was fine, and they went on out to the practice area on the little nine where Hogan usually practiced. After he was through practicing, they went back to the clubhouse where Hogan paid Fred the usual $7 for his hour's work and then took about 30 of his practice balls, basically brand new balls, right out of his practice bag and gave them to Fred.

Fred shagged balls for Hogan fairly regularly for several years. One year at the Colonial NIT tournament, he had seen one of the tour caddies wrap a towel around his hand and catch balls on the first hop. Fred thought that was a pretty good idea; he wouldn't have to bend down to pick the balls up each time. So the next time he shagged balls for Hogan he tried that. Hogan hit about 10 balls then waved him in, and had Fred sit down on the seat of the cart. Hogan took Fred's hand, and pointing to his fingers, said, "Look at your fingers. See how small the bones are? They're very small and catching the balls like that, you could break one of those bones. So just let the ball stop and then pick it up." Fred went back out to shag—without the towel.

In the Shady Oaks pro shop there was an area suitable for swinging a golf club, so on less busy days some of the caddies would occasionally take a golf club and practice swinging. Fred was taking a few swings one day when Hogan walked into the pro shop. Fred immediately quit swinging and started to put the club away when Hogan stopped him. "No, no, let me see you hit it," Hogan said as he approached. Fred took the club down and made a pass at the invisible ball. "Pretty good," Hogan said.

Fred recalled how Hogan could put a lot of spin on his shots. He said one day in the middle of the summer, Hogan was chipping to the green on the little nine next to the 12th hole on the regular golf course. The green was very flat and the ground was hard from a lack of rain, and the little nine didn't get as much water as the regular golf course from the watering system. Hogan was chipping from about 15 yards, and Fred said, "The balls would take two hops and would instantly back up on a flat green in the middle of the summer." Fred was amazed that Hogan could do that with such a short shot to a hard, flat green.

Hogan frequently would play nine holes and walk to get exercise. He usually played the back nine, as it was much flatter and easier for him to walk than the front nine. He usually played three balls on each hole, and on one occasion when Fred was caddying, Hogan was hitting the ball extremely well, even for Hogan. Fred didn't recall the scores he made on the first few holes, but he recalled on the 568 yard, par 5 14th hole, Hogan made 3 birdies. On the next hole, another par 5, this one 531 yards long, Hogan made two eagles and a birdie. And on the 149 yard par 3 16th hole Hogan hit all three of his eight-iron shots within 5 feet of the hole. He was 10 or 11 under par on 3 balls on 3 holes. Given Hogan's putting at that point, Fred was amazed.

Jody Vasquez was a Ben Hogan shag boy who later won the club championship at Colonial Country Club multiple times. He described his first shagging experience in his book, *Afternoons with Mr. Hogan*. Not knowing what to expect after emptying the shag bag balls where Hogan had requested, he trotted out about 50 yards. He watched where Hogan's first shot landed and placed the shag bag there. Hogan hit another shot there, so Vasquez left the bag there and moved away about five to seven yards. The next shot was right at Vasquez, so he walked over and picked up the shag bag and moved it to the new location, and again moved five to seven yards away. Again Hogan's shot was right at Vasquez so he walked over and moved the bag again. Vasquez described the following scenario:

"When I looked up, Mr. Hogan was standing there leaning on his club and staring out at me. He must have thought I was attempting to do my best Charlie Chaplin impression. Then he waved for me to come in. At first I thought he was cutting the session short. But when I stopped in front of him to pick up the un-hit balls, he looked at me and spoke for the first time. 'Son, keep the bag with you. I'm going to hit the balls at you no matter where you stand or put the bag. It would be easier for both of us if you didn't have to move around to find the bag so you can put the balls in it.'

"Until that moment, the idea that he purposely wanted to hit his shots at me hadn't occurred to me. I muttered a polite, 'Yes, sir,' and ran back out to my spot… Oh yes, his final comment to me before I ran back out was, 'and pay attention.'"

Vasquez also told the story of the day Hogan agreed to give 1960 PGA Champion Jay Hebert a lesson. Hebert and Gardner Dickinson met Hogan at Shady Oaks. Hogan worked with Hebert for two hours. Finally, Hogan told Vasquez to get his practice balls and go shag, so Jody dumped the practice balls at Hogan's feet and headed out to the area where Dickinson's caddie had been chasing after Hebert's shots. Figuring he was done, and he was exhausted, the caddie laid a towel down and stretched out on it. Vasquez set his shag bag down and waited for Hogan to hit his first shot. Without a warm-up or a practice shot, Hogan let fly with a shot with his driver. The ball took one bounce and jumped directly into the shag bag in front of Vasquez. Seeing that, Dickinson's caddie exclaimed, "Man, you ain't got no job."

Another time, a different boy shagging for Hogan for the first time kept prancing around, distracting Hogan as he was trying to line up his shot. Frustrated, Hogan waved the boy in. The boy jogged in, "Son, you need to stand still out there," Hogan said. "I'm using you as my target and I can't concentrate if you're going to be moving around like that."

"Mr. Hogan, I can't stand still, cuz you're gonna to hit me every time," wailed the boy.

Hogan, acknowledging the boy's concern, comforted him, "Son, you just watch the ball, and I won't hit you. Just watch the ball." The boy went back out, and Hogan dropped, almost every shot, at the kid's feet. Using caddies as his target put enormous pressure on Hogan to strike each shot precisely, so that he would not hit the boy. It was a way of bringing tournament golf pressure conditions to the practice range.

Hogan did occasionally hit the caddie. Chip Bridges, of the Hogan Company, saw it happen one day when he took some new balls to Hogan at his practice site at Shady Oaks. Hogan was hitting a 4-wood when Chip drove up. Hogan thanked him, and since he knew Hogan fairly well, Chip decided to watch a few shots before going back to the plant.

After he struck a ball, he watched its initial flight long enough to know whether it was to his liking or not, and then went back to a conversation he was having with Gary Laughlin between swings. Hogan didn't have to watch the ball land to know whether he was satisfied with how he struck it. Chip, however, was more curious and watched as each shot landed right at the caddie, where he snatched it and dropped it in the bag. Suddenly, after Hogan had hit a shot and went back to his conversation, Chip let out a loud shout, "He's hit. The ball hit him, and he's down." Laughlin was seated in his cart, so he started to the caddie, Hogan jumped in his cart and both headed toward the downed caddie.

As they reached the caddie, Chip could see the boy was more embarrassed than hurt. The ball had struck him on the chest, on the fly. Coming down at a fairly steep angle it was a glancing blow, causing more fright than hurt. Hogan, though, was upset about it, and after determining the boy was OK, said, "We're done, fella, that's it for the day." With that they all headed for the clubhouse. As usual the shag boy was seated next to Hogan in his golf cart.

Discussing the incident later in the men's grill, Hogan still upset, said, "It was the first time the kid had shagged for me, so I told the little shit that if he couldn't see the ball to take one step backward." Chip was awestruck by the comment. Hogan was dead serious that his distance control was so precise that his shot was intended to land at the feet of the caddie, and thus if the caddie couldn't see the ball, the one step backward, approximately 1 yard, would allow the ball to land right in front of him instead of hitting him.

Chip, never at a loss for a good one liner, shot back, "Yea, then you would have hit him right in the crotch." Hogan studied Chip's expression for a moment, then his serious look turned to a wry smile as he said, "Yeah, I guess you're right about that, maybe I'd better tell 'em to take two steps back next time."

Steve Cain, assistant pro at Shady Oaks and then head professional at the Trophy Club, was watching Hogan practice one day when Hogan flew a 4-wood shot right into the shag bag as it sat upright out on the practice fairway. Later, when Hogan got a new shag bag, Steve kept the old one because it had a mark on the handle where the ball struck the handle on its way into the bag. Steve said Hogan usually hit 6 dozen balls each practice session, and he had watched Hogan on several occasions where the caddie wouldn't make more than 1 or 2 steps to get a ball throughout the entire practice bag of 72 balls.

Randy Jacobs caddied and shagged balls for Hogan in the early 1970s. Like Fred Reynolds, Randy remembered how Hogan could put an unbelievable amount of spin on the ball, even on short shots. "One day he told me to go out about 70 yards so he could hit chips," Randy recalled. "I ran out about that distance, and the first ball he hit was about 15 feet off the ground. It hit the fairway, bounced up to my feet, then sucked back away from me. He then hit five or six more just like it, sucking each one of them back—on the fairway! On another occasion, he was hitting 80-90 yard shots over a tree to the 8th green on the 'Little Nine'. He had hit five balls, and when I got up to the green, three were within three feet and two were in the hole. I finally worked up the nerve to say something to him, 'Mr. Hogan, you know you hit two of those in the hole?' "Hogan responded, 'Yeah,' like it was no big deal."

The underlying mutual respect between Hogan and his shag boys shows in a story told by Randy that took place much later, in 1987, when Hogan had a ruptured appendix. People at the club were saying that he was incoherent and that he would probably not be back at Shady Oaks. Randy thought otherwise, and, in fact, Hogan did come back to Shady, although Randy said he looked the worse for wear.

The first time Randy saw him he walked right up to him and said, "Mr. Hogan, it's sure nice to see you back here." Randy said he could visibly see that Hogan seemed stunned. He looked at Randy with an expression of approval on his face, and in a sincere tone, replied, "Thanks, I really appreciate that."

Randy noted, "I was just a bag boy. I wasn't anyone special, but he really seemed touched by my comment."

HOGAN PUTTING

The logical question is, if Ben Hogan could cure his dreaded hook, if he could eliminate the crowd distraction that plagued him, and if he could master the course management of his game for every tournament he played, why couldn't he cure his putting problems? For determining par, 36 putts are included in the total of 70, 71, or 72 strokes for par on a golf course. Hence, putting accounts for 50 percent or more of the par strokes, so why wouldn't he or why couldn't he fix that part of his game if winning was his goal? Much has been discussed, debated and argued about Ben Hogan's putting.

Early on Hogan was a good putter, but after the late 1940s, some say as early as 1946, Hogan's putting began to deteriorate. Late in his career Hogan had a hard time even

Ben Hogan's putting woes in the mid 1940s. (A/P WORLDWIDE)

drawing the putter back. Eye problems, nerve problems, a result of his accident—all have been theorized as reasons for Hogan's poor results with a putter in his hand, but there is no question that Hogan could have won many more tournaments if he had been a better putter.

Just consider the following 7 major tournaments--

1946 Masters– Hogan 3-putted the 72nd hole to lose by a stroke;

1946 U.S. Open – Hogan 3-putted the 72nd hole to lose by a stroke;

1952 Masters– Hogan started the final round tied for the lead, and three-putted three of the first six holes to knock him out of contention;

1954 Masters playoff with Sam Snead: Hogan reached every green in regulation but took 36 putts. Snead hit fourteen greens in regulation but needed only 33 putts, and beat Hogan by a shot 70 – 71;

1955 U.S. Open playoff with Jack Fleck— Hogan took 5 more putts than Fleck through the first 17 holes, but was only one stroke behind Fleck;

1956 U.S. Open– Hogan missed three short putts in the final round, including a 30-inch putt on the 71st hole to lose to Dr. Cary Middlecoff by one shot;

1960 U.S. Open at Cherry Hills— during the Saturday 36-hole double round finish Hogan hit the first 34 greens in regulation but made no putts of any length on the first 18 holes. It wasn't until the 12th hole on the final 18 (his 30th hole) that Hogan made a 10-foot birdie, then added a 20-footer three holes later at the 15th, yet he still managed to keep himself in the hunt for the title until his 3rd shot on the par 5 71st hole rolled back into the water.

Hogan, particularly in his later days on the tour, was a terrible putter. Jim Trinkle, sportswriter for the *Fort Worth Star-Telegram* and a true friend of Mr. Hogan and the Ben Hogan Company, wrote a story for *Golf* magazine in 1975, in which Hogan described how badly he putted at the British Open in 1953. As Trinkle wrote, "He came from around his desk in his Fort Worth office. He assumed a putting stance and pointed. 'If the hole were over there,' he said, 'Timmy (Cecil Timms his caddie) would stand here. Never behind me, but in my sight. Then when I putted he covered his eyes.'" Later in the Trinkle article Hogan continued, "'I was a fair putter until the last

Ben Hogan and Sam Snead practice their putting at the 1967 Masters. (A/P WORLDWIDE)

few years I played,' he reminded. 'Not a super putter or a super anything. But I was a fairly good putter from inside 10 feet.' Ben thought the real skill in golf concerned the ball in the air, not on the ground." During the six rounds Hogan played at Carnoustie (two qualifying, four tournament rounds) he was in the rough only one time—and that was in a qualifying round.

As he aged, his putting got worse. After the third round of the 1967 Masters, when at the age of 54, he shot the lowest round of the tournament—a 66, shooting the back-nine in a record-tying 6-under par 30—he still had this to say about his putting, "I am still embarrassed to get before people and putt. Hell, I'm even embarrassed to putt when I'm alone, but the only way to beat this thing is to play. I hear children and ladies saying, 'For God's sake, why doesn't he hit it faster?' So I say to myself, 'You idiot. You heard them. Why don't you hit it faster?'"

I witnessed Hogan's poor putting during the 1970 Colonial National Invitation Tournament in Fort Worth, the last time that Hogan, at age 57, played in the event. This is an event he previously won five times. Hogan had finished 9th in the Houston Open at the Champions Golf Club a week or two earlier and had started his final round in that tournament par-par-birdie-birdie-birdie-par-birdie, four under par in his first seven holes and put himself in position to win the tournament until he 3-putted the 8th hole and the magic seemed to disappear. With such play at Champions, Jack Owens, my Hogan Company colleague, and I were excited and eagerly anticipated a good outcome, watching Hogan play Colonial.

Jack and I followed Mr. Hogan for the final two days during the tournament. Obviously, we went with a vested interest to watch the boss compete with the best on the PGA tour. It was disheartening, however, to watch him on the greens, especially during the final round in which he was paired with Ken Still, like Jack an Oregonian, who knew Jack well.

Hogan was driving the ball well, putting his ball in great position for his second shots, and his approach shots were right at or near their intended mark. But, Hogan could not make a putt, or get the ball up and down, even after chipping the ball from the edge of the green or blasting it from a trap to within three feet of the hole. If he didn't put his approach shot within fifteen or twenty feet of the cup, Hogan didn't make par.

Meanwhile, Still was hitting the ball all over the course, but getting it up and down from everywhere, and making putts like crazy. It was demoralizing for us to watch. We couldn't imagine how Hogan could continue to hit the shots he was hitting while carrying such a putting burden. Still's amazing short game just added to the agony of watching Hogan.

Finally, on the par 4 twelfth hole, Hogan hit a perfect drive, cutting the dogleg and putting the ball in perfect position for his approach to the green. He hit his second shot to within fifteen feet just below the hole, so his putt was almost directly up the slope to the hole.

Still pulled his second shot badly to the left, and it came to rest up on the side of the levee that separates the 11th and 12th holes at Colonial, leaving Still with an almost impossible shot. His ball was slightly higher than green level, and he had a 20 yard pitch out of the tough Colonial Bermuda grass rough. He was slightly short of hole, but high, so he had a downhill side hill lie to a near pin on an elevated green. The angle that he had with the side of the green presented another complication as to how the ball would bounce if he landed it short of the green. He pitched the ball just short of the green; it caught up in the rough enough to slow it down, took one or two bounces and rolled straight into the cup. Unbelievably, Still holed out the shot, yet another short game miracle. Rather than going to pick his ball out of the hole, Still went straight over to Hogan and apologized for his uncanny short game that day. It was unbelievable.

Ken Still was totally sincere in his apology to Hogan. Of all the times to have your short game as good as it's ever been and your tee to green game in the tank, you wouldn't pick playing like that with Ben Hogan—but that's golf. You take what you can get on any given day. Graciously, Hogan told him not to worry and went on about his business. Hogan then proceeded to miss his 15-foot straight up the hill birdie putt with a stroke that never got the ball closer than a foot of the hole as it rolled slightly past the cup. We held our breath as he putted the short one out.

Hogan shot 72, but if Still had been putting for him that day, he probably would have shot in the low-mid 60s.

Hogan had noted his putting wasn't very good after 1945. Fellow professionals facetiously praised him as one of the finest putters in the game, but Hogan said, "That started as a joke. I thank them, but it's a joke. I used to be a good putter back in 1938, '39,

'40, and through '45, but from there on I've been a bad putter." Once after a competitive tournament round where Hogan hit sixteen greens and had several birdie putts inside ten feet, but made no birdies during the entire round, Hogan commented, "It doesn't bother me, I've putted so terrible so much, you get to thinking it's futile, all right, but I've gotten to the point where it surprises me when they go in. If Dow Finsterwald had been putting for me, he would have been fifteen under par on the round."

One explanation for his putting problems was that his nerves would no longer allow him to make the smooth putting strokes required to make the putts necessary to be at the top of the professional golf tour. Supporting that theory are several discussions in which Hogan himself admitted that his nerves were the problem.

After his surgeries on his legs, and while Hogan was still in the hospital following his auto accident in 1949, *Chicago Tribune* columnist Charlie Bartlett and *Golfing* editor Herb Graffis visited with Hogan. Noticing the severe swelling in Hogan's ankles and the difficulty that accompanied any movement of his legs, Bartlett asked Hogan if he would play golf again, adding, "Not when, Ben, but will you play?" Hogan responded that he was going to try, but added, "My nervous system has been all shot by this, and I don't see how I can readjust to competitive golf."

In 1974 at his induction as one of the original 13 inductees into the World Golf Hall of Fame in Pinehurst, North Carolina, Hogan commented on his putting during an informal press conference. Admitting that he had received "a roomful" of correspondence on how to improve his putting, he mentioned letters from a national skeet shooting champion who got to where he could no longer pull the trigger, and a violinist who reached a point where he couldn't draw the bow. Similarly Hogan noted that he had trouble drawing the putter back. "I got to where I couldn't get the putter back. I could get it through if I could ever get it back, but I couldn't get it back. I would just stand there and shake, and it wouldn't move. And people would say, 'Oh, for crissake, hit it!' I was saying to myself, 'For crissake, hit it!' I suppose it's a nerve thing, I don't know what it is, but it happens to some people. I think Sam (Snead) and all of us have had a little touch of it from time to time as we get older. Your nerves won't hold still for you. And as a result, you are a terrible putter."

A follow-up question asked whether age or tournament golf had anything to do with deteriorating putting, to which Hogan responded, "I know several 75-year-old men who are very good putters. But had they been playing golf tournaments for 20 years, well, the drop of the water on the rock is going to wear a hole in it, you see. This fellow hasn't been under this pressure all this time, intense pressure. I don't know of any older professional who hasn't had a problem with his nerves. It's a matter of going through the nervous tortures every week. And the people who haven't been going through the tortures haven't had a chance to win."

But if he could master the flight of the ball in the air, why couldn't he control it better on the ground? "Now you can control the flight of a golf ball in the air, but not on the putting surface because you don't know what is going to happen… You are subject to too many undulations and grass changes and things like that…You have to be schooled in how to propel a golf club and a golf ball. And the greens are an intuitive situation—how hard to hit the ball. No one can tell you how hard to hit a putt, or where to aim. It's an intuitive situation entirely."

After missing the cut in the 1957 Masters, Hogan offered another alternative to putting: "I've always contended that golf is one game, and putting is another. If I had my way, every golf green would be made into a huge funnel; you hit the funnel, and the ball would roll down a pipe into the hole."

Hogan later would modify his plan, eliminating the funnel and the hole but retaining the flagsticks. Under the new Hogan plan, the player hitting closest to the flagstick wins—guess who would win that game? Hogan apparently viewed golf and putting as two different sports.

Fred Haas Jr. played on the tour during the Hogan era and had witnessed Hogan freezing over five or six putts inside six feet during a round in the 1953 Masters. Years later, in 1959, he told a reporter about offering Hogan some advice on his putting "I watched Hogan beat Fred Hawkins in a playoff at Colonial despite struggling on the greens. 'Ben, it looks like you're freezing over your putts,' I said when I encountered him afterward. 'Would you like a little observation?' 'I don't want to be remembered as a great putter,' he said. 'I want to be remembered as a great striker of the ball.'"

However, because Hogan prided himself more on his golf ball striking ability it, of course, didn't mean he didn't work to improve his putting or trying new putting techniques. Steve Cain, an assistant professional at Shady Oaks, recalled one Sunday afternoon when Hogan was casually observing a young boy out on the putting green. The boy, about eight or ten years old had his father's putter, which was much too long for him, so long in fact that the lad had it tucked up underneath his armpit to be able to stroke the ball. After watching the boy make several six-foot putts, Hogan mumbled something to himself and walked off. Two days later, Hogan showed up with a putter that he had up under his arm, testing the putting style that he had observed the young boy using. Hogan tried it for two or three days, and finding no success with the technique, quickly discarded it.

Hogan designed a very unique putter called the "Sinker." It had a curved hosel that went over top of the ball with two lines on it for easier alignment. Hogan seemed to putt very well with it; consequently, we sold a lot of them because Hogan was using it; however, when he played in the next tour event, he went back to the center-shafted blade putter he consistently used. He played well, was on national TV with his blade putter and Sinker sales plummeted.

Kris Tschetter, the LPGA pro who knew Hogan well, describes Hogan's old reliable putter this way, "During one of my putting slumps, I was in search of a different putter, and he [Hogan] said, 'Let me see what I've got.' He came out to the putting green with some of the ugliest putters I'd ever seen. I actually laughed when he handed one to me. 'I can't putt with that,' I said. 'It's terrible looking.'"

"'Yeah. It only won sixty-four tournaments. I don't know how you could make anything with it.' He loved sarcasm."

While I had never played golf with Hogan until a couple years after he had finished his competitive tournament career, I had attributed Hogan's putting woes to an indifference toward that part of his game. Watching videos of an earlier Hogan did not reveal the same jerky stroke or the hesitancy in his putting stroke that plagued him in his later years. Having played with Hogan half a dozen times or more and watching him his last two rounds in the 1970 Colonial, I had dismissed his putting to an erratic motion, one that at times was more of a jab than a stroke. His putting stroke was flatter than the putting strokes of other professional golfers or even the good local amateurs I played with, which caused his putter blade to open and close considerably more, which I thought contributed to his problem.

During the rounds of golf I played with Mr. Hogan, I particularly noted his comments regarding a ball in flight—that it would have to "go" or "get down" to land near the target. I was amazed that when someone else had struck the ball and had the advantage of "feeling" how well or how poorly he had hit it, but Hogan usually had such an accurate read on where the ball would land, distance-wise, relative to the flagstick. Consequently, I always thought Hogan had excellent eyesight and depth perception, certainly better than mine or the others in the group, and all of us were considerably younger than he. In surveying the tops of trees, some very distant, for even slight movement to analyze the wind and its possible effect on the flight of the ball it seemed Hogan was particularly meticulous, and particularly good. In turn, I believed he had superior eyesight that might have helped him to be extremely sensitive to even slight details.

Tom Stites, Hogan club designer for the Ben Hogan Company in the late 1980s, agrees. He surmised that Hogan was left-eye dominant and that fanning the toe open reduced any tendency for the wooden club head to look closed (hooked) from the perspective of his left eye. He felt that Hogan's eyesight was OK in his left eye, contrary to opinions expressed in some books and articles that indicated Hogan's sight in his left eye was impaired as a result of his auto accident.

Nevertheless, many people have attributed Hogan's putting problems to his eyesight. If Hogan did have an eye problem from his accident that affected his play, he never commented on it.

John Grace, an excellent putter who played many rounds of golf with Hogan in the 1970s and 1980s, noticed that Hogan, in his later years, stood farther from the ball and was using a putter with a flatter lie. Pictures from his younger days show a more upright Hogan with his feet closer to the ball and an almost vertical putter shaft. As he got older he was more bent over, farther away from the ball and using a putter with a flatter shaft angle. John thought Hogan could see the ball better when it was farther away from his body. Hogan told him, "I never could putt after the accident" and John felt Hogan gradually lost the vision in his left eye.

Curt Sampson in his 1996 book *Hogan* theorized that Hogan's putting woes were the inevitable result of his auto accident and that there was nothing he could do about it: "Hogan's depth perception had deteriorated….He wasn't losing his nerve, he was losing his eyesight."

Jody Vasquez, one of Hogan's ball shaggers, had a conversation with Valerie Hogan in 1994 that included Hogan's putting problems. She told Jody that Hogan couldn't see clearly out of his left eye, and that the eye problem was a result of the auto accident. The vision in his left eye deteriorated badly as time passed. She said that she pleaded with Ben to tell the press about his eye problem, but Ben would have none of that.

Ben Hogan did in fact have an eye problem, but it is unknown whether it was related to his auto accident or just getting older, since it developed later in his life. When I moved to Fort Worth in 1969, I needed an eye appointment to have my eyes checked, so I asked Hogan's secretary, Claribel Kelly, if she would recommend an eye doctor. I told her that I wore contact lenses and was very conscientious about my vision, and my eyes, and I wanted to go to the best eye doctor I could. After giving me Dr. Armstrong's name, she added this eye doctor "was very good. He had recently found a problem with Ben's eye that no other doctors could find." I asked what the problem was, and she said that she thought it was macular degeneration or something like that. I'd never heard of any such thing, so that was a good enough recommendation for me.

I went to Dr. Armstrong until he retired, and in 1999 and again in 2002, he noted that a possible problem might be developing in my eyes, but that at this point he said it was of no concern. I asked what the problem was that concerned him. He replied, "Macular degeneration." Recalling that strange name that I had only heard nearly 30 years previous, I made a mental note of it, and thought it quite ironic that Hogan's secretary would recommend a doctor to me because of the doctor's diagnosis of Mr. Hogan's eye condition that no other doctor could find, and nearly 30 years later that same doctor would tell me that I might be developing the exact same eye problem that he had diagnosed in Mr. Hogan.

He gave me a five-inch by seven-inch Amsler eye chart that consisted of intersecting vertical and horizontal lines, and asked me to periodically check my eyesight by covering one eye and staring at the center dot with the chart about 12-16 inches from my eye. Then, I was to cover the other eye and do the same thing. He told me that if I noticed that the lines started to look bent or curved instead of straight, the condition had gotten worse, and I would need immediate attention. He recommended a combination vitamin and mineral supplement that he said would help slow down, or possibly stave off further degeneration of the macula; however, still a little unsettled, I pursued with him how this macular degeneration would affect my vision if it were to become more serious. The doctor explained that it affects the central vision primarily regarding depth perception and the fine details. He explained that subtle differences in depth or direction would be more difficult to detect.

I had a hidden motive for asking about my condition, but I was uncomfortable about putting him in a situation of unknowingly providing information on Hogan's condition, which I'm sure that he knowingly would not do. So while his comments helped me to understand the problem better, I decided to research macular degeneration on my own.

I learned that macular degeneration is the most common cause of vision loss in the United States in those 50 or older, and its prevalence increases with age, that the central vision deteriorates. In the worst cases, it causes a complete loss of central vision, a dark spot, and makes reading or driving impossible. For others, it may only cause slight distortion. Fortunately, macular degeneration does not cause total blindness, since it does not affect peripheral vision. Genetics, age, nutrition, smoking, and sunlight exposure may all play a role. A first sign of macular degeneration may be a need for more light when doing close-up work. Another symptom is that the patient sees objects distorted. Straight lines may look bent.

Smoking should be avoided by people with macular degeneration and Ben Hogan was a long-time heavy smoker. Sunlight exposure is harmful too and sunglasses that have UV protection from ultraviolet rays should be worn. Hogan was in the sunlight a great

Ben Hogan looks back in disbelief after missing a short putt in '67 Masters. (A/P WORLDWIDE)

deal of time since he was 10 years old, and he rarely, if ever, wore sunglasses. So if details in Hogan's vision were diminished and straight lines may have looked bent, those subtle differences in depth, or direction, or fine details would be more difficult to detect—that's the essence of putting. Being able to see subtle differences in elevations, distinguishing between straight and bent lines and accurately judging distance is vital to read putts to determine both the break and speed. So Hogan's eyesight, if affected by macular degeneration, may indeed have impaired his vision and impacted his putting. However, whether or not his auto accident in 1949 contributed to the macular degeneration is an open question as it was a condition that was detected in the early to mid-1960s.

In March 2006, I bumped into Claribel Kelly's daughter, Colleen Sowden, at Mama's Pizza. After some brief chit chat, I told her I had just come from the eye doctor that her mother had recommended to me some 35 years ago. "Dr. Armstrong?" she asked. Obviously, Claribel's great respect for the doctor was not lost on her daughter.

Art Hall was the head golf professional at the Shady Oaks Country Club when I was a member there during my years at the Hogan Company. While it was an acknowledged fact that Hogan was a very poor putter, very few around the club chided him about it.

Art couldn't wait to tell me one particular putting story. One Saturday morning as our group was finishing our round, Hogan and Art were standing in the men's grill watching through the huge plate glass windows that overlook the ninth and eighteenth greens. As luck would have it, I missed a short, relatively easy putt of three feet or so. Hogan, shaking his head in disgust, turned to Art and matter of factly said, "You know, Scott is the worst damn putter in the club."

Without saying a word Art, who was still gazing out the window, turned toward Hogan. He lowered his head, and adjusted his eyeglasses lower on his nose, and as he peered over the top of his eyeglasses, he quizzically furrowed his eyebrows at Hogan. Almost immediately, Hogan, raising both hands as if caught in the cookie jar, blurted, "OK, OK, he's the second worst putter in the club."

Hogan's facial expression and throwing up his arms in quick admission of his own weakness was so funny that Art couldn't help himself, and he burst out laughing. Hogan did the same. Art said it was one of the best laughs he and Hogan had ever enjoyed together.

FOURTEEN:
BEN HOGAN'S
U.S. NATIONAL OPEN VICTORIES:
WHEN IS A NATIONAL OPEN NOT A
NATIONAL OPEN??

The U.S. Open and Ben Hogan were made for each other, most likely because Hogan's style of precision play matched the exactness Opens demanded from tee to green—the narrow fairways, high rough and firm, lightning-fast greens requiring shot making accuracy, and skilled course management. No other record over an extended period of time in professional golf is as profound as Ben Hogan's record of finishing in the top 10 every time he played in the U.S. Open from 1940–1960. He won the championship in 1948, 1950, 1951 and 1953. He lost four other times, in 1946, 1955, 1956 and 1960 in heartbreaking fashion.

After three-putting the 72nd hole from 18 feet to lose the 1946 U.S. National Open, Hogan won his first "officially recognized" U. S. National Open title in 1948 at Riviera Country Club in Los Angeles.

Eight months later, in February 1949, Hogan was nearly killed when his car was hit head on by a bus. With emergency surgeries to stop blood clots forming in his legs from reaching his lungs, Hogan was given little hope of ever walking again, let alone playing golf, so he was unable to even attempt to defend his title in the 1949 Open at Medina Country Club in Chicago.

In early 1950, less than a year after his accident, Hogan made his famous comeback to the PGA tour at the Los Angeles Open, played at Riviera Country Club, the site of his 1948 U.S. Open victory. He played well, but lost in a playoff to Sam Snead.

Six-months later he entered the 1950 U. S. Open at Merion Golf Club in Ardmore, Pennsylvania, just outside Philadelphia. Until the U. S. Open format was changed in 1965, the Open format called for 36 holes on Saturday, the final day of play. After his accident, playing and walking 36 holes on any day of play was a major obstacle for Ben

Hogan. This was particularly true in the 1950 National Open, about a year after Hogan had to have the main veins in his legs tied off to prevent blood clots from reaching his heart and lungs, which would have killed him. After the operation he had to wear elastic hose from his toes to his waist every round he played, to reduce the pain and swelling in his legs. Following just an 18-hole round Hogan had to soak his legs, so there was serious doubt that Hogan could even complete the Open's final-day, 36-hole grind, let alone come from behind to win.

Hogan trailed by two shots going into the final day, but after 27 holes that day he was in the lead, with nine holes to play. His legs, however, were giving him severe pain, and almost every step had become agony. They were stiff, most likely from the swelling, to the point that Cary Middlecoff, his playing partner for the final 36 holes, had to repeatedly remove Hogan's ball from the hole, and Hogan's caddie had to tee up his ball for him. While his legs seemed to buckle under him as he trudged step-by-step to start through the final nine holes, Hogan's golf swing nonetheless remained intact. Although he was withstanding the pain that grew with each step and he continued to be able to repeat his golf swing with precision, his being able to continue through the final nine holes started to come into question. Hogan years later would admit that his legs felt like they were turning to stone.

Hogan's legs went into spasm several times as he started the final nine holes. At the 12th hole his legs went into severe muscle spasm after he hit his tee shot, and he staggered and nearly fell, having possibly slipped on some new sod inserted in a shady area at the tee. Playing partner Cary Middlecoff thought he was going to collapse. Hogan looked finished, but he continued on. Amazingly, his approach shot was close, only 12 feet above the hole, but Hogan 3-putted the very slick green for bogey, reducing his lead to two stokes. He couldn't even bend over to get his ball out of the hole.

Walking to the par-3 13th tee, his legs again began to spasm, and when they reached the tee, his caddie had to tee up his ball for him. He hit a miraculous tee shot to within 12 feet of the hole, and managed to 2-putt for par. Heading to the 14th tee his legs again began to spasm, and Hogan told his caddie to take his clubs back to the clubhouse, because he couldn't go any further. Amazingly (and fortuitously) his caddie responded, "No, Mr. Hogan. You can't quit. I don't work for quitters. I'll see you at the 14th tee, sir." [While this exchange has been attributed to Merion lore, Merion historian John Capers III confirmed the story during a conversation with Ben Hogan many years later.]

Of the tough final five holes, only on the lengthy par 4's at fourteen and eighteen had Hogan managed to par in all of his three previous rounds. On the treacherous 395 yard, dogleg right, par-4 fifteenth, that had an out of bounds 225 yards straight away, he had twice bogeyed it, and he had one bogey on both the 16th and 17th holes. Needing four pars and a bogey on these difficult final five holes presented severe tests for anyone, let alone a man struggling to play on stiff, painful legs. Now that they were frequently going into a spasm, such that that Hogan, himself, started to doubt that he could even finish the round, as his physical condition presented a monumental hurdle for Ben Hogan to overcome.

He parred the 14th hole, then missed a short 30-inch par putt on the 15th and made bogey. At that point Hogan held a slim one-stroke lead, but needed three pars on, arguably at that time, the three toughest finishing holes in golf—sixteen, seventeen, and eighteen at Merion. After parring the 16th he hit his tee shot on the 230-yard par 3 17th into the bunker left of the green. He blasted his sand shot to six feet of the cup, and his putt rolled true, on-line right to the cup, but stopped on the front lip. Hogan had now bogied three of his last six holes. He reached the tee of the long difficult uphill 458-yard par-4, 18th, needing a par to tie. He had been on the course for six hours and had walked nearly nine miles to get to this point. He was totally spent and in agonizing pain, a pathetic looking figure as he limped along to the final hole.

Yet, on the eighteen, which required a blind tee shot over a quarry, Hogan hit a perfect drive, to the flat spot at the top of the hill rather than driving further and having a downhill lie. Knowing he needed a birdie to win and a par to tie, he deliberated over his options. He had played a Tuesday practice round with Merion member, and local attorney, Francis Sullivan, (more on him in a later chapter) and after hitting his 1-iron shot to the 18th green that day, Hogan hit a second ball using his 4-wood. After hitting the two shots he thought the 4-wood was the right club. Now, with the tournament on the line and after deliberating over the conditions, lie of his ball, position of the flag in the back right part of the green, and noting it waving, indicating a light breeze back there, he mulled over his choices. [The 1950 U.S. Open was the only USGA tournament not to use the famous Merion teardrop-shaped wicker baskets atop the flag sticks.] Going over the green would most likely have resulted in a bogey, whereas a well positioned 1-iron, avoiding the trap on the front right of the green would most assuredly result in a par to tie, and possibly a birdie to win outright. He selected his 1-iron. He then hit one of the most, if not the most, recognizable shots in all of golf—his famous 1-iron to Merion's 18th green, captured on film by *Life* magazine photographer, Hy Peskin (*See NOTE under the "1-iron" photo on page 266). The ball came to rest approximately 40 feet short and left of the flag. While he was safely on in two strokes, giving him two putts to tie, Hogan wasn't satisfied with the shot, as he wanted it 25 feet closer to the hole. He left his first putt a lengthy 4-feet from the hole, and in very uncharacteristic fashion, in about half the time he normally took for his putts, he quickly stroked his second putt. The ball tumbled into the cup for par to tie George Fazio and Lloyd Mangrum, and forcing a 3-way eighteen-hole playoff the following day.

When asked later why he hadn't taken more time on the all-important second putt that he needed to tie Fazio and Mangrum, Hogan said that his legs were aching so badly that he just wanted to get it over and sit down. Acting as host, Francis Sullivan who lived at the Barclay Hotel, drove the Hogans to and from the tournament. On the way back to the hotel the pain in Hogan's legs was so severe it caused him to become sick to his stomach, and after having Sullivan pull the car over to the side of the road, he threw up beside the car.

Back at the hotel he soaked his legs in hot water and Epsom salt to ease the pain and reduce the swelling. His physical condition following his 36-hole round raised the question whether or not Hogan would even be able to answer the starting bell for the 18-hole playoff, but after a good night's sleep, Hogan was rested and ready to play.

The playoff round was a seesaw match: on only 4 of the 18 holes did all three players have the same score. After nine holes Hogan and Mangrum were tied at par, with Fazio 1 stroke behind. Hogan steadily made pars throughout the back nine, and

Ben Hogan's famous 1-iron shot to the 18th green in the final regulation round of the 1950 U.S. Open at Merion Golf Club. (ADRIANA REYNOLDS-PESKIN)

*NOTE: While public information throughout the years has called this Hogan's famous 1-iron shot, others, have said otherwise. Even Ben Hogan in his 1957 book, *Five Lessons: The Modern Fundamentals of Golf*, said on page 13, "I went with a 2-iron…"

Ben Hogan hitting to the 18th green in the playoff round of the 1950 U.S. Open at Merion Golf Club - the day following the shot in the photo on the left hand page. (PHOTO COURTESY OF MERION GOLF CLUB)

through fifteen holes Hogan held a 1-stroke lead over Mangrum and was three strokes ahead of Fazio; however, on the par-4 16th hole Mangrum was about to putt his ball for his par when he noticed a bug on his golf ball. He instinctively marked and lifted the ball to blow the bug off. Mangrum was assessed a two-stroke penalty, resulting in a double bogey six, because he had previously marked his ball on that hole. Marking it a second time was against the rules. The double bogey put Mangrum 3 shots behind Hogan after 16 holes, but left him one shot ahead of Fazio. Hogan then birdied the par-3 17th hole and parred the difficult par-4 18th hole for a total of 69, to beat Mangrum by 4 and Fazio by 6.

Following Ben Hogan's 1950 U.S. Open victory at Merion Golf Club, famous sportswriter Red Smith, in his Monday, June 12, 1950 *New York Herald-Tribune* "View of Sport" column, wrote about Hogan:

> "To say there never has been another achievement in competitive sport comparable to Ben Hogan's victory in the National Open golf championship is not mere understatement; it is practically an insult to language. We shall not live to see anything like it again.
>
> When Ben Hogan talked to the press after the title playoff at the Merion Golf Club outside Philadelphia, he asked the newspaper men to play down the references to the automobile accident that destroyed everything save his life and his will sixteen months ago… He thought the tale of what happened in those four days at Merion should be written simply as a golf story. He did not see that it is something immeasurably bigger than that—the story of a man.
>
> Sporting literature is studded with stories of men who succeeded in spite of great physical handicaps. But what Hogan accomplished was not merely a physical victory but a demonstration of extraordinary recuperative powers. Maybe once in the lifetime of any of us it is possible to see… "a spiritual victory, an absolute triumph of the will!" This is that one time.
>
> Ben Hogan was always tough… To get his first job on a golf course, he had to whip the best scrapper among the caddies. To make his way on the tournament circuit, he had to whip bad luck and failure, and his own temper

and comparative poverty...

By mastering every stroke in the game, he became the most nearly perfect golfer of his time; by mastering himself, the most nearly perfect competitor.

Then a bus smashed his car and him to pieces. There was doubt that he could live, but he lived. It was questionable whether he would walk again. As for playing golf, well... Ben's bones were shattered, muscles torn, nerves ripped.

Before he could learn to walk again, he had to stand. After the months of doctoring, there were months of daily massage, hour upon hour. Then he took a step. Then he walked around the room. Then around the block. Standing in his room, he jogged, up and down, up and down, up and down, clenching and relaxing his fingers with a rubber ball in each fist, rebuilding every muscle, commanding every nerve...

Merion is an exacting, constricted course whose par 70 defeated splendid golfers like Sam Snead and Jimmy Demaret and Cary Middlecoff. Congested as it was during the Open... it was a difficult place to merely to get around. Healthy spectators came back bushed after walking eighteen holes in the punishing sun.

Hogan played eighteen holes on Thursday, eighteen on Friday, thirty-six on Saturday—the first double round he had attempted in two years—and eighteen on Sunday.

He is a golfer who knows exactly what he can do with every club in his bag in every circumstance. That is why he asked the press to play down his injuries. He dislikes to be pictured as a handicapped golfer because he feels, rightly, that he still has all the strokes. The only thing he wasn't sure he had was the stamina, and on Saturday he showed himself that he did..."

Smith concluded his column, "Watching, one thought of the war-time slogan of the Seabees: 'The impossible takes a little longer.' It took Ben Hogan sixteen months."

In 1951 the U.S. Open was played on the extremely difficult Oakland Hills Country Club golf course in Birmingham, Michigan. The course was substantially toughened for the event. Fairway bunkers were repositioned to the landing areas of the pros' tee shots, protective bunkers were added in front of the greens and the fairways narrowed to 22-24 yards wide. The rough was grown to 6-8 inches high, but in actuality in some areas was 12-14 inches high. The course was duly dubbed "the monster."

"The course was so difficult that the golfers were howling and complaining in a way they haven't at any Open since," noted sportswriter/author Dan Jenkins. He also joked that with the golfers giving so many one-line quotes, "More than one golf writer thought he had died and gone to Quote Heaven."

Jenkins wrote that Cary Middlecoff said, "You have to walk down these fairways single file."

He noted that Sam Snead complained, "I thought I was going to a golf tournament, not on a safari."

Jenkins even quoted Hogan as saying, "If I had to play this course for a living every week, I'd get into another business."

Only 2 players finished below 290 (10 over par) for the tournament, and the average score for the week was 77.23. There were only 2 sub-par rounds shot during the entire tournament—Clayton Heafner's closing one-under round of 69 and Hogan's final three-under 67 for a 287 total, beating Heafner by two shots. When asked about his 67 Hogan reportedly replied, "Under the circumstances I think it was the greatest round I have ever played. I didn't think I could do it." At the trophy presentation he uttered the often quoted line, "I'm glad I brought this monster to its knees."

In 1953 Pittsburgh's Oakmont Country Club hosted the U.S. Open. Oakmont was one of Hogan's favorite courses, requiring precise accuracy and excellent course management. The course had 250 sand traps, including pot bunker type traps like those on Scottish courses. Designer Henry Fownes felt a poorly played shot should be penalized, so he made it very difficult to get out of the Oakmont traps. They were dragged with special rakes to gouge furrows in the sand perpendicular to the fairway to make it almost impossible to get out unless the golfer blasted out, and thus sacrificed a stroke.

The USGA tried an unusual format in 1953 to reduce the number of sectional qualifying locations. Only the defending champion, Julius Boros, received an exemption so Hogan, the 1948, 1950 and 1951 champion, had to qualify for the tournament. (The format was so disliked that it was eliminated the following year and never used again.)

Hogan easily qualified.

After shooting 67 in the opening round of the tournament, Hogan led after every round and won by six strokes. Later that year when he won the British Open at Carnoustie, Hogan became the first man to win both the British and U.S. Opens in the same year since Gene Sarazen did it in 1932. Hogan is the first and only man ever to win the Masters, the U.S. Open and the British Open in the same year—a record that still stands 60 years later.

In the 1954 Open at Baltusrol Golf Club in Springfield, New Jersey, Hogan finished tied for sixth, his putter failing him in the third round.

Hogan's next great opportunity to win the Open was in 1955 at the Olympic Club in San Francisco, and this looked to be Hogan's crowning moment, his 5th (officially) U.S. National Open victory. Hogan finished the 72 holes at 287, and appeared to have won. The TV coverage went off the air announcing Hogan as the winner, and Hogan handed his golf ball to USGA Executive Director Joe Dey for the USGA's Golf House museum.

However, an obscure golfer by the name of Jack Fleck was out on the course only two strokes behind Hogan. Fleck managed to birdie the par-3 15th hole and canned an 8-footer for a birdie three on the difficult 18th hole to tie Hogan. The following day he shot 69 to win the 18-hole playoff beating Hogan by three strokes.

Fleck felt that God had played a definite part in his victory, stating that on the morning of the final 36 holes, "I was shaving, and suddenly a voice came out of the glass, clear as a bell. 'Jack, you are going to win the Open,' Fleck recalled. "At first I thought I'd imagined it, or maybe somebody was in the room with me. I looked around then went back to shaving. By golly, if it didn't come a second time—straight out of the mirror. Clear as day, 'Jack, you're going to win the Open!' I had goose bumps on me, as if electricity was going through my body."

On the final round, Shelley Mayfield was in the group right in front of Jack Fleck. According to Shelley, "Fleck played horrendous. Numerous times he hit the ball out of the fairway into the thick, deep rough. His ball apparently ended up on the portion of rough beaten down by the walking of the gallery. He was in trouble numerous times. Shelley, in describing that final day to me, looked heavenward and said, "Sometimes the Man Upstairs just says you will or you won't win." I guess Shelley agreed with Fleck about the '55 Open.

Shelley did mention that Hogan told him that early in the playoff round Fleck had missed the green by quite a distance and that he [Hogan] was fairly close to the flag. Fleck pitched onto the green but was still away, and that moving the gallery for Fleck had caused a delay. On his way to his ball, as he passed by Hogan, Fleck apologized for causing the delay, to which Hogan replied that it was okay, not to worry about it. Hogan told Shelley that his friendly comment, rather than keeping his focused game face or stare, probably relaxed Fleck somewhat and had eliminated an edge that he usually had in such unsettling circumstances.

Amazingly, Hogan had brought Fleck some Ben Hogan golf clubs, made in Hogan's new Fort Worth factory, to the tournament for Fleck. Apparently, Fleck was breaking in those new Hogan clubs during his practice rounds at the Olympic Club.

During a 1983 TV interview Ken Venturi and Hogan discussed the founding of the Ben Hogan Company and Venturi commented that in the 1955 U.S. Open there were two players using Hogan clubs—Ben Hogan and Jack Fleck, the man who beat Hogan in a playoff. Fleck had picked up a set of Hogan clubs earlier that year in Fort Worth during the Colonial. His wedges weren't finished. Hogan commented, "He (Fleck) knew I was coming out to play in the tournament, and he was going to play there, and he asked me if I would make him a pitching club and a sand club, which I did, and I took them out there in my bag and gave them to him before the tournament." Then with a smile, Hogan added, "And ah, apparently that was a mistake."

In the 1956 Open at Oak Hill Country Club in Rochester, New York, Hogan was one stroke behind leader Cary Middlecoff after 54 holes. Hogan was in serious contention until he missed a 30-inch putt for par on the 71st hole. Hogan then missed his birdie attempt on the final hole, and finished one stroke behind the winner, Middlecoff. Limping off the green the disappointed Hogan commented, "I missed three short putts on my last round. You shouldn't win when you miss like that."

Hogan's final opportunity to win his 5th official Open title came at Cherry Hills in 1960. Hogan's 142 total after 36 holes was identical to that of a young, 20-year old amateur named Jack Nicklaus, and the two were paired together on Saturday for the final 36 holes.

In his book, *The Greatest Game of All*, Nicklaus described that day, particularly the final nine holes of the last round. He wrote:

"Some golfers I knew had previously told me that Hogan was hard to play with. He was cold, they said, and he concentrated so explicitly on his own game that he was hardly aware that anyone else was on the course. This, I discovered early in the day, was absolutely wrong. Ben couldn't have been pleasanter to play with. He didn't talk a great deal, but whenever I produced a better than average stroke, he'd say, 'Good shot,' and in a way that you knew he meant it. In a word, he treated me like a fellow competitor, and I liked that. I don't go for the effusive types who are always passing out compliments as if they're going out of style. Ben is also extremely courteous in observing all the little things that add up to golf etiquette, such as standing well outside the rim of your peripheral vision on the tee and the green when it's your shot. The gallery doesn't notice these subtleties, but a golfer certainly does. Not only did I find him friendly and considerate, but, more than this, I have never been partnered in a championship with a man who was in a contending position, as Ben was at Cherry Hills, who was more enjoyable to play with... I was glad I was playing with Hogan. It gives you a firm sense of reality when you look across the fairway and see his familiar figure walking to his ball as you walk to yours."

After Hogan made a birdie at the twelfth hole on the final 18, Nicklaus, noted, "He now had a definite chance to win the record-breaking fifth Open he had been seeking since 1953."

After missing a ten-foot putt for birdie on the 16th (70th) hole, Hogan approached the 71st hole tied for the lead, having hit all 34 straight greens in regulation and having made only two putts of ten feet or more, both in the afternoon round. Hogan arrived at his third shot at 17 with a major decision. Hogan believed (incorrectly) that several pros were tied with him for the lead, so he figured he needed a birdie 4 on the par 5

17th hole and a par on the demanding uphill 468-yard, par 4 18th hole for a 279 total to win the championship outright. His analysis was correct, but, had he finished with two pars for a 280 total, there most likely would have been a playoff, as that was Arnold Palmer's winning score. After playing and walking 36 holes on the final day, Hogan, almost 48 years old, would not have wanted an 18-hole playoff the following day. His legs could barely stand it.

The green on the par-5 17th at Cherry Hills is an island green, totally surrounded by water, and the pin that day was cut dangerously close to the water fronting the green. The green sloped treacherously from back to front, in a semi two-tier fashion, so Hogan decided to go for the flag cut on the lower level front part of the green. Hogan had a good tight lie, so he laid open his wedge and hit a low-flying shot loaded with backspin. Nicklaus thought it was going to be perfect, that the ball would just clear the water and bounce up near the flag, but the ball hit barely short of the green and took the backspin into the water. A few inches more and it would have hit the putting surface and hopped up near the flag, most likely coming to a dead stop at or right below the hole. Hogan took off his shoe and hit the almost totally submerged ball out of the water. While he played the trouble shot well, he missed the putt for par, made a bogey and the tournament for him was over. Totally deflated, according to Nicklaus, "He was completely drained of drive, energy, concentration. It was all he could do to finish the round."

However, during the Hogan-Palmer drama Nicklaus had 3 putted 8 times, 3 times in the last 5 holes of the tournament to finish two strokes behind Palmer. This caused Hogan to remark to reporters who were trying to console him, "Don't feel sorry for me. I played with a kid today who could have won this Open by 10 shots if he'd known how." But Hogan's 1960 attempt to win the Open was a particularly bitter disappointment for him.

In fact, Hogan singled out a single shot in the 1955 and 1960 U.S. Opens that were his greatest disappointments in competitive golf. The first was his drive on 18th tee at the Olympic Club in San Francisco, in the 1955 playoff with Jack Fleck: "When I walked up on the tee, I could see that it had not been watered. I should have worked my feet into the soil just like you do in a sand trap to anchor my right foot. But I didn't." Hogan's right foot slipped, causing him to hook the tee shot and leaving his ball buried in Olympic's deep rough, an almost unplayable lie.

The other was his third shot on the 17th hole at Cherry Hills in Denver: "I laid up to the lake with a four-iron and had the most beautiful lie you could have. The way I was putting, I knew I had to get within two feet, or I couldn't possibly make it. I played what I thought was a good shot, but it hit on the edge of the green and then was drawn back into the water by the backspin. It was hit exactly as I intended, but I just misjudged the shot."

In his desire to be the best, Hogan wanted that fifth "officially recognized" U.S. Open title to set himself totally apart from the two other four-time winners, Willie Anderson and Bob Jones, (and later Jack Nicklaus, who would also win 4). I use the term "officially recognized" because there are those, including Hogan himself, who argued that he won five U. S. Opens. The fifth was also his first—the 1942 Hale America National Open at Ridgmoor Country Club in Chicago.

Claribel Kelly, Ben Hogan's secretary, called me to Mr. Hogan's office one day to help her and Mr. Hogan look up some information. The three of us were searching through some old papers and came across a listing of Hogan's tournament victories that Claribel had apparently put together some time earlier.

She came to the 1942 entry for the Hale America Open and paused. Then, disdainfully, she said, "M'sta Hogan really won 5 U.S. Opens because the Hale America was the U.S. Open of 1942. The event was sponsored by the USGA (United States Golf Association, the ruling body for the U.S. Open), the USGA ran the tournament and they played by USGA rules. They counted Byron's [Nelson] Masters win and Sam's [Snead] PGA victory, but they never did give M'sta Hogan credit for that U.S. Open. They all played in it, and the USGA ran it. So, it shoulda' counted as an Open win, if they're going to count Nelson's and Snead's wins as majors."

Hogan grumbled his agreement: "The competition was as strong as any other Open, and they did count Sam's PGA and Byron's Masters as major wins. And the head of the USGA presented me with exactly the same medal as my four other U.S. Open medals.

Oh, the hell with 'em."

Some who say Hogan's '42 Hale America National Open shouldn't count as an official U.S. Open major championship have used as a major argument that there was only one major championship awarded in 1942-- the Masters, which Byron Nelson won. They're wrong. Sam Snead was credited with the PGA Championship he won in 1942 at Seaview Country Club in Atlantic City, and it qualified as a major.

In fact, in the history of the three current U.S. "major" championships—the Masters, PGA, and U.S. Open, only one year did two of them crown a champion while the third did not—1942, and never since the Masters tournament began in 1934 has a Masters champion been crowned that a U.S. Open champ was not also awarded (officially) the title that year—except in 1942.

Renowned golf writers Dan Jenkins and Charles Price both wrote convincingly that Hogan won five Opens.

According to Jenkins:

"Well, look. Hogan has these five gold medals, see? They still highlight the Ben Hogan Trophy Room at Colonial [Country Club], and all five medals look exactly the same, like the kind of medal they give you when you win a U.S. Open championship. I say a man who owns five gold medals for winning U.S. Opens has won five U.S. Opens....

It seems that a record 1,540 golfers entered local qualifying at sixty-nine sites around the country.... I ask you: What were they doing holding nationwide qualifying tournaments if there wasn't going to be something similar to a U.S. Open at Ridgemoor Country Club in mid-June of '42?....

Here's a paragraph from the Associated Press report of the opening rounds—'There was a furor of excitement in the locker rooms when officials of the United States Golf Association ruled the irons of Sam Byrd of Ardmore, Pa., were too deeply scored, and he could not use them.'

I ask you this: What was the USGA doing inspecting grooves—or ruling on anything else—if this was not a U.S. Open?

The lead on the AP report of June 22, 1942, reads: 'Chicago, June 21 – Tiny

Ben Hogan, never before a winner in a major golf tournament, crashed to a dramatic victory in the Hale America National Open Sunday with a 72-hole score of 271, 17 under par for the distance.'"

Charles Price was even stronger about Hogan's 5th Open in an article he wrote in the November 1975 issue of *Golf* magazine entitled "The Hawk"—

"Speaking of Bob Jones, it has been said that only he, Willie Anderson and Ben [Hogan] have won four National Opens. This is a lie. Ben has won five. Even the USGA, if pressed, would have to admit this." [Since Price's article, Jack Nicklaus has joined the group with four Open victories.]

To get the story straight, Ben played in a USGA-sponsored tournament back in 1942 called, even in the USGA's record books, the 'Hale America National Open Golf Tournament.' Now if that isn't a National Open, I'll kiss Totten P. Heffelfinger's foot…. But the USGA that year, in kind of corporate salute to the war effort, decided to call off the official National Open until the war ended, which turned out to be four years later…. In the meantime, the USGA decided to hold an unofficial National Open for the benefit of the Navy Relief Society and the United Service Organizations at Ridgmoor CC, near Chicago…

To make sure the USGA knows its own record books, the National Open at Ridgmoor in Chicago had 1540 entries, 107 qualifiers and 96 starters, mainly because some of them couldn't scratch up the money to get there… qualifying rounds were held at 69 locations…

The quality of the field entered the tournament, yet only one man managed to break 70 for four straight rounds— Jimmy Demaret. Hogan finished with a 69 and a 68 to win by three strokes—over Demaret."

Price reiterated his above comments contending that Hogan had won five U.S. Opens in his October 1981 *Golf* magazine column "Memories of Ben Hogan." He concluded his argument, "… some people, including Hogan himself, believe he actually won a record five U.S. Opens, the uncounted fifth having been the Hale America Open… and [he was awarded] the standard USGA medal awarded to every winner, but

(CX9) CHICAGO,JUNE 21--HOGAN'S FIRST MAJOR TITLE-BEN HOGAN, HERSHEY,PA. GETS HIS FIRST MAJOR CHAMPIONSHIP MEDAL TODAY FROM THIS TRIO OF GOLF OFFICIALS AFTER HE CONTINUED HIS SENSATIONAL SUB PAR GOLF TO POST A 68 FOR A 72-HOLE TOTAL OF 271 TO WIN THE HALE AMERICA OPEN AT RIDGEMOOR.LEFT TO RIGHT: ED DUDLEY, PGA PRESIDENT; GEORGE BLOSSOM, PRESIDENT UNITED STATES GOLF ASSOCIATION; HOGAN, AND TOM MCMAHON, HEAD CHICAGO DISTRICT GOLF ASSOCIATION.(AP WIREPHOTO)(T11950STF-CEL)1942 (A/P Worldwide)

was a tournament that the USGA, in keeping with the nation's war attitude, chose not to deem a championship. So there you have Ben Hogan's golf game and his championship record—Fred Astaire dressed in short pants."

The *U.S. Open Almanac* of 1995 in its Ben Hogan write up of past champions includes this about the 1942 controversy –

"The Open that year [1942] was cancelled, but the USGA, along with the PGA and the Chicago District Golf Association, decided to stage a tournament anyway, with the proceeds going to the Navy Relief Society and the USO. It was called the Hale America National Open and was held at the Ridgemoor C.C. in Chicago. The tournament drew a strong field, including the long-retired Bobby Jones..."

Golf fans who believe Hogan was unfairly denied credit for a fifth U.S. Open have some intriguing evidence to support their plea. The field was stellar. Hogan was presented a medal for winning the event that looks just like his four U.S. Open medals. The USGA includes the Hale America in the U.S. Open results section of its record book, wedged between the results of the 1941 and 1946 Opens. (The USGA did not, meanwhile, place the results of the Red Cross tournament that was played in 1917 in the Open record books.)"

Even the by-line under the photo of Hogan receiving the medal reads—

(CX9) CHICAGO, JUNE 21--HOGAN'S FIRST MAJOR TITLE-BEN HOGAN, HERSHEY, PA. GETS HIS FIRST MAJOR CHAMPIONSHIP MEDAL TODAY FROM THIS TRIO OF GOLF OFFICIALS AFTER HE CONTINUED HIS SENSATIONAL SUB PAR GOLF TO POST A 68 FOR A 72-HOLE TOTAL OF 271 TO WIN THE HALE AMERICA OPEN AT RIDGEMOOR. LEFT TO RIGHT: ED DUDLEY, PGA PRESIDENT; GEORGE BLOSSOM, PRESIDENT UNITED STATES GOLF ASSOCIATION; HOGAN, AND TOM MCMAHON, HEAD CHICAGO DISTRICT GOLF ASSOCIATION.(AP WIREPHOTO)(T11950STF-CEL)1942 (A/P Worldwide)

Ben Hogan was never a whiner, but he was definitely miffed that the USGA, despite listing the 1942 event in its record books, did not officially recognize his fifth U.S. Open victory. There wasn't any doubt in Ben Hogan's mind that he had won five U.S. Open titles. During his 1983 CBS-TV interview Ken Venturi remarked that Hogan had nearly won his 5th Open medal in 1955, 1956, 1959 and 1960. Hogan responded, "I already have 5 medals, and the president of the USGA has presented each one of them to me. That was the Hale America National Open in Chicago-- it was 1942, I went in to the service in 1943. I played the last 36 holes with Bobby Jones, and I won the tournament. Jimmy Demaret was second, and, ah, Mr. Tufts, Dick Tufts was President of the USGA. [It was actually George Blossom.] He presented me with this medal for winning this tournament, and it's identical to the other four."

Venturi responded, "Then we'd have to call it number five, wouldn't we?"

Hogan added, "Well, Joe Dey does." [Joe Dey was the Executive Director of the USGA (United States Golf Association) from 1935 to 1968—long enough to have an excellent perspective regarding the status of the 1942 "National Open."]

The USGA even helped make the case for Hogan following his victory in the 1953 British Open at Carnoustie. The organization honored Hogan on his triumphal return with a dinner on July 23rd of that year at the Park Lane Hotel in New York City. The dinner program included the menu for the evening, and, on the page opposite, a list of the following Hogan victories:

USGA Open Champion 1948-50-51-53

British Open Champion 1953

Professional Golfers Association of America Champion 1946-48

Hale America National Open Tournament Winner 1942

Masters Tournament Winner 1951-53

It is indeed curious that the Hale America was listed as a "National Open," was not asterisked, and was not qualified with words such as "he also won…." No, the Hale America National Open Tournament was listed right there with only Hogan's major titles—the Masters, PGA, U.S. Open and British Open. Why would the USGA list the Hale America National Open on their own dinner program with only Ben Hogan's other *major* victories if it, the USGA, who called it a *National* Open (isn't that what the U.S. National Open is?), didn't consider it a major title? If the USGA included the *Hale America "National Open"* as a major victory, why hasn't it recognized Hogan's *Hale America National Open* win as his fifth *United States Open* victory? A National

Open that isn't a National Open?

Let's follow this logic. The only professional golf tournament the USGA runs is the U.S. National Open—the USGA ran the 1942 Hale America National Open, but it wasn't a National Open? The Hale America National Open was listed by the USGA as a major championship in their program, but it's not a major championship? Hogan has five identical medals but only four count? With that kind of logic the USGA must be part of the US Senate!

Regardless, the U.S. Open was Ben Hogan's calling card:

23 - Events played in—including the 1942 Hale America National Open

16 - Top 10 finishes (70%)

9 - Top 3 finishes (39%)

5 - Victories (including the 1942 Hale America National) (22%)

1940-1956 – Finished no lower than 6th

1940-1960 – Finished no lower than 10th

1948, 1950, 1951 Won 3 consecutive Opens he played in. (1949-Auto accident)

1948 - 1953 Won 4 of the 5 Opens he played in (Finished 3rd in 1952)

Claribel Kelly's separate stat sheet also has the typed notation "From 1940 through 1960, he was never out of the top ten in the U.S. Open. He was Masters runner-up four times and was never worse than seventh from 1941 through 1956." (It might be noted here that the PGA Championship was a match play tournament until 1958, so from 1948, the 2nd time he won the PGA, until 1958, past his prime, Hogan never participated in the PGA Championship because his damaged legs could not endure the grueling match play format.)

But Hogan never let his disappointment deter his participation for the benefit of golf or the USGA. In 1952 and 1954, as the defending U.S. Open Champion, Hogan challenged amateur golfers in a TV commercial to play against him in the National Golf Day event, designated "Beat Ben Hogan Day." If he held any animosity about the 1942 Hale America not being considered an official U.S. Open, he never let it interfere with his relationship with, or support of, the USGA.

Ben Hogan reveals his Secret in the August 8, 1955 issue of Life magazine. (GETTY IMAGES)

FIFTEEN:
HOGAN'S SECRET

MYTH: *Ben Hogan had knowledge of a special little tidbit of information, a "secret," that was the key to playing par or better golf. All anyone needed was Hogan's one little secret, and he or she could learn to consistently play par golf or better. It was golf's equivalent to the pot of gold at the end of the rainbow.*

MAN: Ben Hogan had vast knowledge regarding the golf swing and other important periphery knowledge that set him apart from other golfers. It was as much Hogan's mental acuity and skills as it was his swing technique that helped to set him apart. And together with his scientific approach to the game to continuously and consistently find improvements, Hogan developed the extraordinary skills to become the best ball striker ever to play the game.

Not to include some of the opinions and stories about Ben Hogan's golf swing and his contribution to the development of the golf swing would be leaving out a major aspect of the man.

Ben Hogan did not have the natural, fluid, graceful swing of Sam Snead or the natural power generated by men of larger build. He was 5' 7" or 5'8" and weighed only about 135–140 pounds when he played, so he developed a very strong, fast, powerful swing that generated as much power as he could muster. He ripped at the ball. Snead, in fact, said he couldn't watch Hogan because Hogan swung so hard that he was afraid it would upset his own smooth, rhythmical swing.

Hogan had to arduously work to develop his swing. His philosophy regarding the secret to the golf swing was that the answers were "in the dirt," meaning on the practice tee. He invented practice as the modern tournament professionals know it today. In his process of practicing Hogan was also experimenting with new techniques, new approaches and theories to find the answers on how to develop the perfect golf swing.

In 1946, Hogan felt he was at a crossroads in his career. His game wasn't up to his standards, and he hadn't won an official major tournament. He believed that he couldn't continue the way he was going and reach the level of success he sought. He was winning money and occasionally a tournament, but that was not good enough for Ben Hogan—he wanted to be the best.

To this point, Hogan's nemesis to a more successful career had been his tendency to hook the ball. He had tried all the conventional cures to eliminate the hook, but they all cut down on his distance by five to ten yards. Hogan wanted every competitive advantage, and being shorter off the tee wasn't one of them, giving up five yards was a big deal for Hogan, and giving up ten was out of the question. Hogan declared, "I was having trouble getting the ball in the air. I had a low, ducking, agonizing hook, the kind you can hang a coat on. When it caught the rough it was the terror of the field mice. I tried all the conventional cures—opening the stance, altering the grip, using more left arm, and cutting the ball. They all worked, but in the process they cut down my distance by five to ten yards. Five yards is a long way. You can't give anybody five yards. You can't correct a fault with a fault." Just eliminating the hook wasn't good enough, he couldn't lose distance, and he needed to be able to land the ball more softly.

Nobel laureate in Medicine/Physiology, Albert Szent-Gyorgyi defined *research* as "to see what everybody else has seen, and to think what nobody else has thought," and *discovery* as "seeing what everyone has seen but understanding it for the first time." Hogan was bent on discovering the perfect golf swing to make the ball do exactly what he wanted it to do. Because he felt his career depended upon it, he was determined enough to research it through: to practice and experiment until he found the answers to the questions that his inquisitive mind kept asking, and his desired level of success kept demanding. Hogan's scientific mindset and his determination to be the best, combined with his will to see it through no matter the cost or difficulties, put him on a lifelong quest for the perfect swing.

Hogan refused to believe that his problem of hooking the ball in his early years on tour couldn't be overcome without compromising his performance-- that he didn't have to "correct a fault with a fault." He believed there was a solution without a loss of yardage.

He also wanted his shots to land more softly, so he had more control over where the ball finally came to rest. Consequently, in 1946 he took time off the tour to find the answers.

When he returned with his new solution, which eliminated the hook with no loss of distance, so slight and obscure were the changes to his swing that while competitors noticed the difference in Hogan's performance, they couldn't pinpoint the change in his swing. And if the technique could help him win tournaments, he wasn't about to share it, so he didn't tell anyone about his new discovery. The "Hogan secret" mystique began to develop. With the strength of his game, and with his opponents believing that Hogan had found some new vital "secret" he wasn't sharing, Hogan had an additional competitive edge, a psychological advantage. Watching Hogan strike the ball, shot after shot, would shake the confidence of most competitors in and of itself. Having the lingering notion in the backs of their minds that Hogan had found some secret, something that no one else knew, that made him capable of consistently hitting his ball farther and more accurately than anyone else could, gave Hogan an additional psychological advantage. Hogan's focus and lack of conversation during his rounds of golf, and his tendency to puff on his cigarette looking directly at you while his thoughts were elsewhere, only added to his psychological advantage. Hogan realized they were giving him a psychological edge, and he was not about to negate that advantage. Make no mistake about it; Hogan was out to maximize his chances to win. Hogan used his mystique to his advantage, and his "secret" just heightened the intrigue. Hogan's amazing record from late 1945 through 1953 had to cause competitors and sportswriters alike to think that Hogan had indeed found something that distinctly set him apart from the others.

During that period from late 1945 – 1953 he did the following:

117 Tournaments entered

102 Top 10 finishes

76 Top 3 finishes

45 Tournament won

18 Major tournaments entered, 9 Major tournaments won

In 1948, the year before his accident—

21 Tournaments entered

15 Top 3 finishes

10 Tournaments won

Realizing Hogan's tremendous performance during that period tour pro Mike Souchak summed it up: "There's something Ben Hogan knows about hitting a golf ball that the rest of us just don't know."

What Hogan developed was a consistent swing that performed exceptionally well under pressure. It produced a high straight shot with a slight fade that caused the ball to land softly and stop quickly.

The golf community was so enamored with Hogan's success and the "Secret" that had set him apart from the others, that *Life* magazine did an article in its April 5, 1954 issue teased on the cover with "Ben Hogan's Secret: A Debate." The article stated that Hogan said "I have a secret." Accompanied by a series of photographs of Hogan's swing, and seven top pros offered their observations and explanations:

Walter Burkemo - "He drops his hands."

Claude Harmon - "The left hip leads."

George Fazio -- "Level shoulders."

Sam Snead -- "Hands never cross."

Fred Gronauer -- "It's his pivot."

Mike Turnesa -- "Twist of the club."

Gene Sarazen -- "It's pronation, a backward roll of the wrists on the backswing which opens the face of the club. Hogan does it subtly and quickly."

The article ended with a picture of Sarazen, pointing to his head, and the caption under it quoting him, "The real reason for secret's success is the intelligence and temperament of the man behind it. He has it up here."

Life published another article in its August 8, 1955 issue. In that cover story, Hogan confirmed what Sarazen had said sixteen months earlier. Pronation was the key. As Sarazen pointed out pronation was a technique old pros had taught decades earlier, but was in contempt by serious golfers. Yet, Hogan had adapted it to his needs, by adjusting his grip and cocking his left wrist. It was, as he said in the article, "like learning to play all over again."

In the article Hogan noted,

"In itself, pronation is no cure for a hook. If anything, it helps promote one. But for me it was the basis for a new experiment, and before the night was over, I added two adjustments, which on paper made pronation hook-proof without any loss of distance....

The two adjustments had transformed pronation into a bonanza for me. They were so delicate that no one would ever think of looking for them, and I certainly was not going to tell anybody where to look. The first was in the grip. I moved my left hand one-eighth to one-fourth inch to the left so that the thumb was almost directly on top of the shaft. The second adjustment, which was the real meat of the 'secret', was nothing more than a twist or a cocking of the left wrist. I cupped the wrist gradually backward and inward on the backswing so that the wrist formed a slight 'V' at the top of the swing... No matter how much wrist I put into the downswing, no matter how hard I swung or how hard I tried to roll into and through the ball, the face of the club could not close fast enough to become absolutely square at the moment of impact. The result was that lovely, long-fading ball which is a highly effective weapon on any golf course.

It took more than one stroke a round off my score. I found that I did not have to work as hard, because I had a ball that was easier to control. I did not have the worry and fright of getting the ball away. I was more secure in my game and did not have to practice as long or as hard as before. In normal tournament play, I used the secret approximately 90% of the time. Whenever I did, there was nothing automatic about it. I was very conscious of cupping the left wrist. In fact, it was the only thing I concentrated on, the rest of my swing operating on muscle memory. I did not use it every time. If a shot required a hook I simply eliminated the twist of the wrist and got it..."

So that was what Hogan revealed as the biggest part to his secret—the combination of pronation with the grip adjustment and the cupping of the left wrist on the backswing.

When John Grace, the 1974 U.S. Amateur runner-up, who played a lot of golf with

Hogan, asked him whether that combination of moves would cause him to "lay the club off," Hogan answered, "So what?" Hogan also mused to John, "The players on the tour noticed after I started hitting the ball that way, but I wouldn't tell them how I was hitting it differently."

Much has been discussed, debated and argued about the "secret." Some thought that Hogan had, in fact, revealed it in the *Life* magazine article, others thought he had not. For example, noted teaching pro David Leadbetter, in his instructional book *The Fundamentals of Hogan*, published in 2000, concluded that Hogan's secret was, in fact, the one Hogan wrote about in *Life* magazine. But Hogan's tour colleague Jimmy Demaret, in a 1978 *Golf* magazine article, said it was "his ready position, when he dropped his hands into the slot." [Dropping the hands into the "slot" is moving the hands at the top of the backswing from the plane of the backswing to the plane of the downswing as the downswing is begun.]

In a book contemporary to Leadbetter's, *The Fundamentals of Hogan*, John Andrisani in *The Hogan Way* writes there was some truth to Hogan critics' criticisms that Hogan had left some aspects of his secret out of the *Life* magazine article because he planned to include them later in his *Five Lessons* book. One of them was a lateral shift of the hips.

Hogan did include the lateral hip movement in his 1957 *Five Lessons* book: "To begin the downswing, TURN YOUR HIPS BACK TO THE LEFT. THERE MUST BE ENOUGH LATERAL MOTION FORWARD TO TRANSFER THE WEIGHT TO THE LEFT FOOT." [Capitals are Hogan's] Turning the hips quickly, but not having already transferred weight to the left side causes "spin-out" slices, because the weight was still on the right side when quickly turning the hips.

In his 2004 book *Afternoons with Mr. Hogan*, Jody Vasquez recounts Hogan telling him his "secret" and it was something entirely different from what had previously been revealed. "The secret is the correct functioning of the right leg, with emphasis on maintaining the angle of the right knee on the back and forward swings. Combined with a slight cupping of the left wrist, it produces optimum balance and control, and allows you to apply as much speed and power as you wish." The left wrist was cupped because it was the only position the wrist could assume based on the position of the right knee. When Vasquez asked Hogan why the right-knee angle was not emphasized in Hogan's instructional books, Hogan barked, "I'm not telling them this." At the end of the conversation that day, Hogan told Vasquez, "Don't tell anybody I told you this."

Dan Jenkins, the golf writer and novelist from Fort Worth, who played many rounds with Hogan, has said Hogan's key secret was over clubbing—taking too much club and hitting it with slightly less than a full swing for better accuracy.

When asked if he thought Hogan had a secret, Mike Wright, Shady Oaks Country Club's current Director of Golf said, "If you had an edge, would you share it? I mean if you thought you had something in business or in athletics that no one else had, would you share it? Hogan's secret was that he left no detail unturned." Wright continued, "Mr. Hogan made two comments to me that will always stick with me. 'You can't depend on teaching tools out on the golf course,' and 'the lessons you learn on your own are the ones you retain.'"

Hogan told numerous people things about the golf swing and told them not to say anything about it. He would say, "This is just between you and me;" "Now don't tell anyone, this is just between us;" "Don't tell anyone I told you this." Perhaps it was just a way for Hogan to share with the individual something the person would remember for a lifetime, and that Ben Hogan had shared a special "treasure" of information about the golf swing with them, something that was just between the two of them. When people found out I had worked for Ben Hogan, even before I started to write this book, quite a number of them recalled such occasions in enough detail for me to believe what they were saying was true. And since getting a pointer from Hogan was the first thing they said to me after they found out I had worked for him, it was obviously the number one thing they remembered about the man.

Ken Venturi, Hogan's longtime friend, had a different take on Hogan's secret. In his wallet Venturi carried with him a piece of paper with two Ben Hogan sayings on it that he thought made the difference for Hogan: "Every day you miss practicing will take you a day longer to be good," and "There isn't enough daylight in any one day to practice all the shots you need to." Many times Hogan had said the secret was "in the dirt," and Venturi knew that Hogan unquestionably lived by that creed. On his practice days during his days of playing tournament golf, Hogan would hit balls for a couple of hours, have lunch, and then go back and hit balls for another three hours.

While Hogan's "secret" did in fact move his game to a higher level, it is my contention that the secret went well beyond the combination of techniques and theories he and others offered. Hogan's vision regarding his success simply excluded nothing– nothing. He explored every possible thing, on and off the golf course that could impact his performance on the golf course.

His true secret was his learning process, his work ethic and the mental acuity, drive, dedication, astuteness, and keen attention to detail that he used to get closer to perfection. Hogan had a philosophy that his search for the perfect swing was a lifelong quest, and he continued to look for techniques that might improve his game. His experimental, scientific mindset kept asking "what if?" "what would?" "I wonder if…," and "why does?" Along with those questions he used science and technology to push his search for knowledge. Some say Hogan sought answers at times when others didn't realize there was a question. By the time LPGA pro Kris Tschetter became friends with Ben Hogan in the late 1980s, he was no longer hitting balls and only occasionally hit three or four at a time. Tschetter wrote, "He also told me that he'd always believed that if the club traveled faster after impact than before impact, the ball would fly farther and straighter. 'I know I saw that once in a physics book.' He said, 'It said that if an object that hit another object was traveling faster after impact, the object being hit would travel farther and straighter. See if you can find me that book. Would you please?'"

Tschetter found such a book, and it had a whole chapter on acceleration and the effects an accelerating object has when striking an object at rest. She gave it to him. He read it, and looking satisfied said, "I knew I'd seen that somewhere. Thank you for bringing it to me." Hogan was over 75 years old and still mulling such things in his mind.

Ben Hogan used technology before technology was cool, and in the late 1960's and early 1970's was definitely in the forefront of the technological development of golf equipment. The combination of lightweight steel shafts, changing the flex point of shafts and adding length to lighter clubs were all innovations Hogan developed with the Apex shaft that Hogan pioneered. He added ½ inch to the length of Hogan irons with the Apex shaft because with the lighter shaft players could hit the ball further without losing accuracy. He lengthened his own driver to gain added distance on his drives. He even checked golf ball quality to see if they would fly true by floating his golf balls in a solution he created with the buoyancy to float the balls.

He was never satisfied, even when he was acknowledged to be the best ball-striker ever to play the game. He kept searching for that next little improvement. If the opportunity existed, Hogan wanted to test it, and if it didn't work under pressure, it was unacceptable. Hogan's inquisitiveness, commitment to continuous improvement and the effort required to achieve it, and his acute observations of all that might affect his game, combined with his mental toughness not to be thrown off track, all contributed as much to his secret as did his swinging a golf club hour after hour after hour.

Joe Mathews and some friends were playing golf at Shady Oaks one day when they saw Hogan out walking on the golf course. Hogan was no longer playing much golf, but when he walked the golf course, he almost always carried a golf club. As they watched, he dropped down three balls and hit them with the iron he was carrying. Hogan hit the first ball about 18 inches to the left of the hole, the second shot went in the hole, and the third ball was two or three feet to the right of the hole. Mathews had known Hogan since he was a young boy, so he rode over and asked him, "How did you do that with all of that wind up there?"

Hogan replied, "You have to find the 'wall of the wind'—having the trajectory and momentum of the ball meet the wind at the apex of its flight, then it doesn't affect the flight of the ball very much at all."

Herbert Warren Wind, the noted author who penned Hogan's *Five Lessons* with him, noted of Hogan's intellectual curiosity, "It would not be remiss to add that the superlative game he ultimately developed depended as least as much on the tireless thinking he put in over the years as it did on his tireless practicing."

From his early days on the tour, Hogan knew his poor results were due to his own poor efforts, and while he quickly learned that in golf, he was the master of his own ship, it took him quite a while to get all the sails fully up. In his 1974 interview at the World Golf Hall of Fame in Pinehurst, N.C., he commented on the development of his golf game, "I've had all the problems. You could run the gamut. There's no problem I haven't had. But, I've worked on every one of them. Not that I've conquered all of them, but I got it to where I could handle most of them. And that's one of the greatest rewards in golf, I think. Learning… I've gotten just great satisfaction, as much as or more than anybody in learning how to swing a golf club and what is going to happen when you swing it this way or that way."

He had this to say about himself regarding his knowing everything about the golf swing: "There's nine jillion things to learn… It's a very complex thing. Some days you react differently, your muscles and your eyes change from day to day. Even a driving machine won't react the same on a cold day as on a warm day. It's utterly impossible. Everything changes… There's always a gray area there. There are so many things I don't know about golf, you could fill a room with them. I don't know them all, and if I did, I wouldn't enjoy practicing. I like to practice and fiddle around and prove or disprove things. I'm a very curious person, and I enjoy that. And if I knew it all, I wouldn't have any more enjoyment."

Hogan, despite being the acknowledged best striker of the ball ever, felt there was still much for him to learn, noting, "Had I, as a young man starting out in professional golf in 1931, known then what I have managed to learn by 1957 and been able to start my experimentation at this more advanced point, I would have been privileged to have possibly made more advanced contributions during my best productive years." So even if Hogan had developed his 1957 swing in 1931, he wouldn't have been satisfied, but would have kept "digging" to be 26 years more advanced in his pursuit of perfection.

In the 1970's, when he was watching a demonstration of the True Temper "mechanical man" that the Hogan company used to test equipment (in addition to Hogan himself), Hogan analyzed the leading edge of the 8-iron that was being swung by the robot from the point of impact all the way back to the top of the backswing. Noting that the machine was hitting at least nine out of ten balls into a six-foot-diameter rubber wading pool filled with water 145 yards away, Hogan wanted to know what made it tick. Methodically he had the machine stopped every few inches to observe the leading edge of the iron and what direction it was pointed. How, where, and why did that direction change? Where was the leading edge pointed at the top of the backswing, just before the downswing was about to begin? Directly at the target? Left or right of the target? Exactly where?

Hogan realized that the mechanical man was a crude, robotic copy of the swing, but he also realized that since the machine wasn't capable of all the movements of the human body, it would have to use a simplified version of the swing to hit the ball consistently. If there was ever anything Ben Hogan said about the golf swing, it was that it was a simple movement, and Hogan's scientific approach to improvement was to simplify the swing by eliminating as many possible opportunities and causes of error as was humanly possible. Chances are, the next day Hogan put his observations of the mechanical man to work with his own golf swing, tinkering a bit here, a bit there.

John Grace, a member of Shady Oaks, observed, "I watched him practice and play every day at the 1961 U.S. Open at Oakland Hills. Hogan hit 250 practice balls before he went out to play his tournament rounds, three to four times as many practice balls as the other players hit, and he was 48 years old. He hit more balls before a tournament round, between two and two-and-a- half hours of practice." Later, in Fort Worth, John recalled Hogan's heavy practicing before a competitive round and asked Hogan why he did that. Hogan responded, "I was practicing the shots that I would hit that day. My round started before I ever got on the golf course." John also remembered that Hogan was practicing from the far right side of the practice range at Oakland Hills, and he asked him about that as well. Hogan replied, "I didn't want to look up and see anybody because it might interrupt my concentration. Hogan also putted for 30-35 minutes every day as well, which was again longer than the other players were practicing their putting before rounds at that tournament.

One day at Shady Oaks, John was practicing chipping. Several people were around him watching him chip and talking with him. After they left, Hogan walked out of the clubhouse and came over to John.

"How would you like to be a good player some day?" Hogan asked.

The question caught John a little by surprise as he was a young amateur who had recently played on the U.S. Walker Cup Team and in two Masters tournaments. But John, eager to learn, particularly from Hogan, said sure he would love to learn and improve, and would greatly appreciate the advice.

"Well," Hogan intoned, "There are two things you need to do to become a good player. First, when you're practicing, don't talk to anyone, and second, every shot you hit is the *most important shot*." To Hogan the saying "Practice makes perfect" was wrong. "Perfect practice makes perfect" was the only way.

John had watched Hogan practice and noticed the time he took between shots. Now he understood more clearly that Hogan didn't just hit *a* shot—every practice shot was *the* shot, so he thought about each one before and after he swung the club to strike the ball. For Hogan each practice shot had a very distinctive purpose, and he thought about it before he hit it and analyzed it after he hit it. Watching Hogan hit practice balls and noticing the time between shots as he stared off into the distance and then very slowly moved another ball into position to hit, he was analyzing the last *most important shot* he had just hit, and preparing himself for the next *most important shot* that he was about to hit.

Another indication of this thinking was at one of our Hogan Staff visits to Fort Worth. Following Hogan's after-dinner speech on the final evening one club professional asked Hogan, "Well, if you just threw down a ball and hit it, without thinking…"

Hogan cut him off in mid-sentence responding, "I don't ever hit a ball without thinking." Focus and concentration were Hogan's watchwords.

John Grace noted, "Distances didn't mean anything to Hogan. He calculated every shot in his head based on the situation. For example, the first hole at Shady Oaks is a very short 320-yard par four, one that in the winter with a north wind and dormant Bermuda grass that allowed more roll, some of the better players at the club could drive to the green (in the 1970s before graphite). But, because the very short par four had a severely sloped green with the grain running straight down the slope from back right to front left, it was lightning fast, and very difficult to put a shot close to the pin. Leaving your approach shot any distance above the hole meant almost a sure three-putt, unless you made a long putt back up the hill. Most of us hit wedges or sand wedges for our approach shots, trying to hit the ball slightly above the hole and ease it back to the cup. Not Hogan. Hogan would hit a little cut 8-iron into the green with a lower trajectory and quite a bit of spin so the ball would check up and stop quickly near the hole, but wouldn't have too much spin to suck it back down the slick, sloping green.

The combination of the lower trajectory from the punched 8-iron and the spin into the sloping green would stop the ball, but wouldn't draw it back like a wedge shot coming in to the green with a higher trajectory with similar spin. That type of shot would also reduce, probably eliminate, the possibility of leaving the ball above the hole any distance. Hogan's objective was for his shot never to go beyond the hole, so that is would always be below it. The one place he did not want his ball to end up was above the hole, so he used his wits to develop the best way to approach the shot. Hogan was using a club he could hit 140-150 yards for a 60-80 yard shot, because that's what he felt was the smartest way to leave his ball where he wanted it, below the hole, and reduce/eliminate leaving it above the hole where he didn't want it. Consequently, you couldn't ask Hogan what club he hit 90 yards, he had to know the situation to give you his answer.

To adequately describe Hogan's golf ball striking ability, well, is almost impossible. I was always amazed at how powerful Hogan appeared at address, during his backswing and then during his downswing and follow-through like a powerful machine concreted to the ground, one that was totally in sync, with every muscle acting in concert, to unleash the power of his entire body. John Grace, like many others who had watched or played with Hogan, noted "Hogan had a unique, distinctive way he hit the ball," Grace said. "The ball had a different crack. It was unlike anyone else I've ever played with."

However, Hogan had to reinvent his swing after his auto accident because of the damage to his left knee, so, if we all thought Hogan tore through the ball in the 1960s, '70s, and '80s, you can imagine what it was like before his accident when he could really shift his weight to his left side. During his 1974 interview at the informal press conference on the eve of the first induction ceremonies to the World Golf Hall of Fame in Pinehurst, Hogan noted, "Well, I have very few or no physical problems outside my knee, and that's the reason I can't play the kind of golf I'd like to play. I have to back up on the ball, and that's not very pleasant because sometimes I hit a little in back of it and sometimes I catch it a little thin. I can't ride it through." Hogan's swing masked that backing up adjustment very well, but on a couple of occasions when playing with him, I saw what he was describing and the pain he felt as he winced during the strain on that left knee.

In 1970, after a layoff of several years, Hogan, at the age of 58, played in the Colonial National Invitation Tournament and the Houston Open. Nick Seitz went to Houston and Fort Worth, and wrote in *Golf Digest* about his observations of Hogan's swing and tactics:

"His yogic concentration, a striking amalgam of intensity and composure that suggests utter transcendence, seem not to have been impaired by the long layoff; Herb Wind's description of Hogan competing 'with the burning frigidity of dry ice' came to mind. Always his own severest critic, Hogan knew better. He devoted months to modifying his swing in favor of his aching left knee, hurt in the automobile accident but no bother to him until the past couple of years. A tendon transplant last year fixed an ailing shoulder, but doctors were afraid to operate on his knee for what probably is torn cartilage, because he might not be able to walk. Hogan had been taking diathermy treatments three times a week and lifting weights on the edge of his bed at night and sleeping with heat pads. A dull pain always was present, and occasionally when he swung, a sharp pain would pierce the knee. 'I wouldn't recommend that anybody swing the way I'm swinging,' he said. 'I used to go in on my left leg as much as anybody, or more. I've had to take the leg out of the swing.'"

In addition to his 1955 *Life* magazine article, Hogan wrote two very detailed books on the golf swing, *Power Golf* in 1948 (with over 18 printings in hardback and later in paperback) and *Ben Hogan's Five Lessons, The Modern Fundamentals of Golf* in 1957. Hogan's *Five Lessons* has been one of the most popular golf instruction books in both hardback and paperback editions.

In 1985, the hardback of *Five Lessons* was reprinted by Digest Classic Books. Nick Seitz, then the Editorial Director at *Golf Digest*, interviewed Hogan in December of

1984 to write the "Foreword" to the book.

In answering Seitz's question if he, Hogan, would write this book any differently in 1985, Hogan responded, "I would write it the same way I did in 1957," he said forcefully. "Everything I know about the full swing is in there. I don't think the fundamentals will ever change. They simply look different because people are built differently. An athletic person who wants to learn and will put in the time and effort, can take this book and become a better player than I was. People are bigger today. I played at 137 pounds. I found no advantage to smallness. It pleases me that the book over the years has helped people improve. Improvement is what the game is all about—the most enjoyable part."

Studying Hogan's *Five Lessons* book yields treasures and tidbits of his secrets for both his unmatched golf swing, and his thinking that might be considered "outside the box" of the golf swing itself. In addition to developing his swing "secret" in 1946, Hogan also developed a different philosophy for his swing process that he later claimed made a marked difference in his level of success. Hogan noted in the "Summary and Review" chapter of his *Five Lessons* book:

"I never felt genuinely confident about my game until 1946... Before a round, I had no idea whether I'd be a 69 or a 79... My friends on the tour used to tell me that I was silly to worry, that I had a grooved swing and had every reason to have confidence in it, but my self-doubting never stopped. Regardless of how well I was going, I was still concerned about the next day and the next day and the next.

In 1946 my attitude suddenly changed. I honestly began to feel that I could count on playing fairly well each time I went out, that there was no practical reason for me to feel I might suddenly 'lose it all.' I would guess that what lay behind my new confidence was this: I had stopped trying to do a great many difficult things perfectly because it had become clear in my mind that this ambitious over thoroughness was neither possible nor advisable, or even necessary. All you needed to groove were the fundamental movements, and there weren't so many of them. Moreover, they were movements that were basically controllable, and so could be executed fairly well whether you happened to be sharp or not so sharp that morning. I don't know what came first, the chicken or the egg, but at about the same time, I began to feel that I had the stuff to play creditable golf even when I was not at my best, my shot making started to take on a new and more stable consistency. THE BASIS FOR THIS PROGRESS, LET ME REPEAT, WAS MY GENUINE CONVICTION THAT ALL THAT IS REALLY REQUIRED TO PLAY GOOD GOLF IS TO EXECUTE PROPERLY A RELATIVELY SMALL NUMBER OF TRUE FUNDAMENTAL MOVEMENTS." [Capitals are Hogan's.]

Hogan listed the eight basic fundamental movements in three parts and listed them in reverse order, but these are listed in the sequence from start to finish:

CORRECTLY POSITIONED AND POISED AT ADDRESS—

1. Correct stance and posture
2. Correct grip

CORRECT POSITION AT THE TOP OF THE BACKSWING—

3. Waggles properly
4. Starts back with his hands, arms and shoulders, and lets his shoulders turn his hips
5. Stays on his plane throughout his backswing

COMES INTO THE BALL AND HITS THROUGH THE BALL CORRECTLY

6. Initiate the downswing by turning the hips to the left
7. Hit through the finish of his swing in one cohesive movement
8. Start to supinate his left wrist just before impact

(CAPITALS are Hogan's)

Hogan then listed a few things to think about and gave a short recap on his five basic fundamentals, admonishing the reader to "SCHOOL YOURSELF TO THINK IN TERMS OF THE CAUSE AND NOT THE RESULT." [Capitals are Hogan's] Rather than looking at where the ball landed, Hogan was thinking about what all he had done that caused it to fly a certain way and to land in a particular spot.

Feel, grip #1 importance: Before Hogan started to give young Joe Matthews a lesson, then a small boy of nine or ten, Hogan told him, "Everything—all your power—

everything, is transmitted through your grip, so let's start on your grip. First thing you need to do is get rid of that glove, it interferes with your contact with your grip."

The only communication the body/brain gets from what happened when the club head strikes the ball is through the shock vibrations sent from the club head, up the shaft, then through the grip to the hands. The feel of the club striking the ball yields different vibrations for the different ways the ball is struck. So, Hogan wanted the best information he could possibly get regarding that impact. His iron heads were blades that offered no compensation for off-center hits, but neither did they yield diminished information via the shock vibrations regarding the impact with the ball. To maximize the vibration his hands felt at impact, Hogan used hard cordline grips on his clubs and did not wear a golf glove. If you hit one of Hogan's clubs slightly off the sweet spot, you immediately knew it.

Indeed, gripping the club was a key to Hogan's "secret" that he began in both of his books with a chapter on the grip, and his 1955 *Life* magazine "Secret" article begins with a slight change in his grip. Hogan noted in a 1987 *Golf* magazine interview, "You can't make those moves unless you have the proper hold on the club… Ability all gets back to the grip, which is the transformer through which the juice flows." In *Power Golf,* Hogan started the book with the "Evolution of the Hogan Grip" chapter that included nine photos with a few accompanying lines of text depicting what was being shown in each photo. "Getting the proper grip at the start is one of the most important steps in learning how to play golf. For that reason, let us first consider the intents and purposes of the grip in relation to golf."

In *Five Lessons* Hogan used the detailed drawings of Anthony Ravielli to show, in detail, how the club should be gripped by both the left and right hands. Hogan suggested practicing this first fundamental, the grip, 30 minutes a day for a week until it became second nature before moving on to the second fundamental.

In a home video taken by friends, Hogan is shown hitting balls with a driver out into the ocean. During the video, he took time to demonstrate his grip position, individually showing each hand's grip position just as it was shown in the book.

"Stance and Posture" is Lesson two of the *Five Lessons* for good reason. Nick

Seitz noted in the "Foreword" of the 1985 edition, "Said Hogan, 'most people are too upright because they disconnect the arms from the body. My left arm swung right across my chest on the backswing, and was the strongest part of my down-swing…. The idea is to rotate the club with the left arm. Poor players, and even some tour players, try to do it with the right arm. You have to do it with the left arm.' Take it from me [Seitz], there is no key on the typewriter to underscore the feeling in Hogan's voice when he emphasizes an instructional point." Hogan maxi-mized his power by utilizing his whole body on his swing—his legs, chest, upper body, and arms were all utilized to their fullest in Hogan's posture and stance.

Elbows. Hogan also had some other principles that he felt strongly about. One was the position of the arms. Hogan felt them to be significant. Hogan has detailed descrip-tions and drawings of the arms, with special attention to the elbows. The description of the elbows in his book is in all capital letters for emphasis. Eldridge Miles, a local Dallas club professional, played many rounds of golf with Hogan, and on several occasions, Hogan noted the importance of the position of the elbows to Eldridge. Once at Shady Oaks, Eldridge was sitting at the round table next to Hogan with several PGA tour profession-als. The touring pros started talking about the golf swing, but Hogan remained silent. Hogan nudged Eldridge and pointed to his elbow and demonstrated one of his "secret" principles—elbow pointed to the target = hook; elbow pointed towards the ground = fade.

Don January related to Eldridge an incident that happened to him in the mid 1950's, when he was paired with Hogan in the final round of the first tournament, the Dallas Open, at Preston Hollow Country Club. On or near the final hole of the tournament, January hooked a tee shot into a trap on the left side of the fairway. January then proceeded to hole out his trap shot for an eagle 2 on the hole, which helped him win the tournament. After changing shoes in the locker room after the tournament, January was about to leave, and he stopped by Hogan's locker to tell him how much he enjoyed playing with him. Hogan thanked January and said that he enjoyed playing with him as well. Hogan asked if January had won the tournament, and January said that he had, so Hogan congratulated him on his victory. Then, Hogan asked, "Say, Don, did you ever have polio in your elbows?" The question puzzled

January, but he just replied, "No" and didn't make much of the question. January told Eldridge it took him 10 years to figure out what Hogan was driving at. January had his elbows pointing out towards the target on his swing rather than tucked in pointing to his hips, and that was Hogan's way of "suggesting" that January might want to consider putting his elbows in a different position to eliminate the hook.

In *Five Lessons* Hogan indicates the elbows should point towards the hipbones, not towards the target or the ground and shows elastic bands holding the arms and elbows in the proper position.

The First Part of the Swing: Hogan not so subtly states in his book "ACTUALLY, THE HANDS START THE CLUBHEAD BACK A SPLIT SECOND BEFORE THE ARMS START BACK. AND THE ARMS BEGIN THEIR MOVEMENT A SPLIT SECOND BEFORE THE SHOULDERS BEGIN TO TURN." [Capitals are Hogan's].

Hogan elaborated on this point in his interview with Nick Seitz, and his comments add clarity to what he was saying when he discussed his search to eliminate his hook and to hit the ball higher. "I would even hook with a weakened grip. I also couldn't hit the ball high enough. Finally I found something that enabled me to stop hooking and hit the ball higher."

Seitz wrote, "What was it he discovered? There followed a long thoughtful pause, Hogan continued, 'It had to do with the face of the club. I rolled the face of the club open away from the ball. That cupped my left wrist. Coming down, the face was moving so fast I couldn't turn it over and hook. I was rotating the club like a baseball bat, and the faster I could rotate, the more distance I got. Training myself, I would roll the face open as fast and as far as I could. With this technique, I could hit the ball straight and farther.' From then on, Hogan quite likely was without peer as a shot-maker. The only part of his clubs that showed wear was the sweet spot."

The Second Part of the Swing: Hogan states this is necessarily the most critical part of the swing from the start of the downswing to the finish or follow-through. It is here where everything pays off or it doesn't. Hogan tells how the hips must initiate the downswing, which automatically lowers the hands and arms to a lower plane than on the backswing. "THE PLANE FOR THE DOWNSWING IS LESS STEEPLY

The greatest ball striker at work. (PHOTO COURTESY DOUG MCGRATH COLLECTION)

INCLINED AND IS ORIENTED WITH THE BALL QUITE DIFFERENTLY FROM THE BACKSWING PLANE… WHEN THE GOLFER IS ON THIS CORRECT DOWNSWING PLANE, HE HAS TO HIT FROM THE INSIDE OUT. When he hits from the inside out, he can get maximum strength into his swing and obtain maximum club head speed." Starting the downswing with the shoulders or the hands will not get the golfer onto the proper plane, so Hogan again emphasizes "THE HIPS INITIATE THE DOWNSWING." Hogan obtained maximum strength into his swing by swinging from the inside out, a swing path normally associated with hooking the ball, but by using his modified pronation of his left hand and a weak grip, he was able to turn the ball slightly left to right from an inside out swing path. Again, Hogan was simplifying dropping the hands into the proper plane by initiating the swing with the hips, which would drop the hands into the proper plane. Thus, the golfer did not have to think about dropping the hands, just focusing on initiating the downswing with the hips.

"To begin the downswing, TURN YOUR HIPS BACK TO THE LEFT. THERE MUST BE ENOUGH LATERAL MOTION FORWARD TO TRANSFER THE WEIGHT TO THE LEFT FOOT."

Focus/Concentration. Another aspect of Hogan's secret was his ability to focus totally on the job at hand. He realized that the crowds bothered him, and he wasn't able to hit the shots he wanted to hit because he was distracted by the galleries that crowded around him as he played. Consequently, Hogan trained himself to focus on the job at hand, the next shot and where it needed to be to give him the best shot after that. He focused on the conditions that could impact his shot—wind in various places, lie of the ball, target elevation, ball above or below your feet, side hill/uphill/downhill, stance, etc., to determine how he was going to play the shot to hit the ball to the exact spot he wanted it to come to rest.

Once in a conversation with a small group of people Hogan was asked, "What could most amateur golfers do to improve their game?" Hogan's response was immediate, "Talk less and pay more attention to what they're doing." It was one reason Hogan didn't like driving a cart or riding in a golf cart with anyone, for it was a distraction that took away from preparing for his next shot. Hogan acknowledged that he could have played more tournaments if he rode a cart, but he responded, "I couldn't play as well. You don't have time to compose yourself."

In addition to building a golf swing like a finely tuned violin, Hogan's scientific approach then left the swing to focus on the golf course. "Course management" Hogan called it, laying out a plan to attack the course shot by shot.

Part of Hogan's course management was to size up the golf course with his own game. To get the number of clubs in his bag down to the club restriction limit Hogan said in *Power Golf*, "I would make my selection on the basis of the clubs which will be the most useful to me during that particular tournament." Consequently, he might leave out the four-iron or even the seven-iron, depending on which club was not called for during the course of his rounds on that particular golf course.

Issue #1 in Hogan's course management—hit the ball to the best possible place to hit your next shot from to maximize your scoring opportunities. Hogan's plan was to move the ball in one direction, left to right, unless the hole layout definitely called for something else.

Why not just hit it straight? Hogan felt that a straight ball was an accident that even the best players couldn't hit it straight every time, particularly under pressure. When asked how often he tried to hit the ball straight, Hogan's answer was, "Never.... It's virtually impossible—at best by accident. Besides you give yourself much more margin for error by maneuvering your shots one way or the other. Much more control...Control is the main thing, and the tee shot is the most important shot in golf. You've got to hit the fairway before you have a good chance of putting the ball close to the pin. You can be the greatest iron player in the world, but if you're in the boondocks, it won't do you any good." By moving the ball consistently in one direction, in Hogan's case from left to right, it gave him the full fairway to work with. If he aimed it down the left side of the fairway that was 30 yards wide, he had the whole 30-yard width of the fairway as a margin for error. Whereas, if he hit it straight down the middle, he had only half of the fairway, 15 yards either direction, in case of error.

Why did Hogan choose to fade the ball, moving it from left to right? Hooking the ball (for a right handed player the ball moves from right to left) produces over spin on the ball causing it to roll further. While roll is good for distance, it is bad for controlling where the golf ball will finally come to rest. The more the ball rolls on the ground, the less control the player has over its final resting spot. Secondly, a fade or slice, moving the ball from left to right (for a right hand player) gives the ball considerably more backspin, meaning it will stop quicker on harder greens. Again, this gives the player more control over the final resting spot of the ball. Hogan once remarked that at the U.S. Opens at Oakland Hills and at Oakmont that "If a ball *even thought* of just leaning left, it wouldn't stay on the green. It had no chance of holding the green." Consequently, if he was going to concentrate on his main strategic shot, the left to right shot made the most sense to him.

Gardner Dickinson commented, "Hogan said he always tried to move the ball one way or the other because he wanted to control its flight and reach the safest part of the fairway. He would no more 'turn a ball loose,' he said, than fly to the moon. 'You don't have to know exactly where your ball is going, but you better know where it's not going,' Hogan once told me. How much lower our scores might be if we all followed this simple yet profound advice."

Hogan also believed a good player needed to have a "safe shot" just to get the ball in the fairway or on the green regardless of conditions. He spent some time on the practice tee with Gardner Dickinson and worked with him on it. "[He] asked me if I had a 'safe shot.' I asked what he meant. 'I mean a shot you would try just to put the ball somewhere on the green with that club, for your very life,' he replied. Without hesitation, I played a rather low knockdown shot with an abbreviated follow-through, and Ben exclaimed, 'Hell, yes!' He asked if I could fade that shot, and I admitted that I couldn't do so at will, so he proceeded to show me how."

Hogan did have a practice routine, though it was not his standard practice routine, to finely hone his shot making by consecutively hitting a straight shot, a fade and then a draw throughout his practice. He would continually repeat that cycle throughout his entire practice session, going through each club in the bag, and hitting each shot exactly as planned—straight shot, followed by a fade, then a draw, going through several bags of balls and using all the clubs in the bag, 9-iron through the driver, without missing a shot. It was Hogan's idea of fine tuning his swing and getting his control as close to perfection as he could.

Hogan paid particular attention to his golf clubs (and his golf balls). Very few, if any, touring pros who ever hit Hogan's driver had much success, because it was made to suit Hogan's flat swing and his desire to make the ball turn slightly from left to right. Hogan noted in *Power Golf*, "In selecting clubs I always look for those which suit my swing. I've spent too long developing that swing to make any radical changes in it merely to fit a new club."

Visitors to Shady Oaks Country Club frequently asked Mike Wright, Director of Golf, (as they had asked Art Hall before him) questions about Hogan's golf swing, but Wright said they very rarely inquired about Hogan's equipment. Noted Wright, "One of the things that impressed me about Hogan's ability to be so consistently accurate with all his clubs was how meticulous he was about his equipment. He had an amazing ability to match his equipment to his swing needs, so he never had to alter anything about his swing to accommodate his clubs. He had the reminders on his hard, cordline grips set at about 4:30, so there was no way he could hit the ball left unless he wanted to. He was always tinkering with equipment."

When it came to his golf clubs, Hogan was very, very precise about every club, particularly his driver. In his chapter on club selection, chapter 2 in *Power Golf*, Hogan immediately discusses shaft flex and club weight. Hogan used the stiffest shaft he could swing. Even when he was in his 60's Hogan swung an X stiffness (extra stiff) in the Apex shaft and had the "X" flex shafts tipped (shafts cut off at the bottom—the club head end) to make them even stiffer. By eliminating any unwanted bending or flexing of the shaft, the stiffer shaft minimized any deviation of where the club head might be from its intended position at the point of contact.

Tom Stites joined the Hogan Company as a club designer in 1987. One day he was in a meeting with Mr. Hogan when Hogan grabbed a nearby club. Holding it by the club head and the butt end of the grip, he put the shaft of the club in front of Tom's face and said to him, "This is 90% of it." Tom related, "He was saying that the shaft was vitally important to hitting the ball the way it was intended to be struck. Tom then impishly inquired, "Well, what's the other 10%?" Without hesitation, Hogan immediately responded, "It's how it goes through the dirt."

To help him move the ball from left to right, Hogan's personal clubs had the reminders on the grips set between 4:30 and 5:00, in an extremely, extremely weak position. Hogan had to get through the ball on his swing or his club face would be left very open, so Hogan had to "stay down and through the ball" to close the club face back to the "square" position.

Hogan did all of these things so he could control the golf ball to its final resting spot as much as was humanly possible. Eliminate as many of the opportunities for error as you can, maximize your feel of each shot, then work on building a repeating swing. Simplify, simplify. Hogan said that he could tell whether or not a player could really play by the consistency of the trajectory of his shots, not necessarily by the consistency of where the ball landed. Repeatedly getting the club head to exactly the same position in the same manner produced consistent golf ball flight trajectories, and that's how Hogan judged a golf swing. When he practiced consistent flight trajectories were his first objective, rather than accuracy of the shot. If he had the proper flight trajectory, and it was consistent from shot to shot he believed he was striking the ball consistently correctly. He felt that if he was striking the ball correctly, the accuracy would be there.

When Hogan stepped onto the first tee, he had perfected as much as possible his swing, his equipment and the shots he needed for this particular golf course, so the first thing he did on that first tee was to mentally focus on the job at hand. He took his time to organize all those aspects of his preparation for the day's round. "I would take longer on that first tee than I would any other place on the golf course. I was gearing my brain, taking a good look at the fairway, taking three or four practice swings. A lot of people wondered what I was doing up there, why I didn't tee the ball up and hit it. I was organizing myself to play this round. I thought harder about that first shot than any shot I played. It set the tone for the day."

Some have thought Hogan found the Holy Grail of golf. In my opinion, it wasn't the neatly packaged little tidbit of information about his golf swing that everyone was seeking to quickly achieve Hoganesque results.

Basic to Hogan's system was his golf swing and how to successfully repeat it as near as possible the same way day after day. While the golf world's focus was on the particular movements of Hogan's swing, Hogan's meticulousness focus was on the "cause" rather than the "results" of his efforts. This caused him to think, to plan, to analyze much more expansively than just on the golf swing. His system expanded to include everything imaginable that might affect a person's performance on a given day. And to help him analyze his performance and the possible causes of his results, he kept meticulous notes that he would jot down after practicing regarding exactly what he had been working on, and precisely how his progress was coming along. Then he might try to relate what things outside of his swing might have caused his performance that day to be better or worse than usual. From there he included the golf equipment he used, to how he felt on a given day, the food and beverages that he might consume or had consumed the night before, or even how the weather might affect him. Hogan searched for and used equipment that fit his swing, even to the shoes he wore. If it would help his performance, he would have it made that way. Hogan always looked bolted to the ground, so strong and stable was his lower body during the swing. His powerful swing pushed off from his right side with great force, so for better stability, he had an extra cleat put in his custom-made golf shoes, right under the balls of his feet, to give him extra holding power into the ground.

Ben Hogan's secret was in implementing to the "nth" degree his all-encompassing game philosophy. He was consistently learning, working, perfecting. He even looked at other sports and how the skills and abilities in those sports might apply to golf, and how the physics of one sport might apply to golf, including seeking information from top athletes in other sports about various habit or techniques that he might apply to positively impact his golf game.

On one occasion Hogan even tried to remake the golf course to fit his swing. When the Tarrant County Water Board decided to reroute the Trinity River in Fort Worth, part of the change was adjacent to the Colonial Country Club golf course, where the Colonial NIT professional tournament is played. Hogan was hired as a consultant to oversee the renovation of the seventh and eighth holes due to the rerouting the river and to see that nothing was done in the river project that would harm the golf course. During the process Hogan decided to do a little landscaping of his own—on the seventh hole, a narrow, straight par-4 hole that was to be changed to a very slight dogleg right. The green on the seventh ran diagonally from left front to back right with a large sand trap in the front right center. The trees in the left rough, some of which were fairly large, reduced the size of the opening on the left side of the fairway for the best approach shot to the green to the point that almost all players used a 3-wood off the tee. That left them with a less than ideal approach shot to the pin. It also negated Hogan's left-to-right ball flight philosophy.

Since the best approach to the green was from the left edge of the fairway, the trees in the left rough were a problem from Hogan's point-of-view as they eliminated the risk/reward payoff of a well-positioned tee shot. To get the ball in the ideal spot would necessitate drawing the tee shot towards the trees and the rough. One of Hogan's fundamental rules was "knowing where he did not want his ball to end up," and using a draw would require turning the ball towards the trouble, the left rough and the trees, and staying out of the rough would be left to chance—how the ball rolled. That, in Hogan's opinion was not the proper layout for the hole, so Hogan began eliminating some of the trees on the left to enable players to play the hole as he felt it was designed to be played, down the left side of the fairway for the best approach to the green. Also, with several of the trees gone, Hogan could hit his fade down the left edge of the fairway and fade it into the perfect position to approach the green. Consequently, with both the seventh and eighth holes being renovated due to the river project anyway, he took the liberty to have a man on a bulldozer, about 200 yards from the tee, start to push over some of the trees in the left rough—several of them good sized trees.

When word of Hogan's landscaping and redesign program reached the clubhouse, the club president immediately went to the seventh hole to see what was going on. There, he saw Hogan, standing on the tee, hand signaling to the man on the bulldozer down in the left rough, as to which tree to push down next. When the club president surveyed the situation and saw a couple of trees down on the ground, he not too politely confronted Hogan, and all hell broke loose. Tree removal at Colonial was a no-no, regardless of who you were. A heated cussing match ensued that finally ended when Hogan yelled at the club president that he quit, whereupon the president barked back in an equally loud voice—"You can't quit, you're fired!"

Hogan's game philosophy was that there are three ways to beat somebody—outwork them, outthink them, and intimidate them. Hogan made a career out of mastering all three. To perfect his golf swing to the very best he could he invented practice as we know it today, working much, much harder than even the hardest working pros on the tour. Even after becoming the acknowledged best ball striker of all time, Hogan continued to practice longer and harder than his competitors. He also knew to compete successfully, he had to think his way through the round or the match. Hogan developed "course management" as a tactical strategy for each round, thinking his way around the course ahead of time as to when and where to take chances and when and where play more conservatively. Hogan also knew other players might be intimidated by his shot-making skills and course management abilities, so he used that to his advantage. With his game face—quiet, stoic, focused facial expressions, his penetrating eyes particularly intimating that all the wheels were turning—he let others try to figure out what he was thinking. When they were thinking about him and his thoughts, they weren't focused on their own game.

Hogan learned that lesson from Paul Runyan during their 1939 PGA Championship match when Hogan, despite consistently outdriving Runyan and repeatedly putting the ball closer to the hole than Runyan, lost 2 and 1. Hogan realized it was Runyan's focus that beat him, as Runyan seemed to be so totally intent on his next shot, blotting out everything else so that Hogan's longer drives and superior approach shots did not faze him. Hogan commented, "Paul's concentration is so absolute that he doesn't seem to see anything but the next shot. He wasn't the slightest bit intimidated by my drives. He controlled his mind and mine. If I'm going to win I've got to be able to do that too." Hogan perfected his ability to focus, so he could also stand there, taking a drag off his cigarette, not looking at anything in particular but with either a slight twinkle in his eye or a more focused, serious introspective look, and have opponents concerned about what he was thinking.

It is important to remember that Hogan stood only 5' 8" and weighed just 137 pounds. He believed someone would come along with the physical size and talent, the mental capabilities, and the internal drive and commitment to push the envelope further. He believed that person would dominate the game because he or she had the physical size and talent that Hogan lacked and would be dedicated to seeking and finding the answers "in the dirt."

In that regard, Hogan advised that anyone desiring to excel or to be the best, "Must be dedicated to what he wants to do, in anything, in golf or anything else, whatever he wants to do. He must be absolutely dedicated. He lives and sleeps golf and dreams golf and he watches everybody. He watches all the equipment, everything. He doesn't miss one thing to make sure he's going in the right direction. He has to train his body and his mind to do this, and it takes a long time to do it. And he'll be so pleased that he took that road."

So, in addition to all the swing fundamentals and check points that he offered in his books and in his magazine articles, Hogan's advice was to take these pieces of information to your swing puzzle and focus on them and work harder on them than anyone else, to achieve the best of your abilities.

Through his books Hogan left significant information to help golfers craft their own swings. He gives insight to the countless hours worked on his swing and his methodology in learning. Hogan gave pieces, significant pieces, for sound fundamentals.

But as Hogan told Mike Wright, "You can't depend on teaching tools out on the golf course. The lessons you learn on your own are the ones you retain." These are but another way of stating Hogan's Rule #1—"It's in the dirt." He gave enough information on the fundamentals to help the individual begin to improve his or her own golf swing, but it was up to each golfer to "get into" his or her own swing and technique intricacies "to learn the lessons on their own that they would retain."

SIXTEEN:
Reverence For The Game Of Golf And Contribution To Golf & Professional Athletes

MYTH: *Ben Hogan cared only for himself, and never gave anything back to the game.*
"Ben's never done anything to help his fellow pros." –Lloyd Mangrum
"Ben Hogan was the most selfish champion I ever knew."—Paul Runyan

MAN: Ben Hogan did as much for golf, and for professional athletes, as any man in the game. Hogan's great respect for the game prompted his efforts to promote the game and to help professional golf become a more viable profession, and played an important part in the growth of the game. His vision to raise the stature of professional golfers made a significant contribution to professional athletes in general.

"Ben Hogan demanded respect for his profession and for his professional skill" –Al Barkow in *Golf's Golden Grind.*

"Man makes laws to order society and to protect what he deems are his rights. Those laws are not static, but to change them is never an easy matter, for men's minds have to be turned to a new light. Those who do alter established concepts are usually of a rather special nature. Ben Hogan is one of them. –Author Al Barkow in *That's Golf.*

When Ben Hogan started playing professional golf, and throughout most of his career, professional tournament golfers were neither held in high regard nor could they make a living strictly playing tournament golf. They had to have other jobs as well just to pay the bills.

Ben Hogan revered the game of golf. While he worked hard for everything he ever had in the game, it was golf that gave him the opportunity to prove himself, to become what he became. Consequently, Hogan regarded tournament golf with respect and dignity, a competition to be treated with honor in a serious, almost religious manner.

When Lloyd Mangrum said, "Ben's never done anything to help his fellow pros," and Paul Runyan called him "the most selfish champion I ever knew," they were wrong. Ben Hogan may have been a solemn, fierce competitor, but he wasn't selfish and uncaring, and he knew exactly what he was doing when it came to professional tour golf and those who played it. Hogan did contribute to golf and to the status of athletes in general. He wanted to improve the livelihood of professional golfers, and he succeeded. Hogan did things during his career to improve golf and the status of athletes in general that received little, if any, fanfare. Indeed, he was maligned by fellow pros and the media for the very things that made those contributions possible, but Hogan wasn't looking for favorable media and accolades; he wanted to improve his lot in life and, in so doing, the livelihood of professional golfers. So in spite of the criticisms and ugly comments, he continued on what he felt was the right path to improve his lot in life, and in the process, the game.

Hogan's family was poor, so Henny Bogan, as he would sometimes call himself, had to start to earn money at an early age. At first, he sold newspapers then began caddying. He saw the type of people who played golf—nice, well dressed people of means, as opposed to the ruffians he competed with selling newspapers or in the caddie pen. So he got a club here and a club there and started learning the game. When he was too old to caddie, he started working in the golf shop, polishing clubs sometimes until two or three in the morning on weekends, yet Hogan never regretted those menial tasks. He relished them for the opportunity they afforded him, an opportunity that he didn't find in his other endeavors.

Hogan had few, if any, things handed to him. The harder road seemed his lot in life, but Hogan didn't complain. He turned pro at the Texas Open in 1931 at the age of 18, but didn't win a tournament until 1940—nine years after his pro debut. Ben Hogan constantly faced an uphill climb. He felt that he didn't seem to have the same natural abilities of his competitors, so he decided that he had to work harder and longer than the rest of the players to succeed. He committed himself to that, to the point that harder, longer work hours became his instinctive work ethic. Some surmise the practice not only helped his golf game, but it perhaps helped an emotional emptiness from his difficult childhood. Hogan acknowledged that he loved to practice, that it helped him clear out everything else on his mind when he focused on hitting the golf ball. Despite his efforts, when he started out on the tour, he failed, and came home broke—several times.

He was fortunate to have a wife, Valerie, who shared his dream. The couple scrimped and saved, and she sacrificed with him in those early years to make the most of his opportunity to become successful on the pro tour. Valerie Hogan provided much needed support and encouragement during those difficult days.

The Hogans didn't party hard, and having a good time wasn't a high priority while Hogan was trying to make it on the tour. The only thing he knew to do when he played poorly was to work harder, practice longer; however, while he was developing the Hogan work ethic, he also was determining that he couldn't succeed by just working harder at the same things that kept failing. His mental make-up told him that he must try to do things differently, to experiment and test, in order to become better.

To hone your skills to the highest level in golf you don't need a partner to catch a ball, hit back a tennis ball or another player to develop teamwork. Hogan could hit practice balls to his heart's content. Alone was pretty much what he'd been dealt in life to this point anyway, so Hogan turned the disadvantage of his lonely, difficult childhood into the advantage of being able to work alone for hours on end, and he made the most of it.

Jimmy Demaret, in his book *My Partner Ben Hogan,* told this story: "In the first round of the Rochester Open in 1941, Hogan burned up the course, shooting a record 64....but the poor guy took a six on the par-four seventeenth. I had a 69, which I thought good enough, and I sat around with the fellows in the clubhouse until it was almost nighttime, gabbing and having a drink or two.

"When I went out to the car to drive home, I noticed a late evening eager beaver all alone on the practice tee hitting wood shots. I didn't have to be told it was Hogan. 'What are you trying to do, man?' I asked. 'You had ten birdies today. Why, the officials are still inside talking about it. They're thinking of putting a limit on you.

"Ben gave me that dead-serious look of his. 'You know, Jimmy, if a man can shoot ten birdies, there's no reason why he can't shoot eighteen. Why can't you birdie every hole on the course?' And then his face took on a look of real anguish, and he wailed, 'And how about that terrible seventeenth?'"

Asked by TV announcer Jim Kelly what drove him, what kept him on the straight and narrow, Hogan answered, "I couldn't veer off. I had nothing. I had to eat, and I didn't want to go to jail—they don't feed you very well in jail. So I had to be on the straight and narrow all my life, and I've loved it. It's the better road to travel. And I had to work so hard, and I'm pleased that I did. I've been rewarded for doing it. And it's a nice thing to have in your life. You can cope with other things—I got enjoyment out of improving. If I just hold my own all the time, it didn't satisfy me. If you improve, you get a great satisfaction of accomplishment."

Similarly during Ken Venturi's 1983 CBS interview, Hogan noted about his journey, "My family wasn't rich, we were poor. I knew tough things. I had a tough day all my life, and I can handle tough things. Every day that I progressed was a joy to me, and I recognized it every day. I don't think I could have done what I've done if I hadn't had the tough days to begin with."

Golf was Hogan's missing friend. It didn't pick on him, it didn't betray him, and it didn't let him down, disappoint him or take advantage of him. The golf course gave and it took away according to the efforts of the golfer; it was the same for every player. Golf enabled Hogan to satisfy many needs, and at the same time become successful. He became known as the most knowledgeable person regarding the golf swing, yet he felt he had an enormous task in front of him—to learn even more. To Hogan, finding the perfect golf swing wasn't a goal, it was a lifetime journey: 18 birdies in a round would be the result of finding the answers he sought.

As Hogan's efforts were rewarded by the game, his respect for it grew into reverence. Golf had afforded him a pleasurable life, success, fame, and that opportunity to prove himself. Golf enabled a poor kid from Fort Worth, Texas to meet and play golf with Presidents of the United States, to be greeted with a ticker tape parade through New

York City, to have President Gerald Ford agreeing to speak at the official opening of the World Golf Hall of Fame in Pinehurst, North Carolina, "…if Ben Hogan was going to be there." Hogan was respected and admired for his great golf skills, and as a champion and an honorable gentleman. He was imperfect, but those who knew him appreciated his character, compassion, sense of humor, and loyalty.

Hogan had two life partners, Valerie and golf, and he treated the two with the same respect. He didn't put up with ill manners or cussing in front of women, and he didn't want to see golf, particularly tournament golf, defiled and turned into a circus, or be demeaned in any way. He tried to protect golf almost like he protected women. When he played on the tour he dressed smartly but conservatively, and used a one-color leather golf bag with no writing on it. When asked to wear a number on his back to enter the richest golf tournament of the day—the George S. May event at the Tam O'Shanter Country Club outside Chicago—Hogan refused. The fact that it was required for entry for the richest purse up to that point made no difference to Hogan. His profession wasn't a cattle show or a rodeo; it was tournament golf at country clubs. He also felt that when you accepted the winner's trophy you should do so with a jacket on your back. Thus, because he felt he had to be properly dressed, he irritated the Scots after winning the British Open in 1953 by making them wait in the rain until he got a sport coat to accept one of the greatest prizes in all of golf.

During a large part of Hogan's professional tournament golf career (1932-1970) not even the best players could make a living from their tournament winnings—they had to supplement that income with part-time club jobs, exhibitions, clinics, appearances, and more. Hogan, as the premier player of his day, was trying to change that. While it would undoubtedly benefit Hogan personally, it also benefited the professional golf tour.

Certainly Hogan had the selfish motivation to make the best living that he could, and to be as successful as possible, but Hogan looked at the sport of golf as a continuum in which he had to play his part to help the game grow and progress. He made TV appearances, appeared in movies, and acted as a salesman for golf in the early 1950s. On the Ed Sullivan show, he did a humorous impression of the host's golf swing, then gave instructions on how to do it right. He clowned with Jack Benny and was in a movie with comedian Jerry Lewis. He appeared on the cover of *Life* and *Time* magazines and promoted golf through the National Beat Ben Hogan Day by playing golf and doing the TV commercial for the United States Golf Association. The movie about his life, *Follow the Sun*, gave more exposure to the professional golf tour and the people involved in it.

In the early 1950s, with Hogan's popularity at its peak and his becoming the top gate attraction at tournaments, he pushed the envelope for appearance fees, exhibition fees and reportedly even sought guarantees when entering a tournament. He was a good, tough negotiator and was not reluctant to push those fees to their upper limit. For that, he was criticized. He did not openly fight back at his detractors, but author Gene Gregston quoted him as saying, "I've been criticized....by the same fellows I'm helping. They don't realize that every time I raise my exhibition fee or the amount of appearance money, it's helping all professional golfers. An exhibition fee of $1,000 was unheard-of until I got it. But you'll notice that when I raise mine, others do the same, and the young fellows coming up in the future will be able to demand more because we've raised the level." Gregston continued, "Hogan was not the least bit reluctant in pushing the price to the limit the market would bear. He became less tractable in golf and other business deals and was a tough negotiator."

Jack Nicklaus noted in his book, *The Greatest Game of All*, "I had certainly chosen the right time to turn professional. Thanks primarily to television, but also to Arnold Palmer's impact on the sports public, to the golf salesmanship of Ben Hogan and General Eisenhower before him, and to our steady national prosperity, tournament golf was entering a prodigious boom period."

Hogan thought the purses should grow, that more of the players should be able to make a good living, not just the elite few at the top. It would be good for golf, and Hogan wanted to see more and more people enjoying the game he loved so much. Later in life he noted that the current tour players had played a great deal of competitive amateur and college golf, so by the time they joined the tour they had a great deal of experience in competing with other talented golfers. It delighted Hogan. For several years in the 1990s,

Hogan and the Ben Hogan Company sponsored the Ben Hogan Tour to help up-and-coming players, as well as veteran professionals who didn't win enough money on the PGA Tour to retain full playing privileges. Hogan wouldn't attend a Ben Hogan Tour event until those players were given more equitable provisions for airfares, insurance, and entry fees relative to the regular PGA tour. When that was improved, Hogan attended the tournament. The developmental tour, under different sponsorship today, still thrives.

In his 1983 CBS interview Ken Venturi noted that Hogan hadn't played golf because he thought he was going to make a lot of money. Hogan responded, "You couldn't make any money. I won 49 tournaments [actually 64], and I couldn't make any money. After the U.S. Open, I used to book 20 to 25 exhibitions. That's the only way I could make a living during the year. And as you say, all the fellas that preceded me, Hagen, Jones, Sarazen, Cruickshank, Armour, those fellas put a rug out for me. Otherwise, there wouldn't be any tournament golf… These fellas that are playing now are better players than we were. Now, my contemporaries, the better players were of course, Snead, Nelson, Demaret, ah, Jackie Burke, and I could go on and on and on. In my opinion, these fellas that are playing now are better players than we were, and I'm delighted that they are. Really! Because if they weren't better than we were, then I would feel like I never contributed anything to the game."

Another time, Dick Harmon noted a conversation that his father, Claude Harmon, and Hogan had after Keith Clearwater had just shot 126 for the first two rounds of a tournament. They were surprised by such an exceptionally low two-round score, yet not totally amazed.

Dick said, "Mr. Hogan said to my father, 'You know, if they're not shooting any lower than we did, Claude, then you and I didn't do a very good job of teaching them. If they're not better than we were, then we didn't add anything to the game.'"

Hogan's quiet cause to make the professional golf tour better wasn't limited to spending endless hours on the practice range, demanding higher fees, or chewing out other tour players about their appearance, attire, and long hairstyles. Prior to the 1952 Masters tournament, he suggested to Bobby Jones and Clifford Roberts that they start a Masters Club and begin a tradition of having a past champions dinner

The 1958 Masters Club gathering, which Ben Hogan founded in 1952. Attendees are -- around the table l to r-- Claude Harmon, Gene Sarazen, Clifford Roberts (Masters Tournament Chairman), Doug Ford, Robert Jones (Tournament and Augusta National Golf Club Founder), Ben Hogan, Horton Smith, Herman Kaiser, Henry Picard-- in the back-- Carey Middlecoff, Sam Snead, Byron Nelson, Jimmy Demaret, Jack Burke, Craig Wood. (PHOTO COURTESY FITZ-SYMMS PHOTOGRAPHY)

hosted by the Masters winner from the previous year. Since Hogan was the defending champion in 1952, he was offering to pick up the tab for the inaugural Masters Club dinner. Jones and Roberts liked the idea, and almost all of the past champions attended. It became an annual tradition that continues today. Hogan felt something special about Bobby Jones, his Masters Tournament and its champions, and he wanted to add to the Masters tradition. Gary Player appreciated Hogan's founding the Masters Club, starting a tradition that was very meaningful to him, noting that "Hogan started something that was a very special part of my career." It turned out that Hogan hosted the dinner two of the first three times (1952 and 1954). "I saw that the dinner was costing me more than I won, so I finished second four times, he joked later."

The Masters wasn't the only event that Hogan made a contribution. Having traveled with Valerie on the tour, he knew how difficult tour life could be, so through his friend Marvin Leonard, Hogan helped make the Colonial National Invitation Tournament a little different. While on the tour, he had struggled in his early years, and wouldn't travel without his wife. So he wanted to help accommodate families that came to play in the Colonial, insisting that during the tournament Colonial Country Club cater to the families of the players. Accommodations such as eating at Colonial for free, even baby-sitting for the families, he felt, would make it easier for families to travel together on the tour. Today, many of the host clubs/courses make similar provisions.

Hogan participated in the Colonial tournament festivities and was always a hit at the Champions Dinner. Rodney Johnston, Chairman of the NIT in the late 1970s and early 1980s reflected, "He briefly touched my life when I was NIT Chairman, and he definitely made an impression." The first year of Johnston's tenure, his wife, Gale, sat next to Hogan, and she was very nervous about being next to him. However, Rodney, recalled, "I looked over and Gale and Mr. Hogan were going back and forth, and Mr. Hogan was doing most of the talking. It carried on for quite some time. After the dinner half a dozen pros from the table in front of them came up to Gale and asked what they were talking about because it was an animated conversation and Mr. Hogan was talking so much." Gale said that Mr. Hogan was telling her how he prepared for a golf tournament shot by shot, going all around the course. Gale said the whole thing fascinated her, and every one of those asking about the conversation was envious of her getting the first-hand details from Hogan himself regarding his tournament preparation.

In 1981, Colonial held a 40th anniversary celebration of the 1941 U.S. Open held at Colonial, in which Craig Wood won the tournament, and Ben Hogan finished tied for third. Johnston said, "When we told him we wanted to hold a 40th anniversary celebration, he kinda' looked at me and asked, 'Why are you doing the 40th?' I said because we were afraid some of the players wouldn't be around for the 50th. He looked at me with a grin on his face and said that it was a pretty good idea, and that he'd be glad to help.

"We had a dinner at Marty Leonard's house with about 26 or so players that came to the 40th, and they had a great time. They all sat around telling stories, reminiscing about those days and how they would drag their putters behind their car or some such thing."

Hogan's tenacity for respect in golf wasn't just applicable to professionals playing the tour. Mike Wright, the Shady Oaks Director of Golf since the mid-1980s, noted, "He respected the many requirements club professionals had and the many hats they had to wear and wear well, beginning with their long demanding hours, and that they were required to be good merchandisers, teachers, managers, and motivators—while at the same time being good politicians to keep many different people happy."

Hogan backed that up with his actions, as evidenced by his insistence on paying Art Hall, the Shady Oaks golf professional from the 1960s to the mid-1980s, the $10 each day he used an electric cart to drive to his practice area. For Hogan, of course, that was virtually every single day.

Unless a money making deal was right in his eyes, Hogan would have none of it. In July 1954, the author of a book sent Hogan a letter, on the stationary of publisher A.S. Barnes & Company, stating that photographs of Hogan had been taken at Baltusrol for illustrations in a book, which the author, Dave Camerer, was writing. (Pictures had been taken of Hogan while he was practicing on the putting green just prior to the 1954 U.S. Open, but Hogan was not aware they were being taken, and had not given his permission to have them taken.) The letter also contained a release form

Ben Hogan and Byron Nelson look through the program for the 1941 U.S. Open, held at Colonial Country Club. (PHOTO COURTESY OF COLONIAL COUNTRY CLUB)

for Hogan to sign. He was promised $100 and two copies of the book when it was completed. The release form provided for the assignment to Camerer by Hogan of all literary rights "in an article to be written under Hogan's supervision;" that Camerer would have the right to use Hogan's name and signature as author, as well as any biographical data and pictures of Hogan. If Ben Hogan had turned down the idea of a chain of Ben Hogan Golf Schools because he wouldn't allow someone else to give golf lessons under his name—which was the case—he certainly wasn't about to let someone write an instructional book-article that he hadn't help write, use pictures of him he hadn't given permission to be shot, or to use his name—something Hogan guardedly protected—without permission, particularly for an offer of $100 and two copies of the book. Hogan's response, sent about two weeks later, contained only three words: "Are you kidding?" Several days later Hogan wrote to the president of the A.S. Barnes & Company, informing him of the letter and asserting that the photographs of him at Baltusrol had been taken without his knowledge and without his consent to their use or publication. He urged the president of A.S. Barnes "not to accept for publication any material written about me, or my golf swing, either from this fellow Camerer or anyone else so far as that is concerned. This goes for photographs also."

Ironically, Hogan found out that the instruction book, *Golf with the Masters*, had indeed been published when someone stuck it in front of him and asked him to autograph it as he was about to tee off against Jack Fleck in the 1955 U.S. Open Championship playoff. You can bet that Hogan didn't sign that book. While A.S. Barnes & Co. had published Hogan's book *Power Golf* in 1948, which meant he and the company were friends, that did not deter him from doing what he had to do. This was a matter of principle to Hogan, and principles meant something to Ben Hogan. So, despite considerable criticism from some of his fellow pros, he sued the publisher.

Remarkably, this example of Hogan's long-term perspective on the game has been overlooked except for one author, Al Barkow. Barkow wrote about the case in *Golf* magazine in 1971, in his book *Golf's Golden Grind; The History of the Tour* in 1974, and in his collection, *That's Golf* devoting an entire chapter, "Ben Hogan's Day in Court," to the reprint of his *Golf* magazine article.

Regarding Hogan's legal efforts to elevate the stature of the professional golfer, and the professional athlete, Barkow wrote:

"In 1921, Honus Wagner, one of the greatest shortstops in baseball history, sued a company for manufacturing and selling baseball bats with his name on them, without his consent or recompense to him. The case went to the Supreme Court, and Wagner lost. Some 20 years later Davey O'Brien, a brilliant football quarterback, brought suit against a beer company for putting his name and picture on a widely distributed calendar. O'Brien received no money, but even more disturbing to him was that, as a crusading teetotaler, he was associated, however indirectly, with beer drinking. O'Brien also lost his case. The decisions against Wagner and O'Brien were based essentially on the legal ground that they were public figures; thus, their name and/or picture could be used for commercial purposes without their being consulted or paid.... At the core of those decisions, which seem so incredible today, was the notion of an athlete's place in society. It seemed to say in effect that when a man exhibits himself on a playing field he lowers himself in the eyes of his fellow men, becomes something of a clown, a second-class citizen who merely entertains and thus can be taken advantage of freely. In 1955 that concept was put to the test by Ben Hogan, and the story is yet another example of this rather unique man's strength of character, and will."

Davey O'Brien appealed the ruling against him and again lost. The majority opinion Judges stating "We think it perfectly plain that the District Judge was right in the view he took that nothing in the publication violated plaintiff's right of privacy and that nothing in it could be legitimately or reasonably construed as falsely stating that he used, endorsed, or recommended the use of Pabst's beer."

However Judge Holmes, Circuit Court of Appeals, Fifth Circuit, in his dissenting opinion wrote:

"The evidence in this case shows that appellant [O'Brien] refused an offer by a New York beer company of $400 for an endorsement of its beer, and the appellee apparently recognized that it was necessary to obtain the consent of the various football players, because it required that releases be obtained from them. This admittedly was not done. The fact that appellant made this stipulation with the publishers of the calendars may save it from the infliction of punitive damages, but cannot relieve it from the payment of actual damages measured by the value of the unauthorized use of appellant's picture….The decision of the majority leaves the appellant without remedy for any non-libelous use made of his picture by advertisers of beer, wine, whiskey, patent medicines, or other non-contraband goods, wares, and merchandise. It also places every other famous stage, screen, and athletic star in the same situation. If one is popular and permits publicity to be given to one's talent and accomplishment in any art or sport, commercial advertisers may seize upon such popularity to increase their sales of any lawful article without compensation of any kind for such commercial use of one's name and fame. This is contrary to usage and custom among advertisers in the marts of trade."

Like Hogan, O'Brien had turned down the offer to use his picture to endorse a beer, yet he was denied damages for Pabst Sales Company using his picture in its beer calendar without his permission.

In the *Hogan v. A.S. Barnes & Company,* Incorporated case, the written opinion of the presiding judge, Judge Hagan wrote:

"This case presents a fact situation which, so far as our research discloses, is dissimilar from any which has ever come before an appellate court in the United States. However, the common law is not static but an ever-expanding body of law, and, therefore, the lack of direct precedent does not necessarily defeat plaintiff's right to recovery. As Chief Judge Biggs stated in a recent decision of the United States Court of Appeals for the Third Circuit, which also involved a relatively new theory of law: 'Concededly, the theory is a somewhat hazy one; but that is not unusual where the laboratories of the courts are working out the development of a new common law right.' In this case the basic facts are not in dispute, but the parties, of course, are not in agreement as to the legal inferences and conclusions to be drawn from the facts."

311

Hogan sought to recover damages on five different theories of liability: 1) invasion of right of privacy; 2) unfair competition, damaging to plaintiff's rights of publicity; 3) an unauthorized and uncompensated appropriation for commercial purposes of plaintiff's right of publicity; 4) libel; and 5) breach of a written contract between Hogan and A.S. Barnes, since Barnes had published Hogan's book *Power Golf.*

On June 19, 1957 the Pennsylvania Court of Common Pleas No. 2, Philadelphia County ruled in Hogan's favor on items 2, 3 and 5 (but noted that Nos. 3 & 5 were variations of No. 2). It determined that Hogan had an enforceable property right in his name and photograph, and as a result, his name and photograph in connection with any aspect of the sport of golf had great commercial value, and that Hogan was entitled to recover compensatory damages for the invasion of his property rights.

It is very important to note that in calculating damages in Judge Hagan's ruling, the Judge wrote in his finding:

"Since the year 1937 plaintiff has earned approximately $1,000,000 from golf, and it is significant to note that of these earnings a little more than one quarter represents winnings from golf tournaments, while almost three quarters represents earnings from exhibitions, endorsements, royalties, personal appearances, motion pictures, magazine articles, etc...From this evidence here emerge the clear conclusions (a) that, by reason of plaintiff's unique position in the world of golf, publications on the subject of his golfing style, and technique are a source of substantial income to him; and (b) that a publisher who makes an unauthorized use of such assets and appropriates them to his own commercial purposes subjects himself to the payment of damages."

All the fees that Hogan had been so harshly criticized for increasing when he was the number one name in golf—fees for exhibitions, personal appearances, clinics, endorsements, royalties, magazine articles, etc.—were deemed to be of significant importance by Judge Hagan in his ruling for Hogan. They accounted for most of the 75 percent of his income. That fact was of major importance in establishing precedent giving athletes new legal standing in the courtroom.

The timing of Hogan's "I have a secret" article in the August 8, 1955 issue of *Life* magazine may not have been just because Hogan felt his career was winding down. Hogan received $20,000 from *Life* and *Sports Illustrated* for the "Secret" article, a considerable amount of money for that day and time. In so doing, Hogan fully demonstrated that his ideas on the golf swing in addition to his 1948 book, *Power Golf,* had significant commercial value, a point Judge Hagan specifically made in his opinion regarding the "Secret" article--"that, in addition to the foregoing sums, plaintiff received $20,000 from *Life* magazine and *Sports Illustrated* magazine, of an article purporting to reveal plaintiff's so-called "secret"... From this evidence there emerge the clear conclusions (a) that, by reason of plaintiff's unique position in the world of golf, publications on the subject of his golfing style and technique are a source of substantial income to him; and (b) that a publisher who makes an unauthorized use of such assets and appropriates them to his own commercial purposes, subjects himself to the payment of damages."

Since other pros were involved in the Camerer book, there were those who said Hogan had selfishly destroyed the potentially valuable publicity the book would have given other pros included in it. Hogan, however, had much bigger issues to prove. He had spent a lifetime developing his swing, and he wasn't about to be financially taken by an author and a publisher who did not understand the meaning of "no." If they could do that to him, the #1 name in golf at the time, they could do it to anybody.

While Ben Hogan was meticulous in everything he did, he was particularly exacting in his record keeping of his efforts on the golf course. Through their "Little Black Book," a 4"x 5 ¾" bound book with a black cover, the Hogans dutifully kept his information, by month and year, regarding the tournaments entered, scores shot, place he finished in the tournament, the money won or earned. and the caddie fee paid. It included tournaments, pro-ams, exhibitions, driving contests, and other related income. Match-play tournaments had the match results, and if he didn't make the cut or made no money it was so noted, as was whether he won or lost in a playoff, or if he had been disqualified (including the round in which he was disqualified). Income was totaled by year, along with the caddie fees. The entry for the 1942 Hale America tournament noted that he won the "Hale America Nat. Open." The "Little Black Book" information became an important factor during the lawsuit.

Ben Hogan had a Little Black Book in which the Hogans dutifully kept track of all Ben Hogan's information, for each tournment entered, scores shot, place finished, money won, caddie fees paid, etc., by month and year. (PHOTO COURTESY HOGAN ESTATE)

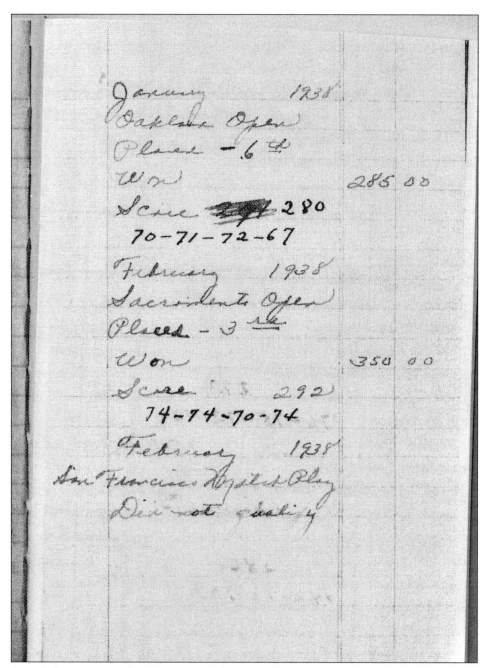

Hogan's Little Black Book open to January 1938, the Oakland Open page, the tournament that Ben Hogan said was the biggest check he ever won-- it kept him from going home and giving up golf for good. (PHOTO COURTESY HOGAN ESTATE)

Hogan's meticulousness was also apparent in his hiring of an attorney for the case. He hired a highly professional Philadelphia lawyer by the name of Francis W. Sullivan who was as dedicated to law as Hogan was to golf. Sullivan was a man of integrity, and was also at one time a scratch golfer, having played with Tommy Armour. Sullivan's single-mindedness to the law had caused him to turn down enticing offers to be proposed for the commissionerships of football and golf, and to being tendered two federal judgeships. The one thing that came first to Sullivan was the practice of law, and his preoccupation with law even caused him to turn down a week of golf with Ben Hogan! That may have been a first for Ben Hogan. Barkow described the Hogan-Sullivan pairing this way–

> "Both take a serious approach to life, particularly the professional end of it. Sullivan, like Hogan, is careful and methodical, as are all good lawyers... and golfers. Both came from similar economic conditions. Sullivan took his bar exam with the last five dollars he owned. Hogan scraped for enough money to hire shag boys and enter tournaments. Both became successful and relatively wealthy by dint of their single-minded sense of purpose and perseverance. They are quietly proud of their achievements and have the same perception of man's rights..."

Hogan was little different in the courtroom than he was on the golf course or everyday life— focused concentration and doing exactly what his attorney instructed him to do. He provided detailed documentation taken from his Little Black Book when he was asked to substantiate his earnings as a professional golfer. The material was so thorough that even his meticulous attorney was surprised, and Judge Hagan later stated that Ben Hogan was possibly the best witness who had ever testified in his courtroom.

That court decision determined that Hogan, professional athletes, and other public figures had value off the golf course, outside the field, arena or the stage. Unfair business competition had damaged Hogan's rights as an author of existing and future literary property and deprived him of income due to the unauthorized and uncompensated appropriation for commercial purposes of Hogan's right of publicity. The court awarded Hogan $5,000, but Barkow further noted:

"The $5,000 was not a great sum, but that wasn't Hogan's main aim. He was out to prove a point. He dispelled the concept of an athlete as it had been directed toward Honus Wagner and Davey O'Brien. He showed that he was not to be taken for a Roman gladiator, performing for his masters solely on their terms and grateful for the few shekels thrown to him. Such an idea is repugnant to the man. He demands the respect he has earned by virtue of his own hard work, and insists on controlling his destiny as far as that is possible. His approach to golf has always been that of a professional in the highest sense of the word. What may be only a game to others, a fine way to avoid work, is to Hogan a life's labor. All the endless hours of practice and play are to him equivalent to the scientist poring over test tubes and equations;"

In a final irony—or just a telling demonstration that while Hogan held to principles he did not hold grudges—it is notable that A.S. Barnes was the publisher of both of Ben Hogan's books *Power Golf* in 1948—before the lawsuit, and after it, *The Five Lessons, The Modern Fundamentals of Golf* in 1957.

Golf writer Charles Price had this to say about Ben Hogan in his 1981 *Golf* magazine article, "Memories of Ben Hogan"—"Ben Hogan was and is the most intense man I have ever known at doing anything. I say this despite the fact I have laughed with him at a locker room story, listened to him wax sentimental at a banquet, and even heard him make a wisecrack or two to a gallery. Until him, nobody in golf shot 66 and then went out and practiced for three hours, and the stories of him slamming clubs into the turf over a shot that would have delighted anybody else are legion."

Price had a conversation with Valerie Hogan regarding Hogan's time in the hospital after his near fatal auto accident that he recounted in the article as well, "When Hogan's body was wrapped in a cast from his shoulders to his ankles at the Hotel Dieu Hospital in El Paso after his grinding car accident in 1949, he continued to play golf in his delirium, his wife, Valerie, once told me. He would go through the motions of gripping a club, twisting and turning his hands to get the proper purchase on it, and then he would make feint motions with an arm, as though waving back a gallery. When you do that on what is thought to be your deathbed, you have come to play for something beyond money."

Despite having his career interrupted twice during his prime taking what could have been his most productive four years out of his career, the severe limitations his near fatal accident placed on his body for the rest of his career, after the countless thousands of hours he committed to practicing and his dedicated self-discipline to train himself, and then retrain himself to be the best that he could possibly be, Ben Hogan looked beyond himself to the reason for his success, even though it took him nine years to win his first tournament. For the immense success he had, winning 64 tournaments, nine major tournaments—six of them in the four years after his horrific accident, Hogan believed there was something stronger at work than a dedicated man succeeding at his chosen profession. He felt things happened for a reason, for a purpose, and he expressed it after winning the British Open in 1953.

Gene Gregston framed it thusly: "Hogan was not sanctimonious, nor a hypocrite, but he said…. 'I don't think anybody does anything unless the Lord's with them. I think it's fate, and supposed to be, that I won these tournaments; otherwise, I wouldn't have won them. All of those victories required more guidance than one human being can give another, and I've been fortunate enough to receive that guidance. I think the Lord has let me win these tournaments for a purpose. I hope that purpose is to give courage to those people who are sick or injured or broken in body as I once was.'"

Later in life, when he was almost 80, during his interview with Jim Kelly, Hogan reflected on his feelings for the sport: "[Being] associated with golf is a life's love of mine. And I wouldn't trade it for anything in the world. And the people I've met, the people I've been with, and what golf stands for is, it's touching the feet of God every day."

Ben Hogan was a man with a purpose that grew as he grew in stature. He didn't start out to change the world, but he used his success to make golf, and coincidentally athletics, a better profession. Indeed. "What Hogan didn't give to his golf, he didn't have to give. Without any question, no other golfer ever dedicated himself so totally to the game." —Herbert Warren Wind, the Story of American Golf

Ben Hogan in front of his new portrait at Shady Oaks Country Club, August 1963. (PHOTO COURTESY, *FORT WORTH STAR-TELEGRAM*, SPECIAL COLLECTIONS, THE UNIVERSITY OF TEXAS AT ARLINGTON LIBRARY, ARLINGTON, TEXAS)

APPENDIX:
BEN HOGAN'S GOLF RECORDS & ACCOMPLISHMENTS

During his career Ben Hogan won 64 official PGA Tour events, ranking him 4th in all-time victories, behind Sam Snead (82), Tiger Woods (79), and Jack Nicklaus (73). However, Hogan's career was interrupted twice in his prime, first for more than two years of military service in World War II, and a second time, for a year, following a near fatal auto/bus collision. The injuries from the collision cut short Hogan's career and severely limited how much he could play following the accident, including not being able to play in the PGA Championship due to the match-play format.

After several unproductive years on the pro tour Hogan finally started winning golf tournaments in 1940. In all, he won 48 events before his accident in 1949. He won the Vardon Trophy, for the lowest scoring average three times and had the lowest average in 1942 when no trophy was awarded.

In the three and one-half years of his prime between returning from the military service in August 1945 until his accident in February, 1949, Hogan won 37 tournaments, and was the top money winner five of the six years he competed from 1940 through 1948, finishing third the only year he wasn't first on the money list, 1947. However, on February 2, 1949, after winning two events on the west coast, Ben Hogan was nearly killed when Ben and Valerie Hogan's car was hit head-on by a bus.

Hogan's victories prior to his accident—

1941 - 5

1942 - 6

1943 - Military Service

1944 - Military Service

1945 - 5 (joined tour in late August, after discharge from U.S. Army Air Forces)

1946 - 13

1947 - 7

1948 - 10

1949 - 2   (Month of January only - bus/car crash February 2nd)

The damage from his injuries so severely limited Hogan's playing schedule that after 1949 he competed in fewer tournaments each year than he had won annually prior to his accident. It took Hogan nearly nine years after his accident to enter as many tournaments as the 37 he had won in the three-and-a-half years after leaving the military in August of 1945.

Tournaments Entered 1950 through the end of his career--

1950 - 6	1956 - 6	1962 - 3	1968 - 0
1951 - 4	1957 - 2	1963 - 1	1969 - 0
1952 - 3	1958 - 3	1964 - 4	1970 - 3
1953 - 6	1959 - 5	1965 - 5	1971 - 1
1954 - 4	1960 - 5	1966 - 4	
1955 - 3	1961 - 3	1967 - 4	

Despite his limited schedule the four years following his accident, 1950 -1953, Hogan continued at his same level of success. During that period he won 10 of the 20 events he entered, including six of the nine major tournaments he entered. Thus from 1948 thru 1953 Hogan won eight of the 12 major tournaments in which he teed it up.

CAREER PERFORMANCE (1932 - 1971)

303 official PGA events entered

64	Victories
45	Finished 2nd or tied for 2nd
28	Finished 3rd or tied for 3rd
137	Top 3 finishes
175	Top 5 finishes
233	Top 10 Finishes

HOGAN'S PRIME YEARS' PERFORMANCE (1940 - 1955)

199 official PGA events entered

62	Victories
40	Finished 2nd or tied for 2nd
22	Finished 3rd or tied for 3rd
124	Top 3 finishes
150	Top 5 finishes
174	Top 10 Finishes

BEN HOGAN'S PERFORMANCE IN MAJOR TOURNAMENTS

Career	**Prime years (1940 – 1955)**
58 Entries	30 Entries
9 Victories	9 Victories
17 Top 3 finishes	16 Top 3 finishes
25 Top 5 finishes	24 Top 5 finishes
40 Top 10 finishes	29 Top 10 finishes

Does NOT include 1942 Hale America National Open as a Major

During his prime years (1940-1955) Hogan finished out of the top 10 in a major tournament only once-- 1947 PGA tournament (match play). During that 16-year period Hogan finished in the Top 6 in majors an amazing 27 times in 30 starts, and in the U.S. Open during that 16-year stretch finished in the Top 6 a truly amazing 11 times in 11 tries. (12 for 12 if you include the 1942 Hale America National Open.)

BEN HOGAN'S MASTERS PERFORMANCE

25	Entries
2	Victories
6	Top 3 finishes
9	Top 5 finishes
17	Top 10 finishes

In the Masters, from 1939 through 1956 Hogan never finished out of the Top 10.

BEN HOGAN'S U.S. NATIONAL OPEN PERFORMANCE+

23	Total entries
4	Victories+
8	Top 3 finishes
10	Top 5 finishes
16	Top 10 finishes

+ Does not include 1942 Hale America National Open as a major

In the U.S. Open Hogan never finished out of the top 10 from 1940 through 1960.

BEN HOGAN'S PGA CHAMPIONSHIP PERFORMANCE

The PGA Championship was a match-play tournament until 1958, when it became a stroke-play tournament. Ben Hogan did not compete in the PGA Championship from 1949-1958 due to his injuries.

9	Entries
2	Victories
5	Top 5 finishes
6	Top 10 finishes

Ben Hogan's match-play record-- wins as a percentage of matches played, was second only to Byron Nelson.

BEN HOGAN'S BRITISH OPEN PERFORMANCE

1953	1st	[Only British Open Hogan entered]

	Masters	U.S. Open	PGA Championship	British Open
1934	---	Missed Cut-	--	---
1936	---	Missed Cut	---	---
1938	T25th	Missed Cut	---	---
1939	9th	T62nd	T9th	---
1940	T10th	T5th	T5th	---
1941	4th	T3rd	T5th	---
1942	2nd	1st (Hale America)	T5th	---
1943	Did not compete - Military Service			
1944	Did not compete - Military Service			
1945	Did not compete - Military Service			
1946	2nd	T4th	1st	---
1947	T4th	T6th	T33rd	---
1948	T6th	1st	1st	---
1949	Did not compete --Auto accident injuries			
1950	T4th	1st	---	---
1951	1st	1st	---	---

1952	T7th	3rd	---	---
1953	1st	1st	--- #	1st
1954	2nd	T6th	---	---
1955	2nd	2nd	---	---
1956	T8th	T2nd	---	---
1957	Missed Cut	---	---	---
1958	T14th	T10th	---	---
1959	T30th	T8th	---	---
1960	T6th	T9th	Missed Cut	---
1961	T32nd	T14th	---	---
1962	38th	---	---	---
1963	---	---	---	---
1964	T9th	---	T9th	---
1965	T21st	---	T15th	---
1966	T13th	12th	---	---
1967	T10th	T34th	---	---

1953 - PGA Championship overlapped with the British Open that year

PGA Championship-- After his auto accident in 1949, Hogan was unable to compete because the match-play format that required a 36-hole qualifying event followed by six straight days of play-- 18 hole matches for the first two, followed by four 36-hole matches. The seven-day grind was too much for Hogan's legs, so he did not play in the PGA Championship again until 1960, after it had been changed to a stroke play tournament.

Hogan's overall accomplishments--

Vardon Trophy Winner	1940, 1941, 1948 (Had low stroke average in 1942, but no award given)
Leading Money Winner	1940, 1941, 1942, 1946, 1948
PGA Player of the Year	1948, 1950, 1951, 1953
U.S. Open Champion+	1942+, 1948, 1950, 1951, 1953
Masters Champion	1951, 1953
PGA Champion #	1946, 1948 (Won 22 of 27 matches)
British Open Champion	1953

Ryder Cup Team Player   1947, 1951 (undefeated)

Ryder Cup Team Captain   1947, 1949, 1967 (won all 3)

(+1942 USGA Hale American National Open)

\# His PGA Match Play win percentage of 81.4% is second only to Byron Nelson's 82.2%)

BEN HOGAN'S CAREER PERFORMANCE RECORD

Year	Entered	1st	2nd	3rd	Top 5	Top 10
1932	4	0	0	0	0	0
1933	2	0	0	0	0	1
1934	3	0	0	0	0	1
1935	--	--	--	--	--	--
1936	1	0	0	0	0	0
1937	10	0	0	1	1	5
1938	19	1	0	2	5	14
1939	18	0	3	1	9	16
1940	21	4	5	1	14	17
1941	27	5	11	3	25	26
1942	19	6	3	1	15	17
1943	--	--	--	--	--	--
(in military service)						
1944	2	0	1	1	2	2
(in military service)						
1945	18	5	2	5	15	18
(in military service until August)						
1946	32	13	6	3	24	27
1947	25	7	3	2	15	20
1948	24	10	3	4	18	22
1949	4	2	1	0	3	3
(Auto accident February 2)						
1950	7	1	1	1	4	4
1951	4	3	0	0	4	4
1952	3	1	0	1	2	3
1953	6	5	1	0	6	6

Year	Entered	1st	2nd	3rd	Top 5	Top 10
1954	4	0	1	0	1	3
(1 WD illness after 2 rounds 69-71)						
1955	3	0	2	0	2	2
1956	5	0	1	0	1	3
1957	2	0	0	0	0	0
1958	3	0	0	0	1	2
1959	5	1	0	0	1	2
1960	5	0	1	0	1	4
1961	3	0	0	0	0	0
1962	3	0	0	0	1	1
1963	1	0	0	0	0	0
1964	4	0	0	0	2	4
1965	5	0	0	0	0	0
1966	4	0	0	0	1	2
1967	4	0	0	2	2	3
1968	--	--	--	--	--	--
1969	--	--	--	--	--	--
1970	2	0	0	0	0	1
(WD Westchester before tournament)						
1971	1	0	0	0	0	0
(WD injury 1st round)						
TOTAL	303	64	45	28	175	233

BEN HOGAN TOURNAMENT VICTORIES/ACCOMPLISHMENTS
Year-by-Year

		Victories
1938	Hershey Four-Ball	1
1940	North and South Open	4
	Greater Greensboro Open	
	Asheville Land of the Sky Open	
	Goodall Palm Beach Round Robin	

Vardon Trophy - 423 Points

1941   Miami Biltmore International Four-Ball   5
Asheville Open
Inverness Four-Ball
Chicago Open
Hershey Open
Vardon Trophy - 494 Points

1942   Los Angeles Open   6
San Francisco Open
Hale America Open (U.S. Open)
North and South Open
Asheville Land of the Sky Open
Rochester Open

[1943 - 1944 Military Service]

1945   (Joined tour in August after military discharge.) 5
Nashville Invitational
Portland Open Invitational
Richmond Invitational
Montgomery Invitational
Orlando Open

1946   Phoenix Open Invitational   13
San Antonio Texas Open
St. Petersburg Open
Miami International Four-Ball
Colonial National Invitation
Western Open
Goodall Round Robin
Inverness Round Robin Four-Ball
Winnipeg Open

	P.G.A. Championship	
	Golden State Open	
	Dallas Invitational	
	North and South Open	
1947	Los Angeles Open	7
	Phoenix Open Invitational	
	Miami International Four-Ball	
	Colonial National Invitation	
	Chicago Victory Open	
	Inverness Round Robin Four-Ball	
	World's Championship of Golf	
1948	Los Angeles Open	10
	P.G.A. Championship	
	U.S. Open*	
	Motor City Open*	
	Western Open*	
	Inverness Round Robin Four-Ball*	
	Reading Open*	
	Denver Open Invitational*	
	Reno Open	
	Glendale Open Invitational	
	Vardon Trophy	
	PGA "Golfer of the Year"	
1949	Bing Crosby Pro-Am	2
	Long Beach Open	
	Automobile Accident - February; did not compete until	
	1950 Los Angeles Open	
1950	Greenbrier Invitation***	1
	U.S. Open	
	PGA "Golfer of the Year"	

1951	Masters Tournament	3
	U.S. Open	
	Tam 'O Shanter***	
	World Championship of Golf	
	PGA "Golfer of the Year"	

1952	Colonial Invitational	1

1953	Colonial Invitational**	5
	Pan American Open**	
	Masters Tournament** (broke Masters record by 5 strokes)	
	U.S. Open** broke Oakmont U.S. Open record by 16 strokes)	
	British Open** (broke tournament record by 8 strokes)	
	PGA "Golfer of the Year"	
	Professional Athlete of the Year	

1956	Canada Cup*** [Now the World Cup - Won with Sam Snead]
	International Trophy*** (Hogan won the individual competition)

1959	Colonial National Invitational	1

TOTAL OFFICIAL VICTORIES   **64**

 *Won these 6 tournaments consecutively (1948)

 **Won these 5 tournaments consecutively (1953)

***Non Official PGA wins (1950, 1951, 1956)

TOP MONEY WINNING YEARS OF BEN HOGAN

Date	Position	Total Purse
1940	1st	$10,655
1941	1st	$18,358
1942	1st	$13,143
1943		$0 (no statistics compiled; Hogan in military service)
1944		$2,750 (Hogan in military service)

1945		$26,328 (Hogan in military service until August)
1946	1st	$42,556
1947	3rd	$23,310
1948	1st	$32,112
1951	4th	$20,400
1953	9th	$16,406

Sources:

PGA Tour Headquarters

Davis, Martin; Ben Hogan, The Man Behind the Mystique

Claribel Kelly's notes (Ben Hogan's Secretary)

Official U.S. Open Almanac – Johnson, Salvatore. Taylor Publishing. Dallas, Texas. 1995

CREDITS/SOURCES BY CHAPTER/SUB CHAPTER

INTRODUCTION

1. Walker, Granville. Speech given at a celebration to welcome Ben Hogan back to Fort Worth from his 1953 victory in the British Open at Carnoustie, Scotland. Fort Worth, TX. 1953.

2. Roberts, Jimmy, ESPN, Fifty Greatest Athletes, April 30, 1999.

3. Curtis, Brent & Eldredge, John, *The Sacred Romance*, Thomas Nelson Publishers, Nashville, TN. 1997. Pgs. 38, 39.

4. Demaret, Jimmy, *My Partner Ben Hogan*, McGraw-Hill Book Company. New York, New York. 1954. Pg. 96.

5. Nelson, Byron, ESPN, Fifty Greatest Athletes, April 30, 1999.

6. Seitz, Nick, *Golf Digest*, "Ben Hogan Today," A publication of the New York Times, September, 1970. Pg. 32.

7. Seitz, Nick, *Golf Digest*, "Ben Hogan Today," A publication of the New York Times, September, 1970. Pgs. 26, 28.

8. Venturi, Ken, *Getting Up & Down* My 60 Years in Golf, Triumph Books. Chicago, IL. 2004. Pg. 258.

HOGAN - CHARACTER TOUGH

1. Snead, Sam. *The Game I Love*, Ballantine Books, Division of Random House, Inc. New York, New York. 1997. pgs. 92 - 93.

2. Davis, Martin. *Ben Hogan The Man Behind The Mystique*, The American Golfer, Inc., Greenwich, CT. 2002. pg. 29.

3. Tschetter, Kris. *MR. HOGAN, The Man I Knew*, Gotham Books, New York, New York. 2010. Pgs. 63, 65.

4. Towle, Mike. *I Remember Ben Hogan*, Cumberland House Publishing, Nashville, TN; 2000. Pgs. 179 - 180.

5. Dickinson, Gardner. *Let 'er Rip*, Longstreet Press, Inc., subsidiary of Cox Enterprises, Marietta, Georgia. 1994. Pg. 33.

6. Dodson, James. *Ben Hogan An American Life*, Doubleday, New York, New York. 2004. Pgs. 37-38, 44-45.

7. Dodson, James. *Ben Hogan An American Life*, Doubleday, New York, New York. 2004. Pgs. 52, 55-56, 59-60.

8. Pate, Russ. *The Legacy Continues - A 50 Years History of Colonial Country Club*. Motheral Printing. Fort Worth, Texas. 1986. Pg. 12.

9. Dodson, James. *Ben Hogan An American Life*, Doubleday, New York, New York. 2004. Pg. 59.

10. Sampson, Curt. *HOGAN*, Rutledge Hill Press, Nashville Tennessee, 1996. Pgs. 18 -27.

11. Sampson, Curt. *HOGAN*, Rutledge Hill Press, Nashville Tennessee, 1996. Pg. 44.

12. Demaret, Jimmy. *My Partner Ben Hogan*, McGraw-Hill Book Company. New York, New York, 1954. Pgs. 71 - 72.

13. Dodson, James. *Ben Hogan An American Life*, Doubleday. New York, New York. 2004. Pgs. 149 - 152.

14. Hogan, Ben. "This is My Secret", *Life* Magazine, Time, Inc., New York, New York. August 8, 1955. Pgs. 60 – 63.

15. PGA Tour. 1946 Tour Schedule and winners

16. Dodson, James. *Ben Hogan An American Life*, Doubleday. New York, New York. 2004. Pgs. 190 - 192.

17. Dodson, James. *Ben Hogan An American Life*, Doubleday. New York, New York. 2004. Pgs. 214 - 221.

18. Dodson, James. *Ben Hogan An American Life*, Doubleday. New York, New York. 2004. Pg. 237.

19. Dodson, James. *Ben Hogan An American Life*, Doubleday. New York, New York. 2004. Pgs. 237 - 243.

20. Dodson, James. *Ben Hogan An American Life*, Doubleday. New York, New York. 2004. Pgs. 247 - 255.

21. "Winners Never Quit…" *Cycler*. Champlin Petroleum Company, Fort Worth, TX. Vol. 20. No. 2 Fall 1972. Pgs. 3-4.

22. Dodson, James. *Ben Hogan An American Life*, Doubleday. New York, New York. 2004. Pg. 262.

23. "Winners Never Quit…" *Cycler*. Champlin Petroleum Company, Fort Worth, TX. Vol. 20, No.2 Fall 1972. Pgs. 3-4.

24. Dodson, James. *Ben Hogan An American Life*, Doubleday. New York, New York. 2004. Pg. 267.

25. Snead, Sam. *The Game I Love*, Ballantine Books, Division of Random House, Inc. New York, New York. 1997 Pgs. 100 - 104.

26. Snead, Sam. *The Game I Love*, Ballantine Books, Division of Random House, Inc. New York, New York. 1997 Pgs. 102 - 103.

27. Dodson, James. *Ben Hogan An American Life*, Doubleday. New York, New York. 2004. Pg. 316.

28. Johnson, Salvatore. *The Official U.S. Open Almanac*, Taylor Publishing Company, Dallas, TX 1995. Pgs. 114-116.

29. Dodson, James. *Ben Hogan An American Life*, Doubleday. New York, New York. 2004. Pgs. 346 - 348.

30. Dodson, James. *Ben Hogan An American Life*, Doubleday. New York, New York. 2004. Pgs. 344 - 345, 356 - 357.

31. Dodson, James. *Ben Hogan An American Life*, Doubleday. New York, New York. 2004. Pgs. 358 - 370.

32. Gregston, Gene. *Hogan, The Man Who Played For Glory*, Prentice-Hall, Inc. Englewood, New Jersey. 1978. Pgs. 142 - 143.

33. Trinkle, Jim. *Golf* magazine, "Ben Hogan Remembers", Times Mirror Magazines, New York, New York, August, 1975. Pgs. 30 - 31.

34. Dodson, James. *Ben Hogan An American Life*, Doubleday. New York, New York. 2004. Pgs. 380 - 382.

35. "Winners Never Quit…" *Cycler*. Champlin Petroleum Company, Fort Worth, TX. Vol. 20, No. 2 Fall 1972. Pg. 6.

36. Dodson, James. *Ben Hogan An American Life*, Doubleday. New York, New York. 2004. Pg. 390.

37. Gregston, Gene. *Hogan, The Man Who Played For Glory,* Prentice-Hall, Inc. Englewood, New Jersey. 978. Pg. 158.

38. Dodson, James. *Ben Hogan An American Life,* Doubleday. New York, New York. 2004. Pg. 397.

39. Dodson, James. *Ben Hogan An American Life,* Doubleday. New York, New York. 2004. Pg. 400.

40. Venturi, Ken. *Getting Up & Down:* My Sixty Years in Golf. Triumph Books, Chicago, Illinois. 2004. Pgs. 60 - 62.

41. Nicklaus, Jack. *The Greatest Game of All*; My Life in Golf, Simon & Schuster, New York, New York. 1969. Pg. 27.

42. Gregston, Gene. *Hogan, The Man Who Played For Glory,* Prentice-Hall, Inc. Englewood, New Jersey. 1978. Pgs. 175 - 176.

43. Dodson, James. *Ben Hogan An American Life,* Doubleday. New York, New York. 2004. Pgs. 484 - 486.

44. Dodson, James. *Ben Hogan An American Life,* Doubleday. New York, New York. 2004. Pg. 490.

45. Dodson, James. *Ben Hogan An American Life,* Doubleday. New York, New York. 2004. Pg. 497.

46. Pillar, Dan. "Ben Hogan Co. to make profit, new owner says." *Fort Worth Star-Telegram*, November 7, 1986. Pgs. 1B - 2B.

47. Sampson, Curt. *HOGAN,* Rutledge Hill Press, Nashville Tennessee. 1996. Pg. 238.

48. Dodson, James. *Ben Hogan An American Life,* Doubleday. New York, New York. 2004. Pgs. 499 - 501.

49. *Golf* magazine, "What a Party". Times Mirror Magazines, New York, New York. September 1988. Pg. 90.

50. Sampson, Curt. *HOGAN,* Rutledge Hill Press, Nashville Tennessee, 1996. Pg. 241.

51. Dodson, James. *Ben Hogan An American Life,* Doubleday. New York, New York. 2004. Pgs. 510 - 513.

52. Dodson, James. *Ben Hogan An American Life*, Doubleday. New York, New York. 2004. Pgs. 511 - 521.

53. Dodson, James. *Ben Hogan An American Life*, Doubleday. New York, New York. 2004. Pgs. 73-74, 98.

A CLOSER GLANCE

Curtis, Brent & Eldredge, John. *The Sacred Romance*, Thomas Nelson, Inc., Nashville, TN. 1997. Pgs. 38 - 40.

CONTRIBUTING TO HIS PUBLIC IMAGE

1. Seitz, Nick. *Golf Digest*, "Ben Hogan Today," A Publication of the New York Times. Norwalk, CT. September, 1970. Pg 32.

2. Gregston, Gene. *Hogan The Man Who Played For Glory*. Prentice-Hall. Englewood Cliffs, New Jersey. 1978. Pg. 128

3. Venturi, Ken. *Getting Up & Down* My 60 Years in Golf. Triumph Books. Chicago, IL. 2004. Pgs. 69 - 77.

4. Seitz, Nick. *Golf Digest*, "Ben Hogan Today," A Publication of the New York Times. Norwalk, CT. September, 1970. Pg. 32.

5. Gill, Howard, Jr. *Golf Digest*, "Publisher's Comments," A Publication of the New York Times. Norwalk, CT. September, 1970. Pg. 4.

6. Sampson, Curt. *HOGAN*, Rutledge Hill Press, Nashville Tennessee, 1996, Pgs. 173 - 175.

7. Gregston, Gene. *Hogan The Man Who Played For Glory*. Prentice-Hall. Englewood Cliffs, New Jersey. 1978. Pgs. 129 - 131.

8. Murray, Jim. *Jim Murray The Autobiography of the Pulitzer Prize Winning Sports Columnist*. MacMillan Publishing Company. New York, New York. 1993. Pgs. 81, 85-86.

9. Murray, Jim. "Sorry, Ben, Jack's the best". *The Oregonian*. LA Times - Washington Post Service. August 12, 1980.

10. Walker, Dr. Granville. First Christian Church of Portland, Church bulletin. August 17, 1980.

11. Gregston, Gene. *Hogan The Man Who Played For Glory.* Prentice-Hall, Inc. Englewood Cliffs, New Jersey. 1978. Pg. 127.

12. Murray, Jim. The *Los Angeles Times*, "Ben Hogan Dies, but Not the Mystique." The Times Mirror Company. New York, New York, July 26, 1997.

13. Tschetter, Kris. *Mr. Hogan, The Man I Knew.* Gotham Books. New York, New York. 2010. Pg 128.

HOGAN CHARACTER

1. Sampson, Curt. *HOGAN,* Rutledge Hill Press. Nashville Tennessee. 1996. Pgs. 247 - 249.

2. The *American Heritage Dictionary*, Second College Edition. Houghton Mifflin Company. Boston, Massachusetts. 1982. Pg. 259.

3. Demaret, Jimmy. *My Partner Ben Hogan.* McGraw-Hill Book Company. New York, New York 1954. Pgs. 98-99.

4. Barkow, Al. *Golf's Golden Grind The History of the Tour.* Harcourt Brace Jovanovich. New York, New York. 1974. pg. 186.

5. Dickinson, Gardner. *Let 'er Rip,* Longstreet Press, Inc., subsidiary of Cox Enterprises. Marietta, Georgia. 1994. Pg. 192.

6. Towle, Mike. *I Remember Ben Hogan,* Cumberland House, Nashville, TN. 2000; Pgs. 180 - 183.

7. Venturi, Ken. *Getting Up & Down:* My Sixty Years in Golf. Triumph Books. Chicago, IL. 2004. Pgs. 180 - 181.

8. Murray, Jim. *Jim Murray, the Autobiography of the Pulitzer Prize Winning Sports Columnist,* MacMillan Publishing Company. New York, New York. 1993. Pgs. 81-86.

THE MIND OF BEN HOGAN

1. Gregston, Gene. *Hogan The Man Who Played For Glory.* Prentice Hall. Englewood

Cliffs, New Jersey. 1978. Pgs. 59 - 60. (Herbert Warren Wind's preface to the final segment of Hogan's *The Modern Fundamentals of Golf*, which was reprinted in Wind's book *The Realm of Sport*.

2. Gregston, Gene. *Hogan The Man Who Played For Glory*. Prentice Hall. Englewood Cliffs, New Jersey. 1978. Pgs. 59 - 60. (Herbert Warren Wind's preface to the final segment of Hogan's *The Modern Fundamentals of Golf*, which was reprinted in Wind's book *The Realm of Sport*.

3. Dickinson, Gardner. *Let 'er Rip*. Longstreet Press, Division of Cox Enterprises. Marietta, Georgia. 1994. Pg. 27

4. Skyzibski, Rich. *Quotable Hogan*: Words of Wisdom, Success Perseverance by and about Ben Hogan, Golf 's Ultimate Perfectionist. Towle House Publishing. Nashville, Tennessee. 2001. Pg. 11.

5. Snead, Sam. *The Game I Love*. Ballantine Books, a Division of Random House, Inc., New York, New York. 1997. Pg. 97.

6. Snead, Sam. *The Game I Love*. Ballantine Books, a Division of Random House, Inc., New York, New York. 1997. Pg. 94.

HOGAN METICULOUSNESS

1. Penick, Harvey with Shrake, Bud. *Harvey Penick's Little Red Book*: Lessons and Teachings From a Lifetime in Golf. Simon and Schuster, New York, New York. 1992. Pg. 151.

2. Hogan, Ben. *Power Golf*. A.S. Barnes & Company. South Brunswick and New York. 1948. Pg 4.

HOGAN TURNED INWARD -- RESPECT

1. Murray, Jim. *The Last of the Best*. Los Angeles Times Publishing. Los Angeles. 1998. Pgs. 15 - 16.

2. Sampson, Curt. *HOGAN*, Rutledge Hill Press. Nashville, TN. 1996. Pg. 135.

3. Barkow, Al. *That's Golf*: The Best of Barkow, "Hogan: Constant Focus on Perfection," Burford Books. Short Hills, NJ. 2001, Pg. 35.

4. Brown, Cal. *Masters Memories*, Sleeping Bear Press. Chelsea Michigan, 1998. Pg 52.

5. *Webster's New College Dictionary*, Random House. New York, NY. 1992. Pg. 1147.

6. Murray, Jim. *Los Angeles Times*, July 26, 1997. "Ben Hogan Dies, but Not the Mystique".

THE BEN HOGAN COMPANY

1. Piller, Dan. *Fort Worth Star-Telegram*, "Ben Hogan Company to make profit, new owner says," Business Section pgs. B1, 3. November 7, 1986.

THE KINDER, GENTLER BEN HOGAN

1. Stewart, Cissy. *Fort Worth Magazine*, "Hogan & Hogan The Man and Woman Behind a Golfing Legend" Fort Worth Chamber of Commerce Publication, Fort Worth, Texas. April 1989. Pgs. 16-17.

2. Derr, John. "This Tournament is Over," *Golf World* Magazine (online), a Golf Digest Publication, Norwalk, CT. February 22, 2003

3. Towle, Mike. *I Remember Ben Hogan*, Cumberland House, Nashville, TN. 2000. Pgs. 185 - 186.

MAX, DUFFER AND BUSTER

1. Friedlander, Andy. Chat Room, *Fort Worth Star-Telegram*. May 20, 2004. Pg. 2D.

2. Cochran, Mike. "Reserved In Honor of Ben Hogan". *Fort Worth Star-Telegram*. May 20, 2002. Pg. 16C.

TOOFIES

1. Barkow, Al. *That's Golf*, "Ben Hogan's Day in Court," Burford Books. Short Hills, New Jersey. 2001. Pg. 35.

PIC & MARVIN

1. Hogan, Ben. *Power Golf,* A.S. Barnes & Company, South Brunswick and New York. 1948, pgs. V – VI.

2. Dickinson, Gardner. *Let 'er Rip,* Longstreet Press, Inc., subsidiary of Cox Enterprises, Marietta, Georgia. 1994. Pgs. 20 - 21.

3. Pate, Russ. *The Legacy Continues A 50-year history of Colonial Country Club* 1936 - 1986. Motheral Printing Company. Fort Worth, TX. 1986. Pgs. 42 - 45.

4. Pate, Russ. *The Legacy Continues A 50-year history of Colonial Country Club* 1936 - 1986. Motheral Printing Company. Fort Worth, TX. 1986. Pgs. 5 - 8.

5. Pate, Russ. *The Legacy Continues A 50-year history of Colonial Country Club* 1936 - 1986. Motheral Printing Company. Fort Worth, TX. 1986. Forward.

SENSE OF HUMOR AND NOTABLE ONE-LINERS

1. Seitz, Nick. *Golf Digest,* "Ben Hogan Today," A Publication of the New York Times, September, 1970. Pg 28.

2. Gregston, Gene. *Hogan The Man Who Played For Glory,* Prentice- Hall, Inc. Englewood Cliffs, New Jersey. 1978. Pg. 133.

3. Gregston, Gene. *Hogan The Man Who Played For Glory,* Prentice- Hall, Inc. Englewood Cliffs, New Jersey. 1978. Pg. 133.

4. Alexander, Jules. Article by Ben Crenshaw, "The Hawk," *The Hogan Mystique,* The American Golfer, Greenwich, CT. 1994. Pg. 31.

5. Bingham, Walter. *Sports Illustrated,* "Welcome Back, Mister Hogan." Time, Inc. Chicago, IL. May 18, 1970 Volume 32 No. 20.

6. Alexander, Jules. Article by Ben Crenshaw. "The Hawk," *The Hogan Mystique.* The American Golfer. Greenwich, CT. 1994. Pg. 29.

7. Alexander, Jules. Article by Dan Jenkins, "Hogan His Ownself" *The Hogan Mystique,* The American Golfer. Greenwich, CT. 1994. Pg. 44.

8. Alexander, Jules. Article by Dan Jenkins, "Hogan His Ownself," *The Hogan Mystique,* The American Golfer, Greenwich, CT. 1994. Pg. 38.

9. Seitz, Nick. *Golf Digest*, "Ben Hogan Today," A Publication of the New York Times, September, 1970. Pg 32.

PRESENCE ON A GOLF COURSE

1. Dickinson, Gardner. *Let 'er Rip*, Longstreet Press, Inc., subsidary of Cox Enterprises, Marietta, Georgia. 1994. Pgs. 69 - 70.

2. Edrington, Tom. Tribune Sports Writer, *The Tampa Tribune-Times*, May 21 1978. Pg. 8-D.

BEN HOGAN WITH A GOLF CLUB – I WOULDN'T HAVE BELIEVED IT MYSELF

1. Nicklaus, Jack. *The Greatest Game of All*, My Life in Golf. Simon and Schuster. New York, New York. 1969. Pg. 21.

2. Nicklaus, Jack. *The Greatest Game of All*, My Life in Golf. Simon and Schuster. New York, New York. 1969. Pg. 28.

3. Barkow, Al. *Golf's Golden Grind The History of the Tour*, Harcourt Brace Jovanovich, 1974; Pgs. 184 - 185.

4. Seitz, Nick. *New York Times*, The Golf Clinic "How to Capitalize On Practice Hints." March 28, 1976.

5. Towle, Mike. *I Remember Ben Hogan*, Cumberland House, Nashville, TN. 2000; pg. 121.

HOGAN AND HIS SHAG BOYS

1. Burch, Jimmy. "Remembering Every Shot, Ben Hogan: A Tribute to a Golf Legend." *Fort Worth Star-Telegram*. Fort Worth, Texas. May 23, 1995. Pg. 6.

2. Vasquez, Jody. *Afternoons With Mr. Hogan*. Gotham Books, Penguin Group. New York, New York. 2004. Pgs. 22 - 23.

3. Vasquez, Jody. *Afternoons With Mr. Hogan*. Gotham Books, Penguin Group. New York, New York. 2004. Pgs. 72 - 74.

HOGAN PUTTING

1. Trinkle, Jim. "Ben Hogan Remembers," *Golf* magazine, Times Mirror Magazines, Inc., New York, New York. August 1975, pg. 29 - 30.

2. Gregston, Gene. *Hogan The Man Who Played For Glory,* Prentice-Hall, Englewood Cliffs, New Jersey 1978. Pg. 152.

3. Gregston, Gene. *Hogan The Man Who Played For Glory,* Prentice-Hall, Englewood Cliffs, New Jersey. 1978. Pg.176.

4. Gregston, Gene. *Hogan The Man Who Played For Glory*, Prentice-Hall, Englewood Cliffs, New Jersey. 1978. Pgs. 164 – 165.

5. Dodson, James. *Ben Hogan: An American Life*, Doubleday, a division of Random House. New York, New York. 2004. Pgs. 254-255.

6. Taylor, Dick - publisher. *The World of Golf* 1974. "An Evening With Hogan." Golf World, A Beckwith Enterprises Company. Southern Pines, North Carolina. 1974. Pg. 98.

7. Brown, Cal. *Masters Memories*, "Mr. Marr, Mr. Roberts, and Mr. Hogan." Sleeping Bear Press, Chelsea, MI. 1998. Pg. 17.

8. Haas, Fred, Jr. Unmoved by all the attention, *GolfDigest.com* - A man apart, February 22, 2003.

9. Tschetter, Kris. *Mr. Hogan, The Man I Knew*, Gotham Books. New York, New York, 2010. Pg. 126.

10. Sampson, Curt. *HOGAN*, Rutledge Hill Press, Nashville Tennessee, 1996. pp. 18 – 27.

11. Vasquez, Jody. *Afternoons With Mr. Hogan*. Gotham Press, Penguin Group. New York, New York. 2004. Pgs. 87 - 89.

12. Various web sites—

The Schepens Eye Research Institute, affiliate of Harvard Medical School, Boston, MA.

American Health Assistance Foundation, Clarksburg, MD.

St. LukesEye.com St. Luke's Cataract & Laser Institute, Tarpon Springs, FL.

Mayo Clinic, Rochester, MN.

BEN HOGAN'S U.S. NATIONAL OPEN VICTORIES:
WHEN IS A NATIONAL OPEN NOT A NATIONAL OPEN??

1. Dodson, James. *Ben Hogan, An American Life*. Doubleday, division of Random House. New York, New York. 2004. Pgs. 293 - 297.

2. Barrett, David. *Miracle at Merion*. Skyhorse Publishing. New York, New York. 2010. Pgs. 184, 205, 249-256.

3. Smith, Red. Views of Sport: "Ben Hogan." *New York Herald-Tribune*, June 12, 1950 from Marvin Davis, *Ben Hogan The Man Behind the Mystique,* The American Golfer, Inc. Greenwich, CT. 2002. Pg. 129.

4. Jenkins, Dan. *Fairways and Greens:* The Best Golf Writing of Dan Jenkins, Doubleday, New York, New York. 1994. Pgs. 92 - 93.

5. Johnson, Salvatore. *The Official U.S. Open Almanac*. Taylor Publishing. Dallas, TX. 1995. Pgs.114-115.

6. Johnson, Salvatore. *The Official U.S. Open Almanac*. Taylor Publishing. Dallas, TX. 1995. Pgs. 290-291.

7. Johnson, Salvatore. T*he Official U.S. Open Almanac*. Taylor Publishing. Dallas, TX. 1995. Pg.118.

8. Dodson, James. *Ben Hogan, An American Life*. Doubleday, division of Random House. New York, New York. 2004. Pg. 423.

9. Venturi, Ken. Interview with Ben Hogan. CBS-TV 1983.

10. Johnson, Salvatore. *The Official U.S. Open Almanac*. Taylor Publishing, Dallas, TX. 1995. Pg. 124.

11. Nicklaus, Jack. *The Greatest Game of All* My Life in Golf. Simon and Schuster. New York, NY. 1969. Pgs. 22-24.

12. Davis, Martin. *Ben Hogan The Man Behind the Mystique*. Dan Jenkins "Hogan Lore Strikes Again" The American Golfer. Inc. Greenwich, CT. 2002. Pg. 65.

13. Gregston, Gene. *Hogan The Man Who Played For Glory*. Prentice-Hall, Inc. Englewood Cliffs. New Jersey. 1978. Pgs. 107 - 108.

14. Jenkins, Dan. *Fairways and Greens:* The Best Golf Writing of Dan Jenkins. Doubleday. New York, New York. 1994. Pgs. 88 - 90.

15. Price, Charles. *Golf* magazine, "The Hawk." Times Mirror Magazines. New York, New York, November 1975. Pgs. 26-27.

16. Price, Charles. *Golf* magazine, "Memories of Ben Hogan." Times Mirror Magazines. New York, New York, October 1981. Pg. 26.

17. Johnson, Salvatore. *The Official U.S. Open Almanac.* Taylor Publishing. Dallas, Texas. 1995. Pgs. 235 - 236.

18. Davis, Martin. B*en Hogan The Man Behind the Mystique.* The American Golfer. Inc. Greenwich, CT. 2002. Pg. 179.

HOGAN'S SECRET

1. Hogan, Ben. "This Is My Secret," *Life* magazine. Time, Inc. Publications. New York, New York. August 8, 1955. Pg. 61.

2. "Ben Hogan's Secret," *Life* magazine. Time, Inc. Publications. New York, New York. April 5, 1954. Pgs. 126 - 134.

3. Hogan, Ben. "This Is My Secret," *Life* magazine. Time, Inc. Publications. New York, New York. August 8, 1955. Pgs. 61 – 62.

4. Demaret, Jimmy. *Golf* magazine Swing Analysis: "Golf's Most Respected Swing," Times Mirror Magazines. New York, NY. April, 1978. Pgs. 78 - 79.

5. Hogan, Ben. *Five Lessons, The Modern Fundamentals of Golf,* 1957. A Golf Digest Book. Trumbull, Connecticut. 1985. Pgs. 90.

6. Vasquez, Jody. *Afternoons with Mr. Hogan.* Gotham Books, Penguin Group. New York, New York. 2004. Pgs. 53 - 63.

7. Venturi, Ken. *Getting Up & Down*: My 60 Years in Golf. Triumph Books. Chicago, IL. 2004. Pg. 95.

8. Tschetter, Kris. *Mr. Hogan, The Man I Knew.* Gotham Books. New York, New York. 2010. Pg. 34.

9. Gregston, Gene. *Hogan The Man Who Played For Glory.* Prentice-Hall. Englewood Cliffs. New Jersey. 1978. Pg. 59.

10. "An Evening With Hogan", *The World of Golf 1974.* Golf World, A Beckwith Enterprises Company. Pgs. 97 – 100

11. Hogan, Ben. *Five Lessons, The Modern Fundamentals of Golf,* 1957. A Golf Digest Book. Trumbull, CT. 1985. Pgs. 110 - 111.

12. Seitz, Nick. *Golf Digest,* "Ben Hogan Today", A Publication of the *New York Times.* New York, NY. September, 1970. Pg. 66.

13. Hogan, Ben. *Five Lessons, The Modern Fundamentals of Golf,* 1957. Forward by Nick Seitz. A Golf Digest Book. Trumbull, CT. 1985.

14. Hogan, Ben. *Five Lessons, The Modern Fundamentals of Golf.* A Golf Digest Book. Trumbull, CT. 1985. Pgs. 113 - 115.

15. Peper, George. "Ben Hogan," *Golf Magazine.* Times Mirror Magazines. September 1987. Pg. 67.

16. Hogan, Ben. *Power Golf,* A.S. Barnes & Company. South Brunswick & New York. 1948, pgs. 3-5.

17. Hogan, Ben. *Five Lessons, The Modern Fundamentals of Golf,* 1957. Forward by Nick Seitz. A Golf Digest Book, Trumbull, CT. 1985

18. Hogan, Ben. *Five Lessons, The Modern Fundamentals of Golf,* 1957. A Golf Digest Book, Trumbull, Connecticut. 1985, Pg. 70.

19. Hogan, Ben. *Five Lessons, The Modern Fundamentals of Golf,* 1957. Forward by Nick Seitz. A Golf Digest Book, Trumbull, CT. 1985

20. Hogan, Ben. *Five Lessons, The Modern Fundamentals of Golf,* 1957. A Golf Digest Book, Trumbull, CT. 1985, Pgs. 84 – 90.

21. Seitz, Nick. *Golf Digest,* "Ben Hogan Today." A Publication of the *New York Times.* New York, NY. September, 1970, Pg. 29.

22. Peper, George. *Golf Magazine,* "Ben Hogan." Times Mirror Magazines. September 1987. Pg. 93.

23. Dickinson, Gardner. *Let 'er Rip.* Longstreet Press subsidiary of Cox Newspapers. Atlanta GA, 1994. Pgs. 332 – 333.

24. Dickinson, Gardner. *Let 'er Rip.* Longstreet Press subsidiary of Cox Newspapers. Atlanta GA, 1994, Pg. 22

25. Vasquez, Jody. *Afternoons with Mr. Hogan.* Gotham Books, Penguin Group. New York, NY. 2004. Pg. 25.

26. Hogan, Ben. *Power Golf,* A.S. Barnes & Company. South Brunswick and New York. 1948. Pg. 12.

27. Skyzinski, Rich. *Quotable Hogan*, TowleHouse Publishing. Nashville TN, 2001. Pg. 11

28. Dodson, James. *Ben Hogan, An American Life,* Doubleday division of Random House. New York, NY. 2004. Pgs. 128 – 129.

29. Kelly, Jim. Video Interview with Ben Hogan. 1991.

REVERENCE FOR THE GAME OF GOLF AND
CONTRIBUTION TO GOLF & PROFESSIONAL ATHLETES

1. Sampson, Curt. *HOGAN*, Rutledge Hill Press, Nashville, Tennessee, 1996, Pg. 174.

2. ESPN Classics TV show on Professional Athletes - Ben Hogan

3. Barkow, Al. *Golf's Golden Grind*, Harcourt, Brace, Jovanovich. New York. London. 1974. Pg. 192.

4. Barkow, Al. *That's Golf,* "Ben Hogan's Day in Court," Burford Books. Short Hills, New Jersey. 2001, Pg. 48.

5. Demaret, Jimmy. *My Partner Ben Hogan,* McGraw-Hill Book Company, Inc., New York - Toronto – London, 1954. Pg. 160.

6. Kelly, Jim. Video Interview with Ben Hogan, 1991.

7. Venturi, Ken. CBS-TV interview with Ben Hogan, May 12, 1983.

8. Gregston, Gene. *Hogan The Man Who Played For Glory,* Prentice-Hall Inc. Englewood Cliffs, New Jersey. 1978. Pg. 131.

9. Nicklaus, Jack. *The Greatest Game of All*, My Life in Golf. Simon and Schuster. New York, New York. 1969. Pg. 128.

10. Venturi, Ken. CBS-TV interview with Ben Hogan, May 12, 1983.

11. Barkow, Al. *That's Golf,* "Ben Hogan's Day in Court," Burford Books. Short Hills, New Jersey. 2001, Pg. 45-46.

12. Judge Hagan, Legal opinion on *Hogan v. A.S. Barnes & Company, Incorporated.* Case # 8645, Pennsylvania Court of Common Pleas No. 2, Philadelphia County 114 United States Patents Quarterly 314, Decided June 19, 1957. Pg. 2.

13. Barkow, Al. *That's Golf*, "Ben Hogan's Day in Court," Burford Books. Short Hills, New Jersey. 2001. Pgs. 45 - 47.

14. Barkow, Al. *That's Golf*, "Ben Hogan's Day in Court," Burford Books. Short Hills, New Jersey. 2001, Pgs. 44 - 45.

15. Judge Foster, Judge Hutcheson majority ruling. Court of Appeals, Fifth Circuit, *O'BRIEN v. PABST SALES CO.* No. 9892. Rehearing Denied Jan. 2, 1942. Appeal from the District Court of the United States for the Northern District of Texas; Wm. H. Atwell, Judge. Dec. 4, 1941. 124 F.2d 167 Pg. 3.

16. Judge Holmes, dissenting opinion. Court of Appeals, Fifth Circuit, *O'BRIEN v. PABST SALES CO.* No. 9892. Rehearing Denied Jan. 2, 1942. Appeal from the District Court of the United States for the Northern District of Texas; Wm. H. Atwell, Judge. Dec. 4, 1941. 124 F.2d 167 Pg. 4.

17. Judge Hagan, Legal opinion on *Hogan v. A.S. Barnes & Company, Incorporated*. Case # 8645, Pennsylvania Court of Common Pleas, 114 United States Patents Quarterly 314. Decided June 19, 1957. Pg. 1.

18. Judge Hagan, Legal opinion on *Hogan v. A.S. Barnes & Company, Incorporated*. Case # 8645, Pennsylvania Court of Common Pleas, 114 United States Patents Quarterly 314. Decided June 19, 1957. Pg. 9.

19. Judge Hagan, Legal opinion on *Hogan v. A.S. Barnes & Company, Incorporated*. Case # 8645, Pennsylvania Court of Common Pleas, 114 United States Patents Quarterly 314. Decided June 19, 1957. Pg. 10.

20. Barkow, Al. *Golf's Golden Grind*, Harcourt, Brace, Jovanovich. New York. London. 1974. Pg. 193.

21. Barkow, Al. *That's Golf*, "Ben Hogan's Day in Court," Burford Books. Short Hills, New Jersey. 2001. Pgs. 46 - 47.

22. Barkow, Al. *That's Golf*, "Ben Hogan's Day in Court," Burford Books. Short Hills, New Jersey. 2001, Pgs. 47 - 48.

23. Price, Charles. "Memories of Ben Hogan," *Golf* magazine. Times Mirror Magazines, Inc. New York, New York. October, 1981. Pgs. 20, 26.

24. Gregston, Gene. *Hogan The Man Who Played For Glory*, Prentice-Hall, Inc.,

Englewood Cliffs, New Jersey. 1978. Pg. 153.

25. Kelly, Jim. Video Interview with Ben Hogan, 1991.

BEN HOGAN'S GOLF RECORDS & ACCOMPLISHMENTS

Sources:

PGA Tour Headquarters.

Davis, Martin; Ben Hogan, *The Man Behind the Mystique.*

Claribel Kelly's notes (Ben Hogan's Secretary).

Official U.S. Open Almanac – Johnson, Salvatore. Taylor Publishing. Dallas, Texas. 1995.